An Australian artist in London

By the same author:

Dorothy Woollard and the etching revival

Front cover: Detail from an untitled oil painting c.1926 by Hewitt Henry Rayner. Sickert's influence is evident. The work probably depicts one of the Chelsea establishments frequented by Rayner and his artist friends. The tall blond figure on the left is almost certainly Rayner himself. The bearded figure reading the newspaper bears a striking similarity to a figure in a Sickert painting '*The old fool*' from 1922. The waitress is modelled on Theresa Rayner. (SW)

Back cover: Oil paintings by Rayner, most from the 1920s when he was a student at the Royal Academy Schools. '*Reclining nude*', c1926 (SW); '*Theresa at the etching press*', c1926 (SW); '*Chelsea lady*', c1926 (SW); '*WR Sickert ARA, 1926*' (RS); '*National Gallery*', c1926 (SW).

An Australian artist in London

The untold story of
Hewitt Henry Rayner (1902–1957)
and his friendship with Walter Sickert

by Roger Staton

with additional research and analysis
by Sheilagh Wilford

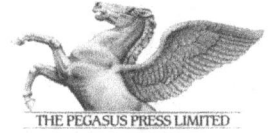

THE PEGASUS PRESS LIMITED

Published by the Pegasus Press Limited, London

First published October 2013 by the Pegasus Press Limited, London

214 Bankside Lofts
65 Hopton Street
London SE1 9JL
United Kingdom
Email enquiry@pegasuspress.co.uk

ISBN 978-0-9558160-1-7

Typography, design and layout: Jim Weaver

Typefaces Minion Pro and Agilita Pro

Printed by LightningSource on 75gsm acid-free paper

Contents

Foreword

This book is full of interest: for its glimpses of colonial Australia in the early years of the Twentieth Century, for its wonderfully detailed description of London's artistic *milieu* (or one of its many artistic *milieux* at least) during the often difficult years of the 1920s, '30s and '40s, and for its poignant portrait of a brave but disappointed life.

But – for me – its great claim to attention lies in the many fascinating side-lights that it sheds upon the life and character of Walter Sickert. Sickert was the supreme maverick figure of the British Art scene when Henry Rayner met him at the Royal Academy Schools, London, in 1925, and fell under his spell.

In this discipleship Rayner was certainly not alone. Sickert had great powers of attraction, and inspired many young artists throughout his long career. Rayner, however, was exceptional in the longevity of his attachment, and the scrupulousness with which he recorded it.

For Rayner, the friendship with Sickert became the great fact of his own artistic life. It was a friendship that continued until Sickert's death in 1941, and the record that Rayner preserved of the relationship – as so deftly woven together by Roger Staton – is rich in telling details. This book adds many things to the record of Sickert's life, his working practices, his teaching methods, his work-spaces, and his character.

Rayner towards the end of his own life set up a school specifically to promote the Sickert tradition. The School – like several of Sickert's own art-educational ventures – was not a great success. (It attracted only one pupil.) But in these pages the Sickert tradition is indeed preserved and promoted and enriched.

Matthew Sturgis, author of 'Walter Sickert, a life' (Harper Collins 2005)

Acknowledgements

A lot of people helped during the research for this book, knowingly and unknowingly.

Sheilagh Wilford merits a special 'thank you'. Without her initiative in rescuing the Rayner archive, allowing unrestricted access to it, and using her art training to help me understand and interpret the masses of material, this book would not have been possible.

Others who helped in various ways are Mark Aston, Adrienne Brewer, Dorothy Carey, Jane and Gerry Dorset, David Edwards, Jean Faulks, Jennifer Gosse, Tony & Sonia Gilderdale, Barbara Griffin, Elizabeth Harvey-Lee, Dominick Jones, Leslie Morris, Pat Northey, Mark Pomeroy, Daphne Searle, Matthew Sturgis, Hylton Thomas and Peter Zecchin.

You can't undertake a research-based historical project like this without calling on the information resources of numerous libraries and museums. I would like to thank the unfailingly helpful staff at the Royal Archives, the Royal Academy, the National Newspaper Library, the National Art Library, London's Guildhall Library, the British Museum, the Probate Office, the Ashmolean Western Art archive in Oxford, Islington Local History Centre, the Brighton Historical Society (whose files held the key – literally – to identifying the artist's family home in Brighton), the V&A Print Room, the National Gallery of Victoria in Melbourne, the Victoria State Library and Public Records Office (both in Melbourne), and the Brighton library.

Online sources also played a significant role in unearthing facts about Hewitt, his family and his achievements, and providing clues to further research. The Trove online archive of historic Australian newspapers came up trumps again and again. It's a tremendous resource for anyone looking into Australian history through the 19th and 20th centuries. *Ancestry.com* and *Findmypast.com* were frequently useful. Even Google, eBay and Abebooks played a part in the constant trawl for information about the artist, his contemporaries, the places he lived and the wider context of the times he lived in.

Permissions

The principal information source for this biography is the manuscripts, correspondence, notes, press cuttings and related material from the artist's estate. This resource, referred to as the 'Rayner archive', consists mostly of material written by the artist himself, and so may be regarded as a primary source.

I am also grateful to the following individuals and organisations for permission to reproduce copyright material:

- Her Majesty Queen Elizabeth II for permission to reproduce extracts from correspondence to and from Rayner in 1945 and 1956, now in the Royal Archives. The relevant references from the Royal Archives are: RA QEQMH/GEN/1945 and RA QEQMH/GEN/1956
- Jean Faulks for permission to reproduce letters from her mother Ethel Mannin to Rayner.
- Dominick Jones for permission to reproduce a letter from his mother Enid Bagnold.
- The *London Evening Standard* for permission to reproduce cuttings from that newspaper and the *London Evening News*.
- Peter Zecchin for Zecchin and Rayner family photographs, and interesting family facts and anecdotes.
- Dorothy Carey (descended from one of the artist's cousins) for Rayner family photographs.
- Pat Northey, from Hewitt's mother's side of the family in New Zealand, for Edwards family photographs and background information.
- Elizabeth Harvey-Lee for access to the Rayner drypoints in her stock, and permission to reproduce some of them.
- Henry Lessore for permission to reproduce Sickert's 1932 letter of recommendation to Rayner.
- Jennifer Gosse for permission to quote extracts from a letter by her mother Sylvia Gosse to Hewitt.
- The Royal Academy of Arts, London, for permission to reproduce extracts from Council Minutes and other records relating to Hewitt Rayner's time as a student.
- The Ashmolean Western Art archive for permission to quote extracts from two letters written by Hewitt in 1943.

Introduction

Towards the end of April 1957, the *East Kent Times* and *Thanet Gazette* published a news story about the death of an Australian artist and printmaker called Henry Rayner at his home in Ramsgate, on the Kent coast. *The Times* and *The Daily Express* also ran good-sized reports.

Who was this artist? What was the Ramsgate connection? What was his art like? More interestingly, perhaps, why had national and local newspapers considered his passing worth reporting?

Details were scant in the press reports. There were mentions that HM Queen Elizabeth II had recently purchased one of his prints for her private collection, and that the Royal collection at Windsor had several of his prints. The few snippets of background information included the fact that he had worked as a motor mechanic when he first arrived in England, and that he had damaged his drawing arm in a wartime accident.

Some readers may have recalled that over the years Henry Rayner had been the subject of occasional press coverage in British and Australian newspapers and magazines. But he wasn't a high-profile artist as far as the general public was concerned. And his chosen speciality – drypoint etching – was well out of fashion by the 1950s.

My own interest in the name Henry Rayner was triggered by the chance purchase of a framed drypoint by him in a charity shop on London's King's Road in 2003. It was a striking image of the Great Hall in Lincoln's Inn, London, still in its original thin black frame. I quickly discovered that there was very little information on the artist in the usual sources, and my curiosity was aroused. The press cuttings about his death were among the first research results. They piqued my interest even more.

It was a long time before I discovered how ironic it was that I had found the print in the King's Road. This is just a few blocks away from the apartment where Hewitt and his wife lived when they were first married in 1926. Had the print spent the intervening 80 years in that area of Chelsea? The framer's details on the back of the picture give an address in Hemel Hempstead. How wonderful to think that by some quirk of chance the print had travelled around the south of England before ending up for sale a few blocks from where it was created.

The research was initially slow going, although I did notice that prints by Rayner were cropping up regularly at local auction houses in London and the south of England. The big breakthrough was when I came into contact with Sheilagh Wilford, a former Head of Art/Textile Departments in Nottinghamshire and Lincolnshire secondary schools. She had discovered a veritable trove of information about the artist, in the form of all his drawings, painting and prints, his original drypoint plates, and his autobiographical writings (never published), correspondence, notebooks and sketchbooks. All this material had been gently deteriorating in a goatshed in Lincolnshire, until Sheilagh rescued it.

Sheilagh has actively supported my research into Rayner's life, not only allowing complete access to this material, but also giving me the benefit of her art training in interpreting it all. Without her initiative in rescuing what I refer to as the 'Rayner archive' in the first place, and then patiently encouraging my research (over a longer period than she ever imagined), this biography would not have been possible.

The mass of information showed that for a little-known artist, Henry Rayner had had a very interesting life, achieved some notable successes, and mixed with some very interesting people. More excitingly for a biographer, he had kept detailed notes of his life and his friendships, and woven it all into various autobiographical manuscripts and essays covering his growing up in Australia and New Zealand, and his life in London after 1923.

From these, it emerged that he had won a place at the Royal Academy Schools, where he was a student and then protégé and friend of Richard Walter Sickert. Through Sickert he got to know some of the leading figures from London's art and literary worlds, including Yoshio Markino, Ethel Mannin, Nina Hamnett, Augustus John, Ethel Walker, Gwen Otter, Philip Wilson Steer and Charles Sims. And they all appear in his manuscripts.

He went against the advice of his mentor, and chose drypoint etching as his principal medium. Between 1926 and 1945 he produced more than 500 original drypoint plates. This constitutes quite probably the largest drypoint *oeuvre* of any mid-20th century artist. Although his public profile is low, there are examples of his drypoint work tucked away in many British public art galleries and museums, as well as in the Royal Collection at Windsor Castle, and galleries in Australia and New Zealand.

Recently there are signs that public interest in his work is growing. In London in October 2005 four Rayner drypoints of Sickert and a pen and ink portrait of D H Lawrence sold for a total of more than £3,300. In February 2008, four Rayner drypoints appeared in an important exhibition at the National Gallery of Australia in Canberra, titled '*Australian Surrealism, the Agapitos/Wilson collection*'.

I feel that the time is right for a biography of this overlooked artist.

Even with the trove of manuscripts and other material from his estate, unravelling the story of his life has required a fair degree of detective work. Basically I wasn't prepared to take his autobiographical manuscripts at face value. What if it was all (or partly) a work of fiction? What if he had grossly distorted events? What if there were gaps to be filled?

I spent a lot of time cross-checking the core facts of his writing against other sources. My conclusion after several years' research is that the written records he left behind are broadly reliable.

Here's an example. One thing that crops up again and again in press cuttings and family documents was the fact that Rayner resorted to selling prints – or even begging – in the street in the 1930s and 1940s. I assumed that this was just one of those things that become part of a family legend, to underline the fact that life was tough. But then, in 2012 I was contacted by a man whose mother had purchased four Rayner drypoints when the artist knocked on the front door of her Hampstead home early in 1942. So perhaps he had never gone around 'selling prints in the street', or even begging, as sometimes stated, but he definitely sold prints door-to-door.

Here's another example. Hewitt wrote that his father bought a yacht, and that it was destroyed in a storm that hit Brighton. Was this true, or a Rayner invention? Thanks to the groundbreaking Trove Australian newspaper archive I tracked down a story in the *Melbourne Argus* from February 1918 about a freak 'tornado-like' storm that had hit Brighton, causing widespread damage to boats and buildings. Once again, Rayner's account checked out.

The worst crimes I found in his written account of his life were a little harmless spin (such as telling people he lived in Hampstead, when in fact the family home was in less-desirable Gospel Oak, on the wrong side of the railway line), the glossing over of some painful family episodes, the occasional 'talking up' of his and other people's status (like describing his step-father as a lawyer when in fact he was a lawyer's office manager), and a sometimes unreliable memory for dates. Additionally, he often changed the names of people and places, in the style of 19th century novelists, creating additional research challenges. But none of these are serious crimes, and nothing emerged from the extensive checking of facts that raised any questions about the general dependability of his writing.

The story of Hewitt Rayner's life in this biography is for the most part told in his own words, extracted from his own writing, and illustrated with his own drawings, paintings and drypoints. I hope that the examples of his drypoint work will give a flavour of the range of subjects he covered.

I'm not qualified to comment on his art. I leave that to others. As for a catalogue of his 500+ drypoints, and his known drawings and paintings, well that will have to wait for another time. To some extent it will depend on how this biography is received.

'Hewitt' or 'Henry'?

One of the dilemmas faced by a biographer is what to do when the subject is known to the wider world by one name, but to family and friends by another. This is the case here. The artist known since 1926 as Henry Rayner was christened Hewitt Henry Rayner. Family and friends knew him as Hewitt, not

Henry. Sometimes this was shortened to Hewie, or Hew, leading some people to mistakenly assume his name was Hugh.

He decided to create a new identity for professional purposes by using his middle name, so 'Henry Rayner' is the signature found on all his drypoints, drawings and paintings from 1926 on.

To family and friends, however, he continued to be known as Hewitt. So I decided in the interests of consistency to use Hewitt rather than Henry throughout this biography.

Sources, attributions and copyright

Although this is essentially an academic biography of the artist Hewitt Henry Rayner, you will notice that there are no footnotes on the pages that follow. Please don't infer from this that there is any lack of academic rigour in the research. It's simply to spare you the tedium of finding the same primary sources repeatedly cited – in particular Hewitt's two unpublished autobiographies.

Wherever I have written 'Rayner wrote' or 'Rayner recalled' or something similar, it signals that the comments come from one of these manuscripts or from other notes or essays in the Rayner archive. Where information has come from other sources, I have generally stated this within the main narrative flow.

I respect the copyrights of others, and have made all reasonable endeavours to seek permission to reproduce material that is still in copyright. In some cases this has not been possible, for example where newspapers and other publications of the period no longer exist, where the literary rights owners cannot be reasonably traced, or where my requests have simply gone unanswered. I have referenced all third-party sources with as much detail as possible, to assist readers who wish to dig deeper into the subject matter. If you are aware of any material herein for which you hold the copyright, please contact the publishers so a suitable acknowledgement can be included in future editions.

Illustrations

All the photographs in this book have come from the Rayner archive, except where indicated otherwise.

All the Rayner drypoints have come from the collections of the author or Sheilagh Wilford, except where stated otherwise. Look for the initials 'RS' or 'SW' at the end of a caption.

Roger Staton
April 2013

I

Growing up in Australia and New Zealand

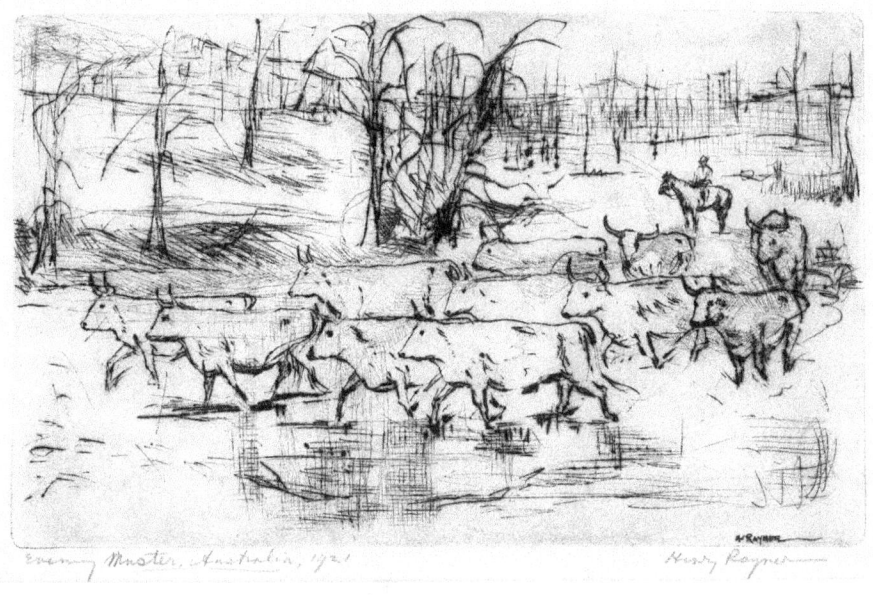

Fig I *'Evening muster'*, Australia, 1921. Drypoint 145 x 229mm. REPRODUCED COURTESY ELIZABETH HARVEY-LEE.

1

Child, when my ship comes in

Hewitt Rayner was born in 1902 near Melbourne, Australia, and did most of his growing up in the town of Brighton, eight miles south of Melbourne on the eastern shores of Port Phillip Bay.

In the early years of the 20th century Brighton was growing. There were new rail and tram services making travel to and from Melbourne easy, and with motor cars appearing in increasing numbers, more and more people saw the town as a desirable place to live. They were attracted by Brighton's invigorating seaside location, its long sandy beach, two piers, two seawater baths, and the elegant legacy of large houses and estates that had occupied the choicest spots along the shoreline since the 1800s.

As the 20th century arrived, these large estates were being broken up, the houses demolished and the land subdivided into building plots to meet the demand for new homes. Weston Bate's fascinating 1962 book [see bibliography] on the history of Brighton records that between 1901 and 1921 the town's population doubled to over 21,000.

By 1908, the pace of new building had slowed down for a while, but for people prepared to work hard and take risks there was still a living to be made from property development in Brighton.

This was the year that a family called Rayner arrived in town. Head of the household was Henry Redstone Rayner, then in his mid-thirties. Born in the village of Shanklin, on the Isle of Wight, he had arrived in Australia some 22 years earlier with his family, at the age of 14.

What he did in the years that followed is not well documented, but it is known that in the 1890s he was in Western Australia prospecting for gold – one of many who followed the Bradlet Find gold rush to Coolgardie. While there he met and married a missionary's daughter. They had two children who died in infancy, and in 1900 his wife died.

Back in Melbourne in 1901, widowed and and describing himself as a plasterer, Henry Redstone Rayner married again. His new bride was Australian-born Emily Ellen Edwards, daughter of a family that

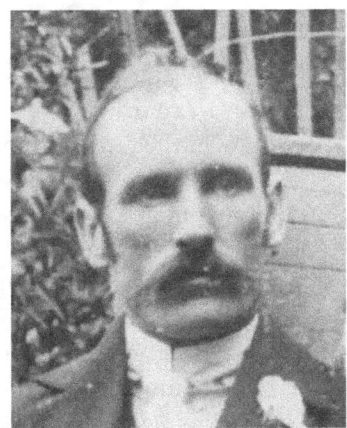

1.1 Hewitt's father in 1901. sw.

3

ran a saddle-tree manufacturing business, making the wooden frames on which leather saddles were constructed.

At first the couple lived in Hawthorn, near Melbourne, where their first and only child – a boy – was born on 19th September 1902. They named him Hewitt and gave him the middle name Henry, after his father. To his family and friends he was known as Hewitt, or 'Hewie', or 'Hew', or occasionally as 'young Harry' or 'Hal'.

This is the boy who 22 years later travelled to England in search of formal art training, and became 'Henry Rayner' the artist.

'I was born in the last years of the great ten-year drought,' he wrote many years later. He and his parents moved around the Melbourne area several times, and also spent some time in New Zealand living with his mother's family. It seems that Hewitt's father was constantly on the lookout for the big opportunity.

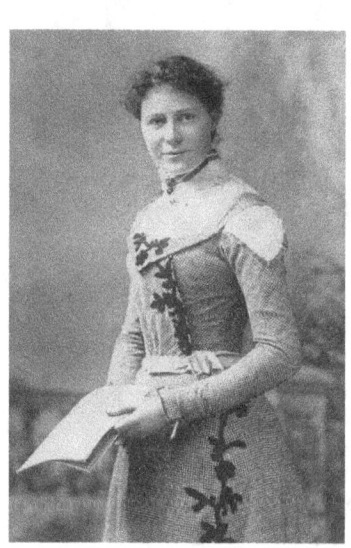

He found it in Brighton in 1908 when they returned from New Zealand. He had spotted in Brighton's New Street a building that he thought could not only provide his family with a home but also be the starting point for his business ambitions.

It was a building with a history. Standing at number 165 New Street, it had originally been built in 1861 as the town's first Mechanics Institute. These were usually financed by benevolent groups or wealthy individuals who saw that an increasingly literate working class needed places where men could meet to improve themselves. The main purpose of these institutes was to host talks on scientific topics, and provide library and reading room facilities. At one stage there were over 1000 Mechanics Institutes in the state of Victoria alone. In the event the, Brighton facility only served for a decade or so in this role, and by the time the Rayners

1.2 Hewitt's mother Emily Ellen (née Edwards) in 1900. sw.

arrived in Brighton it had been rented out for commercial use for 40 years, housing businesses, a school, and quite possibly for a short period serving as the town's courthouse.

On the face of it, the property was an unlikely candidate for a family home. But where others saw a vacant and unloved building, Hewitt's father saw something more. As an accomplished plasterer with ambitions to become a builder, he saw how the property could be converted into a roomy family house.

It was an inspired piece of lateral thinking. The building had an excellent position on a large plot at or near the corner of New Street and Park Street. It was near one of Brighton's main shopping streets and the railway station, close to the Church of St Andrews, and only a short walk to the beach. What's more, the large plot offered the potential for subdivision, and the erection of more houses. The only downside was the fact that the property was down-wind of Brighton's gas works. Hewitt later wrote about 'the swamp reeking with the foul smelling oil from the gasworks'.

Undeterred, Henry Redstone Rayner acquired the land and the building, and divided the property into four rooms with a central corridor running back from the central front door. Then he added an extra room at the back, and a porch and veranda at the front. He re-roofed the whole building in blue slate with red ridge tiles. As a final touch he used his plastering skills to give the building's frontage a thick coat of cement rough-cast, creating the impression it was built from massive stone blocks. Hewitt believed that it was his father who had first introduced this rendering technique into Brighton.

This house in Brighton became the young Hewitt's home for the next ten years. 'I was born there, reared there, and passed my happiest days there,' he wrote. This was a nicely turned phrase, but not entirely true of course, since he had been born somewhere else in the Melbourne area – Hawthorn.

The principal source of information about Hewitt Rayner's early life is a manuscript titled '*Child, when my ship comes in*'. It is essentially the story of the first 21 years of his life. The title was inspired by something his father would say when he wished to sidestep a question from his young son with the word 'when?' in it. Hewitt worked on this manuscript through the 1920s and 1930s. It was never published, but a hand-written copy together with several earlier drafts survive in the Rayner archive.

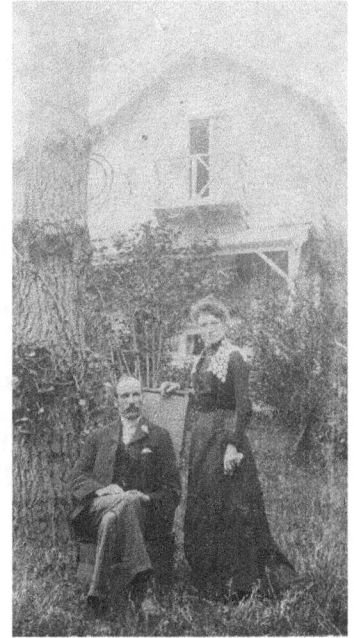

1.3 Hewitt's parents on their honeymoon in Fern Tree Gully, in the Dandenong Ranges east of Melbourne. sw.

This '*Child*' manuscript provides an absorbing account of what it was like to grow up in early 20th century Australia, the people he encountered, and the factors that shaped his lifetime devotion to art. He referred to it as a 'semi-autobiographical' account of his life, and one draft version has the sub-title a 'reconstruction of my life'. This signals that the manuscript should not be taken as a completely true and complete story of his childhood. Its aim was to capture the flavour of what it was like growing up in Brighton between 1908 and 1923, based largely around the events of his own life.

During the research for this biography, it became apparent that there were some painful family events completely missing from his autobiography, and a few instances where he had done some spinning of the facts. Nevertheless, it constitutes an interesting and broadly sound account of his early life. The most significant omissions and factual discrepancies will be explored in Chapter 2.

Hewitt described his father as a self-made man – a labourer and plasterer who became a builder, designing and building houses for the new arrivals in Brighton. Hewitt recalled watching him at work building a new house on a

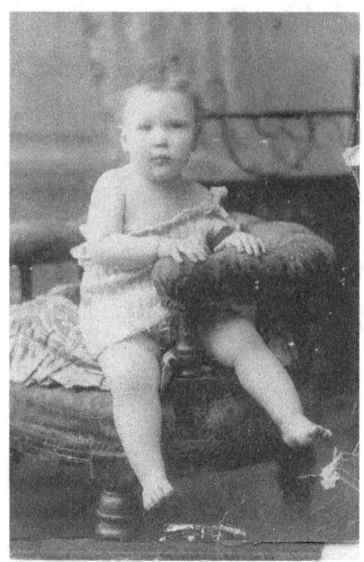

1.4 Hewitt age 1. sw.

nearby plot of land. His clothes were splattered with plaster as he directed his men in cladding the frame of the building with weatherboard. He carried a folding ruler in his waistcoat pocket, and used it as a pointer when instructing his men.

Rayner senior had no time for pro- and anti-union debates. He was only concerned with the quality of workmanship, how hard a man worked, and what he achieved. This brought him into frequent conflict with his employees at a time when unionisation issues were a hot topic. Hewitt wrote: 'Father was perhaps not a born boss. There were frequent setbacks. Men quarrelled and went on strike. He was apt to ignore rules and take matters into his own hands. He was not the kind of man to get panicky when he was intimidated by others. Unionists and non-unionists – father employed them indiscriminately. 'All men must eat', he said.'

His father was evidently a taciturn man, not given to displays of emotion towards his young son. 'Father had never been loquacious. He never had my future in mind. He either did not love me, as his first wife's children had died, or he thought I could push my way better as the labouring masses, of which he was one, did.'

Some notes that were not used in any of his manuscripts paint a rather negative picture of his father. One says 'My father was sadistic and cold. I had been thrown into the sea at two years old by him to swim, and I still see his cold face leering over me as I neared the point of drowning. I remember very little contact with him.' Another cryptic note says: 'My father was sadistic, cold and sought by women.'

But there were good memories as well. Hewitt recalled his father taking him down to the pier one hot summer evening, to look at the 'great white three-masters lying in the bay.' Many years later, he could still recall the sights and sounds that had permeated his childhood. 'The sound of ships' sirens come like deep cello notes across a still bay,' he wrote, adding 'love of birthplace is strong in the Australian.'

On winter evenings when Hewitt was in bed, his father would sit with him and tell stories of his pioneer days prospecting for gold in Western Australia in the 1890s, and of his own childhood on the Isle of Wight. He would sing songs that had come down through the family, including 'roistering smuggling songs.' He recounted stories of the family – several generations of boat-builders, seafarers and fishermen. And he would tell the young Hewitt romantic tales of hidden treasures left on the island by English captains returning from wars with the Spanish, and determined not to deliver all the booty to the court of Queen Elizabeth I.

When the working day was finished, his father would sit and smoke in the back yard; often squatting bush style, rather than sitting on a chair. When he came in from work at the end of the day, his hands would often be lime-bitten from the plastering work. He would wash them carefully, then dress them with mutton grease, before settling down in front of the kitchen fire with his pipe. Dinner might consist of haricot hash or stewed rabbit and potatoes.

Hewitt's father passed on to him the bush craft he had acquired during his gold mining days. This lore was very useful during the years he travelled the bush, when he perfected his 'bushman's eye.'

With hindsight, Hewitt saw that his father had simply tried to build his own life, and make things easy for his wife and son. 'He set no high standards for himself,' Hewitt wrote. 'But he was proud of his reputation.' Hewitt never heard his father use bad language; and if he himself swore, his father would cuff him.

His father was a strong man. Not only able to do endless hours of plastering work on the houses he built, but also able to take part in wrestling bouts. On one occasion, he became involved in a real fight, and was injured by some of his own workers, during a fight about unionisation issues. He spent the following week in bed.

There were occasional outbursts of aggression. Rayner recalls his father hurling a brick at a cat that had come into the yard. It broke the cat's back, and next morning the cat's body was still there, frozen. It was buried in the garden.

Hewitt never saw his father the worse for drink, even though he recorded that he would regularly go to the Marine Hotel at the corner of New Street, St Andrews Street and Park Street on a Friday evening with friends. The hotel building is still there [2004].

His father played a practical joke on him that he still remembered some 20 years later. He recalled it like this: 'Father opened a mahogany box and took out two nickel-silver cylinders attached to strings. He did something with the coils, and I dropped the cylinders. I had had my first electric shock.' His father 'shook with silly laughter'.

The earliest surviving drawing by Hewitt is a pencil sketch of his father dated 1913, drawn on a blank page torn from a book about the Isle of Wight. It shows him as a thin-faced, balding man with a moustache. He would have been 40 or 41 years old at the time.

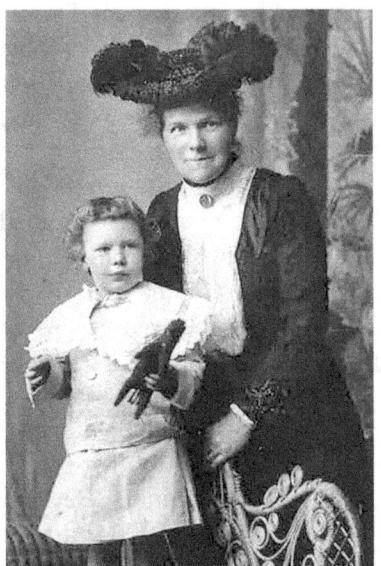

1.5 Hewitt age 3, with his maternal grandmother Edwards. She had just bought him the new coat, and the toy horse was a present for behaving well at the photo session. PHOTO COURTESY DOROTHY CAREY.

Hewitt's paternal grandparents William and Selina Jane had settled in nearby Carrrum, and his grandmother also used to recount family stories from the Isle of Wight. Her favourite was the story of how in 1833 the 14-year-old Princess who would later become Queen Victoria unexpectedly arrived with her mother and entourage at the Rayner family hotel in Shanklin, and stayed the night.

All these tales had a lasting effect on the young Hewitt. Especially when his father and grandmother refused to elaborate on the possible smuggling activities of his great grandfather Jeremiah.

It put into Hewitt's mind an excitement and a curiosity about his forebears and the Isle of Wight that ultimately led to his 'pilgrimage' to the island in 1934, and later visits in the 1950s.

The young Hewitt started attending school when he was five years old, for a few hours a day. He had thick fair curls that his mother had let grow. His main recollection of school was a sense of loneliness. It was evidently mainly a school for girls. He was allowed to join in the games, and wander into any class he chose. He recalled standing in the middle of the dusty playground, feeling the world had rejected him, and watching the big girls in their pigtails, large boots and awkward skirts.

The teacher would take him by the ear to the end of the form and sit with him to see what he had really learnt. 'I longed for her to say a friendly word. I felt like small dogs must feel when they are pulled bodily along on a tight collar by a thoughtless owner.'

The classroom had a bare red-painted brick wall, and an unpainted iron roof. He remembered the teacher moistening the chalk with her lips to prevent it from squeaking when she wrote on the blackboard. Given his first primer, he liked the homely English woodcuts showing farmyard scenes and landscapes, and these images may have laid the foundation for his interest in drawing. 'They captured my imagination,' he wrote

These were years of drought. Hewitt recorded that when the temperature reached 100 degrees (38°C) in the shade, he would 'throw himself on the cool oilcloth of the vestibule, or lie outstretched in the dark passage in the centre of the house'. He recalled blasts of grey dust blowing past the house. The wind would blow from 7am through the day. Water in canvas bags with wooden spigots was hung from the veranda posts, to keep it cool.

In the evenings, when the sun went down children and parents would have an early tea, to prevent cramp when swimming, then stroll down to the beach at the end of Park Street, don their swimsuits and wade out to the submerged sandbanks. On the old gypsy beach [Gypsy Village is today known as Sandringham] they would gather periwinkles to take home and boil.

Occasionally, Hewitt and his parents would catch one of the pleasure steamers from Melbourne to Frankston and Sorrento.

When the evenings were too hot to stay indoors, the family would eat tea in the garden, on the lawn behind the house. On Saturday afternoons, the lawn would be put to a different use, as his father would engage in wrestling matches with his friends and workmates.

On Saturday evenings, his parents would eat shellfish, and drink schnapps from a large dark-green bottle shaped like an old sailing ship. Perhaps the taste for shellfish and schnapps was something Hewitt's father had picked up through working alongside men from Scandinavia in the goldfields of Western Australia.

Sometimes on a Saturday afternoon his father would take him for a walk by the sea at South Brighton. There they would be entertained by an Aborigine who hurled boomerangs far out over the water. They always returned to within a few feet of where he stood.

When he was five or six years old, Hewitt started modelling little figures in wax. 'If I'd starved myself of art, I should have certainly become a morbid introvert, warping my nature

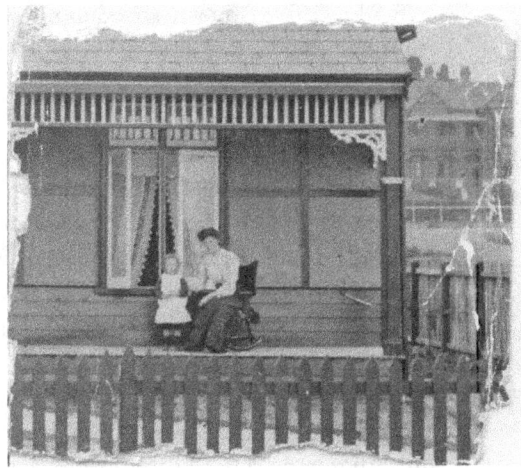

1.6 Hewitt and his mother at the family's first home in St Kilda, 1905. sw.

and destroying my highest gift,' he later noted. 'Chance kindly threw colourful modelling wax in my way. So I made beautiful things to gladden the mind and inflate my pride.'

Then he asked his father if he could have a box of paints. 'Certainly,' his father answered. 'When?' asked Hewitt. 'When my ship comes in,' came the reply. This evasive response was used on other occasions when Hewitt asked questions, and each time the meaning was a complete mystery to the youngster. If he went with his father to watch the boats in Melbourne, Hewitt would ask his father 'Is the ship coming in, Daddy?'

Another of his father's irritating habits when someone said something he disagreed with was to respond 'Pop goes the weasel'. It must have made family conversations rather frustrating.

One of Hewitt's memories of those days was watching three-roomed cottages being 'shifted along the road on large jinker wheels by six sweating horses. A not uncommon sight in those days.' In addition to these low trailers carrying complete houses, in summer the road past Wildways became very busy with crowded chaises, drags and wagons, all caked in dust from the earth roads.

From the garden of Wildways Hewitt could just see the 'turrets and topmost windows' of a large house near the shore, surrounded by beeches, pines and gum trees. This may well have been the mansion built by Henry Dendy, who had purchased eight square miles of land at Port Phillip in 1840, and laid the foundation of what today is Brighton. He kept back one of the best plots, of 72 acres with a mile of sea frontage, for his own use, and named it Brighton Park. The large house he built was locally referred to as the Manor House. It was demolished in the 1920s.

Hewitt described the land immediately behind his home as a 10-acre block that Henry Dendy had put in his wife's name when he got into financial difficulties. The lady who lived here was named by Hewitt as 'Mrs Evelyn Baron' (probably not her real name), originally from Sussex. It's conceivable that this lady was a relative or descendent of Henry Dendy, but Hewitt never stated that.

This 'Mrs Baron' gave his father a lot of work building bungalows alongside the roads that ran down to the sea through her land.

Hewitt wrote a detailed description of the property. 'A veranda and balcony ran round the house in the old style. It had dark & shady French windows, and a tower on one corner. It was a ten-acre property. A long, wide, winding drive led to the front entrance of the house with heavy lamps on carved pillars. Local gossip had it that the old lady was starting to economise, and had come down to the poorer districts to shop. Other rumours said she was about to build. The hedges lining the Barn road through her property were already being hewn away and cart loads of bricks deposited on the green paddocks. It became known that my father had secured the contract.'

Hewitt loved visiting the old house, where he would sometimes be taken up to one of the turrets by the ageing servant and retired British soldier variously referred to by Hewitt as Mr Collins and Mr Lomax, to look out over the harbour. Collins had been a Sergeant Major in the British Army, serving in the Indian and Crimean wars. He drank heavily, according to Hewitt, and was not popular with other adults, which was probably why he 'tried to find favour with us kids'.

He would entertain Hewitt and the other lads by demonstrating how he used to salute when he was in the British army. 'I haven't always been a servant, me lads,' he would tell them. He passed by Wildways twice a day with his quart bottle, to get it filled up with whisky at the pub.

Hewitt visited the Baron house frequently, taking messages for his father. With Mrs Baron lived her two grandsons, and Hewitt spent many happy hours with them. During one visit when he was about seven years old, Mrs Baron gave him a copy of Alice in Wonderland, which prompted him to redouble his efforts at learning to read.

Hewitt described his own mother as 'a young wife in a young country'. Emily had blond hair, which her son inherited. She was a good storyteller, and would regale the young Hewitt with endless fairy tales as she sat by his cot and sewed by the light of an oil lamp. The stories she told were drawn from her own happy childhood. 'Simple bushland scenes with clear running streams, and dark, tree-shaded lagoons. Mother retained a pure and sensitive love for the countryside, where she had been born,' wrote Hewitt later. His mother also sang him a song about the old gold miners.

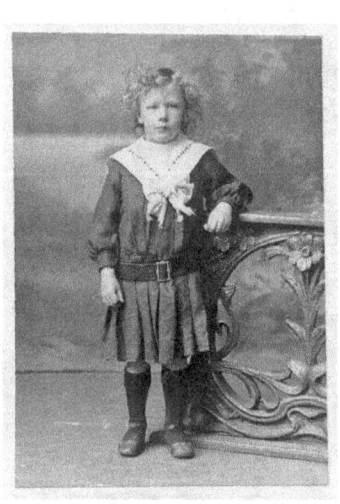

1.7 Hewitt age 5. Photo by Yeoman & Co, Prahran. sw.

She created an imaginary character called Cheribinks, and each night the young Hewitt would demand a new Cheribinks adventure. Later in life, when he had children of his own, he would bring the Cheribinks character back to life, and even write and illustrate little books for his daughters.

He recorded that as a young girl his mother had suffered from sandy blight. This is an Australian term for Trachoma, an infectious eye condition that was widespread among pioneer communities. It could cause complete blindness. After this infection, her eyesight had never been strong. Despite this, she was a keen painter. Hewitt remembered her sitting in the garden, wearing a white cotton dress and large flowered garden hat, her paints beside her on a table. On one such day, the minister from the local church [presumably St Andrews] came and tried unsuccessfully to persuade his mother to have Hewitt baptized. This would have been in 1914 or 1915.

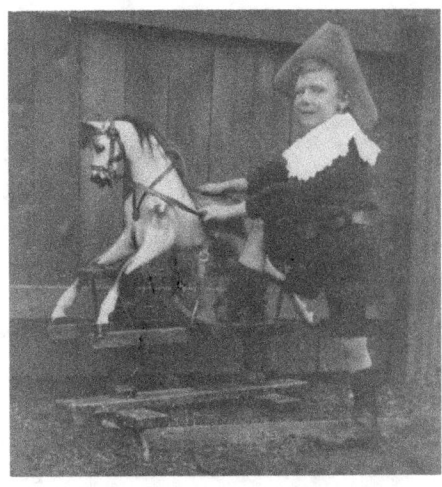

1.8 Hewitt age 6 at his maternal grandparents house in Auckland, New Zealand. sw.

Several paintings by his mother adorned the walls of the Wildways drawing room. 'There was a stag amongst mountains, a scene of Rotorua showing Maori women washing their garments at the boiling springs, and a large canvas of oranges falling from an upturned basket. Finally, a huge canvas of a ship and a desert island.'

Remembering other features of the room, Hewitt wrote: 'On the mantelpiece stood two large pink and white china vases with ovals containing mountain scenes, a reclining dog of Italian lava, a circular silver mounted clock with an irritating tick, two Venetian glass swans, and two ruby coloured glass bowls which seemed to collect all the blowflies as they died.'

It was his mother who looked after the Leghorn hens kept in the chicken run at the bottom of the garden, and carefully nurtured the new broods, transferring them into an oven kept at blood heat. Hewitt's responsibility was to collect the eggs at night from the whitewashed henhouse.

'The place ran with vermin,' he recalled. 'Somehow late one night when Father was away, while mother was attending the chickens the lamp overturned onto the straw. The tinder dry wood caught alight, and the shed was burning before you could say 'Jack Robinson'. We secured the garden hose, and Mother stood with the water playing on the chickens while I dashed to and from the tap and hurled buckets of water on to the burning fowl house. The chickens were in a heap in one corner. The shed was saved but all the chickens were drowned.'

Although he had good memories of his mother, with hindsight he clearly felt that he would have preferred to have brothers and sisters. 'My mother thought I was too good for the world, I think, and tried to keep me to herself.' But Hewitt was not alone in being an only child. He noted that during those years of recession in Australia, people were having few children. 'It was being described as a

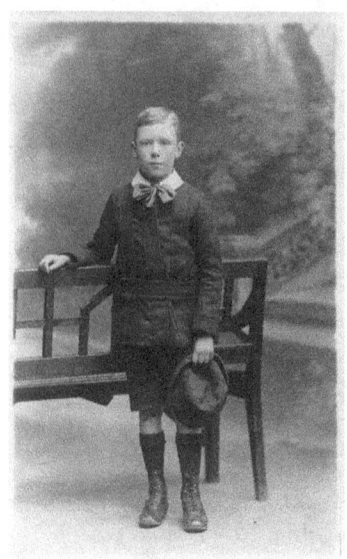

1.9 Hewitt age 8. sw.

'national calamity', he recalled. 'I rather agree. Brothers and sisters are a help, especially where the parents are reclusive and hide away from the polluted world.'

There is certainly a comment in his autobiographical writings that suggests he spent a lot of time at home when he might have been at school. 'I was not strong,' he wrote, 'I was pampered and kept at home, and my education went on within the narrow compass of the backyard. I thought my coloured books and remnants of toys were like no other material on earth. They were mine. The slightest piece of paper, so long as mine own, was rare, beautiful and of profound significance.'

Another memory Hewitt had of his early years was of being taken by his mother down to the docks, where they waited for a ship on which his Aunt Adele, one of his mother's sisters, worked as a stewardess. Then there was a trip to Sydney by train, returning through miles of country blackened by bush fires. And occasional trips by train to Carrum, to see his Rayner grandparents.

He was puzzled by two completely different answers he received to the question 'where do babies come from?'. His mother had told him that babies grow inside cabbages. His Aunt Lucy (one of his mother's sisters) told him babies came from red berries. He spent a lot of time in the garden opening up red berries to see what was in them.

One day his mother took him on a visit to the Botanical Gardens in Melbourne. There he saw a boy painting in a sketch book, and this caught his interest. He wanted to draw and paint like the boy he had seen at the Botanical Gardens.

School life began in earnest for the young Hewitt when he was eight years old, and he started at Brighton State School. His mother had harboured hopes that he might have gone to the Grammar School, along New Street from the Rayner home. There was evidently strong rivalry between the boys of the state school and the boys of the Grammar school, with their distinctive red caps.

During these years, he did all the things that young boys get up to. He pilfered lark's eggs, picked and ate wild fruit (as well as quinces and other fruits from people's orchards), and trapped pigeons. He attended the annual picnic trip organised by the church, when 50 children were taken on three horse-drawn wagons to the estate of a gentleman in Malvern. Tea was brewed in a large washing copper, and the party ate sun-dried fish sandwiches. There was also raspberry vinegar to drink.

Sometimes they would go over to Elsternwick where the Chinese market gardens were. He recalled that the Chinese were able to raise crops of vegetables in all soils and at all seasons. 'They would come to your door with cauliflowers, potatoes and lettuce when no-one else could get them'.

As a youngster, Hewitt helped on his father's building projects, 'picking up all sorts of new knowledge, helping the men mix plaster in large boxes, carrying sacks of red cowhair for binding, collecting fresh sweet-smelling shavings, making up the fire for lunch, and drinking billy tea.'

Then, after all the tasks were done, he would go down to the shark-proof baths (the seawater baths at the end of Park Street) to meet his friends and watch some of the state's swimming champions practise.

But it is apparent that Hewitt was always something of an outsider. His weak physical condition meant that lessons exhausted him, and he was excluded from the games of the schoolyard. He also wrote that his 'puny, resentful nature' did not help. He was bullied by older boys, except when he bribed them with huge pieces of toffee made from molasses. At the age of 10 he was the same height as his mother, and almost as tall as his father. He described his condition as overgrown and frail, which attracted constant jeering from other boys in the streets of Brighton. He found it difficult to ignore and to combat, because of his impressionable nature and desire to please.

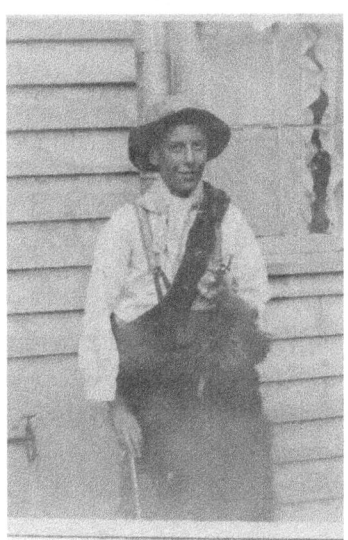

He was happiest roaming the fields of Brighton, observing nature, playing near the Elsternwick Canal. He befriended two boys from the Brighton orphanage, and eventually his circle of friends did start to widen. One of his special friends was 'Tweedie-wee'. His real name was Lionel Dadswell, or Gadswell (but even this may be a Rayner invention). He was one of four brothers. Their father was a salesman for a wine company, and spent weeks at a time travelling around the country. Their mother had once studied art at London's Royal Academy Schools, and may have planted an idea in the young Hewitt's mind. Hewitt wrote that the family lived in a much-neglected Queen Anne villa that lay near the creeper-covered cottage of Margaret

1.10 Hewitt age 11. sw.

Baskerville, the famous Victorian sculptress who at that time had a studio at 24 Church Street. [In 1912 she was commissioned to create a statue of Sir Thomas Bent, late premier of Victoria, which now stands at the end of Bay Street on Nepean Highway in Brighton].

Wildways was constantly receiving visitors, especially on a Sunday when the Rayners seemed to have kept a kind of open house for family and friends after church. Hewitt never stated at which church his parents worshipped. They had been married at the Church of Christ in Hawthorn, Melbourne, and his father would in due course be buried in the Presbyterian and Methodist section of a cemetery. But Hewitt attended Sunday School at St Andrews church across the road from Wildways. This is confirmed by a bible he received from this Sunday School in November 1913, as second prize in that year's class, achieving 385 marks.

The fire in the large room at Wildways would be lit whatever the time of year. Pancakes would be cooked. Hewitt's Aunt Emma (probably one of his mother's sisters) would make devilled almonds in a large frying plan over the fire, frying them in olive oil, salt and cayenne. Mrs Kenning ('fat, kindly-eyed') would come over and make German doughnuts. 'I had never tasted anything so toothsome'.

Among the visitors Hewitt recalled a music-hall artist called Leonard Nelson. He had once worked in the Edwards' saddle-tree factory, and later become a popular entertainer. He wrote and sang songs. 'Goodbye Melbourne Town' was one of his. His real name was Harry Snell. Hewitt wrote that his comedy routines did a lot to keep up the spirits of people during the 1914–18 war.

Another visitor was Bill Parry (almost certainly another pseudonym) whom Hewitt described as a trade union official who would go on to become a Senator and later Minister for State. He recalled 'Parry' leaving labour pamphlets in the house. His father put them in the WC.

One of the most detailed accounts in Hewitt's autobiography of life at Wildways relates to a Sunday afternoon. No date is given, although it was probably a year or two before the outbreak of the First World War. Perhaps 1912 or 1913, when Hewitt would have been 10 or so.

'Father sat on the rough garden seat, cutting tobacco into his hand from a dark oblong plug. His pipe hangs unlit in his thin mouth. He is amusing himself with remarks about my boots. In addition to the many small weekend tasks allotted to me, I was obliged to black my own boots. The blacking was hard to mix, as it had first to be broken from long bars, and then softened with water. The stuff had an acrid smell that I very much disliked, so it is quite possible that I did not give all the attention that I might have given to my footwear.

'That's what they call a soldier's shine' remarked my father, plugging tobacco into the bowl of his pipe, and gazing significantly at my feet.

'Why do they call it a soldier's shine?', I asked.

'Because,' said my father, feeling around his pockets for matches, 'soldiers are taught never to look back, so only the front of their shoes gets polished.'

'Father appeared very soldierly himself, with his sallow, handsome face, waxed moustache and flowered waistcoat. He possessed all the clean movements and ringing command one associates with the drill ground. He had, in fact, been a private in the Melbourne Militia about the time I had been born.

'As the last note of the church bell died away I entered the old burying ground. In the southern corner of the old grass-grown churchyard stood our Sunday School, a battered bluestone edifice that had been the church in the old settlers' days. [This description perfectly fits the

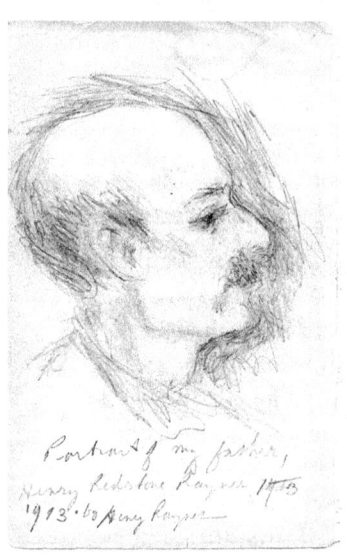

Portrait of my father, Henry Redstone Rayner 1913. by Amy Rayner

1.11 Pencil drawing of his father when Hewitt was 11 years old. sw.

small building that still stands in front of St Andrews church, just across the road from the Rayner home.]

'Sunday usually found Wildways full of visitors', he recalled. 'People who drifted in and never came again. People who hadn't the slightest claim on us, but who stayed on and on. Then there were the uncles and aunts, and mother's friends and father's friends, and a cousin with a mop of shaggy fair hair who came from Blackrock. She never arrived without a few burrs stuck to her stockings or coat. This sturdy country woman was a symbol of energy. No sooner had she entered the house than she rushed into the kitchen to help with the work, and tell all the news in her clear jolly voice.

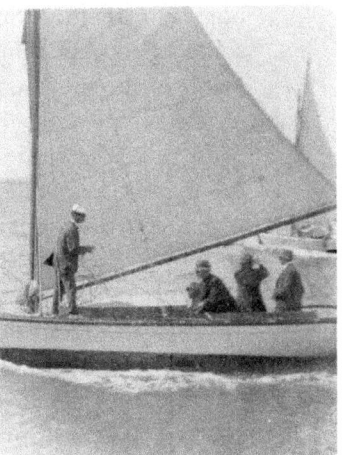

1.12 Hewitt's father on his 25-foot yacht at Brighton. He is the figure on the left. sw.

'Father, at this period, seemed wholly wrapped in himself. Things were going well. He had his hands full. The official architects had inspected his plans for houses to be erected along the new road that cut through the Baron Estate, and a beginning had been made.

'Granny Day' [a Hewitt pseudonym for a widowed lady who ran a small shop popular with the schoolboys, at the corner of Wilson and Carpenter Streets, opposite the old Brighton Methodist chapel] was immersed in one of the armchairs, busily stitching away at an iron holder. She made hundreds of these things, very delicately, of choice designs and colours, and sold them. 'Ah, my precious,' she exclaimed, when I ran into the room. She was wearing a fine lace cap, and looked very happy.

'The flames were flickering cheerily in the grate, multiplying themselves in the blue-glazed tiles of the narrow hearth. Mother, in a voluminous white dress with a high bone collar, sat by the open bay window where a bowl of flowers rose out in a puff of yellow.

'On the other side of the room, half-hidden by a new book case, sprawled Mr Parry, his long legs stretched out beneath a heavy book he was reading. As secretary of the local branch of a Trade Union he found himself on the road to fame, and overworked himself in the effort to keep to that road. But there seemed to be no fun in it, at least that was the impression I gathered from his vastly changed countenance.' Hewitt noted that Parry was studying for the Bar.

Christmas was a traditional occasion with roast duck stuffed with apple, onion and sage, despite the raging hot north wind and dust of the Australian summer. Hewitt noted that the cards from uncles, aunts and cousins in New Zealand all bore images of England.

On Christmas Eve the family would all take the train to nearby Prahran, to do the Christmas shopping. On one such trip Hewitt's mother pointed out a house in Prahran where the singer Nellie Melba had lived as a young girl.

As the years went by, his father's business prospered. The area was attracting more residents, and Rayner senior was winning contracts to build the new homes for them. A Speech given by Brighton's mayor in 1911 noted that by July some 2,600 new homes had been built in the town. This was more than in the whole of the previous year. [Information from an unpublished manuscript *The history of Brighton* by John Butler Cooper (1925), held in Brighton Library].

In the years running up to 1914, areas that had been fields were becoming urbanised. 'Penny libraries and teashops were opening everywhere,' Hewitt wrote. 'Asphalt was laid down, and for miles around lines of red and white villas appeared. The carefully-clipped box trees and hibiscus in the centre of a fresh and fenceless garden betokened a new sort of townsman.'

Other changes were visible in the town. Hewitt recalled that in 1914 a large garage was being built facing the Marine hotel. There is still a garage there today, on the corner site facing the roundabout where New Street meets Park Street. In contrast, at the old coachworks, business was slowing down.

As his father's building activities prospered, there was a little more money available, so Hewitt's mother started going to auctions. She was 'looking for fine old English pieces belonging to families that were selling up and returning to Europe.'

New items appeared in the family home. A red Brussels carpet. A large, round mahogany dining table. Two red plush armchairs to go near the fire. Straight-backed oak chairs ('backcrackers') and a settee.

This new-found financial security also allowed Hewitt's father to buy a yacht. He purchased a 25-foot yacht in Williamstown, and sailed it back. With it came a small dinghy, which Hewitt quickly learnt to handle. He also learnt the rudiments of life-saving, diving and the Australian Crawl from the then champion swimmer of Melbourne.

Rayner senior was a keen sailor, and sailed the bay in all kinds of weather. 'My father could be seen hanging onto the tiller and mainsheet when other hardy yachtsmen were standing muffled up in the bar, drinking whiskies and thinking about it,' Hewitt wrote.

The yacht was destroyed in the freak tornado-like storm that hit Brighton on the afternoon of Saturday 2nd February 1918. Melbourne's *Argus* newspaper reported that 200mph winds hit Brighton Beach and moved on through the town, ripping off roofs, toppling chimneys and leaving a trail of destruction. The Middle Brighton baths where Hewitt had spent so much time in his childhood were extensively damaged.

Hewitt noted that when his father became more prosperous, and owned the yacht, it attracted 'a few questionable friends – town cadgers, and men who saw in him an easy means to cheap fishing excursions, and an introduction to yacht club society.' From one of the brief notes, it is possible that his father also owned at one stage a small off-license.

Hewitt recalled an old photograph album that contained, among others, a photo of his father, with heavy black beard and ragged trousers, standing next to his gold claim in Western Australia. Another photo showed his father as a youth, standing by his boat at Shanklin, Isle of Wight.

Living by the sea, much of the young Hewitt's free time was spent fishing or sailing. Fishing from the pier for whitebait, herring small fry and pilchards was one of the boys' favourite pastimes. Whitebait fried in butter, or carefully boiled in milk, was evidently one of his father's favourite dishes. They would also dive for cockles on the sandy bottom of the bay. Hewitt also went fishing with his father in the dinghy, when flathead and gurnand were the most likely result. On one occasion his father caught a large squid.

Halley's comet in 1910 was an event he recalled. He also recorded that at the age of 10 or 11, he came close to death. The doctors were unable to diagnose what was wrong. He was tested for TB. Daylight was painful. His chest was 'jam-full of pain'. At one point, he was due to be taken away to hospital but his mother insisted on looking after her only son at home.

Whatever the illness, he spent a long time in bed, hardly aware of what was going on around him. His mother fed him milk and eggs beaten with sugar and brandy or wine. She also hung a bunch of onions up in the room, 'to absorb the disease'. Hewitt wrote about lying in bed, just able to see the roof and gables of the house next door – a vicarage according to Hewitt, unusual in that street because it had two stories.

The turning point came (at least according to his own writings) when having exhausted all the usual medical treatments, his mother brought along a local figure who would nowadays be regarded as a faith healer. This was the local character who Hewitt called Frederick Chappy (or 'Chappy' for short) in his writing, but whose true identity has not been identified. Evidently he was a carpenter and joiner by trade, and known around Brighton as the 'stuttering curer'. He seems to have cured Hewitt.

Chappy had a continuing influence on the young Hewitt, with his homespun religious ideas. One day he took Hewitt on a visit to the Melbourne herbarium. 'It was a glorious day. Chappy took me to have a glass of ginger beer and a ham sandwich. Then we went to the aquarium: a stuffy, smelly place. Chappy wore a large white panama hat, and as he shambled along, gazing at things through his strong glasses, and conversing slowly, everyone stared at him. People turned back to gape and grin.'

Many years later, Hewitt still treasured six letters that 'Chappy' had written him when he was away from the Brighton area.

As Hewitt recovered from his illness, his paternal grandmother Selina gave him his very first oil painting set – a large varnished case of Windsor & Newton oil colours, complete with palette, brushes and turpentine. He spent many hours at the kitchen table, happily painting pictures his grandmother would take away.

Hewitt never wrote specifically about the influences that first drew him towards drawing and painting. With a mother who was a keen amateur artist, he had watched her at work from an early age, and her work was hanging on the walls of Wildways. Receiving that box of oil paints from his grandmother must have given him another push in the direction of art. It seems that an artistic flair ran through not only the Rayner family but also the Edwards family. In 2007

David Edwards told the author that Arthur Milner Edwards had three daughters of which Thelma, the eldest, had been a 'reckoned artist'. Her sister Ann was also apparently a talented amateur artist.

By the time Hewitt was at the State School he was showing a flair for drawing. At about this time he also started writing. 'Writing down the things I loved best to remember … painting the things I loved best to see' as he explained it. This is the period when his lifelong habit of jotting down ideas and information on scraps of paper began. It started because he was so impressed by the things Mr Chappy said.

Ill health, however, would dog him for the rest of his life. 'My weak throat and chest were a constant handicap for the whole of my schooling,' he recorded. When he was 11 years old, he was already tall, but painfully thin. He was not academically gifted. He put this down in part to the poor health that kept him away from school for long periods. He and his friend 'Yunker' were 'the dullest louts in our class, so we sat together.'

Hewitt had particular trouble with algebra and history. He envied the bright boys. 'Droning voices, flies and schoolbooks. Who wanted schools?', he later wrote.

He attended 1542 Wilson Street School, a few blocks away from the family home. 'The State schools in Australia have numbers,' he wrote. 'Like convicts. They are compulsory institutions. My school days do not evoke rapturous memories in me. The teacher's life was not an easy one. And the people seemed specifically recruited from the embittered, repressed section of the community. People who were hard upon themselves and others. People who could inflict biting pain. But the pay was low and we were doubtless odious'.

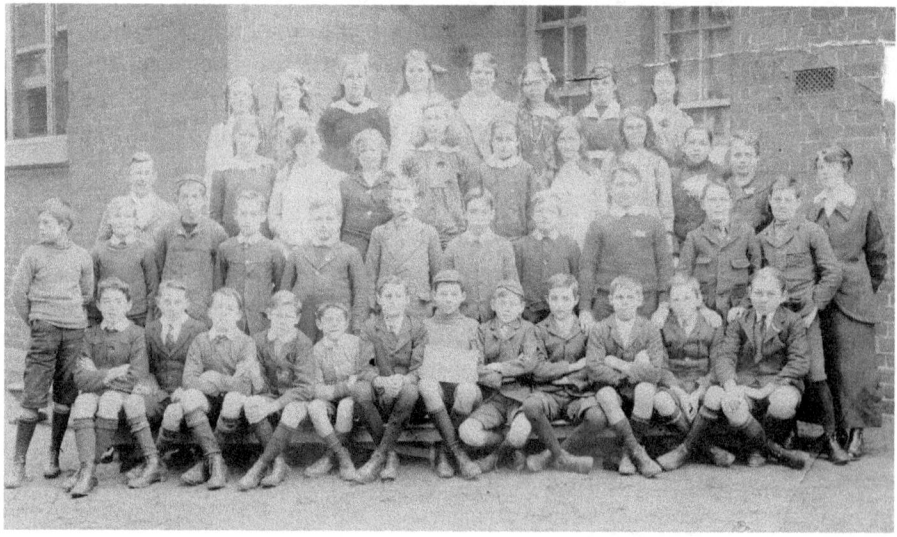

1.13 Hewitt attended the 1542 State School in Wilson Road, Brighton. Here he is in 1914 at the age of 12, on the extreme left in a row of his own, already taller than the boys standing in front of him. sw.

He hated school. He wrote of 'this complete annihilating cessation of all happiness. This awful mechanism of human schools designed to make boyhood miserable and fruitless'.

Freehand drawing was the only subject in which he shone, so much so that he was always top of the class. He had clearly inherited the artistic skills of his mother and his grandmother Selina Jane.

For the rest of the subjects, Hewitt wrote that he was regarded as dull. Many years later he noted with some satisfaction that the boy who won all the prizes at school finished up as a haberdasher. His classmates at the school included Alleyne Monkhouse, with whom Hewitt would briefly resume contact in the 1950s until the relationship went badly wrong.

He recalled a science teacher called Major Wright, who he described as a splendid teacher for the brilliant scholars, 'but I and my dull comrades dreaded him'. Another of Hewitt's teachers was known to the pupils as 'Fairy' Thomas. In the 1950s at the age of 82 she still remembered Hewitt, whom she described as 'my serious and dear pupil'.

Teachers at the school recalled by Hewitt and Alleyne in their letters many years later included Joe Mumby, 'Titsy' Jones, 'Peaky' Obrien the sloyd (wood-working) teacher, and Billy Ellie the gym teacher.

He and his friends were regularly being sent for caning. But they had worked out a solution. Instead of going to the headmaster's room, they rubbed their hands vigorously on the brick wall of the school, then hid in the toilets for a little while, out of sight, before returning to the classroom to show the teacher their red hands. As far as Hewitt could recall, this trick was never discovered.

Although he was not academically inclined, he was an observant child. He was very aware of life around him, noting the effects of the changing seasons, the wildlife, flowers and trees in the area. He was curious about everything (except, apparently, history and algebra). He wanted to capture the spirit of all this in pictures and words, and was frustrated at his early artistic attempts.

The other children, even the brighter ones, would ask Hewitt to help with their drawings. And it was the young Rayner who started a school paper for the boys of the higher grades. For this, he gained the nickname Penny Weekly. He always thought it was ironic that Hewitt Rayner, one of the school's dull pupils, was the only one to come up with the idea of a school magazine, and to make it happen.

The articles in it would address subjects such as school bullies, resulting in threats. In one number, in 1914 or 1915, he had written an article decrying compulsory military drill for 'lads who were weakly, but who were passed as fit by the doctors, and had to walk miles after their days' work in factory or shop, and endure the fatigue of endless marching and standing at attention.'

For this essay, Hewitt was knocked to the ground and beaten and kicked by a gang of youths, resulting in injuries to his arm that needed a sling for several weeks.

He attended woodworking classes, proud of the apron his mother had made, but the sawdust triggered his hay fever, so the doctors prohibited him from attending.

In 1916, when he was 14 years old, he was six feet tall, and worried about certain aspects of his physique. 'I had broad angular shoulders, but the whole of one side of my body did not match the other, through some fault of birth. And all my teeth were falling out. A severe shock to perfection-seeking youth. However, what concerned me most were my lungs. With those cured, I might face the world and be happy.'

A separate note records that a slice of bread and 'good Queensland molasses' formed the greater part of his diet in those days, which probably explains the comment about his teeth falling out.

As well as being a keen amateur artist and a gifted storyteller, Hewitt's mother was also musical. She had a contralto singing voice, and accompanied herself on the elderly upright German piano at Wildways. Hewitt himself received weekly piano lessons from a Miss Williams. These were interrupted in 1914 when her fiancée was killed in action in Europe.

Although a tough, strong man, Hewitt's father developed a slow wasting disease that was first detected in 1914 when he tried to enlist in the Australian Army at the outbreak of war. He was turned down by the Medical Board, and told by his own doctor that he was in the early stages of a spinal disease. Hewitt recounted how his father's health deteriorated. 'First had come fainting fits', he wrote. 'Then enervation and a long course of doctors, reducing the fortunes of the house. He drew himself along on two crutches, painfully'. His father lost the use of his legs in 1916.

Hewitt described his father's face: 'That once confident, handsome face, shrunken to the bone, grey.' On one occasion Hewitt heard his father say 'I have always been prepared to face facts. But I never expected this.'

The family was not rich, and the medical costs left them with very little money. In addition, his father had made some ill-judged investments, including a valueless allotment at Blackrock.

'A dark shadow hung over Wildways,' wrote Hewitt. 'The place had become as quiet as the grave. Father's old fishing cronies no longer bothered about him. No-one ever came to visit us. The white rough-cast walls of the house were beginning to crack, in long ugly rifts. Slates had come loose on the roof, and grass choked the gutters. The yard and sheds were filled with rusting tools – hods, scaffolding, ladders and heaps of grass-grown planks. Father was dying.'

Meanwhile, the young Hewitt had passed his exams to the Prahran Technical College, and was proud of his new striped cap, 'but my clothes were very shabby', he would later write. 'I was perhaps a little too conscious of that fact. And I had grown very meditative.'

At this stage, conscious of the need to earn a livelihood and help his parents, he had given up all ideas of becoming an artist, and got down to his studies in woodwork and metalwork. He regularly heard of people he knew who had gone off to fight in Europe, and been killed or maimed at the Front.

He describes the family home being sold, and extra money raised by selling the lumber that surrounded the house. The furniture was auctioned off, and his father's affairs put in order.

Hewitt recorded being deeply upset at seeing strange people packing the family home, looking for bargains. His mother sat in the kitchen, crying, next to the cold oven. In his parents' bedroom was a pile of postcards and letters.

One of his last memories of the empty house was putting his hands on the windows that his father had recently re-puttied, and seeing his father's fingerprints sealed into the putty. A kind of memorial to his father, Hewitt thought. But one that would mean nothing to Wildways' next occupants.

His father's ship never had come in.

The death of his father meant that Hewitt could not continue his studies at the Prahran Technical College, so he took a job in a nearby garage, overhauling cars for a wage of £1 a week. Then he decided to go up-country to work on the farm owned by Tweedie's uncle. His mother had by this time taken a small house and let a couple of rooms, which relieved him of the need to worry about her.

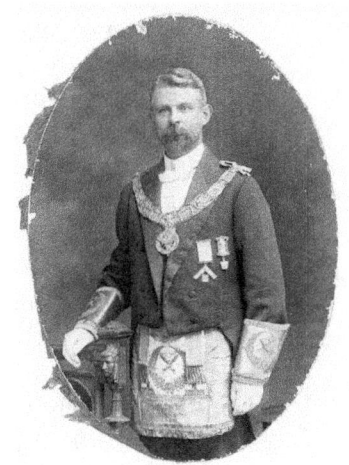

The young Hewitt (now about 19 years old) must for some years have been considering going into the bush. There is an account from several years earlier of how a friend of his father's came round to Wildways with a box containing some ferrets. Having heard that the young Hewitt was thinking of going travelling, he evidently thought the ferrets would be useful for catching game. Rayner senior reacted strongly, sending the man packing, saying that a rifle is all that his son needed for killing food.

1.14 After the death of his father in 1921, his mother remarried. Her new husband was Hal Gillard, manager of a Melbourne lawyer's office, and freemason. sw.

How long this trip up north lasted is not known. In the final 1938 version of Hewitt's 'Ship comes in' manuscript, the story ends as he and his friend Tweedie set off for the country, with a final short section about his return home in 1923.

The earlier 1935 version describes him drifting around Victoria, visiting some of the old gold-mining districts, taking farming and other jobs to earn a crust, meeting people, having visions, even preaching. Sometimes he painted garage and shop signs to earn money. This was clearly an important phase in Hewitt's life, judging by the number of pages he devoted to it in the 'Ship' manuscript. But whether it lasted weeks or months is not clear.

There is a short note recording that in 1921 he would 'tear' down to Melbourne from his retreat in the bush to see Allan Wilkie (Allan Wilkie CBE, 1878–1970) and his wife play Hamlet, Othello and other Shakespearean roles. 'Those were golden days and nights,' he wrote.

Another note records that he took lessons from James Charles Nuttall 'the famous Victorian black and white artist, and wandered around the city of Melbourne sketching. I sold many watercolours and painted a few indifferent portraits'.

At some stage he visited Tasmania. In 1922 he returned to Brighton, and the fledgling motor industry provided him with income for a while. Surviving letters from two Melbourne firms show that he had been employed by Westwood Motor Garage at 102 Chapel Street, Balaclava; and in 1923 at Lanes Motor Property Ltd, at 102 Exhibition Street, Melbourne. Lanes Motors were the distributors for Buick cars in Victoria. There is also a letter from General Motors Export Co, giving Rayner a reference regarding his suitability for working on Buick cars.

Hewitt's job involved driving and testing the new cars. 'Before I left Gippsland, the rugged mountain area of South East Australia, I had become renowned as an ace car driver and tester,' he wrote. 'My long runs were made in the first Buicks to come into that part of the country. And on those perilous mountain tracks I experienced some of the most hair-raising thrills to come the way of any driver of powerful cars.'

In the early 1920s some Buicks were imported into Australia as complete cars, but most had bodies built by Holden (Holden Motor Body Builders Ltd) in Adelaide. Buicks had built up a reputation for ruggedness and reliability, and the Buick Car Club of Australia web site tells how in 1925 one of the cars was driven round the world by relays of local drivers. The cars would have been particularly suitable for Australian driving conditions, and it is not surprising that Rayner was attached to them.

On 7th June 1923, his mother remarried. Her new husband was a Melbourne lawyer's office manager called Harold ('Hal') Gillard. The new family home was at first in Toorak, and a few years later in St Kilda, both near Melbourne. Just four days before the wedding, on 4th June, Hewitt wrote to his mother from Moe, a small town in Gippsland, some 80 miles East of Melbourne. From the content and tone of the letter, a kind of 'goodbye' to his mother, it looks as though he did not attend the wedding. The letter carries a later annotation by his mother (probably added in 1935): 'I was married on 7th June 1923. This is Hew's letter to me.

Hewitt remembered his stepfather as 'a loved and prosperous city lawyer, one of those rare legal men who seem to get every man onto their side by bluff good humour, extraordinary tact and a power to see what the issues are'.

Hewitt recalled Gillard's short white, tidy beard, the fine features and the kindly eyes. He noted that Gillard was a friend of the man who would become Australia's premier, Robert Menzies.

On one occasion Hewitt went with his stepfather to 'Fozoli's' Bohemian restaurant in Melbourne. 'The diners sat on long benches and rubbed shoulders with the great and the near-great. A plain wine was set on the board for those who had not the wherewithal to order their own. It was a happy atmosphere, and as many actors and actresses patronised the place, the atmosphere was usually hilarious.'

Perhaps influenced by his mother's new-found happiness, and the knowledge that she now had someone to look after her, Hewitt felt able to turn his attention to his main ambition – to further his artistic training in Europe.

In October 1923, in the Australian Spring, he sailed for Britain, paying his passage with some of the money he had saved from his employment in the motor trade.

This, then, is the story of Hewitt's growing up in Australia, based largely on his semi-autobiography. Hewitt had been a compulsive writer and hoarder, so the archive rescued by Sheilagh Wilford also contained masses of items ranging from scribbled notes on cigarette packets to long typewritten articles. There were also press cuttings from British, Australian and New Zealand newspapers and magazines, as well as letters he had received from family and friends.

Often, as if anticipating that one day a biographer might read the material, he added pencil notes to manuscripts, providing some background context such as why he had written them and how they had been used. He also helpfully annotated incoming correspondence, especially if it was from someone famous.

As all this material was studied, and original research was undertaken in Britain and Australia, it became clear that the story told in the 'Child' manuscript was incomplete. Some important events had been completely omitted, some had been sanitised, and others were complete invention. Hewitt had done what today would be described as a little spinning – glossing over uncomfortable events, protecting the identities of characters that appear in the stories, and allowing his imagination to create the story of what he would like to have happened, rather than what actually happened.

There is only one passing mention of the fact that his father had been married before. The bitter break-up of his parents' marriage gets no mention at all. And it turned out that he had created a completely fictitious name for the family home in New Street, Brighton.

2

Some uncomfortable truths

Press cuttings and other documents from the Rayner archive confirm that Hewitt lived and worked in New Zealand from 1918 until he returned to Australia in 1921. Some of the truths – for example relating to his father's first marriage, and death – emerged only as a result of research into official records in Australia. Some were found in papers buried in the Rayner archive, and never intended for use in anything Hewitt wrote.

His father's first marriage

The Australian birth, marriage and death records show that Hewitt's father had married a girl called Alice Elizabeth MacDonald when he was living and working in Western Australia. She was the daughter of a missionary, and had been born in Penang Straits Settlement. The couple were married on 18th March 1897 in Perth. On the marriage certificate, he gave his name as Harry (rather than Henry) Redstone Rayner. They lived in Cottesloe, between Perth and Freemantle. In 1898, their first child, Donald Henry, was born in Cottesloe. He died one year later.

Then the family moved to Melbourne, where their second son, Allan Garfield Redstone, was born on 25th January 1900. He too died in infancy, at the age of four months in May. On 10th June, Alice herself died. The death certificate gives 'Cardiac Syncope and Phthisis Pulmonalis' [Pulmonary TB] as the cause of death, and states that she had been suffering from this for the past three years. Her death was reported in the Melbourne Argus on 12th June 1900, with the words: '*RAYNER: On the 10th June at Kew, Alice Elizabeth Rayner, wife of Henry Rayner, and daughter of' Wm Macdonald of Penang*'.

Mother and son were buried in Boroondara cemetery, at Kew, on the outskirts of Melbourne. The death certificate shows that the family was living at Kew, in Walpole Street. Henry's occupation was given as 'plasterer'. At what point he acquired plastering skills is not known.

By the time he married again in April 1901, he was not yet 30 years old, yet had experienced the deaths of two young children and his wife.

His parents' breakup

There is plenty of documentary evidence to confirm that Hewitt lived in New Zealand in his late teens, and then had to return to Australia. But it cannot have been in order to see his dying father. His father's death certificate shows that he died in January 1921. Yet according to the reference letter from Lester & Bell, Hewitt didn't leave New Zealand until March 1921.

In fact, the circumstances surrounding his father's death were very different from the versions written by Hewitt. So bad, in fact, that this is almost certainly the reason Hewitt invented a more palatable version. In the 'Child' manuscript, he movingly describes his father's deterioration at the family home at Wildways, in Brighton, his transfer to hospital where he died, and the auctioning of the family home and contents.

The first clue that this was far from the truth came when his father's death certificate was located. This shows that his father died, not in hospital as Hewitt had written, but at an address in East Malvern, near Melbourne. The address was 33 Coppin Street. Cause of death was given as Paraplegia, Enteritis and Exhaustion. He was 49 years old.

Probate was granted to his older brother, Frederick Charles Rayner, rather than to his wife or son. The probate documents reveal that the day before he died, Henry Redstone Rayner made a will giving all his assets to his brother. In other words, he disinherited his wife and son. The will was dated 14th Jan 1921, and was witnessed by Harold Thomas Lawrence of Main Street Mooroopna, a railway employee, and Myra Hendrey, of 33 Coppin Street, where Rayner was living at the time.

The probate file still contains the hand-written will, dictated by Henry Redstone Rayner, and signed by him in a shaky hand. [The Victoria PRO reference for the will is VPRS 007591/P/0002, Unit 000638, descr 177/98]. It reads:

> This is the last will & testament of Henry Redstone Rayner made fourteenth day of January 1921.
>
> I do give and bequeath to Frederick Walter Charles Rayner all my worldly possessions after my funeral and all debts are paid.
>
> [Not legible] savings bank Elizabeth Street Melbourne also monies in State Savings Bank, Caulfield East, and remainder of purchase money of house situate in Brighton being paid off by Vivian Bell.
>
> Signed H R Rayner
>
> Witness H T Lawrence
>
> Witness (nurse) Myra Hendrey

The solicitor, Alfred Pearce, of 'Whitehall', Bank Place, Melbourne, advertised in the *Argus* on 20th May 1921 as follows:

> Last will and testament of Henry Redstone Rayner, late of 33 Coppin Street, East Malvern, in the said State, plasterer, deceased, may be granted to Frederick Walter Charles Rayner of 38 Corsair Street, Richmond, in the said State, builder, the executor according to the tenor of the said will.

Probate was granted to the deceased's older brother Frederick, following affidavits made by him, Myra Hendrey and Alfred Pearce, on 5th July 1921.

Frederick's address was Corsair Street, Richmond. He gave his occupation as 'builder'.

The Affidavit of Execution states that Henry Redstone Rayner was married at the time of his death, and left a will dated 14th Jan 1921. The will had been witnessed by Harold Thomas Lawrence of Main Street Mooroopna, a railway employee, and Myra Hendrey, of 33 Coppin Street. The deceased had left no real estate in Victoria, but had left property [meaning assets] valued at not more than £890–17–2.

There is also a signed statement from Mrs Myra Hendrey stating that the will shown to her is the one she wrote down on 14th an 1921 under instructions from Henry Redstone Rayner. Evidently no will had been deposited with the Registrar General, so the will written the day before his death was accepted.

The inventory attached to the probate document makes sad reading. All the possessions Henry Redstone Rayner left were a metal watch and chain, clothes, rug and an invalid chair worth £7. Financially, however, he was well off. The 'property' mentioned in the Affidavit of Execution comprised two savings accounts holding (with interest due to date of death) £373.14.6 and £219.0.0, and a debt due to the estate of £291.0.0 from a V. Bell. This latter was the balance of purchase money owing on a house in Selwyn Street, Brighton, that Mr Bell had purchased from Rayner. The Brighton Rate Book for 1921 shows that the house was indeed owned by a Vivian Bell, engineer, of 40 Hambleton St, Albert Park. The house no longer exists, having been replaced by a more modern building.

For Henry Rayner to disinherit his wife and son in this way, just a day before his death, indicates that the marriage break-up must have been bitter.

The final discovery in Melbourne seems to confirm this. In addition to cutting his wife and son out of his will, Henry Redstone Rayner chose to be buried in the same grave as his first wife Alice and his son Allan, in Boroondara cemetery, Kew, on 17th January 1921.

It takes considerable perseverance to find the grave plot, number A005 in the Presbyterian and Methodist section at Boroondara cemetery. It is completely unmarked. Hewitt's older brother had clearly not spent any of his inheritance on erecting a lasting gravestone. Or even any gravestone at all.

Exactly what went wrong in the Rayner household in the years running up to 1920 is unknown. A small handwritten note found among Hewitt's papers states that his parents' marriage was dissolved and they were legally separated in 1917. However, during the execution of his will, Hewitt's father was described as married, so it seems that the marriage had not, in fact, been legally ended.

In the circumstances, it is not surprising that Hewitt glossed over these events in his own autobiographical account, and presented a gentler (but untrue) version of a family that stayed together until his father's decline and death at the family home in Brighton.

The truth seems to be that Hewitt's parents had split up in 1917 or 1918, and this is why he went to New Zealand with his mother, to stay with the Edwards family in Auckland. It is a matter of record (from the Brighton rate books) that by 1918 Grey Lynn was no longer occupied by the Rayner family.

Hewitt's father, left alone in Australia, suffered a painful and crippling illness that left him wheelchair bound. He died alone, cut his wife and son out of his will, and chose to be buried with his first wife.

Hewitt's mother looked back on the years of her marriage to Henry with a bitterness that extended to all the Rayners in Australia. Many years later, in November 1936, when Hewitt was enquiring about the past, she wrote in a letter: 'It was miserable enough for me. If you weren't sick, your father was, and I had to work and scrub, and pack and unpack. Nineteen moves in 17 years, dragged from pillar to post, and all I got out of it was kicks. I wish you'd let the past die.'

Hewitt himself recalled one incident that confirms the state of his parent's marriage. 'I was beginning to realise that my parents were not happy; had never been happy together, in fact. One dreadful night I found mother lying hysterical on the floor, and father standing by the dressing table. She was threatening to shoot herself. The drawers father was leaning against held his revolver. 'What should I do', he said coldly, 'throw a bucket of cold water over her?'.

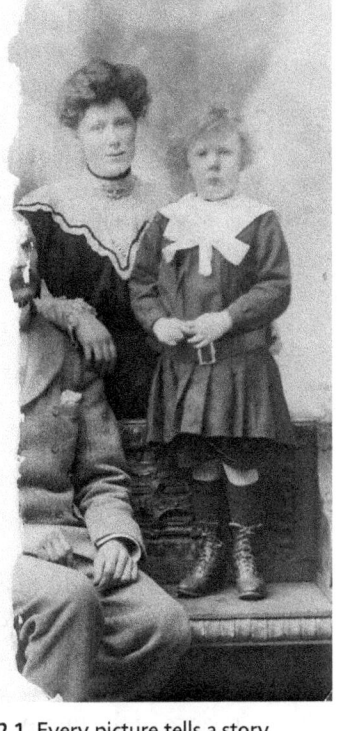

2.1 Every picture tells a story. Hewitt's mother ripped her husband's image from this 1907 photo after their separation. sw.

Hewitt's mother wanted a social life. 'She loved society, loved company,' Hewitt wrote. 'There were times when she read the papers and paused on the notices of concerts, balls, dinners and other exclusive assemblies in Melbourne, all of which were denied her. She could not resist reading them aloud when in this mood. She had wanted to join the Ladies' Church Tennis Club, but father had hummed and hawed until she became infuriated and avoided the subject.'

To make up for it, his father took his mother out to a Ladies' Evening at the yacht club, but this turned out to be a disaster. 'Mother returned very miserable, and a most frightful row resulted. She had been cut, snubbed, cold-shouldered, sneered at – the wife of a plasterer who came to the event in a lounge suit. And she in an ordinary frock – unheard of. What was the club coming to?'

In the afternoons his mother would hurry through her work so she could play to herself on the piano. 'In the silence of the house her beautiful voice sang forth, a mellow contralto. Always the old beloved songs of her youth. This and her painting were her only recreation.'

Hewitt jotted down several other notes about his parents that were never used in the 'Child' manuscript. He recorded that his mother and father had frequent rows. 'At night they quarrelled bitterly. They were a wilful and full-blooded pair. I feared them and loved them in terror.'

On one occasion his mother said that she hated being called a 'wife'. 'The terms man and wife are repugnant to me, if we can't be friends' she declared. 'Rot', his father replied. 'Your ideas are absurd. I know those sorts of la-de-dah wives; the sort who come home late every day and feed their menfolk up with cold polony [a type of pork-based luncheon meat] and German sausage. The Colonies are full of them.'

Hewitt wrote that his parents were disappointed in their son. Hewitt's sickly constitution contrasted sharply with his father's strength and fitness. At least in the early years.

'They took everything'

When his parents' marriage broke down, Hewitt's mother fell out with the rest of the Rayners as well. In later life she clearly hated it if she discovered that Hewitt had been in touch with any of the Rayners in Australia. References to 'they took everything' indicate that nothing of Henry Redstone Rayner's estate reached his former wife or his son. Including the former family home, Grey Lynn. This is why Hewitt's mother had to move into rented accommodation.

It may well be that the marriage was flawed right from the start. There is a photograph taken during Henry and Emily's 1901 honeymoon in Fern Tree Gully, some 30km East of Melbourne in the Dandenong Ranges. It shows the two of them in the garden of a house. He is seated, she is standing. On the reverse of the photograph, Hewitt's mother had written:

> 'I was only 22 years of age when this was taken, staying in Fern Tree Gully. Distracted and nearly out of my mind by this man's ill treatment. I had just returned from a long lonely walk to find this man posing all smiles for this photo, & when the owner of the house saw me returning insisted I should stand. The result I'll leave for a reader of character to comment on.'

More tellingly his mother's copy of her wedding photograph from 1901 has been torn in half so that Henry Redstone's image is no longer there. Similarly there is a group photo of Hewitt and his parents, but it has been torn in two so that only Hewitt and his mother remain.

In later years Hewitt's mother blamed her husband for poisoning their son against her. In an undated letter from around 1938 she wrote: 'My whole life was devoted to you, and as you grew up I can see now, [you] hated me all the time. How that devil must have lied and lied behind my back while I was going without clothes or any pleasure, & barely food. He started a quarrel every mealtime, I can see now, so that I shouldn't eat. I hate him more every time I think of the crawling beast. I can't help it. I can't get over the horrible past, and it has even come into Hal's life.'

Outbursts like this are a regular feature of her airmail letters to her son. So it's perhaps surprising that as the years rolled by Hewitt would develop an increasing sense of identity with his Rayner forebears on the Isle of Wight. As we shall see he made several visits to the island starting in the early 1930s, digging into the Rayner family history, meeting distant relatives, checking out the family legends he had heard as a child, and looking for clues to his own personality.

Growing up in New Zealand

Hewitt's account of growing up in Australia, as told in the 'Child' manuscript, completely omits to mention that in his late teens he spent two and possibly three years living in New Zealand, between 1917 and 1921. This is a strange omission, as towards the end of his life he would sometimes say that he regarded New Zealand as his spiritual home.

After his parents' separation Hewitt went there with his mother to live with her family. The main source of information on this phase of his life is a two-part article he wrote for the *Waikato Times* in May 1952. There is also corroboration for his New Zealand years in the form of letters to him at New Zealand addresses during this period, later letters to him from people in New Zealand, and various reference letters from employers he worked for in New Zealand.

This is the essential story he told in the article he contributed to the *Waikato Times*, where it appeared in two instalments on Thursday May 15 and Saturday May 17 1952.

In 1918, age 16, he was working for a jeweller in Auckland. His job was to 'furnace gold in a dark little shed, and create in silver precious little gems and gold at the bench'.

He described himself in those years as 'sensitive, delicate, reticent to a too high degree'. He was finding that the jeweller's bench had tired him. 'The people of New Zealand were hard-working, quiet and strong' he later explained. 'I knew that wherever I drifted I would find work and friendship.'

The trigger for his unrest was his discovery of Impressionist art, and the work of Degas, Cezanne and Sickert. Then he discovered the work of Van Gogh. 'Poor Van Gogh set me painting and drawing in a passion, with *Thomson's Anatomy* by my side, and a clutter of dead animals, birds, fish, human bones, fossils and machine parts, absorbing the essence of life and freeing myself from a mixture of State school mental incompatibilities.'

He was also fascinated by the greenstone art of the Maoris, and had started carving in this translucent jade.

Hewitt had wide interests. He says that his mother had wanted him to study medicine, as she was convinced he had healing fingers. He was teaching himself French, through reading and translating French plays. One of his goals at that time was to go to Paris and enter the studio of a master. He purchased a big engineering book so he could 'gain a sounder understanding of the aesthetics of machinery, and to have a side craft.'

One spring day in 1918 at the age of 16 he left Waikato and went into the countryside. In an interview given to the *Auckland Herald* in June 1947, Rayner described this act as 'running away from home'.

He was employed as a farmhand on a farm called Spion Kop, outside Cambridge. Many years later the farmer would write to Rayner saying 'I remember you being a better artist than farmer.'

At this time, Hewitt was conscious that he was not receiving any tuition in art. 'So much of a young artist's time is wasted without adequate schooling,' he later wrote. 'Students must be taught the rudiments of the craft, the way to tread.' Rayner himself did not receive any formal teaching in art until he was 20 years old.

Even without formal art tuition, back in 1918 he was nevertheless busy drawing and painting. 'My little room on the hill farm was soon more like an alchemist's study,' he recalled. He was busy sketching nomad Maoris as they dried their eels by the roadside, and 'snatching time off from the heavy tasks of the day to catch the growth of the plants, grasses and trees and the animals and the light falling on them.'

'Often I wandered into the mysterious, silent hills, and sat watching the story of it all. I was quite at home with the wild life of this place, even the wily deer and the hare allowed me to approach near them.'

Moving into Cambridge itself, Rayner found work at Wilkinson's motor garage. A reference letter written by Wilkinson's shows that he worked there from March 1919 to March 1920. When not working, he painted – on larger canvases that he bought on frequent visits to Hamilton.

He joined the 1st Waikato regiment, attaining the rank of Corporal, and the 3rd Auckland Regiment. Surviving orders show that in October 1919 and January 1920 Hewitt received orders to attend parades with A Company of the 16th Waikato Regiment in Cambridge Drill Hall. He was part of the 1920 guard of honour formed to welcome Lord Jellicoe to Auckland as Governor, as a photo records.

All this is in marked contrast to the story he recounted in the 'Child' manuscript. In that, he gives the impression that he stayed in Australia, moved from the state school in Brighton to the Technical College in Prahran, and then when his father died he abandoned his schooling to earn money by working in a local garage. There is no mention of New Zealand. And no mention of travelling and working prior to his father's death.

The article in the *Waikato Times*, written by Rayner himself, tells a very different story. According to that, his plans to settle in Cambridge were thwarted by a message from his dying father, following which he returned to Auckland. Then he 'followed' his father to Melbourne.

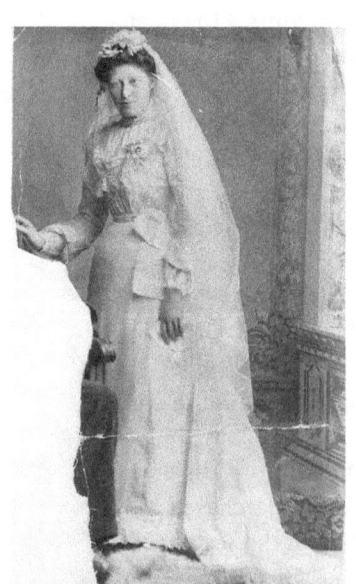

2.2 Hewitt's mother's wedding photo after she had torn off the portion with her husband's image. SW.

In March 1920 he was employed by the Lester and Bell Hire Garage at 3 Lamps Garage, 4 St Mary's Road in the north Auckland suburb of Ponsonby. The garage ran taxi services, undertook car servicing and repairs, and sold petrol. It took its name from the distinctive ornamental three-lamp street light that stood in front of the garage at the intersection of Ponsonby, College Hill, Jervois and St Mary's Roads. [The original lamp was removed in 1934, and a faithful reproduction erected in July 2012, to much local acclaim].

Hewitt described his position there as chief mechanic, although the reference letter when he left one year later (dated 11th March 1921) gave his position as 'improver motor mechanic'. It was nevertheless a glowing reference:

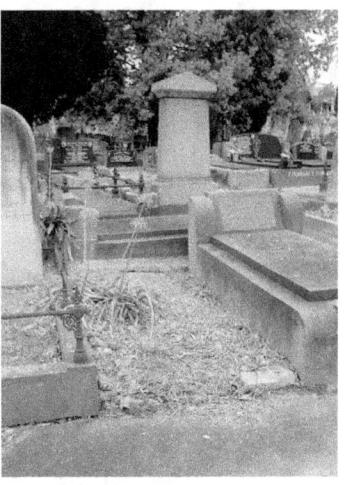

2.3 The unmarked plot where Hewitt's father was buried in Boroondara cemetery in Brighton, next to his first wife and their son. PHOTO RS.

> 'We have pleasure in stating that we have at all times found him thoroughly capable and conscientious – the makings of a first-class mechanic. In fact we have, in the variety of work he has had to undertake in this garage, found him equally as capable as the average full-time journeyman. Apart from his ability as a mechanic, we may state that he is abstemious, of punctual habits, and of excellent character.
>
> We have no hesitation whatever in recommending him for motor-mechanical work of any description. We regret very much losing his services, but he leaves us entirely of his own accord, owing to his departing for Australia. We wish him every success.

He returned to Australia, and continued working in the motor trade. A reference from Hoe Motor Garage dated 12th October 1923 states that he had worked there for two years until his departure for England. This doesn't quite tally with the reference letters from Westwood Motor Garage in Balaclava and Lanes Motor Property in Melbourne, which cover more or less the same period. It may be that he held down two jobs, in order to save for his trip to England.

Whatever the detailed dates and employers, it is evident that for four years from March 1919 to October 1923 he earned a living working in the motor trade in New Zealand and Australia.

Many years later, in 1953, a press article about a pre-Cook shipwreck in Ruapuke Bay brought back a memory for Hewitt, relating to his motoring days, and he wrote a letter about it to the editor. It is not known whether the letter was ever published.

> Apropos of Ruapuke Bay wreck, I was working in the Three Bells Garage, with Lester, in Auckland in 1920, and it was one of my hobbies to act as driver-mechanic in the races that went on at Muriwai.

Sometimes I helped to tune the engines of the then crack British entries, Rolls and Daimlers etc, and at one time we all went down there with our new Chalmers stripped for the race. The great white Daimler had taken the bend of one of the cliff hairpins and had slipped over into the dense undergrowth. I was looking around for some likely timber for jacking, and came upon what seemed to be the remains of a door, just below me the beach gleamed white, streaking out to the ocean.

I broke up some of the timber and we had the chassis back on the narrow road again, but I, with my student's curiosity roused, went back to the rotting wood. It was all in strips, I found, and very old. I was needed for the race and had not much time to dawdle.

I kicked up as much of the earth as possible and came upon a small shaped strip of wood which, from the modelling of its base and rivet hole three parts of the way up, and hollowing, told me that it was the remains of a crucifix, about eighteen inches long, such as Catholics have always carried for ritual purposes.

I took the piece and left for the beach. I afterwards cleaned the piece, and found that it was of oak, European or English. The metal attachments had long corroded away.

Was that an old coffin I had found? And was it from an early European ship, years before Cook? Your story of the ship remains of Ruapuke Bay roused all the old memories. I had intended to return to the spot and make my own investigations, but I was required in Melbourne, and never returned to New Zealand.

Muriwai Beach is on the west coast of New Zealand's North Island, only 40km or so from Auckland. The first New Zealand Motor Cup was held there in 1921, but Hewitt's story shows that the beach was already used for motor racing events in earlier years.

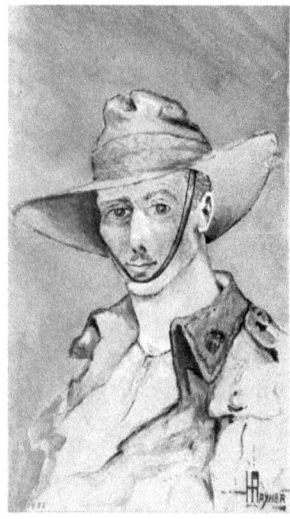

2.4 This cartoon self-portrait from 1922 shows Hewitt in New Zealand army uniform. sw.

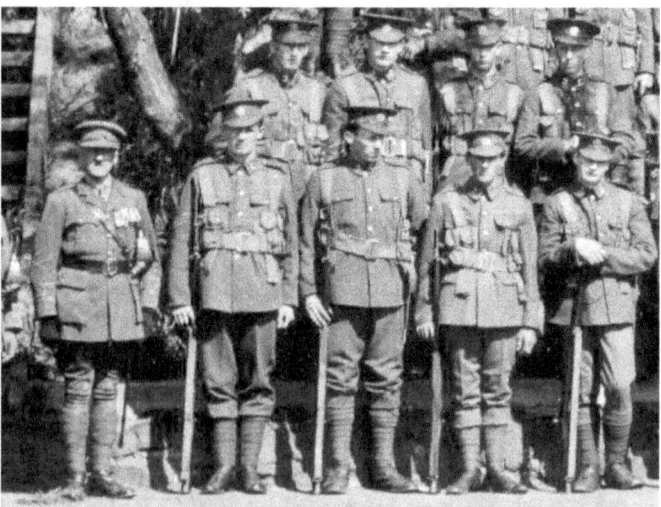

2.5 Hewitt joined the 1st Waikato regiment, attaining the rank of Corporal, and the 3rd Auckland Regiment. He was part of the large guard of honour formed to welcome Lord Jellicoe to Auckland as Governor in 1920. Here he is in the centre, front row. sw.

While he was in New Zealand he formed a friendship with a girl called Gwendoline Walker, who lived in Auckland. When he left for Britain in 1923, she obtained his London address from his mother, and this started an exchange of letters that continued until August 1926 when Hewitt told her of his impending marriage.

Whatever happened in the Rayner family as Hewitt was growing up in Australia and New Zealand, he always looked back fondly on his days in New Zealand. 'His happiest days were spent there,' his wife Theresa would write 40 years later. Hewitt himself described New Zealand as 'my spiritual home' in one of the biographies he penned for the press.

The Walhalla scam

Hewitt's mother was outraged in 1913 when her husband decided to invest £500 of their hard-earned money in what turned out to be a gold-mining investment scam. Although this story was never mentioned in Hewitt's 'Child' manuscript, there are numerous versions of it in his preparatory notes, so clearly at one stage he had been planning to include the Walhalla incident.

Walhalla was a township that had sprung up during a gold mining boom in the mid 1800s. Located in the remote Baw Baw range of mountains in Gippsland, about 100 miles to the east of Melbourne, it had grown to a town of some 5000 people at its peak. But extracting the ore and crushing it turned out to be a costly undertaking, and by the turn of the century it was clear that gold-mining in Walhalla was becoming uneconomic.

By 1913 the gold mining activities at Walhalla had shrunk to a shadow of their former scale. This was the year that a friend of Hewitt's father approached him with an investment opportunity that 'couldn't fail'. Bill Closter (probably not his real name) was apparently a former engineer and a prospective parliamentary candidate.

This was the tale he told. A group of businessmen had formed a new private company called Blue Reef Mining to exploit a new gold discovery in Walhalla's northern ridge. The find was being kept secret, which was why there had been no press coverage about the discovery. Just a few selected individuals were being invited to invest in it.

Hewitt's father had been a gold miner in Western Australia in the 1890s. This new investment opportunity re-awoke the gold bug in him. The 'gold digger's disease', as Hewitt called it.

His wife was dead against the whole idea. The argument raged back and forth in the Rayner household, and was the only topic of conversation at the dinner table for many days. Hewitt recalled that his father was so passionate during these discussions that he 'even put away his pipe'.

In the end, against the wishes of his mother his father paid £500 for 500 shares in Blue Reef Mining. It is possible that there were further calls on his money, but Hewitt did not record (or did not know) how much was invested in total.

It turned out to be a scam. Initially, Hewitt's father was given reassuring accounts of the progress of the new mine in Walhalla. The front man for the business was a smooth talker called 'Connelly', who Hewitt recalled as 'cool as a cucumber, a man with a Chinese gleam in his eye, a gentleman.' Rayner senior visited him in Melbourne, and was shown samples of the gold allegedly taken from the newly discovered reef.

At last, after several months, and increasingly worried, Hewitt's father decided that the only way to reassure himself that everything was in order would be to visit Walhalla. He took Hewitt with him. His wife's parting words were: 'I suppose you think you're going to return with a wheelbarrow full of gold. Well, we could do with it.'

They travelled by train from Melbourne to Moe where they were met by an old horse-drawn coach for the final leg of the journey along the road via Erica. On the way they encountered a bush fire that delayed them. Fallen trees had to be cleared from the road, and they arrived black with the ash. They ate in the hotel in Erica, where their driver Wally was well known. To the north, Hewitt could see the snow-capped Baw Baw range of hills.

They arrived in Walhalla, which was little more than a single street. There were few people around. They asked an old man for information on the new Blue Reef mine. He knew nothing of any new mine, and was sceptical of the whole story. He took them to the only recently opened shaft. 'You'll wait until doomsday afore ye'll git paydirt out of that hole,' he said.

Hewitt and his father spent the night in Walhalla, then set off back to Melbourne. Hewitt's father had been unable to find the promised workings. He was never able to track down the mysterious Mr Connelly again.

'Father's ship had struck another calm,' noted Hewitt.

It seems that Mr Closter, the family friend who had first brought the Blue Reef Mine company to Rayner senior's attention, also lost money in the venture, to the tune of £1800. No mention of this investment fraud has so far been traced in the Australian newspapers, so the perpetrators seem to have successfully kept it away from public gaze.

The real 'Wildways'

Hewitt's description of the family home in the '*Child*' manuscript was correct in every aspect except the name. In reality it was called 'Grey Lynn'. Hewitt thought that this was an old name from the Isle of Wight, but it's more likely that the house was named after the district in Auckland where his mother's parents lived.

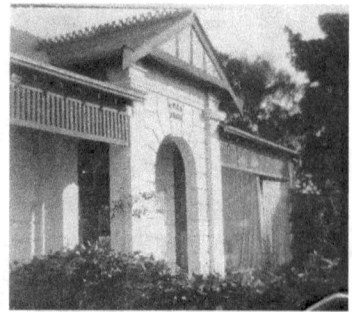

2.6 Grey Lynn as it was when Hewitt grew up there. Note the curtains on the north, sun-facing, side of the property. Hewitt's father was a plasterer, and the stone-effect porch rendering with the name Grey Lynn was his work. sw.

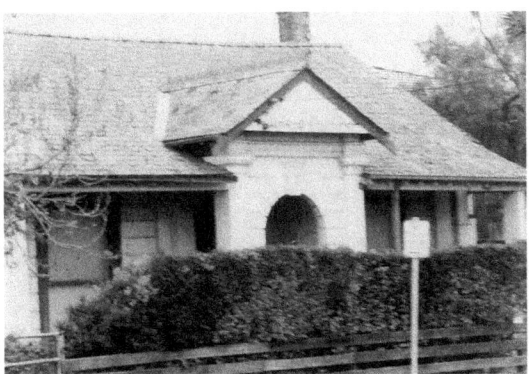

2.7 Still little changed by 1983 when there was an unsuccessful campaign to prevent the building being demolished. PHOTO COURTESY BRIGHTON HISTORICAL SOCIETY ARCHIVES.

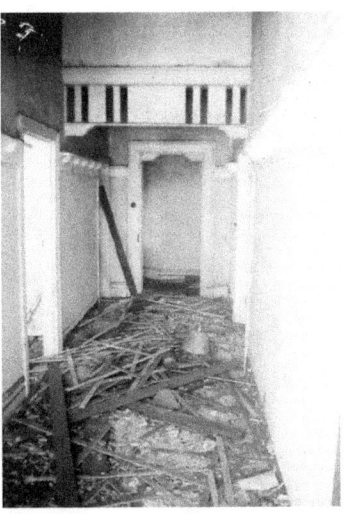

2.8 The main passageway of the property looked rather sad after several years of neglect and vandalism. PHOTO COURTESY BRIGHTON HISTORICAL SOCIETY.

Exactly why he felt it necessary to give his early home a completely false name in the 'Child' manuscript is not known.

Finding the location of the property during the research for this book was also made more difficult because at some stage since the 1920s all the homes along New Street in Brighton had been renumbered. The plot that was number 165 New Street in Hewitt's day is now number 231.

Yet another obstacle in identifying the property was the fact that the building itself is no longer there. It was demolished in the 1980s after a controversial and much publicised court battle to preserve the historic building. Fortunately, the local Brighton Historic Society has a file on the property, with photographs taken during the conservation battle. No-one at that time was aware of the property's link with Henry Rayner the artist.

Once the location in Brighton was confirmed, it did tie in completely with the clues in Hewitt's manuscripts. It *is* near Park Road. It *is* near St Andrew's Church, where he attended Sunday School. And the gasworks *was* upwind of the house.

It may be that the family always called their home Grey Lynn. The Sands & McDougall Directory for 1907 shows a Henry Rayner living in a house called Greylynn on Narong Street in Caulfield. The Caulfield Rates Book for that period doesn't give a house name, but does give the occupier's full name – Henry Redstone Rayner.

[For more details on the history of the Rayner home in Brighton, see Appendix 7].

II

London: the Sickert years

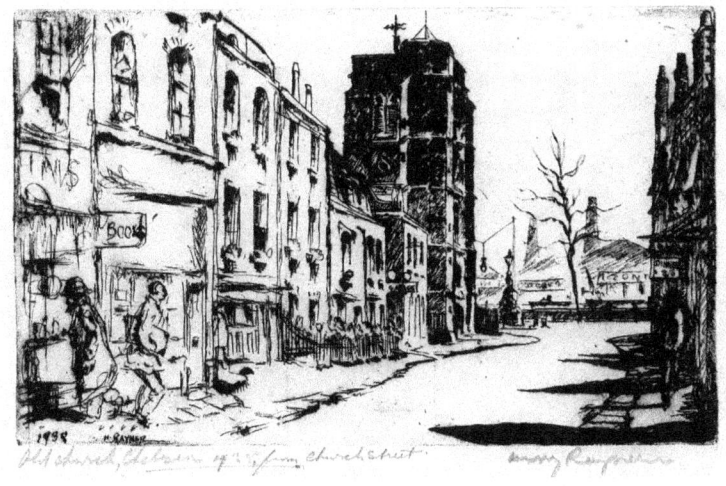

Fig II *'Old Church, Chelsea, 1925, from Church Street'*, drypoint 116 x 177mm. RS.

3
From art student to artist

Hewitt Rayner arrived in London on Monday 24th December 1923 on board P&O's 9000-ton *SS Khyber*, a freighter that also carried a limited number of passengers. He was one of only seven passengers to disembark – five had joined in Sydney, and one in Gibraltar. Their route to Britain was via Colombo, Suez, Port Said, Naples and Gibraltar. A small watercolour by Hewitt of his ship in Gibraltar harbour is dated 21st December 1923.

Hewitt was 22 years old. For the passenger list he had given his occupation as *engineer*. Unlike his fellow travellers he had not given a UK contact address, implying that there was no relative or friend waiting to welcome him to England. In the space for an address it simply says c/o P&O, Cockspur Street, London. Where he first lodged is not recorded.

He attended evensong in St Paul's Cathedral on Christmas Day, and kept the printed Order of Service for the rest of his life.

He needed to earn money in order to survive while he pursued his ambition of getting into a top school of art and becoming an artist. Using the references he brought with him from the General Motors Export Company, he quickly secured a position with General Motors, Hendon, where he tested and drove new models from America. He later wrote: 'The old 1914 Graham White airfield [the airfield in Colindale, north London, that later became known as Hendon Aerodrome] where we kept the superseded cars in their hundreds, was littered with the wrecks of the first British war planes – great rugged monsters, clumsy and fragile'.

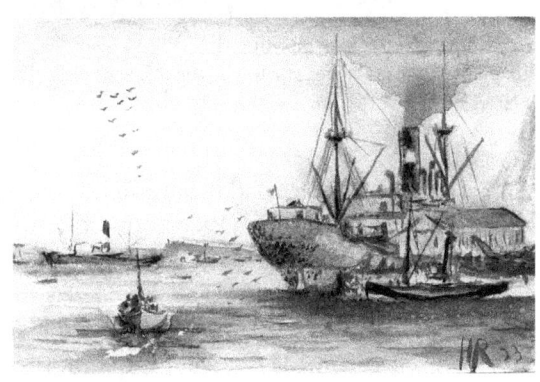

3.1 This small work from Hewitt's sketchbook shows his ship, the *SS Khyber*, in Gibraltar on 21st December 1923. Watercolour, 87×135mm. sw.

Virtually nothing is known of his movements during this period, apart from the fact that on 19th April 1924 he made a trip to Birmingham to visit some cousins.

The reference he was given when he left General Motors has survived:

General Motors Limited, The Hyde, London NW9
30th May 1924

To whom it may concern

This is to certify that H H Rayner was employed by this company from 10th January 1924 to 17th April 1924 as a driver tester in our Sales Department. During this period he worked satisfactorily and was discharged upon the rearrangement of the work of this department.

F W Beard, Secretary

Next, he took a job at the Daimler Works as a tester. 'I was employed by Commander Piper (an Australian) of the Tank Corps. But one day I threw everything up to become an artist wholetime. It meant giving up a lot.'

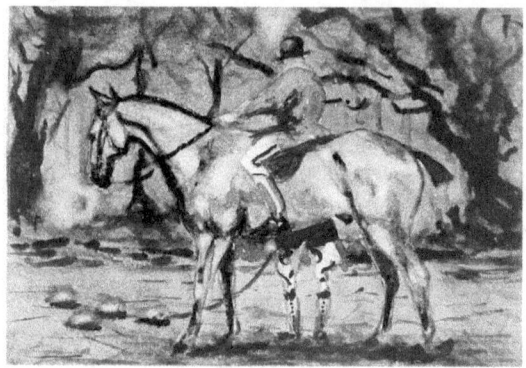

Commander Piper had evidently tried to persuade the young Rayner to give up his plans to change careers, with the words 'Where you are going there is no bed of roses. Get down to blueprints instead'. But to no avail. Art was what had brought Hewitt to Britain, and art was going to be his life.

He started his studies at the St John's Wood Art Schools under Leonard Fuller, in readiness for applying for a place at the Royal Academy Schools. By September 1924 his finances were poor, and he pawned a gold watch at

3.2 A small sketchbook painting dated 1924 from the period before Rayner started at the RA Schools. Watercolour, 85×113mm. sw.

a pawnbroker in Edgware Road, obtaining £3. He gave his address as 3 Alma Square, in St John's Wood. This is to the north of Paddington station and west of Regent's Park.

St John's Wood Art Schools was in those days regarded as a stepping stone for aspiring artists planning to apply to the Royal Academy Schools. An advertisement in the March 1914 edition of *The Studio* magazine makes this clear, stating: 'Students specially prepared for the Royal Academy Schools, where forty four have been passed in since July 1910'. The school had an honorary advisory council that included members of the Royal Academy.

Another practical attraction was that students could start their training at any time of year. Term started from the day of entrance, according to the school's advertising. This must have been especially attractive to someone like Hewitt Rayner, in a hurry to get to the RA schools.

The location of the school at 29 Elm Tree Road, right next to Lord's Cricket Ground, was very convenient for his lodgings in Alma Square. By 1925 he had moved a few blocks eastwards to a room at 18 Culworth Street – still only a few blocks from the school. Culworth Street is near Regent's Park and the Regent's Canal – both locations that would feature in his etchings through the 1920s.

While studying at the St John's Wood Art School he met Alfred Munnings, who spent a term as visiting artist.

Hewitt must have stayed in touch with Frederick Walenn, Principal of the school. Four years later in January 1929 Walenn wrote inviting him to make use of the school's life model during a period when there were few students. 'I have lost most of the men to the RA,' Walenn wrote, 'and I must tide over this empty period until I get more in. I wonder whether you could make use of the model to paint something for exhibition or for some other purpose of your own. You are welcome to make what use you can of the model.'

In the Spring of 1925 came the breakthrough he was hoping for. He won a place at London's Royal Academy Schools, with a five-year studentship starting in May 1925. In 1960 his widow wrote about him receiving an ivory medallion from the schools. This is a reference to the ivory discs or 'bones' that served as students' entrance tickets to classes.

Hewitt had been recommended by a Lt. Col. N. Hillary. 'I did not pass in without a struggle,' he recorded in an early note. 'The Royal Academy is a jealous institution and at this time over-careful in its choices [of student].'

The primary source of information about Hewitt's experiences at the Royal Academy Schools is his unpublished auto-biographical manuscript titled '*Red Violet*', completed in 1954. This chronicles the years from his arrival in England up to the 1940s. Unlike the earlier '*Child when my boat comes in*' manuscript it is a more factual and less varnished account of his experiences. Supplementary information has come from the RA's archives.

Hewitt entered the RA schools on 19th May. The usual academic year ran from September to July with a two month summer break, and there was an annual examination at the beginning of November. However, in those days students could be admitted at one of six dates through the year.

Starting at the RA Schools with Hewitt in May 1925 were four other students. Ralph Fisher Skelton (1899–1930) was a 25-year old American who had studied at the Chicago Art Institute and The Slade. Henning Alfred Nyberg (1903–1964) was a 22-year-old Norwegian. The other two were fellow Australian Jean Sutherland (1902–1968) and Rosalind Mayne, both aged 22.

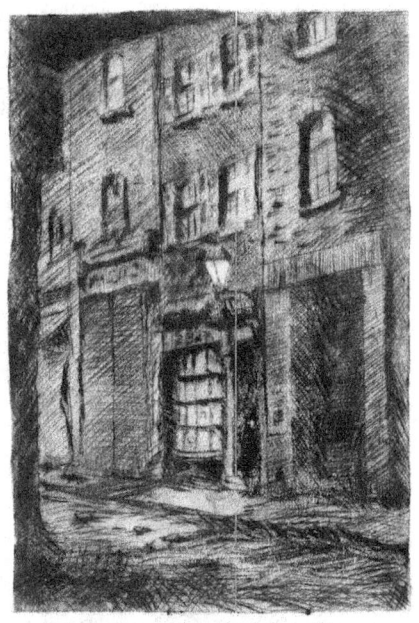

3.3 One of the earliest known London etchings by Hewitt Rayner, before he adopted his 'Impressionistic' style of drypoint and settled on the professional name 'Henry Rayner'. An unknown London location at night. Untitled drypoint 130×90mm. COURTESY ELIZABETH HARVEY-LEE.

Among the students already at the Schools when Hewitt started were René Quinn, son of the Australian artist James Quinn, and Edwin John, son of Augustus John. Edwin had enrolled at the schools in February 1924 at the age of 17, and remained a student until January 1928, when the official Council Minutes record that he was expelled for 'improper conduct', having posted in the common room some unflattering comments about the RA President, the Curator and Members. Another student Hewitt became acquainted with was Clifford Hall (1904–1973).

René Quinn and Henning Nyberg struck up close friendships with Hewitt, and both figure in his autobiographical writings. Strangely, he never referred to Nyberg by name, simply calling him his 'Norwegian artist friend'.

Hewitt's mother and stepfather sent him a Reuters telegram on 24th May: '*Overwhelmed good news. Our united congratulations. Don't fail to have furlough. Love.*'

As a new arrival at the RA Schools he recorded his first impressions of the place: 'Its fetid corridors were sweet to me; its dust delicious.' He was charmed by his new surroundings. He settled down to life as a student, making pencil drawings of statues and plaster casts in the RA, and copying paintings by the Masters. Some of his student works have survived – mainly life pencil drawings and oils. Some of the oils are copies from old masters, and some are contemporary scenes. He seems to have been particularly interested in the works of Jean Francois Millet.

Hewitt was especially thrilled to discover that one of the visiting teachers for the month of June that year was Walter Richard Sickert. It was a dream come true – the work of Degas and Sickert had appealed to him ever since he discovered impressionist art while he was living and working in New Zealand.

According to Hewitt, Sickert's arrival at the schools 'broke the refined melancholy of the painting and drawing rooms, including the smelly corridors. It had introduced an electric touch not too pleasing to many of the elegant students and some of the academicians. He added to the 'Modern Left Wing' of which I was a member.'

Sickert liked being in the company of younger artists, and was generous in his encouragement to them. He was a good host and kind friend to the young, as Osbert Sitwell wrote in the preface to '*A free house! Or the artist as a craftsman, being the writings of Walter Richard Sickert*' [Macmillan & Co, 1947].

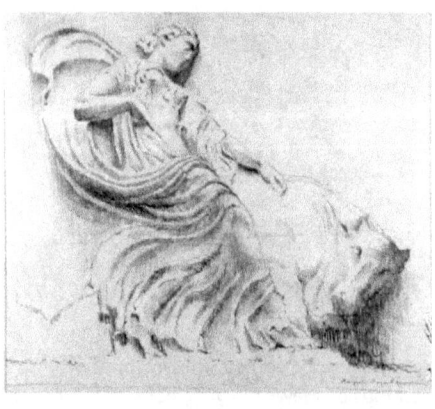

3.4 Students at the RA Schools routinely had to copy plaster casts. This is Hewitt's drawing of 'Europa and the Bull' – the RA's cast of an original in the Vatican Museum. Pencil, 425×325mm. sw.

Unlike his own former teacher, Whistler, Sickert evidently did not become jealous when one of his students achieved success. Hewitt benefited greatly from Sickert's support for younger artists, as subsequent events confirm.

Hewitt was not blind to Sickert's failings. He knew that Sickert was not universally admired by his peers. 'He had earned the reputation among his colleagues of being the ruin of all his pupils,' Hewitt noted. 'They doted on his Indian reds and yellow greens, and went cheerfully to ruin under the tragic (fatal) spell of his strange personality.'

'I had heard so much of Sickert, so-called 'one of the greatest living artists, a pupil of Whistler'. Now came my chance to meet him.'

Sickert's classroom technique was often to set up a *tableau vivant* of several models posed together, dressed in costume. This was in marked contrast to the usual approach at the Royal Academy schools – described by Hewitt as 'a stiff solo bout of 'classical' pose, with faded, moth-eaten draperies arranged in the ancient manner of the Greeks, too often verging on the comic.'

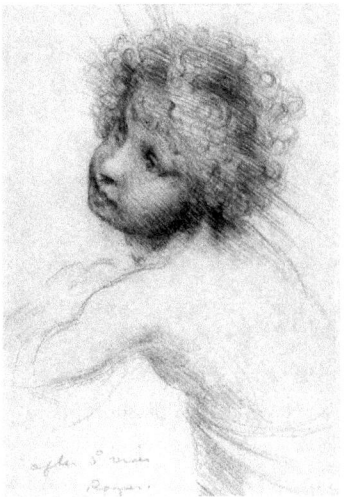

3.5 Hewitt studied the drawing techniques of Leonardo da Vinci. Pencil, 240×160mm. sw

Sickert's own views on how best to arrange lessons have also survived in a hand-written report to the Royal Academy following the month he spent as a Visitor in 1925. In it he says: 'I believe that the maximum benefit to be derived from models will be got by engaging them for the month and posing them in a kind of knot in the centre of the room, so that the whole resulting *chiaroscuro* can be studied all round'.

In this letter Sickert also makes a case for giving students easels at which they can sit rather than stand. He felt so strongly about this matter that he donated 12 easels to the School.

Thinking back to the Sickert lessons, Hewitt wrote: 'He would abide no opposition to his methods and was often harsh to both the men and women pupils under him. His retorts were quick … penetrating … final. Everything started from the two-tone *camaieu*. Two colours, black and brown barred. Out of this any picture could, in his opinion, be built up. 'Any drawing holds infinite possibilities', he said.

'Sometimes I think he did not give sufficient consideration to promising individuals, and the inherent tendencies of certain pupils who by gift and inclination found it impossible to work from a monochrome basis. And he seemed to take it for granted that everyone understood what he said in both his fluent French and English disquisitions.

'Sickert never concentrated on the work of students he considered to be wasting their time, be they rich or poor. They were just wasting their own good time, in class and in studio. Equally, he held no brief for the scruffy artists, the rich pretentious ones with the long and matted hair, who drank cherry brandies in Chelsea.' 'They are a drug on the market,' Rayner recalled him saying.

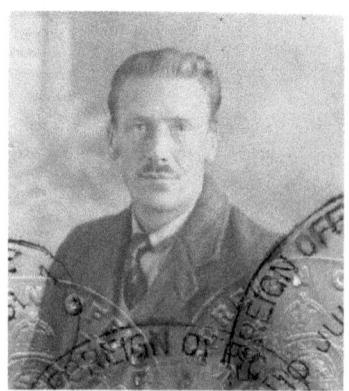

3.6 Hewitt's 1929 passport photo.
sw.

One incident involved a young lady student who had brought two dogs into the class with her. 'One of the setters began nosing Sickert's coat,' Hewitt wrote. 'This incensed Walter. He quickly applied his monocle to an enraged eye, and bawled: 'Take those animals away madam! I do not teach dogs! Take them to the London University … to the philosophers!'

Hewitt responded well to Sickert's eccentric teaching techniques. His tutor's frequent use of the French language was not a problem, thanks to Hewitt's studies of French books in New Zealand. Sickert in turn seems to have seen something special in the young Australian's work, and taken him under his wing. His 'capacious' wing as Hewitt commented in a letter to Osbert Sitwell in October 1955. There was a rapport between Rayner and Sickert, perhaps helped by the fact that neither had been born in the UK. The full story of their decade-long friendship is told in Chapter 6.

This special relationship did not, however, mean that Hewitt was safe from Sickert's occasionally biting criticism. On one occasion early in 1926 when Sickert was evidently in a fit of deep depression, he took a look at Hewitt's current painting and commented: 'Is your name Mr Cadbury or Mr Fry? There are no plain chocolate shadows in nature! Go off to the Tate Gallery and see my *Café des Tribuneaux*. There are shadows painted with stark common sense. I was only a mere youth, but I worked with pigments, not chocolate soufflé!' With that, Sickert took a large brush and swept a passage of violet-red into the canvas.

It may be Sickert who drew Hewitt's attention to the works of Millet. Sickert is known to have been an admirer of Jean Francois Millet (1814–1875), whose pioneering portrayals of ordinary working people probably also appealed to Hewitt's ideals. Among Hewitt's effects rescued in 2003 are three copies in oil of paintings by Millet, including *the gleaners*.

Hewitt's studentship at the RA Schools should have lasted until May 1930, but things did not go according to plan. His record card, still held in the RA's archives, shows that his studentship was terminated in November 1927. The reason given was 'non-attendance and failure to submit'.

The card also details his attendance record at classes. This is very revealing. From May 1925 to the end of that academic year in July, he attended 53 of the 79 morning classes, and all of the 65 evening classes. In the following academic year, however, he attended only 26 of the 241 morning classes and only one of the 201 evening classes. In the next academic year he didn't attend any of the 212 morning classes and he only attended one of the 178 evening classes.

He failed to submit a work for the annual November examination in either 1926 or 1927. It seems that for all practical purposes Hewitt had stopped attending classes by the end of the 1926 academic year; and even during that year he attended only five percent of the classes. What had happened?

Student unrest at the RA Schools

The circumstances of Hewitt's departure from the Royal Academy Schools are not entirely clear from his own written account. According to that, events at the schools led to him being branded a troublemaker, and as a result the British art establishment cold-shouldered him for the rest of his life. He wrote that he had been accused of deliberately smashing a plaster cast of a statue in the sculpture room. His attitude when taken to view the damage in the presence of the Academicians didn't help. He laughed.

'A cultivated assembly of ARAs and RAs stood by with set lips (one smoked a cigarette and smiled). And I was upbraided for a crime I did not commit. And as I was young and happy of soul, I laughed out loud; and was thereupon accused of being full of contempt and guile, and a danger to the other students.' He later wrote that this was the first occasion he had seen the statue or the pieces.

'I was made to feel as lonely as possible, and poor Charles Sims, RA, the Keeper of the Schools, was sent to rebuke me. That constituted the beginnings of the now famous Royal Academy Student Strike.' In an interview he gave to a journalist called F L McIlraith for *Smiths Weekly* in May 1939 Hewitt stated that René Quinn and Augustus John's son Edwin were also part of the student strike.

How reliable is this account of events? If there was a 'student strike' in 1925 or 1926, it was not reported in the newspapers of the time. But new research for this biography has shown that there had been a period of student unrest that worried the School's authorities. The first clue came from '*The history of the Royal Academy 1768–1986*' by Sidney Hutchinson [Robert Royce, 1968] in which there is a passing reference to 'serious disorder in the Schools' in 1926.

The records held by the Royal Academy Library – in particular, the minutes of RA Council meetings and the officially published annual reports – provided a lot more information on the matter. Information gleaned from these official records is reproduced here with the permission of the Royal Academy Library.

In 1925 pressure was building up among Academicians and Members for changes to be made in how the RA Schools were run. It surfaced as an issue at that year's General Assembly, held in May, when there was 'some discussion of questions of method and discipline', ending in a decision to ask the Schools Committee to consult Members and prepare a report on the organisation of the schools.

At this same General Assembly, Charles Sims was re-elected as Keeper of the Schools, but only on condition he accepted a significantly lower salary than in previous years. No reason was recorded, but it must have been a real slap in the face for him.

The nub of the challenge facing the RA was, in the words of R Blomfield (Chairman of the Schools Committee) a 'recognition that conditions have altered in recent years, and we fear it must now be recognised that the Royal Academy is not quite pulling its weight as an educational institution'.

One perceived problem was a lack of policy regarding the purpose of the Schools – were they for elementary students, partially trained students, or advanced students? There was also a general feeling that the standard of admission was too low, and that students were allowed too much freedom in their methods of study.

The years immediately following the 1914–18 war had been challenging for the RA Schools, with a big drop in student numbers. It had been left to the Keeper to build up the student numbers again. 'This has been done successfully under difficult conditions, but the time has now come to aim at quality rather than quantity', wrote Blomfield.

Sims noted in his report at the end of 1925 that: 'The level of accomplishment is not as high as could be wished in the Painting School. This is owing to the inability of students to support themselves by daily work and continue their studies in the Schools at the same time. Most of the clever students stay but a short time before leaving to earn their living.

Following the request from the General Assembly, Blomfield arranged meetings in November and December 1925 to canvas the views of Academicians and Members on the Schools. The resulting report was submitted to the RA's Council in early 1926. It proposed that 'Studentships should be limited to three years instead of five as at present. Students no longer come to the Schools at an elementary stage, but have all attended some art school for years; and after three years in the Schools they naturally wish to begin work for themselves.'

Another proposal was a three-month vacation beginning in July. 'This would give the students more time to begin work on their own account, and particularly those students competing for the Medals'. Other recommendations included a probationary period of six months, and the automatic striking off of a student who failed to attend the School for a period of three months.

This is how G. Clausen described the situation. 'The old system, which came to an end with the war, was perfect of its kind. Attendance was enforced, lectures were regularly given, models were engaged by the visitors. The Schools were if anything overstaffed and the system was too rigid. But it worked without much difficulty because of the prestige of the Academy, and because at that time its teaching had not been seriously challenged or questioned.

'Contrast this with what now exists – not so much a School, as a rather freely-run life class. The attendance is somewhat casual – this is due to some extent to the necessity of earning money – and the students work to a great extent as they please. I have no fault to find with them: they are well-behaved, orderly and on the whole steady at their work. But they are impatient of control; and it must be recognised that the younger generation no longer accept the old ideals: a different spirit exists and must be reckoned with.

... 'I think that the admission tests should remain as at present, but that a higher standard for admission might be required, and that students who habitually fail to attend should be struck off the School Register.

At the same time as all this focus on the management of the Schools, behind the scenes another drama was being played out. This didn't directly concern the School's affairs, at least not initially, but it would eventually have a big impact on the students – and on Hewitt Rayner in particular. It concerned Charles Sims and a large oil painting he had done of King George V in 1924. The story is told in Sidney Hutchinson's 1968 book, and this is the gist of it:

Sims was an Academician and a successful painter in his own right, as well as being Keeper of the Schools. He had been commissioned by the RA to paint a portrait of the King that would be hung in the Academy. Unfortunately the King didn't like the painting, feeling that it didn't display the appropriate sense of dignity, so he didn't want it to be hung in the RA. This had put the Council in a difficult position. They decided that the solution was to pay Sims the agreed fee of 250 Guineas on the understanding that the picture would not be hung at the RA.

There seems to have been an assumption and possibly a verbal agreement that the picture would be destroyed. However, this didn't happen, and in the autumn of 1925 it was shown at a gallery in New York. When the Royal Academy found out, a few months later in the Spring of 1926, they were understandably furious. To resolve the situation they appealed to Sims to accept a very generous offer of a further 750 Guineas on top of the fee already paid, in return for which he would hand over the picture to the Academy. This happened in June 1926. According to a pencil annotation to the Council minutes for 1927 the picture was cut up and burned in the Academy's boiler room.

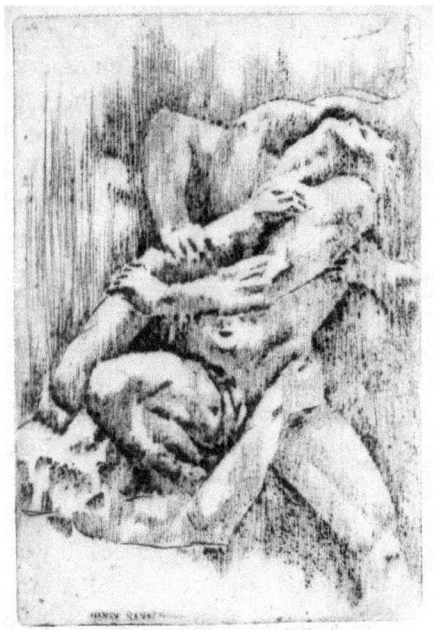

The relationship between the Academy and Sims had been terminally damaged. He was still Keeper of the Schools but as the examination date of November 1926 approached he was nowhere to be seen. He was still in the USA. The Council grew increasingly concerned that Sims was to be absent in America until the beginning of November, and the Schools would effectively be left without direction at a very important time of the year. Things came to a head on 2nd November when the Annual Examination had to be conducted without Sims' assistance. The Council sent him a telegram.

The official records state that 'disorder subsequently arose in the Schools owing to the failure of a number of Students in the Examination, and the President and Sir R Blomfield (Chairman of the Schools

3.7 *'The wrestlers'*, a student work by Rayner dating from c1926, before he had developed his 'Impressionistic' style. Drypoint, 233×156mm. RS.

Committee) had to intervene on November 4 and recall the Students to a proper sense of their privileges and duties.'

Hewitt had failed to enter a work for this examination. So had several other students. This was the 'student strike' that he talked about. A boycott of the annual exam.

On November 8 the Council received a letter from Sims, 'enquiring if his resignation would be acceptable'. They accepted and appointed an interim manager. Their anger may be seen in their decision to consider Sims' salary as being payable only up to the previous Christmas – almost a year before his resignation. They did, however, allow him to use the Keeper's House with its large studio until Midsummer 1927.

With all this going on it is not surprising that there was 'student unrest'. And there was Hewitt Rayner right in the middle of it all. Whether he was simply caught up in events or, as he suggested, an instigator of the student unrest is not clear. It is likely that he was more outspoken than the British students, simply on account of his new-world background. And his height would have made him stand out (literally) in any student gathering.

A completely unrelated source also throws some light on what was going on at the RA Schools in 1926, and confirms Hewitt's account of a student strike. It is an article in the *The Argus* newspaper in Melbourne, Australia, in 1936 about an exhibition of paintings by James Quinn at the Fine Art Society's Galleries at 100 Exhibition Street.

Most of the article is devoted to Quinn recounting anecdotes about painting portraits of various members of British Royalty including the then King and the Duchess of York. But there at the end is an account of the student strike at the RA Schools. This version of the story suggests that there had been a full-scale revolt, resulting in the expelling of students.

The way James Quinn told the story, it was his son René and Edwin John who led the 'one and only strike at the Royal Academy'. Quinn stated that the two students had been reprimanded by RA president Frank Dicksee for having used methods of drawing that he considered 'too modern'. When they resisted his authority, he expelled the two of them together with an unknown number of sympathisers from the Academy.

It was a step too far. As recalled by Quinn, among the expelled students were prize winners of the year before, and the most brilliant students of the current year. Furthermore, the authorities realised that the students were serious about the strike so Dicksee asked them to send a deputation 'for a parley'.

According to Quinn it was his son and Edwin John who led a procession of students bask into the RA, singing a witty reinterpretation of a popular Victorian minstrel song – 'We're gwine back to Dicksee ... to the picture-postcard land'.

Quinn stated that all the striking students had been reinstated.

Taking this independent account by James Quinn, together with the information from the Royal Academy's own archives, it does seem that Hewitt Rayner's tale of a student strike in 1926 is true. But as to how prominent was his role in the affair, we only have Hewitt's own recollections for that.

The tightening-up of methods and discipline at the Royal Academy Schools would continue through 1927 and 1928. The question of poor student attendance at classes was raised again by the RA's Council in early 1927 when they asked for an explanation for 'the large number of students whose names remained on the books although they had absented themselves for some time from the schools'. Hewitt was one of them, and in due course he became one of the students who had their studentships terminated in November 1927.

Hewitt had been badly affected by the treatment received by the Keeper Charles Sims whom he regarded as a personal friend and supporter. In earlier, happier times at the RA Schools Sims had taught him egg tempera in his Academy Studio, and drawing at the night classes held in the schools. 'Sometimes I went up to his great studio situated at the top of Burlington House and painted with him. Crippled in one foot, he could be heard hobbling along the silent corridors. At his death I lost one of my best friends. It had been he who had come to plead with me to return when I left the schools, but Sickert was against it.'

It is clear from Hewitt's writing that Sims was in a disturbed state of mind. Hewitt wrote: 'One morning just before I left the schools of the Royal Academy, I was on a bus in congested Bond Street on my way to the morning class. From the open top I suddenly saw my dear old friend Charles Sims, Keeper at the schools, one of the great painters of the period, passing blindly through a crowd that pushed him right and left.

'His morning jacket and trousers were muddled, his hair dishevelled, his eyes staring unseeing ahead of him. He dragged his lame foot behind him carelessly.

'We were near the schools and I jumped off the bus and rushed into the porter's lodge to get help, but none arrived. I went up to Sim's studio where a great canvas hung askew on the giant easel, and I waited, not daring to approach him in the Burlington House entrance.' [Students were not allowed to use the public front entrance to the Academy – they had their own entrance to the Schools, from Burlington Gardens].

'But he did not come, and was away all that day. We knew that his last pictures at the Summer Exhibition had been severely criticised, and that his summer of paintings had undergone an unusually rapid change. We did not know how bad things were with him. One evening the newspapers announced that he, poor gentle Sims, had jumped from a bridge up North, his pockets weighted with stones'. Sims died in April 1928 in Scotland. The *Canberra Times* of 19th April described it as 'a tragic end to a career of strangely recurrent triumphs and defeats'.

Hewitt noted: 'For some days before his death he had worked on fourteen pictures, strange mystical creations in an entirely new colour harmony. These were his last masterpieces. Some were hung at the next Academy Exhibition, others went all over the world: the final salute of a fine English gentleman and artist. I missed him greatly, as he was an immaculate draughtsman and was teaching me a splendid line method when he died.'

Nearly 20 years later Hewitt described this period of his life in a letter to Mr Williams, curator of Merthyr Art Gallery, dated 6th February 1944. He wrote: 'I was the man who led the student strike at the Royal Academy Schools, 1925–26, for better teaching conditions, treatment etc. I achieved my aims, but walked out of the Academy because of official opposition to me and my principles. Walter Sickert stood behind me in this and made me his pupil. … I won my fight. I suffered for it later. Petty enemies made my career almost impossible. I kept on.

'I had just come over from Australia penniless, but with a mad absorption by art. I saw a great artistic future for Britain, if the freer open methods of Impressionism and the sciences (new) were followed. Sickert continued to instruct me. Charles Sims, my painting master, worked out of the Academy by miserable gossip and jealousies, took his life. I was grieved very much by that.'

'Paint yourself into a career'

Hewitt did not decide to quit the Royal Academy Schools without considerable anguish. He had had to fight hard to get into the school, and it involved sacrifices. On the other hand he found the physical environment of the schools, and the culture, stuffy. He was under pressure from his mother to return home to Australia. He was upset by the way Sims had been treated. He needed to earn money. And then there was the episode of the smashed statue, which had given him a reputation (rightly or wrongly) as a rebel.

He voiced his anguish to Sickert at a meeting in Kensington Gardens in the spring of 1926, telling him he was planning to leave the Royal Academy and return to Australia. 'My mother wants me back,' he said. 'I don't feel free.'

Sickert was horrified. Not so much about Hewitt's plans to leave the RA Schools, but about his plans to leave Britain. He urged Hewitt to think again. 'Go back to Australia? You've only just begun! Give yourself five years, then think about going back. All mothers are like that. They want their sons back.

'You're gifted. You can draw. You can paint. Come to me and I will help you when you need it. Your stand at the Academy has evidently shaken an RA or two, but don't stop on if you have a large painting room where you can get down to hard work, and sell, as quickly as you are able to.'

'Go out naked and fight for your gifts. Paint yourself into a career. The schools are filled with genius without talent. You're not an art student, you're an artist.'

Bold advice indeed for a young artist who had no wealthy family or private funds to fall back on. But Hewitt followed the advice. He had been copying pictures in the National Gallery at Fildes' suggestion. 'I stopped that, and tried expressing myself.'

Financial pressures were mounting on Hewitt. He had no source of income. And recurrent illness meant spending more of his dwindling money on doctors and medications. 'I could not be a student for much longer,' he confided to his notebook. He had moved out of his room at 18 Culworth Street, near Regent's Park, to a room in Wellington Square, just off the King's Road in Chelsea, where he drew and painted. By his bed was a real human skull complete with jawbone, that he used for anatomy purposes. At some time it had been used in a school play, where it had acquired a covering of phosphorus paint that made it shine in the dark.

He worked well into the night. He lived on sardines and stale bread. The combination of burning the midnight oil, poor diet, the dampness of the riverside area and the dampness of his rooms affected his health.

In the *Red Violet* manuscript Hewitt listed the artists whose work he found especially inspiring during this period – Corot, Millet, Courbet, Ingres, Delacroix, Degas, Monet, van Gogh, Picasso, Pissarro, Sisley, Segonzac and Dufy. 'My introduction into England's Impressionist school had been the most natural thing in the world,' he wrote. 'I held the Impressionist philosophy instinctively. I felt a close kinship with the movement.'

In a note that was not used in any of his autobiographical manuscripts, he recounted the occasion when he first saw a work by van Gogh. It was 1925. 'I remember walking through the Tate Gallery with Clifford Hall, the young London painter who was just beginning to make his mark, and seeing post-Impressionist works. I was a pupil of Sir Luke Fildes at the time, and he thought Sickert was a madman. I remember walking through one of the rooms and seeing, or being struck by, van Gogh's '*Sunflowers*' for the first time in one of the dark South rooms. It was like a blow in the chest to me. The yellow sunlight, the rich light, life and flowers in the pot. This was art. It was the work of an artist I was looking at now.'

He launched his career as a drypoint etcher. 'I had made three portraits of Sickert and these were converted into drypoints,' he wrote, commenting that he was surprised that so few artists had drawn Sickert. 'My Chelsea set was commenced – river and street scenes from the Reach to Pimlico and Old Belgravia. It meant a good Christmas for us, shopping along Old Fulham Road in the rosy lights and blue mist'.

His first real art patron was the wealthy partner of a firm of antique dealers, not named by Hewitt in his writing but said to be patronised by the Royal Family. Evidently the man would pay the lowest possible prices for Hewitt's prints, saying that 'it is bad to pay a young artist too much'. There was some compensation in the form of dinners at the man's apartment on The Embankment, at which they would drink Veuve Cliquot champagne.

Hewitt came to know the roads from Chelsea to Hammersmith very well. He frequently walked to Richmond, where he painted in Kew Gardens in all weathers. 'I was working at Richmond, painting in the fields and lingering beneath the Japanese cherry blossom at Kew. Painting in the Ilex groves through the summer; and in the winter snow painting in the pine woods, inhaling the cold perfume of the trees I loved, my fingers frozen to the brush. I would take my small packet of lunch and repair to the tropical warmth of the huge glass

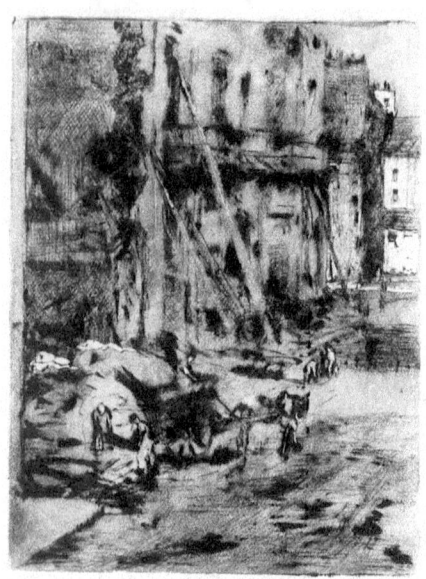

3.8 *'Demolishing Devonshire House, Picadilly'*, second plate, 1926. Signed Gillard Rayner. 102×77mm. RS.

houses, and sit munching behind a banana tree or an oriental bloom, bashful of the dark eyes of South African planters' daughters.'

In autumn he would sit in the secluded garden of Queen Mary's childhood Cambridge Cottage, 'sitting beneath the old chestnut tree she loved so much'. Sometimes he travelled further to Hampton.

His love of the River Thames and its artistic legacy also took him eastwards into the docklands areas. He did two drypoints of The Old Turk's Head Inn at Wapping. On a print of one of them, dated 1927, he wrote in pencil that this was 'where Whistler drew and etched'.

Most but not all of his etchings during this period were of riverside scenes. Dating from 1926 there are a few small prints of grimy urban scenes. These include Charing Cross, Limehouse Basin, the demolition of Devonshire House, and an untitled night-time street scene. Some of these early etchings are signed 'Gillard Rayner', as he endeavoured to work out what he should call himself following his mother's recent marriage to Hal Gillard.

In the event, he decided to use his middle name Henry for professional purposes, so from 1926 onwards all his drypoints, drawings and paintings carry the signature Henry Rayner. To his family and friends, however, he continued to be Hewitt, or 'Hewie' for short.

Sickert visited Hewitt's Wellington Square room, looked through his work and commented that he should get a bigger studio and a drier one. Not a very helpful suggestion to an impoverished student.

Hewitt regularly visited Sickert at his Fitzroy Street studio, and true to his promise Sickert continued to tutor the young artist in painting and etching. In a letter written two decades later Hewitt recalled that this was a period when 'Sickert had been ill and was then approaching a breakdown'.

By the time he left the RA Schools, someone else had entered Hewitt's life. Someone who believed fiercely in his talents and ambitions, and cajoled and encouraged him through the worst times, financially and emotionally. Someone who would nurse him through his almost constant illness and wartime injuries, and continue to promote his reputation even after his tragic death in 1957.

That someone was Theresa Zecchin.

4

Theresa

Theresa Maria Charlotte Zecchin was an artists' model. She was two years younger than Hewitt, born in London on 4th May 1905 to Italian parents. She met Hewitt in the summer of 1925.

When Hewitt left the Royal Academy Schools, Theresa left with him. She would become his wife and devote the rest of her life to helping him achieve his ambitions as an artist. She helped him print his drypoints. She sat for drawings, watercolours and oil paintings. She cheered him up and encouraged him through his many low periods, physical and mental. She bore him two daughters. 'She acted as his second mind', wrote one of their daughters many years later.

Theresa helped him cope with years of intense poverty in the 1930s, and for long periods was the family's main breadwinner, sometimes holding down a day job and also doing dressmaking in the evenings. She wrote to Hewitt almost daily while they were separated on three or four occasions during the 1939–45 war, when she and their two daughters were evacuated from London to escape the bombing.

And all the time she worked tirelessly to promote her husband's reputation and put his work in front of the widest possible audience.

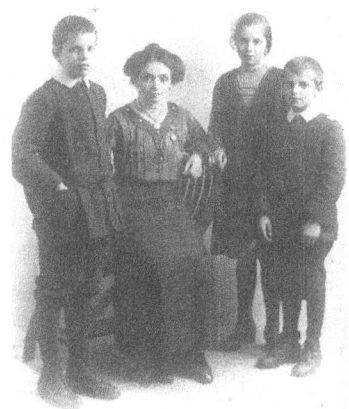

This work continued after Hewitt's death in 1957. The 1960 retrospective exhibition in Richmond was her idea. And right up to her own death in 1996 she carefully kept together the archive of letters, plates, oil paintings, press cuttings and other material covering the period 1924 to 1957. Without that archive, this book would not have been possible.

All this was in the future, of course, when Theresa and Rayner met. This happened when she was sitting for one of the night classes during Hewitt's first few weeks at the RA Schools. By then she was already a well-known and popular model. Hewitt described her in a letter to his mother as 'a fair-haired Italian from the North, of rare loveliness. One of the most beautiful models in London.'

4.1 Theresa Zecchin aged around 14 with her mother and older brother Richard (left) and younger brother Severin (right). PHOTO COURTESY PETER ZECCHIN (SEVERIN'S SON).

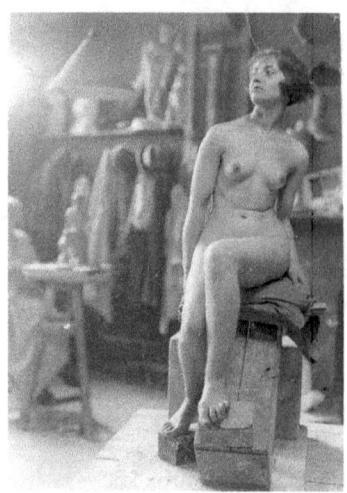

4.2 Theresa modelling at a St
Martin's School of Art sculpture
class in 1925. sw.

She lived with her parents Giuseppe and Caterina, and two brothers Richard (Riccardo) and Severino, at 20 Tottenham Street, off the Tottenham Court Road. Her father was a skilled mosaic worker from northern Italy who had come to Britain around the turn of the century in search of work. All three of his children were been born in England. The family took in lodgers to help pay the running costs of their large four-storey terraced house.

Rayner noted that Theresa had been first 'discovered' by Professor Tonks at the Slade School. Evidently he had been so eager to obtain her services as a model that he personally went to see her mother to make arrangements. Later she also became a popular model at other art schools including the Central School of Art, St Martin's School of Art, the Polytechnic, the Westminster Institute (where Sickert had taught), the Boltcourt School, and the Kennington School.

She had posed for several well-known artists and sculptors. According to Hewitt, Wilson Steer drew her when he was teaching at the Slade. Painter John Wheatley, a former pupil of Sickert, spotted her at the Slade and invited her to pose for him in Chelsea. Sculptor Pegram 'made some of his best work from her figure'. [Hewitt never clarified which Pegram this was – Henry Alfred or Alfred Bertram].

She had sat for John Sargent's niece in Chelsea, and Sargent himself came to draw her. Hewitt also recorded that a photograph of her by the celebrated photographer Yvonne was used in a magazine advertisement by Pears, although no confirmation of this has yet been found. It was Sims who had arranged for her to sit for classes at the RA Schools.

Rayner was smitten by Theresa, describing the effect when she took up her pose during an art class as 'it was as if a classic beauty from the golden age of Art had come amongst us. Other models 'posed', but she, in her posing, was the most natural thing in the world.

'Strangely, as one worked, one could see the likeness of the women of the Great Italian painters coming to life. She appeared to contain the essence of that artistic past. The eyes did not pop at us as they usually did from other models. Her eyes were those we had seen in the Masters' works. She wore a lovely fringe like Trilby, the heroine of the novel I read over and over again. [Hewitt was referring to the 1893 novel about a beautiful artists' model called *Trilby* by George du Maurier].

'One could not imagine this girl growing old. She had already inspired some of the finest work by the students in the RA sculpture room; young Gilbert, grandson of the famous sculptor, made an especially noble work that was exhibited for the Prix de Rome.' This 'famous sculptor' was Alfred Gilbert, 1854–1934, whose work included the Shaftesbury Memorial Fountain in London's Piccadilly Circus. Which grandson Hewitt is referring to is not known.

Hewitt plucked up courage to ask Theresa to pose for him. She said yes and a date was agreed for her to visit his boarding house in Wellington Square, Chelsea. That posed an initial problem because the landlady's rules forbad ladies to visit the rooms of her gentlemen guests. Special permission was given for the two of them to use the front parlour for an hour.

No painting was done during that first visit – they just talked. They found they shared many views and tastes, and quickly became inseparable. She gave up sitting for any other artists, and devoted herself to helping Hewitt's artistic ambitions.

In a letter to his mother dated 20th August 1925 Hewitt wrote: 'I am still in love and have gone out and captured that Italian girl (she is not German as I thought). I love her, she assists me and is too beautiful to be knocking about going to waste – considered one of the leading models – and is a full-blown dressmaker – a queen of taste and tone.

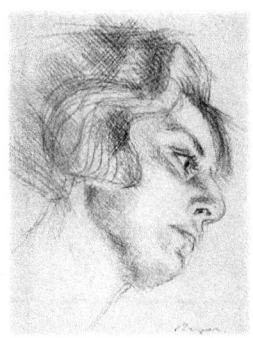

'I'll swear upon it, mother, she is the most well-formed and beautiful faced creature in London today, sent to me to be my help. I cannot but say we are naturally becoming, as gossip has it, a 'perfect two'. You, my darling mother, would love her, for she is born a lady, a queen, and will be a good woman, I am sure. She visits me and we are very quiet and peaceful together, and learning to not love but respect and adore one another'.

Hewitt wrote more about this episode of his life in the *Red Violet* manuscript: 'Nights were spent by the river at our old Chelsea, dining at the Blue Cockatoo and preparing our plans', he wrote. The Blue Cockatoo was a popular Chelsea haunt for artists, located next to the Pier Hotel at the junction of Cheyne Walk and Oakley Street, facing the Albert Bridge across the Thames. The restaurant building was demolished in 1968 to make way for an apartment block.

4.3 Pencil drawing by Hewitt of Theresa from c1926. 170 by 128mm. RS.

'One evening she returned to my room, which she was only allowed to visit briefly, and announced that she had found a wonderful little place at the World's End, half a mile along the road'.

This was in May 1926. They were married at the Chelsea Register office in the King's Road later the same year, on 4th October. The witnesses at the marriage were K B Cosgrove and K Malyard.

Hewitt gave his address as 28 Whiteheads Grove, Chelsea, probably the 'wonderful little place' found by Theresa. Theresa gave her parents' address of 20 Tottenham Street.

Not recorded in anything Hewitt wrote about Theresa is the fact that Theresa's family disapproved of their marriage, and may not have attended the wedding. By 1932 things would become so bad that Theresa ceased all contact with her family.

Hewitt put a happy spin on his wedding day. He wrote: 'The day was chill and it tried to rain. All our belongings had gone on to the new flat at the World's End – our first little home. But I carried a large portfolio of precious drypoints and etchings – all my first proofs, things which subsequently found their way into museums all over the world.

'Before we stepped for the first time over the threshold of our flat, we went to sit on the Embankment at Cheyne Walk to silently watch the water and the boats and the birds. It was one of our favourite spots just opposite Wilson Steer's house, and by the small building once occupied by the great painter Turner'.

From then on the pair worked very hard at making Hewitt's career a success. 'I was now driven to work twice as hard,' he recalled. 'The heavy winter fogs and mists settled down over Chelsea. The nights were spent at the small press, Theresa wetting the rich hand-made paper and passing it to me when it was ready for placing against the etched plate. Each 'pull' was a thrill. Would it be fine or just a dud? Most of the work came out well. The rich burr of drypoint soon deteriorates, and if the impressions do not yield well the edition is small and a dead loss.

'Theresa was highly gifted. She knew the faults and the excellence of fine etching and engraving. She was a good critic of painting, and could design her own needlework, create her own and my garments, and was able to cut my hair in a fashion that passed my barber by and saved us a lot of money'.

It was Theresa's skills as a seamstress that through the next 30 years would keep a roof over their heads and food on the table.

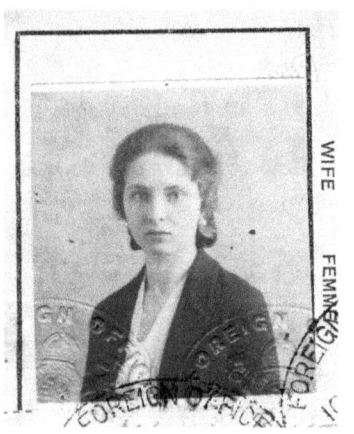

4.4 Theresa's passport photo from 1929. sw.

Their occupation of the apartment in Chelsea turned out to be short lived because Theresa fell ill with TB. 'The wet, low-lying mists of Chelsea had helped to include a tubercular spot on one lung,' Hewitt wrote. 'She began to lose weight and to grow listless. The final X-ray plates determined me to get her out of South London, so we took a flat nearer to the heights of Hampstead'.

Their first accommodation in this area is not known, but a surviving letter from Dame Nellie Melba's private secretary dated 13th February 1929 is addressed to Hewitt at 20 Princess Road, near Regent's Park, so it is possible that this was where they moved first when they left Chelsea.

'They were anxious months. I tried to earn more by selling bundles of my work, and by bringing my engraving to a standard that would equal and even surpass the best on the British market. I sought to cut new ground, to introduce new excellences. In one day I would pull eighty prints from the press, Theresa still helping me to prepare the papers and to dry the proofs and store them'.

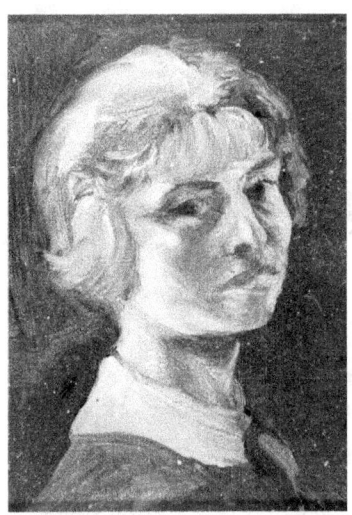

4.5 An early oil of Theresa, c1930. sw.

'Sitting out in the open river bends and on the windy hillocks of the countryside had created trouble in my own chest; but my first care was to see that Theresa had all the attention that medical science could offer. It went to my heart to see her face becoming so thin and pale-hectic.

'Few there were to buy my work as the great art slump approached. But the works went out to rich and poor, and hundreds were sold. At last I was able to send Theresa to Italy'.

She returned to the mountains of Maniago in the north-east of Italy, accompanied by her father, who had been in the UK managing one of his mosaic installation projects. While in Italy, Theresa visited Venice and saw some of Sickert's work, and the paintings of Tintoretto in the Scuola di San Rocco.

When Theresa returned to London, the doctors in Italy had passed her fit and free from TB.

It seems that she suffered further lung problems in early 1932, judging by a letter dated 11th February 1932 from Hewitt's stepfather Hal Gillard, in which he wrote:

> We were pleased to get your last letters and to glean therefrom the pleasant news that an examination by X-Ray disclosed no very bad intrusion on her lung and we can only hope that it will soon respond to treatment. We cannot however too strongly impress upon you both the very great care which must be taken to prevent any inroads upon an organ which has such an important function to perform during our short term here on earth.

5

Chelsea days. Chelsea nights.

Hewitt had felt drawn to the River Thames at Chelsea, almost from the moment he arrived in London. He loved the water and the river traffic. He loved the sunsets. And he felt a sense of connection to Turner, Whistler and other artists who had lived in Chelsea in the previous century.

'Wonderful old Chelsea,' he called it. He would recall 'the haunting notes of a Thames river tug', a sound that took him back to his childhood in Brighton, listening to the ships as they crossed Port Phillip Bay to and from Melbourne harbour.

He was acutely aware that by the time he arrived in England, Chelsea's heyday as the bohemian art centre had passed. But this didn't deter him. On the contrary, he saw it as an advantage. 'Coming in as I did at the end of the Grand Period,' he wrote, 'I gathered a richer harvest than I might have done had I appeared earlier. I reaped all the experience and memories of the last living members of a time that had brought into the world of British art a rare collection of men and women of extraordinary gifts and genius. The skill and teaching of such unusual and highly-gifted personalities threw an exciting colouration over one's young mind and feelings. One knew that this occasion could not be repeated.'

Certainly, in 1920s Chelsea it was still possible to bump into people who had known and worked with Whistler. Although it has to be said that by the 1920s the gentrification of Chelsea had begun, and the old riverside strip had been transformed by the construction of the embankment.

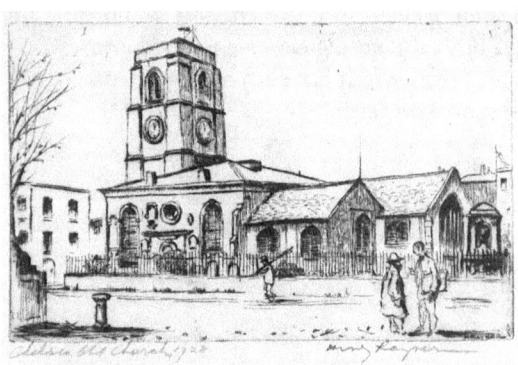

5.1 Rayner did at least three etchings of Chelsea Old Church. This one dates from 1928. Just visible on the extreme left is the end of Old Lombard Terrace. The tall figure carrying an artists' portfolio may be Rayner himself. Drypoint, 118×160mm. RS.

When Hewitt stopped attending the RA Schools in 1926 it was perhaps inevitable that he would immediately move to Chelsea. He took a room in Wellington Square, off the King's Road. When he married Theresa and settled down with her, it was in Chelsea. And even when the two of them moved away from the river on account of health problems, he regularly went back to his old haunts to draw and paint. Not only in Chelsea but further upstream in Richmond and Putney. In the evenings, when he returned from his painting trips along the Thames, Theresa would sit for portraits.

Success with sales of his prints allowed the two of them to splash out a little. One of their haunts was the Caledonian Market, originally a livestock market in Islington but by the 1920s a popular bric-a-brac market. Sickert was also a regular visitor. Hewitt and Theresa purchased a gramophone – 'A quaint old gramophone with a massive green trumpet', he recalled, 'which my friends would detach and use as a megaphone when calling up the road for a newspaper from the man on the corner.

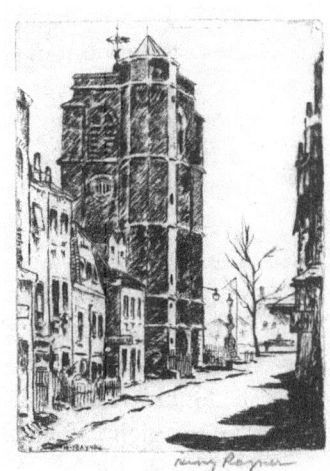

5.2 A view of Chelsea Old Church looking down Church Street towards the Thames. Drypoint, c1928, 145×104mm. RS.

Hewitt would later describe these as his happiest days in london.

'It had been our great happiness to frequent the Proms at the Queen's Hall on Saturdays and watch Sir Henry Wood conduct, and meet our friends to enjoy the world's best music. Now we could buy records of the same and paint and draw to Beethoven and Schubert – his Trout Quintet being my favourite, cracked in two places though the record was'.

Hewitt and Theresa's friends were mostly other art students, working artists, writers and poets. Some were from an earlier generation of artists. One of the latter was the Japanese artist and writer Yoshio Markino. Markino had taken London by storm in the early years of the century with his book '*A Japanese artist in London*'.

Hewitt described Markino as 'ageing but child-like; a gentle, loveable person, wise and full of rich Eastern humour'. Markino lived in the 1920s in a block of flats in Notting Hill Gate. One of his neighbours was Wyndham Lewis. Hewitt was a regular visitor to Markino's apartment, who he said was a born philosopher. If things were not going as they should, 'little, grey-haired Markino' had the answer – 'Times are not good. How pity! Let us make gramophone.' Whereupon he would put on a record of what Rayner described as eerie oriental music. One evening as the music was playing, rather loudly, Wyndham Lewis appeared in the doorway of the apartment, nodded, and left. Markino said 'How nice.'

He introduced Hewitt to the Japanese wine, saki. One evening Markino talked about sincerity. 'It is so agony for some people to be sincere,' he said. 'The little childrens have not to learn this arts. They come into world with it. I have teach myself this is same all world over. Peoples grow from sincere to insincere. Artists have to know to grow into higher sincerity and do works to put down all inferior feelings and forget the dirty commercials.'

Markino was evidently a good cook and Rayner recalled him running down the road to the shops, returning with a few mushrooms, some cream, an egg or two and a few greens, and producing a very appetising dish. He was aware of his shortcomings with the English language, but philosophical about them. He said to Hewitt : 'I never master your language. How pity! The John Bullses always make try to teach me. So charming. But it's a great shame.'

A friend of Hewitt's own age was fellow student Henning Alfred Nyberg. The two of them often ate together. 'We often pooled our resources and bought smoked salmon, mettwurst sausage and salami from Fred Schmidt's restaurant and delicatessen in Charlotte Street when funds allowed. At other times, we frequented the little workmen's cafes in Chelsea side streets', Rayner recalled. [Schmidt's restaurant at 35–37 Charlotte Street survived into the 1970s].

One night, after selling a bundle of six paintings, Hewitt and Henning ate at a café near the Lots Road power station where they had an unsettling encounter with a man who turned out to be a hangman.

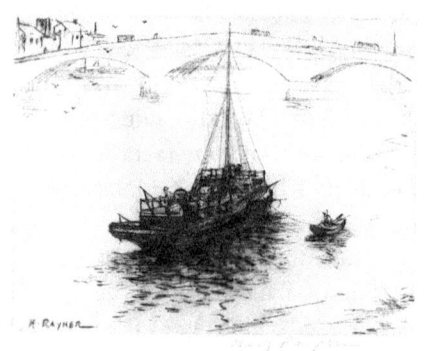

5.3 *'Chelsea'*. Drypoint 122×154mm. RS.

Henning evidently had eccentric eating habits. Hewitt remembers him eating not only the sausage from Fred Schmidt but also the skins and the string endings. When he came to breakfast with Hewitt at the lodgings in Wellington Square Henning would eat his boiled egg, carefully clean out the shell with a spoon, then proceed to eat that as well.

It is notable that most of the friendships Hewitt struck in his early years in London were with students and artists who, like him, had been born elsewhere in the world. The bond they shared was that they were all foreigners in London.

Many of Hewitt's reminiscences of Chelsea involve eating and drinking places. There was the Good Intent, which he described that as 'renowned for its Bohemian clientele'. Twenty years later he still remembered 'the shaded lights and copper mirrors'.

The Good Intent had started out in life in 1908 in premises at number 64 Cheyne Walk, on the corner of Cheyne Walk and Church Street, and had been a popular haunt of Chelsea's art community. Around 1917 it moved to 316–320 King's Road, and that's where it was in Hewitt's day. Found in his effects was a card from the restaurant, offering 'Excellent cuisine, fully licensed, luncheon 12–3, dinner 6.30–10.30, morning coffee, afternoon teas, light refreshments'.

In his *Red Violet* manuscript Hewitt recounted a story of dining at the Good Intent one summer evening in 1927 with Sickert and two others. One of the other diners was Australian portrait painter James Quinn (c1870–1951), then working on his portrait of the Duchess of York. He had evidently walked over from his studio at 15 Crookham Road, Fulham, a handsome four-storey house where he lived with his wife and son René. Quinn had lived and worked in London since 1902. He had been one of ten Australian artists in London to be appointed Official War Artists during the 1914–18 war. According to a note on the National Gallery of Australia website, he was a lover of good food, wine and conversation. Like many London-based artists of his generation he frequented the Chelsea Arts Club and the Café Royal. In his 1992 book about the Chelsea Arts Club [*Artists and bohemians: 100 years with the Chelsea Arts Club*, Quiller Press, 1992], Tom Cross noted that Quinn was one of many expatriate Australian and Canadian artists who frequented the club.

Quinn's son René was a fellow student of Hewitt's at the RA Schools, and the two were good friends.

The fourth member of the group was someone who Hewitt carefully avoided naming in his *Red Violet* manuscript, preferring instead to describe him as 'an author whose books are read in hundreds of thousands'. He also described him as 'a short and melancholy man with the air of a restauranteur'.

By chance, the identity of this author was discovered from one of the many scraps of paper that had been used by Hewitt for jotting down notes. The hand-written note says simply: 'Bennett – he had the air of a restauranteur'. So the un-named author was actually Arnold Bennett, then aged 60 and one of the wealthiest journalists/playwrights/authors of the day.

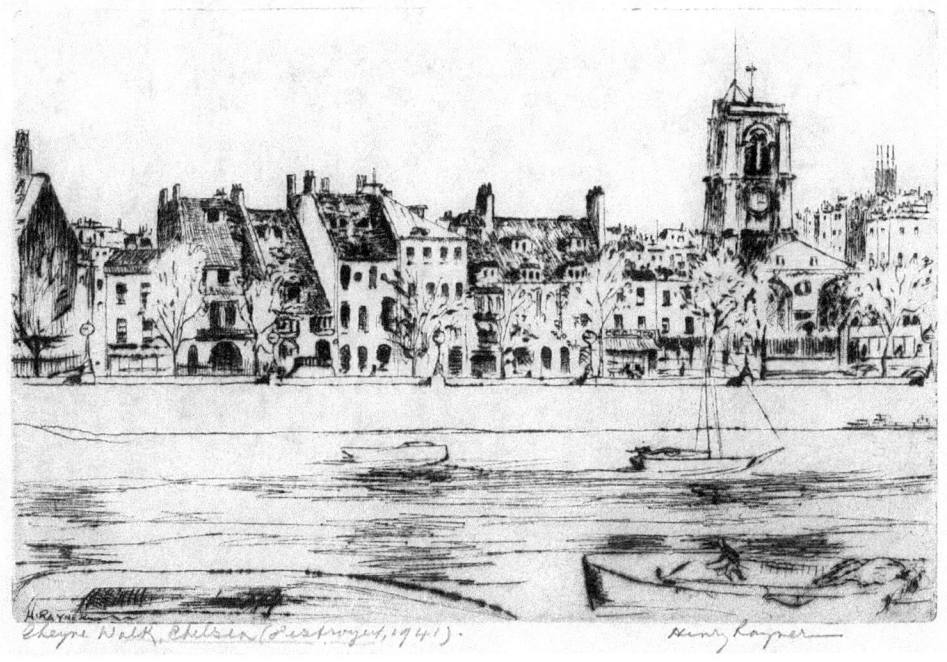

5.4 *'Cheyne Walk'* showing Chelsea Old Church on the right, and the old Lombard Terrace with the canopy over the Old Lombard Café clearly visible. There are other Rayner drypoints that show this same scene, as well as slightly different perspectives on the same stretch of Chelsea's Embankment. Drypoint, 1927, 201×275mm. IMAGE COURTESY ELIZABETH HARVEY-LEE.

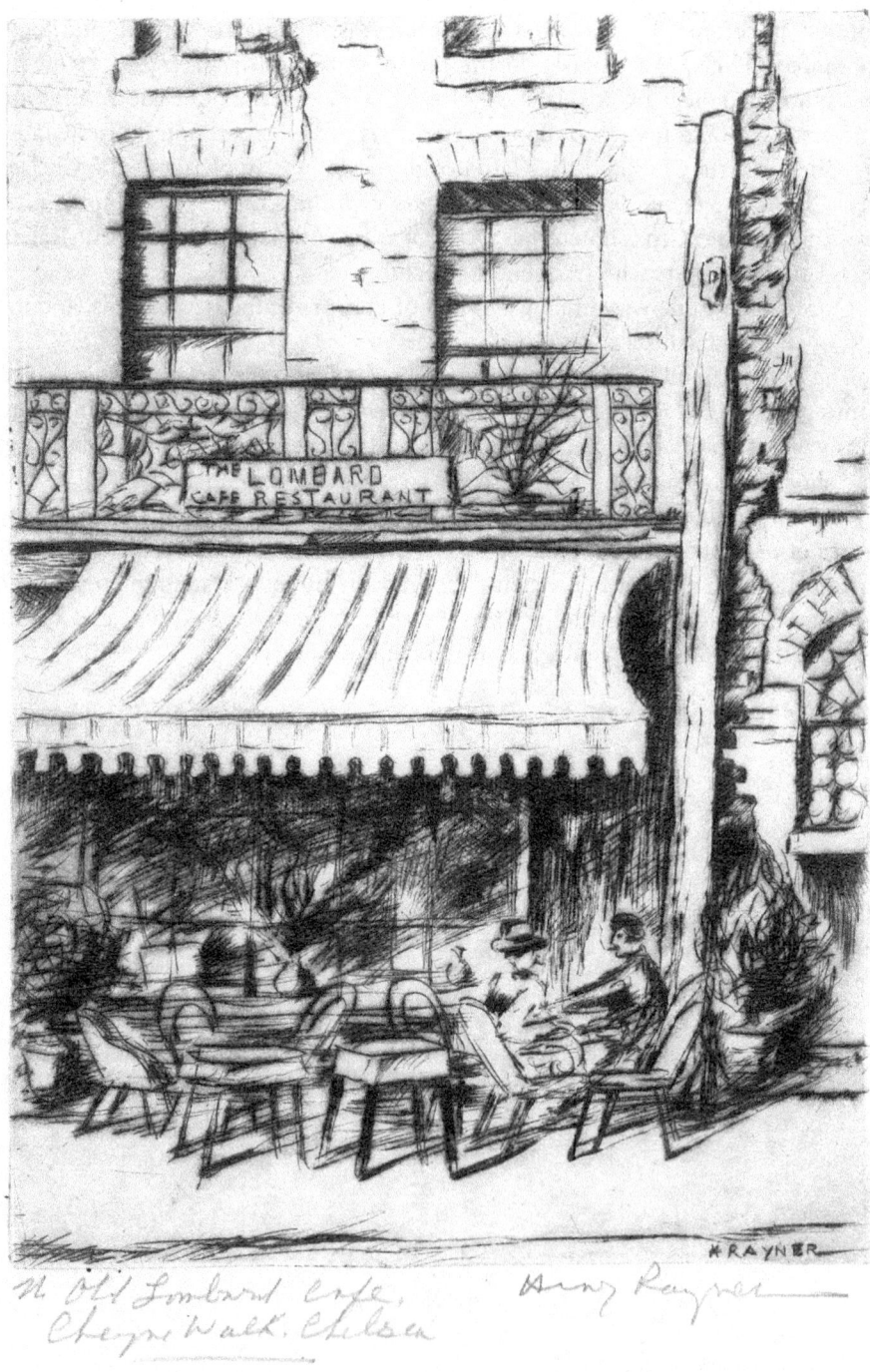

5.5 *'The Old Lombard café'* was one of Rayner's most successful works. He etched the same scene at least three times – some proofs are confusingly titled *'Cheyne Walk'*. The café was a regular haunt of Hewitt's in the 1920s and 1930s. Drypoint 210×145mm. RS.

Hewitt recalled that Bennett had arrived at the restaurant in a chauffeur-driven car, and the chauffeur had brought in a bottle of vintage Moet & Chandon champagne purchased from the Six Bells public house at 195 King's Road. Evidently in Hewitt's day the Good Intent did not have a wine list so diners brought their own drinks with them.

Bennett said that he had seen a painting of cheese similar to that in the Tate gallery by Sickert. The painting he had seen also bore Sickert's signature. 'How many cheeses are there, Walter?' Sickert chose to misunderstand the question and proceeded to list all the types of French cheese. Bennett asked more specifically: 'What I meant was, how many copies do you generally make of these things?'

Sickert's reply was unexpected. 'Imitators must eat,' he says. 'And so long as the forgers keep up to standard, I don't object. They might have attempted a more adventurous canvas, but they usually paint me small. The chances of sale are better.'

Hewitt noted in his *Red-Violet* manuscript that the number of forgeries of Sickert's work was known to be very large. 'The artist's [Sickert's] view was – the more the merrier'.

Another topic of conversation that evening was Oscar Wilde. Sickert commented that Wilde might be considered one of the first Impressionist writers in Britain, emulating the French style, and that many people had missed that knowledge in their judgement of him. Bennett on the other hand held the view that Wilde was 'witty but insular, and dead as mutton'.

During the evening Sickert mentioned that Ellen Terry had frequently dined at the Good Intent, and that he had met her on several occasions but never had the chance to paint her.

Sickert was as usual smoking his Manilla cheroots, lighting them back-to-front, which he claimed gave a more satisfactory 'draw'. He was smartly attired in evening dress, and it was only as they all left the restaurant that Hewitt noticed he was wearing carpet slippers.

Sickert had arrived by taxi, and the cab had waited for him as he dined. His use of taxis was legendary.

Other Chelsea eating and drinking places frequented by Hewitt were the Buttery, The Lombard café and the Swan wine house, all in Cheyne Walk along Chelsea's Embankment.

The Lombard Café has a dual significance to Hewitt's career. It was a regular meeting place for Chelsea's artistic community. Characters such as William Orpen, Augustus John and Philip Wilson Steer were often to be found sitting at the pavement tables under its awnings. Hewitt and Theresa would sometimes meet up for a meal there with James Quinn. The café was also the subject of one of Hewitt's drypoints – one that sold so well he had to repeat it several times.

But even as Hewitt enjoyed the Lombard Café in the late 1920s, its days were numbered. He later wrote that the building was demolished because of its dangerous condition and because the owner of the site had redevelopment

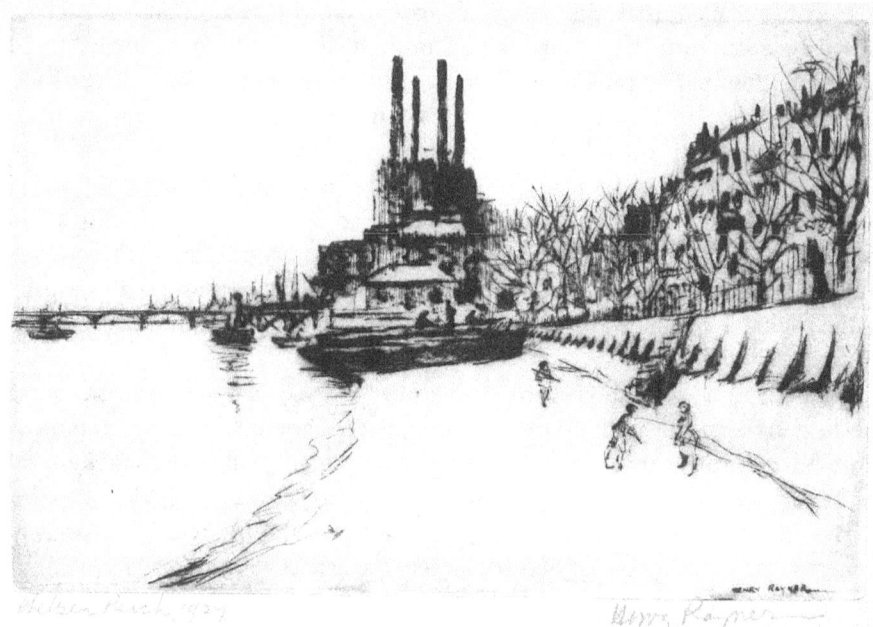

5.6 *'Chelsea reach, 1927'* shows a view along the river bank, with the Lots Road Power Station in the background. Drypoint, 150×218mm. RS.

plans. 'The more allergic among us would hold our breaths as we mounted the wobbly stairs to lunch in the beautifully Parisian-Victorian atmosphere'. The first floor dining room had crettone curtains and wide windows overlooking a large balcony.

Sitting at the first-floor window of the Lombard was a favourite evening haunt for Hewitt. He liked to watch 'the last rays of the sun pass orange, gold and red along the gaunt sides of the factory walls and chimneys on the Battersea shore. Here, at ease, one could again picture Whistler's camel trains following him as he returned from a painting expedition up the Thames – the students doing all the carrying, James doing all the talking and whipping.' It is likely that some of Hewitt's drypoints of the river and its barges were done from this window.

The Lombard café was one of a group of four terraced properties facing the river on the corner of Cheyne Walk and Church Street. These 16th-century buildings with their decorative lace-like metal balustrades and Georgian windows were all that had survived of Lombard Terrace when the Chelsea Embankment was created. The Lombard café was most likely at number 65 Cheyne Walk, in a building that had formerly been the home of The Chelsea Book Club.

The corner property, number 64, with its distinctive curved window that followed the line of the building, was The Swan Inn in Rayner's time. A decade earlier it had been occupied by The Good Intent restaurant. In the flat above number 64 lived artist Marion Dawson.

It is sometimes said that this old terrace was destroyed in the same bombing raid that demolished Chelsea Old Church in April 1941. However, it may have already been demolished before the outbreak of war, judging by a very public campaign waged by some well-known Chelsea figures.

In *The Times* newspaper of 26th November 1926, Reginald Blunt (a prolific writer on the subject of old Chelsea) revealed that the little terrace was to be demolished, partly in order to widen Church Street. On 3rd January 1927 the newspaper reported that a petition signed by well-known Chelsea residents including Philip Wilson Steer, Ellen Terry and Sybil Thorndike had been delivered to the land owner, protesting at the plan to demolish the terrace. On 2nd February, a letter from William Orpen in Paris added to the debate.

The petition was not successful. The terrace was demolished and replaced with new buildings in an 18th century style. Hewitt wrote that this happened in 1939, and that it was these replacement buildings that were destroyed in the 1941 bombing raid. His recollection is born out by the 1964 booklet 'Chelsea Old Church, bombing and rebuilding, 1941–1950', which refers to '.... The Old Café Lombard, demolished before the War'.

Although the campaign to prevent the demolition of this historic terrace failed, it did have one useful spin-off. It led to the founding by Reginald Blunt of The Chelsea Society in 1927.

In the chronology written by Theresa Rayner she notes that in 1927 or 1928 an exhibition of Rayner's drypoints of Chelsea was held at the Lombard café.

Across the other side of Old Church Street from these buildings was Chelsea Old Church – the subject of several Rayner drypoints. An etching by Hanslip Fletcher of this stretch of Cheyne Walk shows neatly how Lombard Terrace and Chelsea Old Church sat either side of Church Street. You can also just make out the end of Lombard Terrace on the extreme edge of Rayner's own drypoint of the church as viewed from the river.

When the Lombard was finally pulled down (or pushed down, in Hewitt's words) he recorded that all the staff went round to Whistler's old house, a little way up Cheyne Walk, where they ate oxtail soup in the first-floor room where the artist used to paint his *nocturnes*.

The Buttery, by comparison, was a more modest place with just a single ground floor room. The name had nothing to do with butter, but was derived from the butts used to store wine in. More correctly called The Cheyne Buttery, it was at number 77 Cheyne Walk, next to Crosby Hall – the 15th century building that in 1910 had been relocated from its original position in Bishopsgate.

The Buttery can be seen in one of Hewitt's 1927 drypoints of Cheyne Walk (see Fig 5.4). This shows the view from across the river with Chelsea Old Church on the extreme right and Crosby Hall on the extreme left. This print also shows clearly the Old Lombard Café with its distinctive awning. Hewitt noted that a proof of this drypoint was in the collection of Lady Freyburg. He repeated this scene in later drypoints, probably indicating that it sold well.

Rayner described the Buttery as 'an eating house where the indigent and the affluent of Chelsea Bohemia could hold an inquest on roast lamb with a bottle of lager, or toy with a crème caramel on summer days at reasonable cost and in good company. It was a place where you could rub shoulders with writers, poets, painters, actresses and actors.'

Sickert, in one of his word-plays on the real name, had evidently christened it the '*bouteillerie*'.

Hanging on the walls of The Buttery was a collection of drawings by Walter Greaves. 'Large, splendid interpretations of the Thames,' as Hewitt remembered them. 'I openly admired these works, and ate there purposely to enjoy them. Then one day as I sat down by the window I saw that a new picture had been added. One of my own, showing the Lombard Café as it was a few years before. I could not have been more honoured if I had been shown in the National Gallery.'

The night that Chelsea Old Church was destroyed by bombing, the Buttery was reduced to a deep hole, and the new building that had replaced the Lombard café was also destroyed. Amazingly, the Greaves pictures that had been hanging on the wall of the Buttery were saved, and so was Rayner's picture of the Lombard Café.

The loss of this bit of Chelsea had a deep effect on Hewitt. On post-war proofs of his etchings of Chelsea Old Church, for example, he would carefully write 'destroyed in 1941' or words to that effect.

Remembering earlier, happier days, he recalled one evening in 1925 or 1926 when he had been in the Lombard with René Quinn. The two were sitting at the balcony window. Hewitt was smoking a cigarette after a hard day's painting. Quinn had recently taken to smoking a pipe and was doing so now with uncertain enjoyment.

With hindsight, Hewitt felt he should have been aware of how frail Quinn was becoming. Quinn would die tragically young at the age of 31 on 7th June 1934 in Hanwell Mental Hospital, Uxbridge Road, Norwood, suffering from schizophrenia ('dementia praecox' as it was termed at the time). His occupation was given on the death certificate as 'formerly an artist'. After René's death his father returned to Australia. He exhibited a large oil painting of his son at a 1936 exhibition at the Fine Arts Society Gallery in Melbourne, 4–15 May. Rayner noted that Quinn had grown a beard in the period before his death, and this is how he appears in the oil painting.

Quinn, 'a quiet and even-tempered lad, delighting in witty conversation', was devoted to Sickert, according to Hewitt. 'And Sickert was very fond of him, treating him with special courtesy and respect as if sensing that the boy would soon be taken away from our midst by fatal illness.' That evening, Quinn waited until after the meal then told Hewitt that Sickert would like to see the two of them the following evening. The next evening, before travelling to Sickert's house at 15 Fitzroy Street the two of them dined at Bassi's – later to become the Caletta Restaurant, near Markham Square, in the King's Road.

'Whistler's London seemed not far away then. One often ran into people who had known him well. Ordinary folk who had worked for him, who had sold him tintacks and run errands for him.'

One of these people was the man who ran a business called The Mangle Works at the World's End. Hewitt remembered him as 'an old fellow with his ancient cut-away coat that had one vast button, and a habit of addressing his wife as 'you fool'. Evidently he had known Whistler well and had repaired the artist's etching press on more than one occasion. 'A very fussy man was Mr Whistler', the man said to Hewitt, 'a very fussy man.'

Years after the antiquated, tottering Victorian buildings had been pulled down and replaced with concrete shops, Hewitt could still remember how the place looked. 'Over the shop, with its high balcony of rusted fancy ironwork, was hung out on a pole a large piece of sacking painted white, and on this was written in tar: The Mangle Works. In front of the shop lay a twisted conglomeration of mangle parts hedged off with barbed wire.'

Hewitt had his own press repaired at the Mangle Works. The man came and took away the pieces of the press 'in an ancient perambulator, at a funereal pace'. It took three trips. The cost, when the press was returned, was two shillings and sixpence.

Hewitt did a drypoint of the Mangle Works, and a proof was acquired by the British Museum.

From the late 1920s to the 1950s, he got to know several figures from the world of art in and around Chelsea. One was Dame Ethel Walker. 'Please don't call me Dame', she would say to visitors,' Hewitt remembered. 'Ethel lived on the first floor of 127 Luna Street, Cheyne Walk, on the Embankment facing the Rising Sun. It was not far from Steer who lived at 109 Cheyne Walk, facing a mass of old hulks, yachts and crumbling barges at the point where old man Greaves used to have his hire boathouse, later to be Swan Jetty.

'Her painting room overlooked the river, the wind and the birds. The room was full of pictures, picture debris, easels, frames, dust and discomfort. One had to pick one's way with delicate care through the labyrinth of stools and tables and painter's gear, following secret tracks known only to Ethel. She had bought several of my works, chiefly river scenes. Tea was always served with all the care of a woman well bred. And she showed me her early *pochades*, made in Italy, delicate, precious little pieces.

'One terrible day we left her studio to procure cakes and bread in the King's Road. A special visitor was coming to tea, and Ethel found the cupboard bare. There was a high wind, and Ethel prattled away and scampered about the streets completely heedless of passing traffic. In the middle of the main road a bus came tearing down upon us, and with a dexterity that afterwards astonished me I took Ethel up bodily and planted her clear of the great red vehicle just in time – she still gabbling away about the sort of loaf she wanted. It became a matter of pride for me to think that, in this act, I had saved for the nation one of its greatest women painters, and all the beautiful works she subsequently made.'

Another well-known Chelsea figure Hewitt used to visit was Gwen Otter. Hewitt said: 'She had known practically every great personality in art from her girlhood days in the last part of the 19th century. She was a famous hostess, a wit, and a friend of Beardsley, Beerbohm Tree, Ethel Mannin, and George Moore. Her house stood in dreamy, reposeful Margaretta Terrace, renowned for the variety of trees that lined the walks and the variety of celebrities who lived there. She owned one of the best John drawings I have ever seen, and had perhaps the kindest eyes, which she waved away as 'beery'.

'She loved coffee, and relished salads, which she made to perfection, not forgetting plenty of olive oil. And one was expected to help in the bright little kitchenette where wonderful dishes were concocted. She was always prepared for those who preferred the cuisine of France, and her dainty dishes, especially pastry, were renowned.

'After luncheon I would sometimes use her sitting room on the first floor overlooking the Terrace. Here I could study in peace. She possessed a very fine collection of 19th century French classics and some rare books on British Victorian art, including de-luxe editions of Beardsley.

'These were hours of rest for me as I was working very hard on my first drypoint editions of Les Sylphides and the Swan Lake ballet sets.

'It was through Gwen that I came to know Ethel Mannin, the well-known novelist and reformer, and James Laver, the brilliant writer and keeper of prints at the Victoria and Albert Museum, where I often studied and lunched in solitude.'

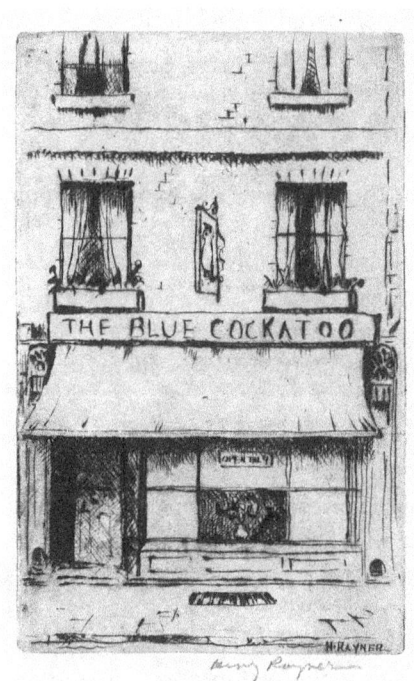

5.7 Another Chelsea eating place popular with Rayner and other artists was the Blue Cockatoo. Drypoint, 1942, 170×107mm. IMAGE COURTESY ELIZABETH HARVEY-LEE.

Virginia Nicholson referred to Gwen Otter's inexhaustible hospitality towards the younger generation in her 2002 book *Among the Bohemians: Experiments in Living 1900–1939*. In the book there is a description of Gwen's house by Ethel Mannin.

Another celebrated figure from the art world who Hewitt knew at that time was Nina Hamnett. She talked to him about Henri Gaudier-Brzeska, who she had known and sat for. She had been the model for Brzeska's '*Torso*' sculpture, and later wrote a book '*The laughing torso*' tracing the lives of Gaudier and Miss Brzeska.

This may have been the trigger for the drypoint portraits Hewitt did of Gaudier Brzeska. They must have been based on a photograph since Gaudier Brzeska had been killed in the war in 1915. There were three different versions of the Brzeska portrait, indicating either that it sold well or that Hewitt was unhappy with his first versions.

Hewitt must have been fascinated to hear Nina Hamnett reminisce about her years in Bohemian Paris, holding parties attended by artists such as Picasso. She had been photographed by the celebrated photographer Man Ray.

Surviving letters and postcards from Nina to Hewitt from 1946 talk about visits she was planning, to make drawings of Hewitt and Theresa. Hewitt had obviously also asked he if she had any photographs that he could use in his 'Red Violet' manuscript, then in progress. In August that year Nina (then living at 31 Howland Street) wrote back: 'Thank you for your letter. I enclose the proofs of the Sickert letters, which I am not supposed to show anyone. Everyone who should have seen them has done so, so what the hell! I know where the photos [are] so will dig them out & bring them with me for you to choose from. I will be with you about 10.30 on Wednesday.'

In a later letter, she said she would bring them with her when she came to sit for Hewitt on 4th September. 'I have an old one taken about the time that Sickert wrote the letters'. She offered Hewitt a choice of three photos of Sickert when she visited him, and he chose a picture that Nina said had been taken in Dieppe around 1922.

By the year end Nina had been forced to move as a result of a fire. Her books and her few remaining paintings survived, dirty but intact. On 9th December she wrote to Hewitt from the Kent coastal town of Broadstairs, (where she had gone for a two-week break, staying at 93 Bradstow Way) to tell him she had moved to 'two splendid rooms at the Harrow Road end of Westbourne Terrace, near the canal ... no landlords on the premises ... 17/6 a week.'

In the same letter she proposed a date to come to the Rayners' home and do the drawings. 'I am drawing my nephews every day, drinking and smoking nothing, walking in the icy blast and generally boring myself, which is a change.'

By January 1946, Nina was writing to Hewitt from 43 Windmill Street, Charlotte Street, near Goodge Street in Fitzrovia. She gave him a photo of herself taken in the south of France 20 years earlier. On the reverse she had written: 'To Henry Rayner from Nina Hamnett. On the rocks 1924. Still on the rocks 1946.'

Hamnett had also known Sickert for many years. She had owned some of Sickert's best paintings and drawings, according to Hewitt, 'but these had been sold at different times to keep the wolf from the studio door.' Nina told Hewitt that she had sold ten sketches and drawings by Sickert for £40 to the Leicester Galleries, and had sold a painting of an Italian woman for £500. At the time, she declared it to be the highest price ever paid for a Sickert painting.

According to Rayner's notes, this picture was the oil painting titled 'La Giuseppina', executed around 1903 in Italy. It appeared as the frontispiece in the Lillian Browse book on Sickert published by Faber and Faber in 1943.

Another figure Hewitt got to know was Ambrose McEvoy, best known as a portrait painter. Like Sickert, he had come to the Royal Academy to teach.

Although McEvoy had been a pupil of Sickert in the Camden Town days, Hewitt noted that the two of them had little in common, and McEvoy never spoke of him.

Hewitt did a drypoint of McEvoy at the latter's Pimlico Studio. The work was later acquired by the Cheltenham Art Gallery, which also acquired an early Rayner picture of Sickert. McEvoy had done watercolour studies of Theresa, as had his wife.

McEvoy introduced Hewitt to Sir Luke Fildes, who had been Charles Dicken's last illustrator. Fildes himself had done an etching of Dicken's study and chair, titled '*Empty chair*', which had sold in thousands. But the first time Hewitt visited Fildes' home in Kensington, the meeting was almost a disaster. When Fildes, then about 80 years old, discovered that Hewitt was a pupil of Sickert, he reacted violently. Hewitt wrote that 'he rose from his chair, drew himself slowly to his full height, and exploded: 'Sickert! That man is mad. His paintings are rubbish.'

Hewitt managed to turn the conversation away from Sickert, whereupon Fildes told him a story about a meeting with Whistler. Fildes also spoke favourably of the work of Walter Greaves.

Hewitt had already become interested in the work of Walter Greaves whom he felt was seriously unappreciated. He would go and look at a large river scene in oils by Greaves that hung in the reading room of the Chelsea Library. 'The delicate silvery tones and complete technical mastery caused me to wonder at the artist's obscurity. I saw where Whistler was influenced, and I went everywhere seeking this strange and unknown master's paintings and drawings.'

Hewitt found plenty of people in Chelsea and Fulham who remembered Greaves, the son of a Chelsea boatman. They told him that the artist would go out day after day with an old portfolio filled with drawings under his arm, and hawk them for bread and painting materials. 'Sometimes he wore an old-fashioned hat, a boater, varnished in the sailor fashion of many years before,' Rayner learnt.

'Always alone, he trudged the streets of London trying to sell the treasures in the tattered portfolio – Chelsea boats and Chelsea bridges, Chelsea skies and Chelsea Blue. One publican would buy a watercolour of the old Swan Jetty. Another a sketch of the Old Chelsea Church (a favourite subject with Greaves).'

A decade later Hewitt himself would adopt Greaves' sales approach and tour the streets of London, selling his prints door-to-door.

The Chelsea Library seems to have been a regular destination for Hewitt. Its Chief Librarian from 1929 on was Armitage Denton, who by the time of his retirement in 1939 had worked for the library for 43 years. He was popular with the public and by all accounts with the local artistic community. As well as managing the library's book collection Denton also devoted much time to building up the 'Chelsea Collection'. This was (and is) a priceless collection of prints and pictures showing old Chelsea. Started in the late 1800s it contains work by artists such as Whistler.

When Denton retired on 10th June 1939, he received a retirement gift from a group of Chelsea artists, in the form of a framed copy of Rayner's drypoint of the Old Lombard Café in Cheyne Walk.

Chelsea was a constant source of inspiration for Hewitt. His first drypoints of Chelsea were done in 1925. A proof of Chelsea Reach was bought by Philip Wilson Steer. Then in 1927 and 1928 he started his Chelsea set, which was completed in 1934. He was still capturing Chelsea river scenes in drypoints in the late 1930s.

'Night after night I would stand and draw the river from the Embankment at Chelsea,' he later wrote, 'and watch the boats and the swans and harsh-throated sea-gulls, the great river with its mysterious blue mist flowing into my heart. Only by making hundreds of sketches could I hope to feed myself and Theresa. When an exceptionally good piece of drawing was pulled off, I placed it on the pile of colour notes and pencil work and later took the lot round to Walter's studio.'

Two decades later when the Brook Street Art Gallery staged a one-man exhibition of Rayner's work there was an entire section devoted to Chelsea scenes,

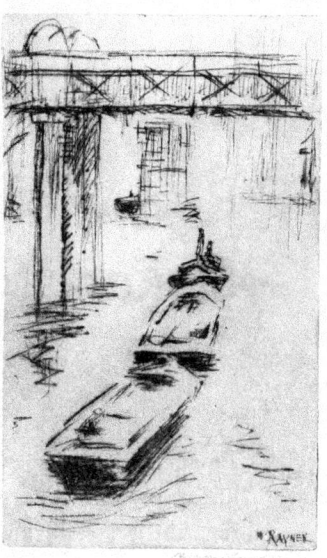

5.8 The sights and the sounds of the Thames delighted Hewitt, and this is one of a number of etchings showing river traffic. Drypoint, 1940, 212×125mm. RS.

containing 12 works. At the present time there are over 30 known drypoints of Chelsea scenes by Rayner.

A framed copy of the Thames barges drypoint has Theresa Rayner's name and Twickenham address on a label on the back, indicating that it was one of the prints on display at the Richmond Hill Gallery exhibition of 1960.

A telling recollection comes from a long essay-like letter Hewitt wrote for his mother in October 1951, in which he related this story:

'… Last Christmas, it was exactly Christmas Eve, an American came to my small studio [at 121 Mansfield Road] with his young son, and he asked to see my river scenes. He had been sent by Mr Child, a friend and Librarian at the American Embassy. This man looked at my scenes up river on the Thames and he said: 'I reckon you must love that old place.' That was one of the best compliments I had been paid that year, or any other year.'

In the same letter he talked about his deep love for Chelsea, adopting the rather literary style he sometimes used for these rambling essays: 'Yes, my heart is in the river down to Chelsea … my lovely old Chelsea, where I hope when my time comes they shall bury me. Close by the river at Cheyne Walk where my friends Sickert, Wilson Steer, John and McEvoy used to meet, where Quinn, Hall, Ethel Walker and I met and talked of the things we loved, the things that we considered fine and beautiful.'

6

Red-Violet – the era of the Sickert touch

Hewitt's friendship with Sickert was to have a strong and lasting effect on his life and work. As far back as his days in New Zealand, he had developed a high regard for the ways in which the French master artists would set up 'ateliers' in which students could work and study. He saw Sickert in this way, as a Master.

The two of them first met in 1925 when Sickert took classes at the Royal Academy Schools. It was in the early summer of 1925 that Sickert first took Hewitt for tea at the kiosk in Kensington Gardens. Subsequently they saw each other regularly until Sickert left London for Kent in 1934.

Hewitt saw Sickert as a role model ... a father figure ... and a direct connection back to Whistler and the mid-1800s era. 'Sickert was for me the compère of the great entertainment I was enjoying,' he wrote, referring to the people he met through the things he learned through his new-found mentor and friend.'

Hewitt made copious notes about the things Sickert said and did, and incorporated the information into several autobiographical manuscripts that have never been published. He was already a compulsive writer before he met Sickert, and the friendship only strengthened his resolve to record the important events in his life.

'Few people who have written about Sickert and his intimate life give many details about his personal attitude to his own painting, and the things he liked to eat and drink and see and feel,' Hewitt wrote.

'I had the invaluable experience of seeing Walter at work and play under many conditions. Of seeing him teach and lecture at the Royal Academy. Of receiving from him personally in fair mood and foul the 'chips' from the workshop – advice on systems and theory and methods of work. And of benefitting from his patient watching of my own progress and development, as my self-appointed master.'

Hewitt's note-taking system was to scribble down in pencil his observations, thoughts and ideas onto anything handy. 'Sickert advised his pupils to keep notes in laundry books,' he recalled.

Hewitt himself used virtually anything at hand to record his notes. There are small notebooks from stationers. There are endless scraps of paper; even an old cigarette packet. Some of his pocket sketchbooks contained more notes than sketches. And he wasn't averse to using a sub-standard proof from his etching press as the carrier for some important thought. In later years his older daughter Frances made small notebooks for him as Christmas presents.

As he incorporated the information from his initial notes into a more substantial piece of writing he would put a pencil line through the note. But he kept all the original notes, many of which still survive. These have provided useful snippets of information that for one reason or another he chose not to include in the final drafts.

As a manuscript took shape he used large-format notebooks he had made himself from large sheets of paper, hand-stitched together. Only the *Red-Violet* manuscript chronicling the Sickert years, and a few letters and short articles from the 1940s and 1950, were typed.

As well as writing about the things Sickert said and did, Hewitt also did numerous drawings, etchings and paintings of his mentor and friend, starting in 1925 when Sickert lived in Fitzroy Street and taught at the RA Schools, and continuing up to 1934. Sickert was rarely drawn or painted by other artists, so it may well be that the Rayner drypoints and paintings constitute the largest collection of works featuring Sickert.

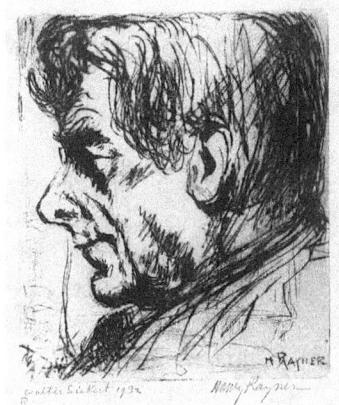

When Sickert arrived at the RA schools it seemed to Hewitt like a breath of fresh air. He noted that Sickert's position as a visiting teacher to the painting schools was over a longer period than has generally been recorded by biographers. A surviving letter to Hewitt from the Royal Academy dated 14th January 1954 confirms this, recording that Sickert began teaching there in 1925 when he made 13 visits in February. Then 24 visits in June the same year and finally 22 visits in April and May 1926.

6.1 *Walter Sickert 1932*. Drypoint, 165×140mm. sw.

Denys Sutton's 1976 biography of Sickert ['*Walter Sickert, a biography*', Joseph] throws an interesting light on the nearly 12-month gap in Sickert's visits. He suggests that Sickert took offence at press reports that he was teaching his pupils to work from photographs, so withdrew his teaching services until the spring of 1926.

The Sutton book also includes a comment about Sickert that seems perfectly in tune with Hewitt's feelings towards his mentor, describing him as '… a notable figure in the none-too-exciting English art world of the 1920s … something of a hero to the younger generation, and his sense of fun made him appealing.'

To appreciate Sickert's appeal to the students at the RA schools it is worth reviewing his background prior to 1925. The most interesting biography of Sickert in the present context is probably *The life and opinions of Walter Richard Sickert* by Robert Emmons, 1941, Faber and Faber (reprinted in 1992 by Lund

Humphries Publishers). This was the first biography of Sickert, written when the subject was still alive by someone who knew him and had studied under him. Furthermore, the author would have known Hewitt, as the two of them had frequented Sickert's short-lived school at Highbury in 1927.

What Emmons wrote about Sickert's views was largely based on first-hand experience, together with information he obtained from Andrina Schweder, Sickert's sister-in-law. [Interestingly, many years later in the 1950s when Rayner asked Andrina Schweder for some background information on Sickert's earlier life, she responded by giving him a copy of the same typewritten pages she had prepared for Robert Emmons].

The most recent addition to the literature about Sickert is the authoritative 2005 biography by Matthew Sturgis [*Walter Sickert: a life*, Harper Collins]. The most comprehensive illustrated collection of Sickert's work is Wendy Baron's 2006 book *Sickert paintings and drawings* published by Yale University Press.

When he started teaching at the Royal Academy Schools in 1925, Sickert was 65 years old. He was an inspiring and romantic figure to young would-be artists. For one thing, he provided a direct link back to the French avant-garde, and was seen by many as the link between them and Britain's Camden Town Group.

As a young man in 1881, at the age of 21, Sickert had quit the Slade art school after just one year to become an assistant to Whistler. He worked at Whistler's studio in Tite Street, preparing canvases and helping print Whistler's Venice etchings. Through Whistler he met Degas, with whom he worked in Paris in 1883.

It was from Whistler that Sickert picked up the idea of starting with the chief point of interest of a drawing, drawing this in detail and then working outwards from it. In this way the picture would be complete 'even if one were to be arrested in the middle of it'.

Interestingly, being an artist was not Sickert's first career. He began as an actor, which perhaps explains his later oratorial skills and his interest in drawing and painting music hall and ballet themes. 'The best of Sickert's nature was in his stories and the way he told them,' Hewitt noted. 'He sang and acted and quoted Shakespeare and music hall.' On one occasion in class Rayner heard Sickert comment to a student: 'Your vocabulary is better than mine but you do not use it to effect.'

Sickert had a passion for art education. He had set up numerous private art schools in his life although few had lasted long. He had strong views about the deficiencies in art education in Britain at that time and he was dismissive about idlers who were only looking for fame and 'promotion to the Café Royal'.

In her 1992 book *Walter Sickert and the Camden Town Group*, (David & Charles), Maureen Connett described Sickert as having 'everything that was needed to make a brilliant teacher: a deep love and mastery of his craft; a profound knowledge and understanding of *la peinture* and the tradition which had nurtured it; a lucid and racy style of exposition, and the authority that comes from first-hand acquaintance with the great French painters.'

What was it like being at one of Sickert's classes? His method of teaching was apparently based more on talk than engaging in practical workshops. He didn't give individual criticism of student works – in this respect he had adopted Whistler's teaching technique. What he did was encourage his students to rely on themselves and not on direction. At the RA Schools he often dressed and posed his models in *tableaux vivants* and tasked the students with capturing the scene.

Sickert had few pretensions about his art, or art in general. He gave freely of his knowledge and experience. And he constantly stated his view that it was the work rather than the artist's name that attracted his attention. 'Drawings or paintings by unknown artists often gave him as much pleasure as those by well-known names', wrote Emmons.

He seems to have also had a relaxed attitude about imitations of his work.

Sickert was also, of course, an etcher, though his side of his output was largely overshadowed by his paintings. He started doing etchings when he worked with Whistler. He was against limited editions of prints, opining that 'the edition of a print should be unlimited, or limited only by the demand, the price low, and all incentive to speculation avoided.' It seems that in later life Sickert refused to sign

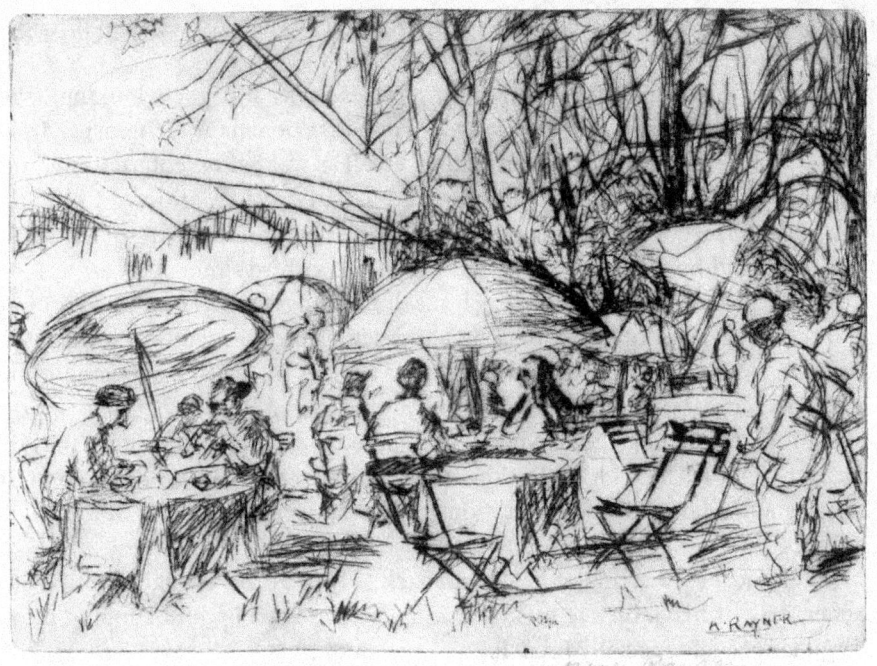

6.2 '*The tea house in Kensington gardens, 1925*'. The bowler-hatted figure on the right with the artist's gear slung across his shoulder, is almost certainly Sickert, who was working on his '*Serpentine*' painting during this period. Drypoint, 140×193mm. RS.

his own prints, on the grounds that 'they should be bought and sold on their own merits, and not on that of the name.'

There was an exhibition devoted to Sickert's etchings, titled 'Walter Sickert as printmaker' at the Yale Center for British Art in 1976. In the exhibition catalogue, Andrew Wilson, Curator of Prints and drawings, wrote: 'His [Sickert's] dismissal of the Whistlerian aestheticism, and of the dogma embraced by the Society of Painter Etchers that each impression is 'unique', looks forward to the highly commercialised print workshops of our day.'

Sickert did not see etchings as a separate activity, but rather as reproductions of his favourite drawings. This is why many of his 200+ etchings depict the same scenes as his paintings.

In 1925 when Hewitt Rayner met him, Sickert was gaining recognition from the etching fraternity. From 1923 on the authoritative annual publication *Fine Prints of the Year* included Sickert etchings. In 1925 the Leicester gallery held a retrospective of his etchings. Later, in 1926 and 1928 he would even be invited to submit etchings to the exhibitions of the Royal Society of Painter Etchers.

This, then, is the background to the man who stood in front of the students at the RA Schools, following his election as a Royal Academician.

A real legend. An engaging teacher who talked from experience, and taught in new ways. An artist and etcher. A writer. A story-teller. A man who provided a direct line to Whistler and Degas.

Sickert in his sixties cut a striking figure. He was still good looking, even though his wavy brown hair had greyed. He had a penchant for wearing frock coats and other fashions from an earlier era. He was witty, entertaining, and engaging. He chose his clothes carefully, and would dress up or down to suit the occasion and the company. He mixed easily in the highest levels of society – and the lowest. And he was about to get married for the third time.

By 1925 Sickert had begun getting himself back together. He travelled around the UK to deliver lectures. In 1924 he had been elected a member of the Royal Academy. He was writing regular newspaper articles on art that appeared in the *Daily Telegraph*, the *Manchester Guardian* and *Morning Post*.

He took up teaching again. And he took up etching again. In January 1925 the Leicester Galleries held an exhibition of his etchings from 1884 to the present. In February and May 1926 two exhibitions of his paintings were held at the Savile Gallery.

Walter Sickert was making a comeback. He was an engaging and witty teacher, even if his audience was occasionally perplexed by him slipping into a foreign language, especially French.

There was nevertheless a darker side to Sickert. Hewitt wrote: 'We who knew him in those days (1925) felt the intense mental agitation and heart despair of a man who had become a voluntary recluse for five years – the world's greatest artist a recluse at the height of his fame. Many have missed the point and the reason for his turning inwards and painting memories – 'Echoes' – for the rest of his life. I was close to him at this time. I witnessed the moments of his deepest despair. ... his strange moodiness, his sudden irritable, insulting behaviour to women and students.' Hewitt was convinced that it was his grief over the death in 1920 of his first wife Christine that was still affecting Sickert.

The incident that started the friendship between Rayner and Sickert arose from a morning class at the RA Schools in June 1925. Sickert, as usual, had set up one of his *tableaux vivants*. The tableau that day consisted of three figures. One of them was a woman, bending over a figure dressed as a clown on the floor. Against Sickert's wishes, Hewitt chose to paint the scene from a good height, unlike the rest of the students who were following Sickert's instructions to paint at what Hewitt described as 'uncomfortable little floor easels'. Ironically, these were probably the easels that Sickert himself had donated to the schools, as noted in the Annual Report of the Royal Academy Council for 1925.

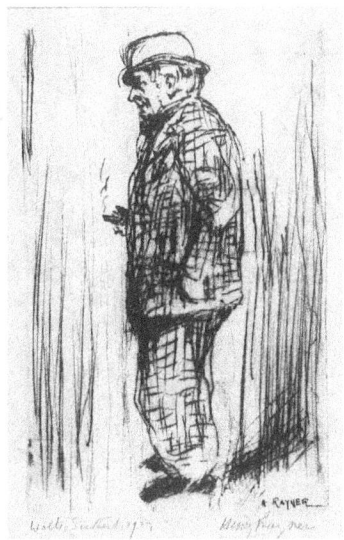

6.3 One of the earliest of Rayner's drypoints of Sickert, titled *'Sickert in Kensington Gardens, 1925'* and also *'Walter Sickert 1927'*. RS.

Hewitt painted the scene in an Impressionist manner, using a system of three colours for tones and shadows. Rayner christened this technique a 'trichrome' *camaieu*. He titled the resulting work *'The dying clown'*. Sickert held the work – at that stage only in its *camaieu* form – up to the class as a fine example of tone and composition.

The morning session didn't go smoothly, as Hewitt recalled. 'The first soul to rebel was one of the models, the tall, strapping woman with the long black tresses,' he wrote in *Red Violet*. 'As morning class began she stood up against the south wall and declared she would not take the pose of bending over the jester with her face almost against his for two hours.

'The poor little jester had not minded as far as I could determine, but the lady continued to stand rigid against the wall until Sickert appeared, beautifully attired, as if about to step onto the stage of a musical revue. Indeed, the next few moments were not unlike one. Walter, advancing to the elderly woman model sitting on the side of the throne, girt in chemise, made a gallant flourish with his right arm and kissed her hand.

'Then, noticing that something was amiss he turned and stepped quickly over to the distressed lady. Her eyes were darkly blazing; her hands were clenched. It seemed to many part of a natural Sickert act. Walter spoke. But his charm could not prevail on this occasion. A man was procured, and a wig, and the painting went merrily on.

'To those among us who enjoyed what Walter termed 'a slice of Life' this demonstration was precious, helpful, for we now had a variety of models, which meant that new life could be given to our drawings and new colour to our paintings. They were Sickert's models and I expect he, as usual, paid.' Sickert

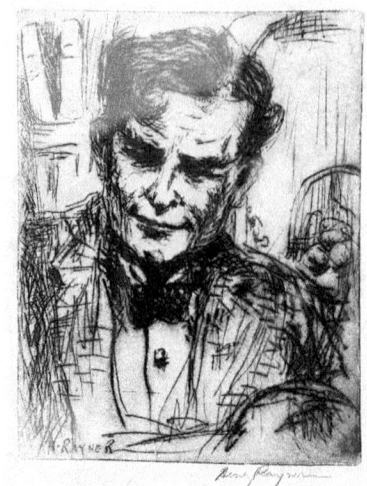

6.4 'Richard Sickert ARA'. Drypoint, 193×148mm. sw.

was renowned for not using establishment models, preferring instead acquaintances and people he had met in various circumstances.

Confirmation of this classroom incident comes from Marjorie Lilly's 1971 book *Sickert: the painter and his circle*. In the book, Rayner's fellow-student and friend Clifford Hall (1904–1973) described the same incident. Since Hewitt's account written in the 1950s was never published, and the story told by Hall appeared some 14 years after Hewitt's death, neither can have copied the story from the other.

A few days after this classroom incident, Sickert sent a note to Hewitt via Clifford Hall. The note invited Hewitt to meet him at the Kensington Gardens tea house at 3.00pm and to bring his paint box and any drawings from the tableau session. The note was signed Richard Sickert.

Hewitt recalls what happened next. 'I was given the note just in time and rushed off down to the Serpentine to find Walter shuffling into the tea gardens garbed in a grey cut-away coat, black cravat, a grey bowler and spats. He appeared as if he had only just left the Private Enclosure at Ascot, but over his bent shoulder was slung a heavy paint-box and other sketching devices, constituting quite a cumbrous load for so aged a man. This image of Sickert was later captured in one of Hewitt's drypoints of his mentor.

'He gave me a tired friendly grin, not his usual Asiatic sort, behind which he disappeared like Alice's cat. His first salutation was 'Have you brought the drawings with you?'

'I had. And we sat at one of the shady tables and Walter ordered tea for two, bread and butter, cakes, jam, cream. He came to the point without waiting. 'I should like to buy your *tableau vivant* painting. May I have it?' I agreed to sell it and he immediately gave me a cheque on an Islington Bank. Later on he took the drawings for the picture'.

'This was out first *tete-a-tete*. I had heard so much about him, the great painter, the great wit, the great legend. It took me all I could do to refrain from wiping my eyes to clear away the vision I swore could not be true. Walter Sickert sitting here beside me, pouring out my tea as delicately as a woman, and pressing bread, jam and cakes upon me.

'I thought of the picture I had just painted. Three figures. One, a male garbed as a jester, lying outstretched, with a female, whose black hair streamed down, bending forward over him. An elderly female in a chemise sitting at the head. Merely a student's work. What was there so marvellous in it? The years were to show'.

What did this cryptic comment 'the years were to show' mean? The explanation is that a celebrated work by Sickert two years later used a composition and perspective that Hewitt believed took its inspiration from his '*Dying clown*' work.

Hewitt recalled in a 1955 letter to Andrina Schweder that '*The Dying clown*' was a large canvas. What happened to it after Sickert acquired it is not known. It's also not known how much he had paid Hewitt for the picture.

'I shall remove the painting by taxi tomorrow,' said Walter. And he talked about my future. We left the tea garden and went to sit near the Serpentine where he continued with a sketch he was making. I began work as well.' Sickert was, as usual, smoking his Manila cheroots, scattering ash all over his drawing as he talked.

Sickert duly took away the painting, still in its *camaieu* form. But this was not the end of the *Dying Clown* story. In 1926 Sickert asked him to make an underpainting of the picture.

Hewitt recorded that the day after this meeting over tea, cream and strawberry jam in Kensington Gardens, Sickert gave a lecture on the merits of the 'Dying clown' picture to the students of the Academy. 'A fact which did little to further my popularity among the young brothers of the brush,' he later wrote.

There were more visits to Kensington Gardens. On one visit, Sickert sat on the grass overlooking the Serpentine and said to Hewitt: 'I have painted here for 38 years, and the only drawback of this place is the nursemaids. But I am not a *plein air* painter.'

'This time period was important to me,' Hewitt wrote. 'I had become undecided whether or not to remain in England. I knew that the new renaissance of art had been incalculably enriched by Sickert, and as a thinking mind he was no mere intellectual gas-works. He was making a big come-back in his art, and looking for fresh ideas, and I was a raw young painter and etcher coming onto the scene for the first time studying old ideas. To me it was all as mysterious and undefined and beckoning as the wind on the sail of a boat.'

The two of them met again in Kensington Gardens a few days later. The weather was very fine, and Sickert was evidently in a communicative mood. They took up positions in the same location as before. Sickert was working on what would become his famous '*Serpentine*' painting, in front of a great oak.

Indicating the big tree in his drawing, Sickert said 'You see, I have to make up my mind about what I'm doing here. The Old Masters for the most part had their minds made up for them. The Church gave orders for another St Peter or St John, and off the painter went, altar-piece-wise, working under precise directions. Now we have all the world to choose from, but numbers of my brethren, knowing this, have not the sense to paint a piece of bread properly. Painting in oils requires just that thing, common-sense and a grip of the subject. There is too much talk about natural refinement of mind.'

Instead of eating at the kiosk that day, Sickert took Hewitt for lunch at a little place in Shepherd's Market, Mayfair. It was Hewitt's first experience of Hungarian Goulash. To wash it down they drank Chateau d'Yquem, 1911 vintage.

There was an amusing misunderstanding in the afternoon. Sickert came over and stood watching Hewitt paint. After a while he wanted to make a correction and took the palette of oils. Then, after trying to work out how to hold Rayner's palette and spilling most of the oil medium onto the grass, he criticised him for putting the paint on the wrong side of the palette. Hewitt had to point out that he was left handed, prompting an immediate apology from Sickert who added: 'Of course, many great artists have been left-handed.'

[As a side note, it seems that left-handedness is a trait that runs through the Rayner family, according to Dorothy Carey. Dorothy is a grand-daughter of Amy, one of the Rayner children who arrived in Australia in 1886, and an Aunt of Hewitt's. Evidently Amy was left-handed, as are Dorothy's sister, her son and one of her nieces.]

By way of compensation Sickert then gave Hewitt some tuition in the correct use of mineral violet and violet cobalt to express shadows. These were colours the young artist had never seen before. 'It was a mild revelation,' he wrote later.

Sickert finished the session with the words: 'Now, paint with feeling! God has given you emotions. Use them, for your painting. When you paint, don't think, feel. And for mercy's sake, don't wear your heart on your sleeve.'

When they left the Gardens, they walked together as far as the Bayswater Road, where Sickert left him and then in Hewitt's own words 'shambled towards a taxi'.

There are three Rayner drypoints that emerged from these meetings in Kensington Gardens. One is the full-length portrait showing Sickert in his characteristic check-patterned suit and bowler hat (see Fig 6.3). There is also a close-up of the bowler-hatted Sickert, titled 'RW Sickert ARA, Kensington gardens, 1925'. (See Fig 6.5).

The other Rayner drypoint to result from these visits to Kensington Gardens has never previously been recognised for what it is. Titled simply '*Old Kensington Gardens*' it shows people sitting at tables under large parasols, taking tea (see Fig 6.2). The interesting feature from the perspective of the Rayner/Sickert friendship is the bowler-hatted figure on the right of the picture. This is Sickert, with his cutaway coat, carrying his artist's portfolio in his left hand and a bag over his right shoulder,

In early 1926 Sickert's health deteriorated sharply. Hewitt and René Quinn had been invited to visit him at his home in Fitzroy Street, near the northern end of Tottenham Court Road. Hewitt described Fitzroy Street as 'a gloomy, rain-covered landscape where garish red and green lights reflected sharply into the greasy pavements, and dark figures hurried along with heads bent low. Number 15 was one of a row of smart grey stone buildings standing in the centre of London's West End Bohemia. Whistler had once lived opposite at Number 8, and Augustus John began his career in one of these houses.'

Therese Lessore opened the door, and before they went into Walter's room warned them that he was not well and needed rest. Then she left and headed across the road to the studio flat in which she was living at the time. 'We found

Walter sitting in the corner of his front room, writing,' Hewitt recalled. 'He was dressed in his familiar cut-away coat, his neck free of a collar, which he usually seemed to find an encumbrance. His face was grey and tired looking, and he greeted us with a wan smile.

'We sat by the empty fireplace and he went through some work we had: the last drawings for my '*Dying Clown*', and the first of my Thames set in drypoint. Walter spoke to René about his future, and soon afterwards Quinn left. Walter began speaking of the increasing embarrassments he was having to face in the house. He could not work for the street noises and the house noises. He was suffering from nervous exhaustion. He explained that he had no doctor and would abide none. He was against any sort of treatment and loathed drugs, finding solace alone in an endless chain of Manilla cheroots. He could not sleep, he said. '*On me derange tout le temps*'. Work had become impossible and he had been trying unsuccessfully to finish the last Serpentine picture.'

Before he left that evening Hewitt persuaded Sickert to take some paraldehyde (a drug he was familiar with from his days in the Australian bush) obtained from a chemist in nearby Goodge Street. Relaxed by the drug, Sickert talked about his teaching work which he said would have to stop. His Manchester school was to close. Changing tack, he advised Hewitt to go over to Paris where 'his English style would suit French connoisseurs'.

This was the last time Hewitt would visit Sickert in Fitzroy Street. Therese Lessore, shortly to become Mrs Sickert, was doing her best to get him out of London. Hewitt wrote: 'It was Therese Lessore who first told me of the forthcoming marriage between herself and Sickert. She seemed to be thinking more of his health than herself or her future, and was eager to get him out of London.' Her idea was to go to Margate but the next thing Hewitt heard was that they had settled in Brighton. At around this time Hewitt was starting his *Les Sylphides* set of drypoints.

Hewitt does not mention anything specific about the nature of Sickert's ill health, but in his 1976 book about Sickert, Denys Sutton states that during the Brighton days Sickert was recovering from a stroke.

There are no records of contact between Hewitt and Sickert for the next year, but in the late spring or early summer of 1927 Hewitt learnt that Walter and Therese had returned to London and purchased a house at 15 Quadrant Road in Islington, north London. Quadrant Road no longer exists, having been replaced by a housing estate in the 1960s. One of the residential blocks is called Sickert Court.

Hewitt didn't hear of the new address from the Sickerts themselves but from Major Lessore, Therese's brother. He was a sculptor, as well as founder and proprietor of the Beaux Arts Gallery in London's Bruton Street.

There is one Sickert painting that shows the back garden of his home at Quadrant Road. It is the one titled '*Garden of love*'. Hewitt happened to be visiting Sickert one day when he surveyed the view from the back window and described it as 'the garden of love'. Hewitt remembered the scene with a small lawn, behind which were three trellis arches covered with roses. In the centre of the lawn was a sundial. Several years later, when the Sickerts had moved to a house in Barnsbury Park, he found that Sickert had captured the scene in a painting.

Major Lessore invited Hewitt to accompany him on a visit to Quadrant Road where he was hoping to see Sickert's latest works. The most notable picture they saw was a portrait of Admiral Lumsden. 'The biggest, the bluest, the best of the new pictures,' recalled Hewitt. This work had caused a little problem at the RA earlier in the year, when the Hanging Committee considered it 'in too unfinished a state' to be exhibited, and invited Sickert to withdraw it. As noted in the minutes of the Council meeting of 12th April 1927, Sickert gracefully obliged.

Over tea in the kitchen, Sickert told Hewitt and Lessore that he planned to set up a new art school in a big studio he had taken at number 1 Highbury Fields. This is not far from Quadrant Road, and its location right opposite Highbury Station would make it easy for people to travel to the school, in Sickert's view. An advertisement in *The Times* launched the school.

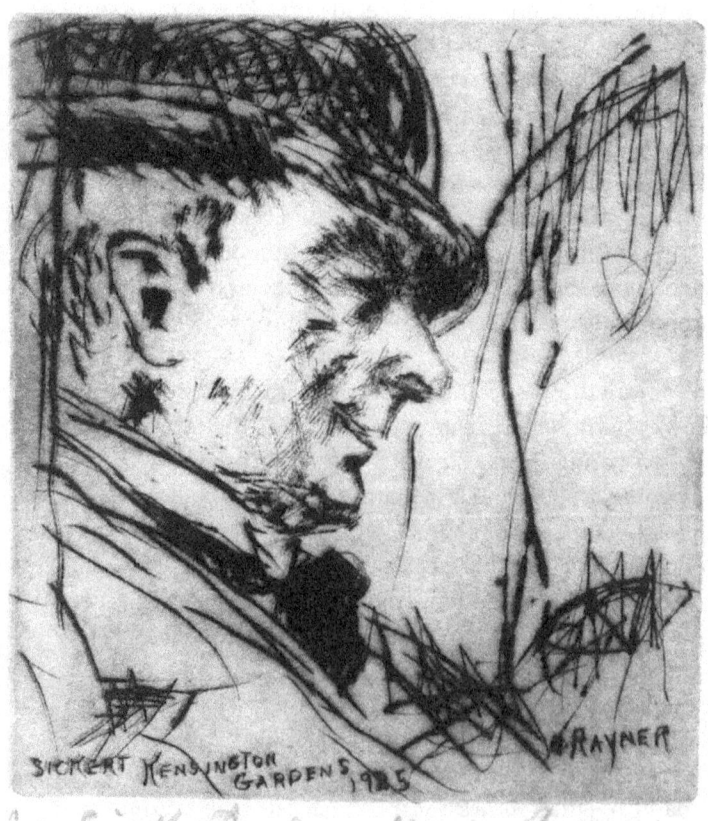

6.5 *'RW Sickert ARA, Kensington Gardens'*, 1925. Drypoint, 120×106mm. sw.

When the school started in October Sickert invited Hewitt to come along. It's not clear whether this invitation was intended to attract Hewitt as a student or teacher, or both. Hewitt found that the students included Lord Methuen, Mark Oliver, Morland Lewis, and Robert Emmons (who 14 years later would publish his biography of Sickert). Sickert continued to get the students to paint from press photographs or from drawings they had done elsewhere.

However, the school did not last long. A kind of apathy seems to have set in, and when Sickert stopped attending so did the students. Hewitt says that the school only lasted one month. Sickert continued to use the premises for his own work.

Hewitt noted that Sickert's wife Therese would accompany him back and forth between Quadrant Road and Highbury in taxi cabs. 'Few in those days could easily gain access to the great artist,' he commented.

It seems that Sickert also had an extra layer of protection from unwelcome visitors to his Highbury studios, in the form of a peanut seller called Johnny. His stand was just outside the front door of the Highbury premises. 'Walter was very fond of this man,' explained Hewitt, 'who warned him of the approach of undesirable visitors and pestering callers by running into the studio yard and making a certain noise.'

Hewitt wrote about the Highbury premises. 'The large dark red brick studio jutted out from behind a decorous Victorian house – an ugly contrivance. It possessed three big windows faced with inlet arches. From these, one could look out over the St Paul's Road, the station and its busy populace, the end of the Holloway Road and a part of Upper Street.

There were two entrances to Sickert's studio. One was via the main entrance shared with the residential apartments in the building. This involved going through the charming old Victorian portico, up a short flight of steps in the vestibule and along a passage. The other entrance was via an iron staircase that led up from the back yard.

Hewitt noted that the main entrance was used primarily for Sickert's VIP visitors – important people who wanted to buy a picture, or share a cheroot with him. Everyone else – students, models and heavy canvasses – was supposed to use the iron staircase.

'The lights would be glaring from the windows. The door would open at the top of the thin iron stairway. The great, heavy, shuffling figure would shout *'Bonsoir Monseigneur.* Enter!'.

There had been unfortunate incidents. Sometimes, models seeking the studio would by mistake knock at the doors of other residents of the building, causing alarm and suspicion. On one occasion pictures of nudes painted by his students had been carried down the main stairs and out through the front door, causing great distress to a most devout elderly lady who lived on the front ground floor.

Hewitt wrote about one cold, wet day when he and Sickert collected five large canvases – two still sticky with paint – from Sickert's studio in Noel Street and home in Quadrant Road, and took them by taxi to the Highbury studio. With the help of the cabman they managed to get them up the narrow iron stairway, although at one point Sickert actually fell down the steps. The story ends with Sickert inviting the cabman in for a brandy, and inviting his opinion of the '*Front at Hove*' painting.

Hewitt said that Sir Hugh Walpole was a close friend of Sickert and was a frequent visitor to the Highbury Fields studio. Sir Hugh had written the preface to the catalogue for an exhibition of Sickert's work at the Saville Gallery in 1926.

Today the property carries a historic building plaque from the London Borough of Islington noting that this 'WR Sickert (1860–1942) had his school of painting and engraving here 1927–1934'. These dates don't tally with Hewitt's recollections. The structure containing Sickert's studio is no longer attached to the property.

As a student of Sickert's at the Royal Academy schools and later at the short-lived Highbury art school, and during visits they made to each other's homes, Hewitt had plenty of opportunity to absorb Sickert's ideas and techniques on drawing and painting. He took scribbled notes during classes, and also documented the thoughts and ideas Sickert put forward during conversations. Later, as part of his *Red Violet* manuscript Rayner assembled all the information to form a unique record of Sickert's painting and teaching technique as seen through the eyes of a student and protégé.

Recalling Sickert's RA lessons during 1925, Hewitt wrote: 'At this time his teaching prescribed the squaring up of large and small canvasses and under-painting from small drawings or photographs which were interesting tonally. A sample *camaieu* construction at this period under his guidance would be of two colours, either cobalt blue or indian red. He instructed me that back in his Bath and Neuville days it was indian red and cobalt in the one *camaieu*.

'Walter used absorptive and unabsorptive canvas, and often a quick-drying *siccative: siccative de Coutrai Blanc* or *siccative Lechertier Barbe*, procured from the firm of that name in Jermyn Street, near the Royal Academy.

'Sometimes a violet and indian red was used for the underpainting and mixing together in the right proportion with white in a series of tones. He instructed me to work the *siccative de Coutrai* well down with turpentine, saying that the painting would crack badly if very great care was not taken and the quantities were not right.

'This method gave him the fast drying he needed, and as he had numerous canvasses on the stocks at the same time, a not unusual feature with him. He required a crisp surface, a sparkling and lasting patina.

'His touch was extremely quick, pushing and lightly dragging the pigment. He used to say that one could not paint satisfactorily in the street or countryside, on account of the dust and the wind and the changing light, and the cars and horses that will not stand still while the painter struggled to apply pigment to canvas.

'The highest course was to make a variety of quick sketches in pencil and wash, brief colour notes, and square up, then build the composition up on to a large squared canvas properly primed with either a tint or white alone. Now the artist may commence his *camaieu* in two or three colours. This monochrome method, Walter insisted, was for the man who conceived in terms of light and shade, painting from drawing, and not to be used for direct painting from nature. This advice he always considered most important, as there had been much misunderstanding about it.

'A very clear plan was needed for this *camaieu* method that produced such great results in the studios of Sickert. When the monochrome was dry it could, according to an earlier method of his, be re-squared with a piece of white chalk, and another more precise drawing worked in, and a two-colour painting made for the final correction of drawing. Everything had to be kept continuously loose and moving.'

The rest of the instructions, Hewitt put into Sickert's own words

> Keep it on the move, but keep it firm. You can shove the paint about, and alter freely to the advantage of the texture and luminosity. This adds weight and quality. Scrub with undiluted pigment as it comes out of the tube, if necessary, using equal proportions of turps and unbleached linseed oil. Scrub until the last touches on the final underpainting get flat, as they will do. You are then ready for the true colour, and a thin runny paint.

> When you have sufficiently and succinctly expressed yourself in that drawn *camaieu*, stop. Let it get bone dry, with its face to the wall. A little dust won't hurt it. You wouldn't believe it, but there are some people who are afraid of their painting collecting a little of God's healthy dust. We swallow vats of it. Remember, as the painters say, knock it about a bit.

> The monochrome needs shoving vigorously to live and grow, and move as a complete study for final working. The result of this initial stage is a precision and an uncertainty of form that is in itself not unpleasant. The tentative part of your picture.

> Experience in nature sketching will teach you what and what not to draw in strongly at the initial working. Some of the finished surface may require just that loosened and tentative appearance. But keep the whole thing fresh with your first crisp drawing from the sketch or print or photograph. A photograph is not a furtive object. It can be and often is a very beautiful one-eyed drawing of nature that we artists are privileged to exploit.

> An agreeable quality and surface may be achieved by the application of undiluted paint scrubbed hard over a bone dry and coarse *camaieu*, that is painted best in light tone arrangements – nearly all white, with just enough colour-tone to define and create light and shadow. This is the last monochrome coat. The lights may be one colour, the shadows another. White-indian red for shadow; white-French cobalt for the lights. Little medium may be used.

> Four tones have been my practice for years. For the lights, white coloured with red cobalt. For shadows, white mixed with indian red. White mixed with more Indian red. And White mixed with a further lot of red. The two white-blue tones mixed the same way. If the study is begun in just two colours, white and another, make four tones of this colour, and begin painting.

Hewitt noted that Sickert's plan of *camaieu* formation became 'very simple in the end when his hand grew technically perfect; and he seemed not to want such a defined underdrawing (or at least not such a precise *camaieu*). But he was a Master, and could dispense with much scaffolding.'

The notes return to Walter Sickert's own voice, as remembered by Hewitt:

> The more you push about and alter, the more luminous and solid the paint becomes. This is the advantage. The more you redraw, the better the resulting quality of paint in the first two-colour applications. But in the last coats of the true colour, the more you shove it about and overwork, with dark piled on dark, the more unsatisfactory and jammed the study becomes. All luminosity is lost.
>
> If the paint is too thinned at the initial stage of the monochrome, the surface becomes poor and wispy. If the paint is allowed to become too fatted up at this stage, by heavy pigment, the thickness will prove fatal to the ultimate working.
>
> It is this study of the beginning in oils that we must all look to. The transparency given by the camaieu I have described, worked over with little dilutant, and painted intelligently, reveals qualities in the undercoats which make for a blessedness in the last touches worked for translucence, opaque against the semi-transparent early underpainting shows a richness. This whole method for success depends on the coarse tooth of the canvas, and is for painting from drawings, and not from life.'

Looking back at these painting principles as taught by Sickert in 1925, Hewitt noted that the system was very tantalising to those young painters who wanted to splash about a bit. 'It would have driven Whistler into hysterics,' he observed. 'But what suited Sickert never suited James.

'Many of the best artists of the day worked from a clear untouched canvas base to a direct finish. But Walter was sound in his manner of instruction, covering a very wide ground for any type of painter student. In class he admitted that the wisest men make the silliest mistakes.'

One of Hewitt's own *camaieus* for a painting of Theresa from this period has survived. Executed on the reverse of an earlier oil of a Victorian gentlemen (artist unknown) the unfinished work shows Theresa sitting in an upholstered armchair.

Evidently, many students were shocked when Sickert brought along the daily newspaper, and asked the students in solemn tones to square up a newspaper photograph of a fashionable wedding, and transfer it to a prepared canvas. 'Many of them thought Sickert was trying to lead them into a painting short cut, whereas he was merely endeavouring to inculcate a knowledge of tonal relationships, composition, exact squaring up, and *camaieu* construction in a new way.' This practice also resulted in critical comments in the media.

Hewitt himself sometimes used newspaper images as the inspiration for drypoints.

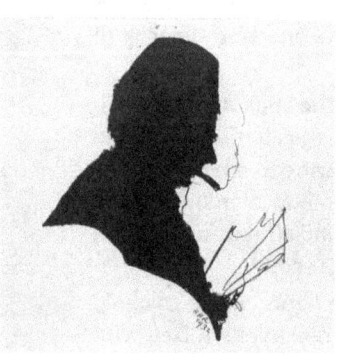

6.6 Silhouette of Sickert by Rayner, 1932, probably at the Barnsbury Park house. Ink, 180×160mm. sw.

Sickert would say: 'Who is to say when a painting is finished? Who is to say when the last touch is to be applied? That is the most difficult decision of all for any artist.'

Hewitt pointed out that the *Red Violet* era (which he attributed to Sickert) 'was not born, shaped and yielded in proud solitude. Two women of great brilliance and originality stood by the Master. Not only influencing him with their own bright, highly-keyed and finely-coloured works, but by their labours in working on some of his best pictures, painting in the first coats and bringing the canvasses to a pitch that needed only the final throwing in of those incidentals which create the tour de force, the Touch that only Walter could give with precision and definite completion.'

The two women were Sylvia Gosse and Therese Lessore, both of whom had known Sickert since the Camden Town Group.

'These three artists formed a triple strength of which Sickert constituted the main supporting part,' Hewitt wrote. 'It was a strange union, and I do not suppose we shall ever know the true, full influence one had upon the other. It is certain that Walter derived much strength from Sylvia Gosse, and she from him. And it is equally certain that the French Therese Lessore supplied lights and shadows from her undisputed artistic resources.'

Strangely, perhaps, for one so talented with the tools of the artist Sickert was not renowned for his handwriting. 'His penmanship was as obscure as his brushwork was clear and bright,' is how Hewitt put it, adding, 'it has ever been a puzzle to me to know how the press deciphered that script.'

Sickert's sister-in-law Andrina confirmed just how bad his handwriting was when she wrote to Hewitt: 'We were rather glad when Dr. Emmons published the letters Walter wrote to me, as for the first time we were able to understand what they contained. We had never been able to decipher them.'

One wet November evening in 1927 Hewitt responded to an invitation from Sickert to go to Highbury and show him the new canal and river set of drypoints. Arriving via Highbury station, Hewitt was directed to Number 1 Highbury Place by a taxi driver. He was amused but not surprised to see that there was a cab rank right in front of Sickert's address.

Inside, Sickert was working by the light of an electric lamp. 'A cheerful fire blazed in the small grate,' Rayner wrote. 'The big room retained its Victorian atmosphere. It had been alternately dancing academy, music academy, studio and club. The place was snug, and filled with the rich smell of turps and linseed oil, a joyful odour to all painters born.

'Walter was smoking and painting. Cigar ash was falling generously on to his palette, the quick brush mixing ash and paint into fine tone that was deftly swept into the tooth of the canvas. A study for Noel Street stood in the corner, its low green and brown tones shining. The great portrait of Admiral Lumsden towered its length between the windows that faced to the south – Walter had a contempt for the north-light painters.

'His painting rooms were ever very warm. Sickert was the type of painter who needed a hard ground for working: thus he must have a drying atmosphere. As Walter had many canvasses drying on the stocks at the same time, he required an intense heat. 'Bone dry', was the term he used, 'and have as many drying at the same time as possible.'

'There were photos and paintings and prints scattered about the room, much of it Therese's work. A great round-topped mirror rested on the mantelpiece, and I imagined her arranging her beautiful hair in front of it.'

Sickert evidently did not spend money carelessly on his studio environments or his homes. 'Glamour was sadly missing at Highbury and at Quadrant Road', Hewitt recorded. 'where simplicity, commonsense and Degas reigned. One could smell greatness in the very bareness of the sanded floorboards (some of the rooms being purposely stripped to an ascetic barrenness).'

The last time Hewitt saw the Highbury studio, probably in the winter of 1941, it was a bomb-shattered ruin. 'The mirror is in fragments all over the room. The ceiling is falling in. The walls are damp and cracked, the windows paneless and open to wind and rain. The grate is black and cold. The door where the Master stood so often to bow his visitor in with a roguish smile and witty greeting, is walled up. It is hard to realise that those great pictures: 'She stoops to conquer', 'The raising of Lazarus', 'Barnet Fair', 'Lazarus breaks his fast', 'Sir High Walpole', and many 'Echoes' were made in this bomb-shattered ruin.'

Rayner and Sickert shared a strong interest in France and French art. They both spoke French – indeed it was evidently necessary to speak French in order to study with Sickert and talk with him.

The things that Sickert said to Hewitt during their friendship would have a lasting impression on the young man. On one occasion when he was visiting Sickert at home he asked the older man whether he agreed with Carlyle's dictum that 'genius is the art of taking infinite pains'.

'Genius is not the art of taking pains', replied Sickert. 'It is the art of incurring pains'. Hewitt thought of this during his struggle through the 1930s. 'Hunger whipped the inspiration into me on more than one occasion.'

On models, Sickert said: 'Models can't get model expressions. You are your own best and cheapest model. You've got to fizz when you paint.'

On writing, he said: 'Writing is good when one is not painting, but writing must not be allowed to obtrude on painting. But philosophy is no good. I shall have no philosophers in my class. I want painters and draughtsmen or nobody. Take your philosophers and 'argumentators' out of my sight'.

Hewitt also recalled that in all the years he knew Sickert, he only saw the man really angry on one occasion. It concerned a taxi trip. Sickert had ordered a taxi from the rank near the studio at Highbury Field, to take him home to Quadrant Road. The man who responded was a new driver who had earned the nickname 'the wrecker' on account of what Rayner termed 'his ruthless handling of the steering wheel'.

This is the story in Hewitt's own words:

'The great artist, all unsuspecting and faultlessly attired, stepped into the taxi and was almost immediately hurled to the floor as the machine appeared to leap from its wheels and fly around Highbury Corner. Walter had as a rule been able to control his multitude of cab drivers but on this day the worst happened.

'Thrown to the floor, he made gallant efforts to rise to the window to yell at 'the wrecker' but as he gained his foothold the car took the St Paul's Road turning on two wheels and Sickert was hurled onto the other side of the floor with greater violence. From this position he bawled to the driver to stop but 'the wrecker' had not begun.

'Down Canonbury Road they went, taking part of the road on no wheels at all. Up the Essex Road, threading the heavy traffic at unprecedented pace. Walter got up from his hands and knees and managed to get his head out of the door window, his favourite position. The taxi turned up Quadrant Road and came to an abrupt stop at number 15. Sickert was thrown back into his seat for the first time.

'Walter, ignoring the grinning face of the wrecker, staggered into the house, speechless, *dedaigneux*.' The next time he ordered a cab from the same rank, he shouted over the telephone: 'And do not send that man with a face like a bull.'

Sickert enjoyed wordplay humour. On one occasion as he and Hewitt were leaving the Highbury studio together by taxi, and heading for the Tate to see an exhibition of work by the East London Group, Sickert spotted a man pushing a street piano along the pavement. On the high back of the instrument was written in chalk 'Wives and children to support.'

Sickert liked the humour and commented that Phil May [a humorous artist of the time] would have made something of it. As they passed the man Sickert stopped the taxi and put a bank note into his hand.

At The Tate that day, after looking at the East London Group pictures, Sickert took Hewitt to the room where his '*George Moore*' and '*Café des Tribuneaux, Dieppe*' paintings hung. Commenting on the George Moore picture, he told Hewitt: 'I painted that portrait of Moore when I was very young. It was made in four sittings. Three for the underpainting and one for the last quick finish from life. I employed much the same technique then as I do now.

'I did not find Moore a particularly good sitter. He talked a lot, which is a bad thing in any sitter. If I had had my way I would have employed a photographer to get a couple of fair shots of the head.'

Hewitt wrote that this painting had caused some public comment when it was unveiled, with some people saying it made Moore look 'like a drunken cabdriver'.

Sickert hed been keen for the East London Group to grow, and in 1929 made several visits to give talks to its members at the evening institute in Bow where they met. At the first visit, he was sporting a huge chest-length beard, wearing a great coat with brightly-coloured lining and matching socks. For the next visit he had adopted a different guise – the beard had gone (because of the warm weather, he said) and he was wearing a shabby grey suit, heavy boots and thick woollen socks. Evidently he felt that as he was planning to talk about the craft of painting he should dress like a workman.

This information comes from an article written by one of the East End Group members, Cecil Osborne, for the March 1955 edition of the *St Pancras Journal*. It's worth including here because in the Rayner archive is a copy of the two-part article, heavily annotated by Hewitt. One of the notes records that in 1929 during one of his visits to Sickert's Highbury studio, Sickert had suggested he become involved with the East London Group. There is nothing to show that Hewitt ever followed up the suggestion.

One interesting piece of information in Osborne's article is the fact that Sickert's concept for the exhibitions planned for the Lefevre and Whitechapel Galleries involved more than having no selection jury and hanging the pictures in alphabetical order around the room. He also proposed that the pictures should be unframed. Osborne remembers Sickert saying that if a picture sells, the buyer is much more able to pay for a frame than the artist. In the event, the oil paintings were hung unframed but the drawings were framed – partly because that's how they had arrived and partly because the consensus was that it was the only practicable way to hang them.

Among the 60 or so pictures were one by Sickert and one by Therese Lessore. Nine sold during the exhibition.

Towards the end of Sickert's life Hewitt visited the 1941 Sickert exhibition at the National Gallery. This was a year before the artist's death, as it would turn out, and Sickert himself was unable to attend. Rayner wrote in a diary intended only for the eyes of his daughters:

> We who were present in 1941 were witnesses to the greatest tribute a nation can pay its premier artist, a tribute few artists live to enjoy.
>
> One hundred and thirty two paintings and drawings by Sickert were exhibited at the National Gallery, works from every period of his life. The Queen, who had lent pictures, visited the show, and thirty thousand people were to follow her.
>
> Walter had come home; this was his crowning victory; and as I walked round the mighty exhibition, dressed in rough battle dress or boiler suit, I felt his presence by me, cheroot in hand, slippers dragging along the floor of the gallery. 'One of the secrets of painting is to keep it fresh. Some like their herrings kippered, some like 'em fresh. I belong to the latter clique...'.

7

'Hanging gardens' and 'Raising Lazarus': What was Rayner's influence?

In early 1927 during a visit to Sickert, newly-returned from Brighton, Hewitt showed him the 'Regent's Canal' work he had just finished. Sickert responded by inviting his young protégé to go with him to Islington where he was working.

On the appointed day Hewitt went round to Sickert's home and the two of them took a taxi to Noel Street not far from The Angel underground station. Sickert had taken a room in a house owned by a Mrs Spencer. The three-storey house (nowadays number 54 Noel Road) is situated at the eastern end of the road next to Danbury Bridge, and the rear of the house overlooks the Regent's Canal.

This area evidently held good memories for Sickert. As a young boy he had lived with a great-aunt in nearby Duncan Terrace, while he was recovering from an operation for a fistula. 'On Sundays I would wander down along the canal and watch the barges float away into the dark recesses of the tunnel – a scene worthy of the hand of Meryon,' Hewitt remembered him saying.

Sickert's habit of renting studios in various locations in London was well-known. 'It was his method to have rooms where he could enjoy peace and paint at leisure without interference or interruption,' says Hewitt. 'I doubt whether even his most trusted friend, Miss Sylvia Gosse, would have intruded into this holy of holies.'

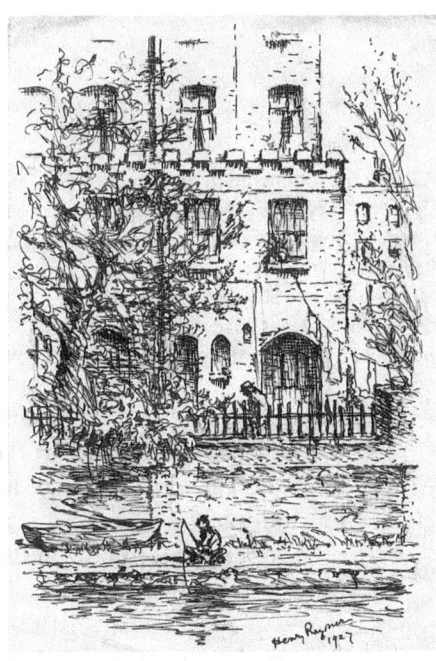

7.1 Drawing by Rayner of number 54 Noel Road as seen from the south side of the Regent's Canal, with a straw-hatted Sickert at work in the garden. Ink, 260×180mm, 1927. SW.

The monthly rent he paid his landlady for the room also gave him the right to move freely around the house and the garden that sloped down to the canal edge. According to Rayner, Sickert painted many of his '*Echoes*' in this studio, which he says was on the first floor at the rear of the house overlooking the canal.

The landlady's daughter and a young friend sat for Sickert in the front parlour of this house, for the picture that would become '*Laylock and Thunderplump*'.

Hewitt accompanied Sickert across to the other side of the canal on at least two occasions. One of the days, Sickert was working on drawings for what would become his '*Hanging gardens of Islington*' works. On the other he was working on drawings for '*The fading memories of Sir Walter Scott*.'

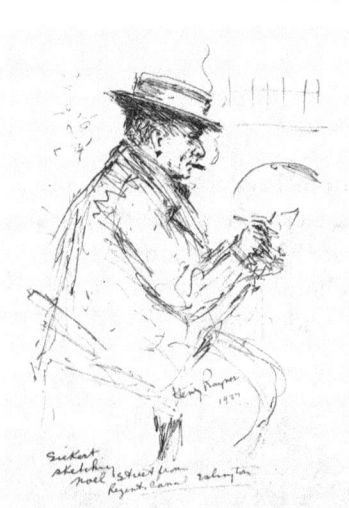

It has to be said that there seems to be a discrepancy in the dating of these meetings between Hewitt and Sickert. Dr Wendy Baron has pointed out that Sickert's '*Hanging gardens*' work was shown at an exhibition in 1926, in which case he cannot have been working on this picture in 1927 as Hewitt recalled. However, Hewitt's two pen and ink drawings of Sickert and the Noel Street house, as far as we know done on the spot, are clearly dated 1927. And in the *Red Violet* manuscript he ties this episode in with the year in which Sickert returned to London from Brighton. That was definitely 1927.

Hewitt made more than one visit to see Sickert at Noel Street, so it may be that when writing about the incidents some years later he simply mixed up what had been discussed during which visit. Hewitt's memory for dates was sometimes unreliable. For example he gave the year in which he and Theresa visited Australia variously as 1930, 1931 and 1932. In reality it was 1931, as the ticket receipt and passport entries confirm.

7.2 Pen & ink drawing by Rayner of Sickert as they sat by the Regent's Canal in Islington in 1926 or 1927. Behind him is the entrance to the Islington Tunnel. Sickert is sketching the rear of 54 Noel Road, where his studio was. Ink 255×180mm. sw.

While the two of them worked side by side, Sickert talked about how to determine the 'cut' of a picture, or how the scene to be depicted is to stand within the four sides of the canvas.

Sickert explained how in the Impressionist manner, you needed to eliminate unnecessary objects and detail. 'Understate or overstate masses, and study the shapes they create against the background,' Sickert explained. Hewitt thought that the delicate washes Sickert made while they worked together on the canalside were 'a perfect demonstration of his old method of direct drawing from nature. And I was watching, incidentally, some of the last work he was to make from nature. Noel Road was the first of the semi-*Echoes*, half from life and half from a hidden past.'

Two pen and ink sketches done during these visits by Rayner have survived. One shows Sickert at work, wearing a straw boater and smoking one of his cheroots. Visible behind him is the entrance to the canal tunnel.

The other is a drawing of number 54 Noel Street, with a straw-hatted Sickert at work in the garden. Hewitt wrote on the reverse of this drawing:

> The original Hanging Gardens of Islington and Last Memories of Sir Walter Scott by Sickert. No 54 Noel Street, Regent's Canal, Islington, 1927. Walter Sickert's studio (first floor) 1927–1930 showing Sickert sketching in garden. House was blitzed 1943 Hitler war

Hewitt's account of his visits to Noel Street throw some interesting light on how the rather unusual titles for Sickert's two paintings evolved. Hewitt said that 'one always waited with some interest for Sickert's picture titles, which he would change as the mood took him. This method of changing the titles of pictures infuriated many of the serious-minded devotees of Art; but the artist took it as a quite normal thing to do. He held no brief for sentimentality. Paint was what mattered.'

Back in Noel Street the emphasis of Sickert's work-in-progress was clearly on hanging garments and bedsheets, and Rayner recounted the following conversation 'I asked what he intended to do about a title and he jocularly answered: 'The hanging garments of Noel Road.' I suggested a much more noble name, and one with as much humour – '*The hanging gardens of Islington*'. Thus the matter rested.'

Only later did he discover that Sickert had adopted his suggestion. If this account is correct, it seems that Hewitt had a hand in the titling of one of Sickert's best-known pictures (and one of his last etchings).

Hewitt revisited this title idea later in his own career with a drypoint showing a house in Flood Street Chelsea with window boxes overflowing with flowers. He titled it '*The hanging gardens of Chelsea*'.

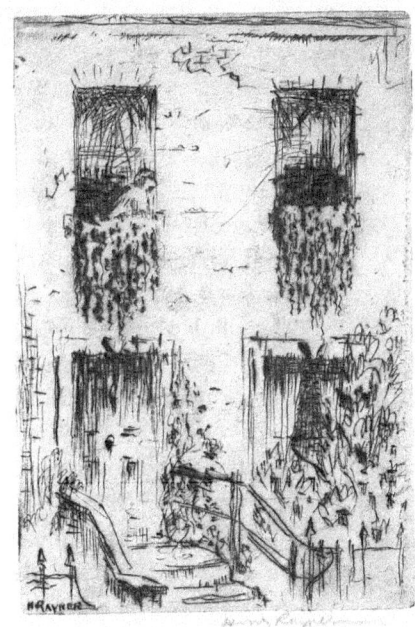

7.3 Rayner later returned to the 'hanging gardens' idea in one of his own etchings titled *'Hanging gardens of Chelsea, Old Flood Street'*. Drypoint, 178×110mm. IMAGE COURTESY ELIZABETH HARVEY-LEE.

The other important work by Sickert to emerge from this Noel Road period, '*The fading memories of Sir Walter Scott*', also has an interesting tale concerning its title. Hewitt learnt what title Sickert had given this work one day during a later visit to the Sickerts' home. He asked how Scott came into the canal scene. Sickert laughed, and explained that it was a play on words. The Sir Walter Scott could be interpreted as Si R. W.S., or Si Richard Walter Sickert. An old man painting a location that brought back fond memories of his childhood.

After work on the last morning, Sickert took Hewitt into Islington Upper Street, to the Peacock Tavern [just a block or two away from Noel Street] for lunch in the large back dining room. 'This place is bristling with history,' said Sickert. 'It was from here, the Peacock, that Tom Brown boarded the coach to take him to his famous school. All fields around here, then. Highbury Corner, the place of my new studio, was a wild cross-roads of ill repute.'

As well as recounting how he was involved in the titling of Sickert's 'hanging gardens' painting, Hewitt also believed that he made a contribution of a rather different sort to Sickert's 'Raising of Lazarus' picture.

The widely accepted story behind this painting, first told in the Emmons book on Sickert, is that the artist got the idea when he saw a life-sized wooden lay figure being carried up the stairs to his studio. The lay figure was a gift from Sickert's brother-in-law Major Lessore, and had allegedly once belonged to Hogarth.

Hewitt gives an alternative explanation. He wrote that Sickert had played with the idea ever since purchasing his composition 'The dying clown', and that he had used the same composition, attitude and lighting for his own masterpiece.

'I saw it boiling in his mind ... this tour de force, this Islington resurrection,' Hewitt wrote. He described Therese swathing the huge figure in white cloth in the Highbury studio. Sickert set to and painted the first sketch directly onto the wallpaper of the room.

'The whole thing (was) limned as a purely mural effect, as was the later large panel of the same subject,' Hewitt wrote. 'He worked quickly to a rapid completion; grey-whites and shimmering greens and carmines of glowing Italian richness.'

Hewitt also noted that when Sickert gave up this Highbury studio in 1931, he had the original wall painting of Lazarus cut away from the orange-red wallpaper and laid on prepared canvas. He recalls that Therese kept the picture, later taking it to Bath with her. Meanwhile Sickert worked on the other painting from the latter part of 1928 to 1929, and it was finally exhibited at the Royal Academy in 1932.

If Hewitt is right in his belief that Sickert's 'Raising of Lazarus' composition was inspired by his own student work 'Dying clown', then there is a certain irony in what subsequently happened to Sickert's painting. Since 1947 it has been in the collection of the National Gallery of Victoria, in Melbourne, Australia – just a few miles from Hewitt's birthplace in Hawthorn and childhood home in Brighton.

8

Back to Australia

Hewitt Rayner was determined to make his way financially on the basis of his art alone, and as far as is known he never took a salaried job in order to supplement the family income. 'I was obliged to work with redoubled speed to keep the wolves and the landlord from our door,' he later wrote. 'Every piece of paper with an imprint from a new engraved plate meant money and continuance at my art. It meant bread.'

The economic recession of the 1930s created a tough environment for a young artist to make his way by art alone. As if that wasn't enough, as 1930 gave way to 1931 Hewitt also started to feel that his health was deteriorating.

'I had the feeling that a terrible and protracted illness was stealing upon me,' he wrote. 'Asthma had me in its grip. All I thought about was the sea. It could save me. I must go away, anywhere across the water. At last it was determined that Theresa and I would go to Australia for my health.'

There was another motive behind his planned return to Australia. He was hoping that the chill economic wind blowing across Europe and the USA might have missed Australia, so perhaps he would have greater success there.

He was under pressure from his mother and stepfather to return to Australia. Not just for a visit, but permanently. In April 1931 his stepfather Hal wrote that: '… little seems to be gained by your remaining in that dank, dark and germ-laden atmosphere when you could be here in a nice comfy home.' This is a reference to another issue that Hewitt and Theresa were dealing with. Theresa had been diagnosed with TB.

She evidently spent some time in hospital, but X-rays showed that there was no major lung damage. In a letter dated 11th February, Hewitt's mother advised Theresa to tell no-one what she was suffering from, in case it scared the neighbours and they were forced to leave their house.

With all these problems, it's not surprising that Hewitt's thoughts had turned to the land of his birth.

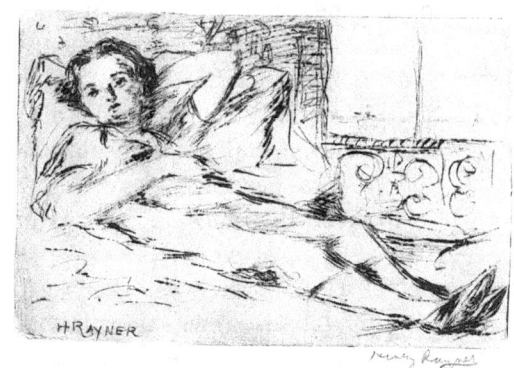

8.1 *'Theresa going East',* from the Rayner's outward journey to Australia. Drypoint, 118×175mm. RS.

One night a few weeks before his departure Hewitt was in a taxi with Sickert, travelling along the Caledonian Road. He was in difficulty with an asthma attack and he needed to give himself an injection in the wrist. As he did this Sickert said: 'What are you doing? Are you a cocaine addict?' Breathing with difficulty, Hewitt explained that he was injecting 'an expensive German adrenaline preparation.' Sickert asked the taxi driver to slow down.

Despite his ill health, along with Major Lessore and Therese, Hewitt helped Sickert move from Quadrant Road into his new home in Barnsbury Park. Sickert had picked this place because it was 'higher up, healthier, and quieter. Age produces a natural desire for rest and quiet.' He evidently referred to the street as 'a muddy backwater of Islington'.

'Barnsbury is not a park but a quaint little street leading up from the Liverpool Road to Barnsbury Square,' Hewitt wrote. 'Its houses are of many strange designs and Victorian shapes, inviting in their various little mysteries. Number fourteen was a bare expressionless façade of sooted yellow stucco, one worn step led up to an old wooden door from the days of good Queen Victoria, needing a coat of paint. It was as good a disguise as Walter could have wished.

'I was to grow to love Barnsbury Park. With its crazy passages upstairs, its dark mirrors, and quaint old Victorian furniture, and the Sickert atmosphere it had quickly assumed.'

The location of Sickert's new home was conveniently close to the Caledonian Market, 'a cold, exposed spot, but a hive of activity on market days,' wrote Hewitt.

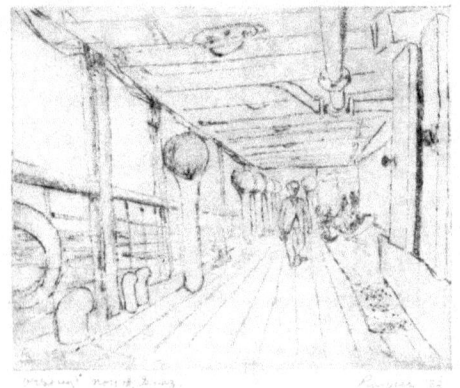

8.2 'Orsova off Aden', 1931, Suez. Drypoint, 110×133mm. sw.

'Artists flocked here and could furnish a new studio for ten shillings. Sickert was often to be seen fossicking about the stalls and making his minute drawings. He would either be taken for an eccentric farmer or a pensioned naval officer. It was often thought that he was a retired music hall artist. He must have been known to hundreds of Caledonian habitués. There was always the famous taxi waiting, and a heap of junk for Barnsbury Park. Where all this material was eventually lodged, I was never to know.'

Early on the morning of 26th July, some three weeks before his departure for Australia, Hewitt walked over to Barnsbury Park from Gospel Oak to say goodbye to Sickert. 'I went over the hills of Tufnell Park, Holloway and Islington on a dazzling summer's morning when the dew blazed from the grassy edges of pavement and in the gardens of still-sleeping citizens,' he recalled. 'I was to breakfast with the Sickerts. I approached Barnsbury from Liverpool Road.

'The good housekeeper, with eyes as sharp as Sickert's, let me in. 'Which room has Mr Sickert chosen as his studio?' I asked by way of conversation. 'The whole house has become a studio', the keen little woman replied. 'He has even knocked part of the staircase wall out to put a wretched window in for more light. He is ruining the place.'

'This in a loud voice, irrespective of the fact that Walter was in the adjoining room reading *The Times*. Mrs Sickert, wearing her white sari, helped to serve breakfast in the kitchenette that lay at a lower level than the other rooms. We discussed the morning over boiled eggs, French bread and brioches, and her incomparable bowl of coffee.

'Later, Walter and I adjourned to the Red Room, so named from the new wallpaper of his design, still in existence I believe' [this was written in 1954].

Then they moved through to the library, overlooking the garden, and Sickert wrote a reference for Hewitt, endorsing his capabilities as an art teacher. 'You were an indefatigable worker there [at the RA] as a student,' he told Hewitt, 'and I shall place that on record in the credential you ask for. It will carry you as a teacher. If you remain in Australia I should like you to have a letter from me, to enable you to approach more confidently the authorities in teaching departments. For as you recover, in the new country you will discover that you want to teach, for which you are eminently gifted.' The original reference letter is lost, but Sickert wrote a second letter in 1932:

14 Barnsbury Park
Liverpool Road
London N

Mr Hewitt Henry Rayner was a very able student at the Royal Academy Schools. There I formed a high opinion of his character and ability. He would be perfectly fitted to teach drawing and painting and etching.

I am asking Messrs Brown and Phillips of the Leicester Galleries, London, to handle his output in drawing and engraving, and I feel certain that the results will be satisfactory.

Richard Sickert, LL.D., A.R.A., etc

'That,' said Walter, throwing the scrap of paper over to me, 'will be currency anywhere in the world.'

Sickert also wrote a letter to his dealers, recommending Rayner's work to them. The letter to the Leicester Galleries read:

To Messrs Brown and Phillips, Leicester Square

My Dears

Will you please give careful and kindly consideration to plates of my pupil and friend Henry Rayner, which, without any bias from friendship, I think very able and brilliant.

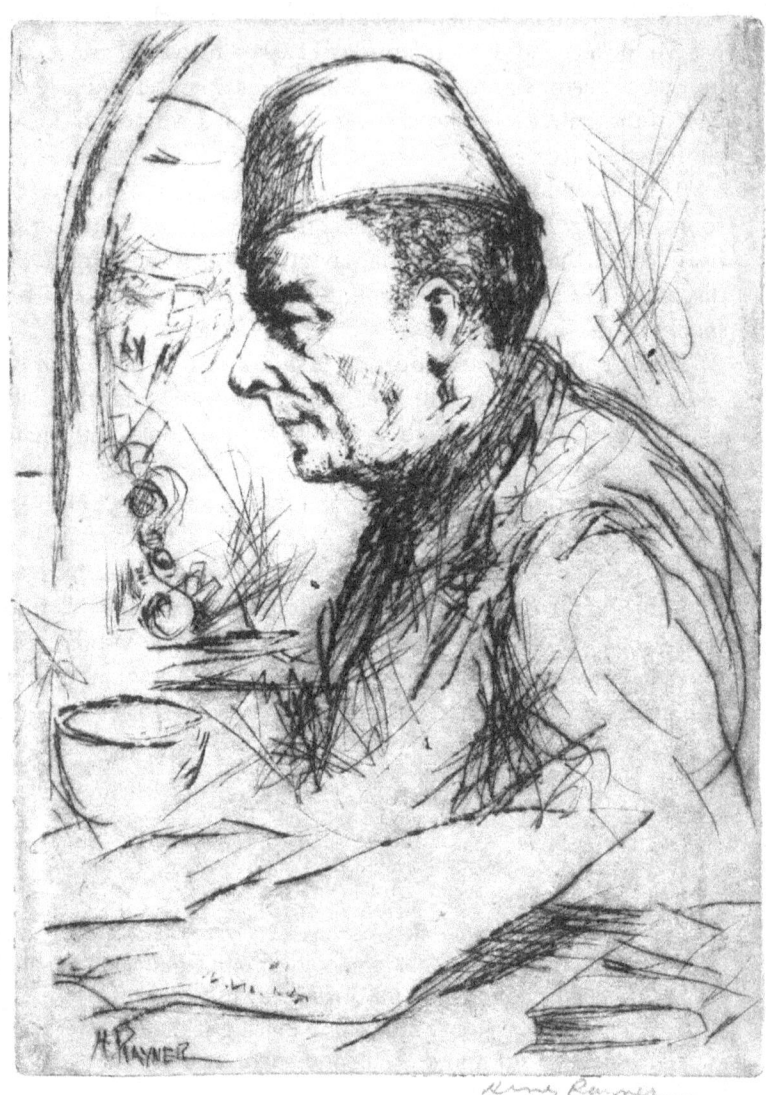

8.3 *'Richard Walter Sickert, Barnsbury Park, 1931'*. Note the coffee bowl rather than a cup. The British Museum took a proof of this work, as did the Russell Coates Museum & Art Gallery in Bournemouth. Drypoint, 215×150mm. sw.

He is going back to Melbourne next month. I have suggested that you might be kind enough to allow him to leave his plates with you so that you might print a few proofs and judge how they go. Being, let us say, on my lines. Things that might not be liked in the colonies might be a great success in London.

Richard Sickert, LL.D., A.R.A.

During the conversation that day, much of it concerning Sickert's plans for the garden, Hewitt again sketched Sickert. 'As he rambled on I began drawing him again in his red fez and brown cutaway coat, big enough for two men.

'The Manila smoke twined up, filling the room with an odour that I have come to associate so strongly with the great artist that when I am suddenly immersed in the sweet odour I instinctively look up and expect the conversation to continue and the old carpet slippers to drag across to me.'

The Victoria & Albert Museum has a copy of one of the drypoints that resulted from this visit.

Before Hewitt left for Australia he had several farewell parties. One was at Jesus College, Cambridge, with some medical student friends. All his friends believed this was the last time they would see Hewitt and Theresa.

Sickert invited him to a farewell dinner at the Café Royal. 'Let us toast your diffidence away before you flash across the skies of the South,' his mentor said. Wilson Steer had also been invited, but did not attend. Hewitt wore a hopsack jacket for this last *tete-a-tete*. But he was in a bad way that evening, and before setting off he gave himself an injection of adrenaline in the muscles of his forearm and took a dose of ephedrine. Then he took a bus to Piccadilly Circus, arriving at the Café Royal just as Sickert stepped out of his taxi 'to be greeted like royalty by the restaurant staff'.

'We dined, or rather Walter did, as my medical advisers had laid down strict rules about eating at night for asthma. But also, I knew my master had an overdraft at the bank at this time, the period of the great Art clean-out. '*Lazarus*' still lay on his hands, as did many of his great pictures.

'I drank vintage Bollinger, and nibbled piquant crab *hors d'oeuvres*. Walter got up and walked about through the assembly, speaking to those he knew with all the old zeal and crispness of wit. Walter appeared again young and glowing.

'The huge calf-like head. The serio-comic eye. The massive bowed shoulders. The tripping feet. The carefully considered comic coat for the occasion. A glove that seemed to be on the wrong hand. Cigar ash falling onto the manager's outstretched hand. That was Sickert, whose *savoir faire* and *savoir vivre* made him the most acceptable man in London's social and artistic salons of the great period of red-violet, which was his own invention and enjoyment.

'Then he seemed to fall into a sudden melancholy. A cab was ordered. In the cab, he was silent. Just sitting back, his eyes closed.'

The taxi took them to Rowlandsen House, at number 140 Hampstead Road, opposite Mackworth Street. 'My old school,' said Sickert, clearly emotional. 'It wants a wash and brush-up.'

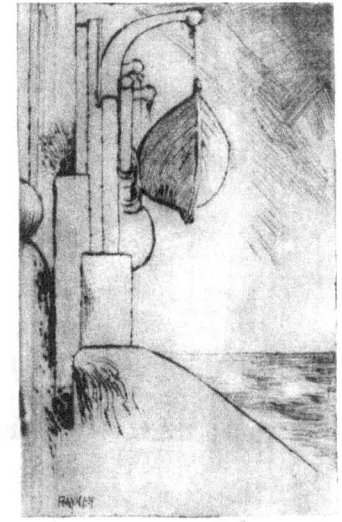

8.4 *'SS Orsova, Indian Ocean'.*
Drypoint, 145×88mm. SW.

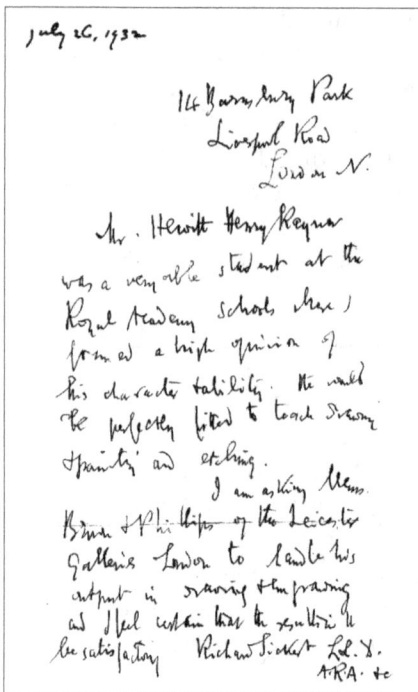

8.5 Sickert's duplicate letter of recommendation to Rayner, dated 26 July 1932. sw.

Hewitt noted that Sickert had a reputation for riding off in taxis in the night, 'visiting the studios and rooms of his past, as if trying to call back the dead and the forgotten to his own ache. I was to be a mere witness, his chosen audience for the night.'

Hewitt and Theresa obtained their joint five-year passport on 10th July 1931. He was described in the passport as painter (artist), height 6ft 1.5in, blue eyes, very fair hair. Theresa's description was height 5ft 4in, blue eyes, blond hair.

The couple sailed from the Port of London (Tilbury) on 15th August 1931 on the Orient Line *RMS (Royal Mail Steamer) Orsova*. They had one-way tickets, costing £82.10.0 in total, purchased by Hewitt's mother and paid for via cable from Melbourne. This was the *Orsova's* first trip since it had been converted into a single-class ship, so Hewitt and Theresa would have been able to enjoy all the public rooms and decks. The route took them via Gibraltar, Toulon, Naples, Port Said, Suez, Colombo, Fremantle and Adelaide.

They weren't intending to return. The passenger list shows that in answer to the question 'country of intended future residence?' they had answered 'Australia'.

Two days before they departed, Hewitt wrote a short airmail letter to his mother, which he said he hoped would arrive before he and Theresa did. In it he told her that he had recently been spending time with his father-in-law, who was laying mosaics in the National Liberal Club in Whitehall Place. He promised to write again and post letters when their ship docked in Toulon and Naples.

They arrived in Melbourne, in the second half of September – the Australian Spring. According to the account in his *Red Violet* autobiography the two of them stayed with his mother and Hal Gillard at their home in Toorak, Melbourne, and he worked in a room his mother had set aside for him as a studio. They travelled around, with Hewitt showing his wife the places he remembered from his childhood, and they visited Sydney. Then, after an unspecified amount of time, they changed their plans and returned to the UK.

When the passenger lists for ships arriving in Britain became available online, it revealed a startling fact – Hewitt and Theresa were on the *Orsova's* return trip to Britain, arriving in Plymouth on the 18th November 1931.

At first when this data was uncovered it was assumed that it was an error of some kind. If true it would mean that Hewittt and Theresa spent a matter of three weeks in Melbourne before re-embarking on the *Orsova* and sailing back to Britain. This made no sense at all, until their passport was re-examined.

The port-of-entry stamps record their outward journey, with entry stamps for Naples (23 Aug), Colombo (5 Sept) and (Fremantle, the first port of call in Australia, 15 Sept). There is no entry stamp for Melbourne but the *Orsova* usually took six days for the trip so they probably arrived in

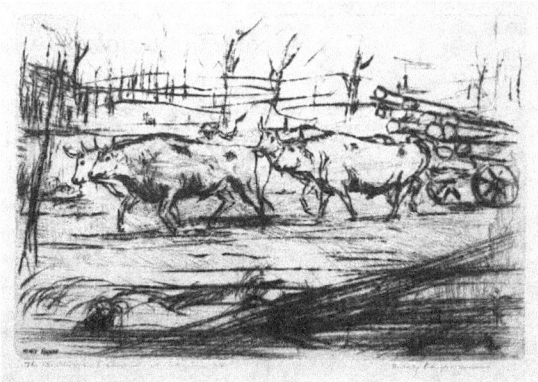

8.6 *'The bullock team'*. Drypoint 155×230mm. sw.

Melbourne on 21st September. The *Orsova*'s schedule then took it on to Sydney and Brisbane, where it turned around for the next trip to England, passing through Melbourne again some three weeks later.

In the passport there is an entry stamp for Colombo dated 28 Oct 1931. Earlier in the research this had been ignored on the basis that it was some kind of mix-up. In the light of the new passenger list information, this Colombo date-stamp makes complete sense – Hewitt and Theresa were on their way back to Britain. They had re-boarded the *Orsova* on 13th October, when it passed through Melbourne on its return journey to England.

What had happened? When they left Britain, they were planning to settle permanently in Australia. They had just spent six weeks travelling there. Hewitt was hoping the Australian climate would restore his health. He was carrying Sickert's letter of recommendation so he could look for a teaching job. And he was keen to see whether he could achieve the commercial success and recognition that had so far eluded him in Britain.

Yet here they were, just 21 days after arriving, heading back to Britain. A sudden and complete reversal of their grand plan.

It seems that there had been some furious rows between Hewitt's mother and Theresa, because of their religious differences. Emily's father Jabez had been a 'devout and conservative Methodist type', explained David Edwards (a descendent of Jabez) in 2007. With this family background it was not altogether surprising that Emily found it difficult to cope with her daughter-in-law's Catholicism. The issue became almost an obsession with her. Hewitt never wrote about it, but his mother did, in her letters to him over the years. The wounds must have been deep, because even 15 years later she was still angry. This letter is from October 1945:

> Hal said he could not leave anything to you. When Tess was here he saw her take the money he gave you out of your hand, and before Tess came out she wrote and said she had given up that awful religion. Creatures that make people give up all to say prayers all their lives to let others out of purgatory and other such penances.

And when Tess saw Hal in his house she told him she would not give it up, and as they hate the freemasons with a deadly hate, Hal said he would not leave anything as you would let them take it all from Tess, and you'd be just as poor, while it would only go to people who were only laughing at you.

Why I am once again telling you this is Tess still never says she will go to English church with you and the children. Not that I go often. I could at my death make arrangements somehow, that you all could be comfortable, and leave the children something if they take an oath to be protestant.

Hewitt and Theresa were back in London by the end of November. Their stay in Australia had been for a stressful few days rather than the leisurely few months suggested in Hewitt's *Red Violet* manuscript. What did their friends think, when just three months after all those farewell parties, Hewitt and Theresa reappeared in London?

Hewitt was a proud man, so in his autobiography he did a little spinning of the facts. He wrote the story of how the Australian visit *should* have been, rather than how it actually turned out. It's consistent with how he handled other uncomfortable truths from his life. At least the visit provided him with material for drypoints of Australian scenes.

In 2012 Peter Zecchin (Theresa's nephew) told the author an amusing story that shows how strong-willed his aunt was, and how capable she was of changing her mind in a dramatic way. Evidently she once took both daughters on a trip to visit the Zecchin family in Italy. The trio arrived at Venice airport, where Theresa felt unwell. So all three of them turned round and flew back to Britain without leaving the airport, and without visiting the relations at all. End of story.

It's not difficult to imagine her in 1931 quickly deciding that Australia wasn't for her, and more specifically that Hewitt's mother wasn't for her, and insisting to her husband that they must return to Britain immediately. The *Orsova* was the first available boat destined for England, so they took it. There is no evidence to show who paid for the tickets.

Hewitt's back-to-Australia idea had come to an unexpected and premature conclusion. This 1931 visit was the last time he would see the country of his birth.

It's likely that they moved in with Theresa's parents when they arrived back in London. They were certainly living there in September 1932, because one of Hewitt's sketchbooks from that period gives his address as 'care of 20 Tottenham Street'.

Hewitt and Theresa were occupying one of the rooms that were normally used by paying guests. But they weren't contributing anything to the household running costs, and ultimately this led to them being asked to leave. Theresa's older brother Richard (Riccardo) had felt particularly aggrieved, and accused them of taking advantage of his parents'

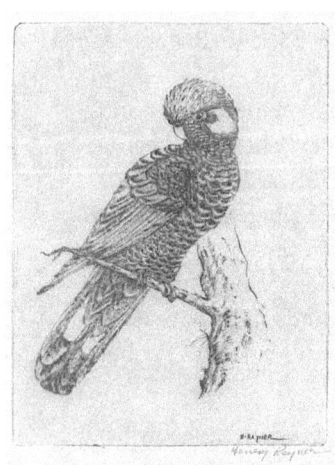

8.7 *'Bush bird'*. Rayner took proofs of this work in sepia and in black inks. Drypoint, 170×123mm. RS.

generosity. Feelings were running so high that from that date on Theresa broke off all communications with her parents and brothers.

She and Hewitt were in dire financial straights, effectively homeless, so they turned to a charity-run hostel in Soho for help. In November the Principal of St. John's Wood Art Schools, Frederick D. Walenn, wrote a letter of reference on Hewitt's behalf to the hostel, run by 'The House of St. Barnabas' in Soho. Addressed to the Sister, The Hostel, 1 Greek Street, Soho, it said:

> '… I have known Mr Rayner for some years now, and can assure you that I consider him a sincere and reliable man in every way, and deserving of any help you can give him. He was a student of these schools, and I had a good chance of getting to know him. I feel quite confident that you will not regret giving him assistance, believe me.'

It is not known how long they spent living in the hostel. There is only a passing reference to it in one of Theresa's letters to Hewitt from hospital in 1936 when she referred to everyone meeting in the dining room 'after the style of the hostel'.

While the Rayners were away on their ill-fated Australian trip, Sickert had given up the Highbury studio and taken instead a studio in Whitcher Place. Hewitt described this as a 'mews within a mews' on the fringe of Camden and Kentish Towns. The premises had previously been a taxi garage, and he was surrounded by taxi cabs and horses. There was a room upstairs that Sickert also rented and where he occasionally slept. Hewitt also noted that sometimes Sickert slept in a room at Sylvia Gosse's house 'in the beautiful old crescent that sweeps back on the Camden Road opposite Cantelowes Road'.

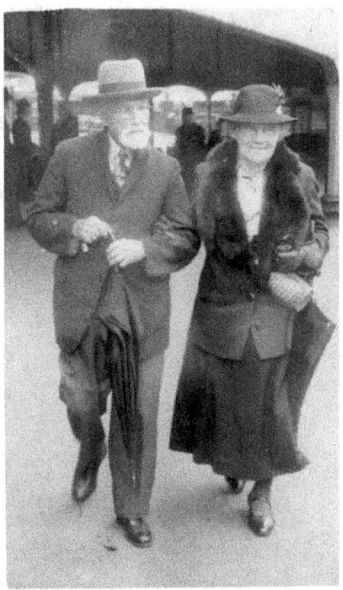

Hewitt recalled that the studio was the fourth building from the bottom of the mews on the right. Evidently Sickert would tell the taxi drivers: 'fourth garage from the bottom, and mind the gutter!'

'He bought a peaked motor cap, and painted in a frocked coat, cap and carpet slippers,' recalled Hewitt, 'one day frightening away a young lady who had knocked at the large double door in search of a horse'.

Sickert retained this studio until 1934. 'Whitcher Place saw the completion of some of the loveliest 'Echoes' he was to paint.'

8.8 Hewitt's mother and her second husband Hal Gillard in Melbourne in the 1930s. sw.

9

Doctor Sickert's Pink Pills for Pale People

Sickert's new home in Barnsbury Park was just a few blocks from Pentonville prison, which amused him considerably. Matthew Sturgis recounts in his 2005 biography that Sickert would take taxis from the West End and ask to be taken 'to Pentonville'.

He often went off to the West End, recalled Hewitt, and forgot all about the taxi he had left ticking away. 'He always turned up at the rank a few days later and paid the man. Everybody in Islington with whom he had dealings, indeed everyone who knew him, including the schoolchildren whom he used to treat to char-a-banc rides, loved the man.'

Sickert's house was at number 14 Barnsbury Park, and that is the number visible over the front door in two drypoints by Hewitt of the property. However in later years there was some renumbering of the houses in Barnsbury Park.

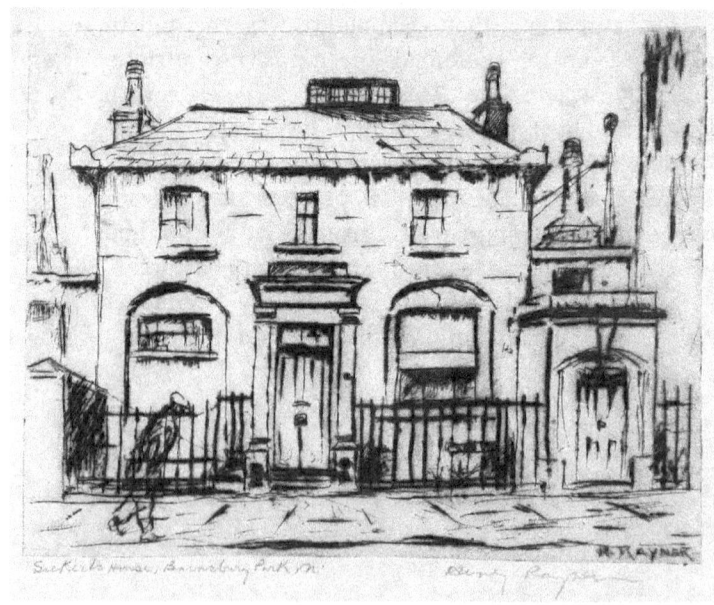

9.1 Hewitt's drypoint of Sickert's Barnsbury Park house, c1932, enabled the correct property to be identified as Sickert's home. In Sickert's day this was number 14. Today it is number 12. Drypoint, 125×158mm. sw.

Rayner's drypoints make it clear that Sickert's house was the imposing detached property that is today number 12.

It is likely that Hewitt's etchings of the Barnsbury Park house are the only record of Sickert's home at that time. Proofs of the main drypoint (showing the whole house) may exist with varying titles: '*Sickert's studio, 14 Barnsbury Park*', '*Sickert's Old House*, '*Walter Sickert's red studio, 14 Barnsbury Park, 1931*', and '*The red house*'. This last title can't be a reference to the colour of the house, which Hewitt recorded was yellow. It probably referred to the distinctive rich red wallpaper Sickert had hung in one of the rooms.

There is also a close-up etching showing the doorway, with Sickert waving to the artist.

What was the house like on the inside? In 1942 Hewitt received a visit from an unidentified Mr. B who had 'come over from Kensington' [probably a reference to the V&A] to talk about Sickert, and in particular to hear about his home at Barnsbury Park'. This prompted Hewitt to write about the house in one of the 'War letters' he wrote for his children.

> The only indication of big work in the Barnsbury *menage* consisted of two large oblong canvasses of lobsters and crabs in a rich reddish brown (probably the work of Therese Lessore) hanging in the Red Room, a place made more dark by his rich red wallpaper of his own design.
>
> The library floor was bare and sanded, as he usually preferred it to be in any of his houses. A watercolour by, I think, Morland Lewis, a close friend and one who assisted him with his underpainting at times, hung unframed on the west wall.
>
> A fine set of etchings on silk hung on the staircase walls, French I believe. He had bought these from an old antique shop at the bottom of Barnsbury Park, on the corner of Liverpool Road. I remember the old fellow who kept the place coming to Sickert for the money, almost in hysterics. Walter said: 'When I sell a picture you shall have your money. You may go to bed and feel quite at ease about the deal.' The old chap got his money all right.
>
> Therese, who loved him dearly, was ever at his side; she struck me as being a mysterious person, of strong mystical tendencies. She would wear her hat on indoors in the manner of cockney women, and frequently a white dressing gown.

Some separate jottings on scraps of paper add further to Hewitt's recollections of the interior of the house. 'In the west room at Barnsbury Park Sickert had it papered with a design of his own which was very effective. It was much better furnished than his study, which had bare boards and a rather monkish austerity of decoration. His small library was of course well chosen, consisting of old and modern French classics – Verlaine, Baudelaire, the Yellow Books and bound copies of *Punch*. [There was] a small rolltop desk in the corner by the window where the Master wrote, usually in the mornings.'

In London's National Portrait Gallery there is a group of press photographs dating from March 1934, showing Sickert and Therese in this library. At this point he was again sporting a bushy beard.

It seems from some of Hewitt's notes that Sickert's studio was on the top floor, in the attic. The special rooflight that Sickert had installed, to allow more daylight into the studio, can be seen in Hewitt's drypoint, protruding above the roofline.

The well-known Rayner close-ups of Sickert at breakfast, wearing his trademark fez, drinking coffee from a bowl and reading *The Times* newspaper, were done here. Hewitt also started work on an oil of Sickert at Barnsbury. This became one of the pictures sold at auction by Bonhams in 2000, described as 'Lot 155: '*My Last Portrait of Walter Sickert at Barnsbury Park 1934*', finished 1955, oil on board, signed, inscribed on label verso, 56×39cm.'

There may also be an oil painting by Hewitt of the house itself, but if so its whereabouts are not currently known.

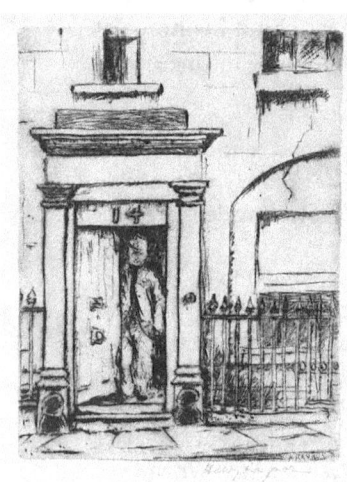

9.2 Sickert at the door of his Barnsbury Park house. Note the partially bricked-up ground floor windows – Sickert did this in order to increase his privacy. Drypoint, 169×126mm. SW.

Hewitt made several visits to Barnsbury Park. On one visit he had a specific agenda. He was worried about stories he had heard on the grapevine about his own alleged misdemeanours at the Royal Academy Schools, and he was concerned that these could affect his career. There is nothing in his autobiographical notes to clarify what these rumours were about but presumably they related to the allegations that he had smashed a statue – something he always strenuously denied.

He thought it would be helpful in stopping the stories circulating if he got Sickert to write to the RA to set the record straight. But he didn't get the response he hoped for. Sickert simply smiled and said: 'The Academy is a limited company. You will grow to learn the ways of its strange inhabitants. They mean no harm. They repulse me with kindness and I kindly repulse them; it is a mutual agreement. We have to earn our living. You were an indefatigable worker there, as a student, and I shall place that on record.'

On one visit Hewitt found that Sickert had engaged not one but two French maids. This followed an unfortunate culinary incident when he had been forced to employ a 'raw-boned lassie from Clerkenwell' to look after the kitchen arrangements while his usual housekeeper was away. On the whole, Sickert evidently found French staff more to his liking.

From the visits to Barnsbury Park Hewitt recorded the flavour of Sickert's conversation. 'Honours came, honours went,' Hewitt wrote. 'Money came, money went (and lavishly) but Art went on forever. Nothing must stand in the way of the Idea, the realisation. The painting had to sing, and it sang.'

Mediocrity in art was a recurrent theme of Sickert's. 'Some are handicapped; some are handcuffed; but most labour earnestly but inexpertly at their task,' he asserted. 'I am a subject painter, but the subject matters very little if the essence of the craft is lost in the attainment of this point of view.

'In fact, the subject matters very little. It misleads. No matter how we weave the pattern in our work, we cannot hide ourselves in the warp and weft – especially in our more serious canvases, and in our writing, where we expose ourselves beyond prevention. Those of us who can encompass the Idea in painting and drawing must go on.

'We are steadily approaching the age of the predominance of the least fit. When the freedom of the individual in the State will be more restricted, and science less beneficial. Our age is the last of the Independent Artist, the Free Creator.

'For nearly 60 years I have taught the sickly and the pampered, finding a flash of talent here and a modicum of genius there. Dedication is not enough. It is not enough to stop a crack on a salon wall. What did Balzac say? He drew to our notice that the desert of Art was thickly strewn with the bones of those who unsuccessfully sought the goddess of that desert whose mirages are only real to men of real talent and genius. Talk of an aesthetic creed is not enough. The things about us are in themselves beautiful. It is our own most grievous folly if we mistake this beauty for something else.

'Do not depend on society to give you that to which your talent alone can give you *entrée*. Whatever may be said of the artist, that reporter-pestered creature, he is able to throw off his complexes by his creative ability.'

Sickert's wife, Therese, was present during this conversation, which amused her. 'Dr. Sickert's Pink Pills for Pale People, Mr Rayner,' she commented. [This was an allusion to a popular newspaper advertisement of the time, 'Doctor Williams' Pink Pills for Pale People', from the Doctor Williams Medicine Company in London]. 'You will never grow old and indolent.'

On another occasion Sickert raged about the way old masters were being cleaned. 'The machinery of State is always a cumbrous elephant. In Art matters it is deplorable and compromising to the highest degree. The nation has collected a very wonderful assembly of Old Masters, and the works are cleaned and retouched, in many cases by mishandling house-painters, we should imagine. Impasto is pressed on with wild indiscretion. These abuses should be limited by statute. Who is it that has power to pass our national treasures into the clutches of unlearned daubers? The counsels of the National Gallery are sadly failing.'

One day the conversation turned to health. Hewitt explained his experiments with Calcium Gluconate as a remedy for hay fever. Sickert responded with his own views on how to stay healthy: 'I can recommend the shunning of a state of purposeless emotionalism and nerves,' he said. 'Leisurely contemplation brings more peace and security than all your clinics, and all your physicians. A *tete-a-tete* with a good friend or lover does more in the way of health than is commonly thought to be the case.

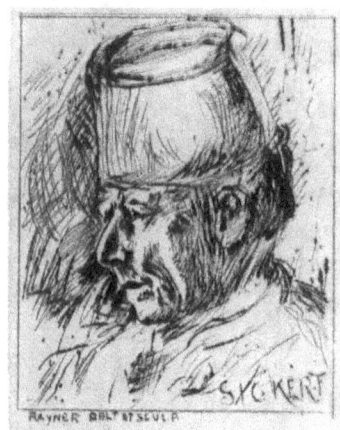

9.3 *'Portrait of Richard Sickert at Barnsbury Square'*, c1932. Drypoint, 116×90mm. RS.

'If you make yourself the rag-tag of any person you lose your own personality plus health. Be very exacting in this matter of rights over your person. Friendship is the most refreshing recreation in the world. We who have hard work to do need most of all this exhilarating companionship, which is nourishment to mind and body.

'I used to make it a point to systematically measure my appearances at tea parties, dinner parties, supper parties, assemblies, visitations to my men and women friends, theatres, music halls and picture galleries. I took each in small doses, and was very exacting about the settled hours, and the rights of one over the other. It was a deliberate and conscious planning for my recreation, amusement and mental rest. Without it I could not have continued. I should not have continued to possess a masterful ability to cut away what was undermining and debilitating.

'The early days in Dieppe were for me my hours of gruelling test. I found myself thrown out into the world, deprived of an elegant living, and forced to greet my destiny by hard living and cool reflection.

'No. Do not stand any nonsense from life. You must either master it or be mastered.'

This philosophy evidently included his approach to picture dealers. He said: 'Nothing is to be gained when interviewing picture dealers by appearing shabbily Bohemian and on the verge of bankruptcy, as so many artists are accustomed to doing. One must be the man-about-town and take the initiative. Always take the initiative. Do not show feeling. Feel nothing.'

Hewitt noted that around this time Sickert had been painting on gesso surfaces: a technique introduced to him by Therese. Hewitt also noted that she worked with Sickert on most of the gesso examples attributed to him.

One day in April 1934, Hewitt was at the Barnsbury Park house putting the finishing touches to a painting of The Red Room (*la chambre rouge*), and made a wash for an etching of the house itself 'showing the little top light for the attic studio'. That day Therese's brother dropped in with a young French woman artist – a friend of Therese's. At one point, the question was raised, half jokingly, as to why Sickert had not made any wall paintings or large murals.

'Diamonds are not made as large as bricks', was his answer. 'Why should I pin myself to a brick wall when I find more comfort and profit standing or sitting at an easel? Vermeer, Rembrandt and Degas were satisfied to create diamonds of full carat at a small easel, and neglect the immovable slab of wall so cumbrous that only an American would bother to carry it away'.

III

The struggle for success

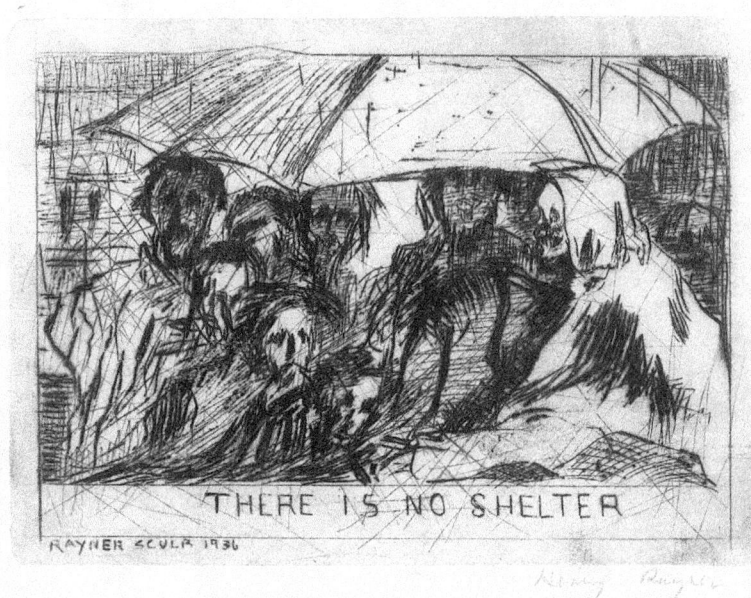

Fig III '*There is no shelter*', 1936, drypoint, 138×191mm. RS.

10
Pilgrimage to Vectis

The 1930s were tough for the Rayners, as for many people in Britain and the rest of the world.

Evidence for their dire financial situation in 1933 comes from a comment Hewitt made to a journalist in 1939. In a report in the *Canberra Times* of 20th April 1939 the journalist wrote '[Rayner] struck a bad patch in 1933 and was reduced to street begging, trying to sell his paintings.'

This reference to Hewitt begging in the streets stayed on file in press clippings libraries, and unfortunately became one of the most frequently-quoted facts about him in press reports. Even today it is usually mentioned in online references to Rayner.

It is unlikely that he ever resorted to begging in the street. What he did unquestionably do was sometimes go round knocking on people's doors and trying to interest them in his prints. This was, to Rayner, an acceptable way for a penniless artist to promote his art. After all, hadn't Walter Greaves – a Chelsea artist for whom Hewitt had enormous respect – done exactly this a few decades earlier? And as a sales technique it undoubtedly worked for Hewitt, as later events will show.

By 1934 Hewitt and Theresa had sorted out their finances and were renting a flat at 13 Great College Street [nowadays called Royal College Street], Camden, in a house that stood facing the Veterinary College. As usual, Hewitt explored the area on foot looking for locations to draw. Three of the drypoints showing local streets are '*Kelly Street, Kentish Town*', '*Kentish Town*' and '*Georgiana Street*'.

That year both Hewitt and Sickert were planning to leave London. Hewitt was planning a trip to the Isle of Wight to research his family history. Sickert was planning something altogether more permanent. His plan was to spend the summer in Margate, then move to Dieppe in France. Hewitt's impression was that Sickert wished to spend his final days near to Christine. 'He had long aired his view that Dieppe would be his last resting place,' Hewitt wrote.

'There is not much that holds me to this country any longer,' Sickert said to Hewitt one evening at his Barnsbury Park home. 'I am not becoming younger, and I have to watch the issues of every action more carefully. After the summer at Margate we shall be going to Dieppe.'

Sickert was clearly expecting Hewitt to join him in France. 'I can give you a letter of introduction to Jacques Blanche,' he told Hewitt. 'He is a very good friend of mine; a very fine painter of portraits. I am sorry I sold the *Maison Mouton*. You will find the little British colony there very interesting.'

When Sickert realised that Hewitt was unlikely to follow him to France, he made an alternative suggestion – that the Rayners should move into the Barnsbury Park house, renting it from him. 'I intend to keep Barnsbury Park on,' he told Hewitt. 'It is still open to your wife and you, otherwise it goes to Lessore [his brother-in-law]. You could grow asparagus and tulips in the garden, and you could shut it up when you felt like it and come over to France.'

The Rayners never did rent number 14 Barnsbury Park from Sickert. It would have been way beyond their means. Sickert's brother-in-law took it over.

Of course, Sickert never did go back to Dieppe – or anywhere else in France. He went to Margate for the summer as planned, but then instead of moving to France he rented an imposing house in St Peter's-in-Thanet. Matthew Sturgis noted that the rent Sickert earned from letting the Barnsbury Park house went on renting this 'unnecessarily large' house in St Peters. The Sickerts stayed living in the area until 1938 when they made their final move to Bath.

By the middle of 1934 a project that had been in Hewitt's mind for a while came to fruition. As a child in Brighton, Australia, he had listened to his father's and grandmother's tales of pirates and smugglers who used the Isle of Wight for their activities. He had not been allowed to ask about his family's possibly murky past, including his great grandfather Jeremiah's activities as a smuggler. This, of course, aroused his curiosity. There were, he suspected, dark secrets to be uncovered. He was right.

Hewitt was deeply interested in how people may be shaped by hereditary factors. He regarded the Isle of Wight as 'the home of my people'. By finding out more about the Rayners on the Isle of Wight he hoped to find out more about where his artistic talents may have come from, and also gain some insights into his various physical ailments. Particularly the asthma and seasonal hay fever.

In the early summer of 1934 his health had again started to deteriorate. Asthma was the problem. 'I could scarcely walk,' he wrote. 'Doctors proved of no avail. Vivid and startling visions filled my nights. I cut down drugs to a minimum. The dreams grew more fantastic and unreal.

'I knew with a sure instinct now that my health lay in this return to the ancient home of my people,' he wrote. 'It seemed to me that in the family cupboard was a jangling skeleton, and until I discovered it I would be ill. Some mighty salvation lay there, in the chines and downs of Wight.'

Hewitt and Theresa decided it was time to make the trip to the Isle of Wight.

A few days before they set off from their back-room flat at 13 Great College Street (in Camden Town), they were visited by Sickert. He arrived by taxi to return some books he had borrowed. Theresa was using a sewing machine to make a tent from an old sheet, and a young girl suckling a baby was helping hold the fabric.

As Sickert sat and recounted a story about a visit he had made to the next door house to visit poet Paul Verlaine in 1894, Hewitt sketched Sickert and the young mother. This later became the '*Mr Walter Sickert and the lady*' drypoint.

Sickert's tale concerned a speech Verlaine was preparing to make at Oxford or Cambridge, having been given an academic honour. Sickert had commented that Verlaine did not speak very good English. And he was ill, having wandered for years after being released from prison for attempting to shoot a friend. [The friend was fellow poet Arthur Rimbaud, who in the 1870s had shared a flat with Verlaine at number 8 Great College Street, across the road from the Rayners' home].

Sickert was evidently a regular

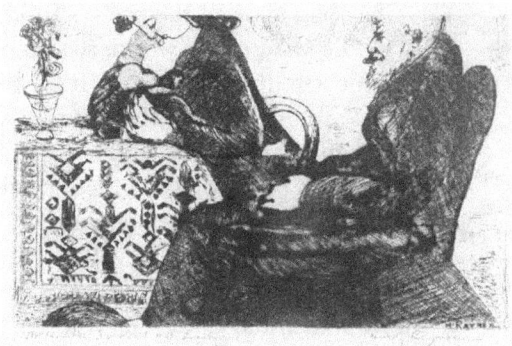

10.1 '*Mr Walter Sickert and the lady*', 1934. From a visit Sickert made to the Rayner's flat in Great College Street while Hewitt and Theresa were getting ready for their expedition to the Isle of Wight. The young girl suckling her baby was helping Theresa make the tent for their trip. Drypoint, 115×184mm. sw.

visitor to the Rayners' studio flat in Great College Street, to dine and to borrow from Hewitt's collection of old journals and prints. Hewitt recalled that Sickert would take taxis down to the District Post Office in Eversholt Street, where he would send off telegrams 'of staggering length'. Then he would buy all the daily newspapers and a dozen crumpets, and arrive at the Rayner's door.

Several weeks earlier, knowing that Hewitt was planning his trip to the Isle of Wight he had given him an old engraving by Hogarth of Wilkes, purchased from Horace Lewis's antique shop on Liverpool Road at the end of Barnsbury Park. [The print was among the ephemera in the Rayner archive]. 'You should find some interest in Wilkes, now that you are going to the Isle of Wight,' Sickert explains. 'He began Sandown as a tourist centre, and was the first Londoner to build a holiday villa there. A *morceau* of remembrance, Rayner.' Another illustration of Sickert's wide-ranging knowledge.

Both Hewitt and Theresa later wrote about their 1934 trip to the Isle of Wight. Hewitt's account was largely devoted to his family history. Theresa's was more about the details of the first couple of days of the journey. Both are interesting from a biographical perspective.

In the first sentence of Theresa's account, without any explanation she gives an alternative name for the isle of Wight – Vectis. This is the old Roman name for the island.

There's an amusing conflict between Hewitt's and Theresa's accounts. Hewitt said he carried a rucksack weighing 60 pounds. Theresa's account says his rucksack weighed 40 pounds. Whatever the truth, Theresa's was lighter at 23 pounds.

Hewitt also carried a cold joint of beef in a small canvas bag. Theresa wore 'a new sea-blue rambling blouse, and a bright blue beret.' Among the items they carried were the tent Theresa had made.

They had allowed themselves three weeks for the trip. They took with them £4, all they had in the world, according to Theresa. They set out on foot at 5am on Sunday 14th August 1934 from their flat. Their route took them through Hyde Park to Chelsea. Their aim was to get to Putney Bridge by 8 am. Then they headed across Putney Heath and on to Kingston on Thames, where they experienced the first signs of foot trouble. Then to Esher, where they witnessed a car crash that left one person dead.

It was a very hot day. Hewitt's feet started giving him problems. His own fault really, since he had decided that to signify that this was something really different from their day-to-day lifestyle, he would not wear socks.

In the late afternoon they reached Cobham and rested up for a while. Their aim had been to reach Ripley by the end of this first day, but the state of their feet made this impossible. At Wisley Common, the blister on Hewitt's foot burst and started to bleed. They had little choice but to stop.

They were directed to Pound Farm and they made it there by 5.30pm. They were given a choice of field in which to pitch their tent, and the farmer provided

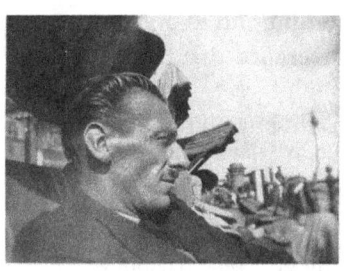

10.2 Hewitt Rayner on Sandown seafront, Isle of Wight, 1934. sw.

eggs and bacon. Hewitt later recalled: 'I shall never forget that first night. Cream, fresh eggs, fresh milk. A miraculous savoury vegetable soup to begin with, brought over by the good farmer's wife who insisted it would just go to waste if we didn't have it.'

In the night it started to rain, and Theresa rushed out to throw her husband's coat over the tent, since she was not sure that it would be waterproof.

They had made 24 miles in their first day – for people with no regular long-distance walking habit, this was a real achievement. Although as Barbara Griffin recalled many years later, Hewitt tended to walk everywhere in London. And he was an energetic tennis player. So notwithstanding asthma attacks he was quite fit.

Perhaps not surprisingly, the next day they decided to stay a while to recover their strength and give their blisters a chance to heal. They also stayed a second day, setting off on the Wednesday morning. There had been a heavy dew, and the morning was misty. They set out towards Guildford, six miles away. As they reached Ripley, the rain started.

This is as far as Theresa's account covers. At least, this is the only part that has survived.

Hewitt's account goes on, and he talks about making sketches at Ripley in watercolour and pencil. As they travelled they obtained fresh honey from farmers, home-made bread, and local bacon and eggs. They cooked on a tiny stove that used methylated spirits and weighed only three ounces. Finally they reached the summit of Portsdown Hill, and saw the Isle of White.

Once on the island the couple camped on Rew Down near Rew Farm, above Ventnor bay, and made this their base for the first part of their Isle of Wight visit. Later they moved to a more central location and pitched their tent in a field at the village of Lake, between Sandown and Shanklin. Rayner referred to the noise of the 'five-shillings-a-trip planes from the nearby Isle of Wight airfield circling over our heads' as he sat in the sun, writing and drawing. In the evenings the pair would go down into Sandown and mingle with the crowds.

While at Lake they were visited by two friends, one a fellow artist from Hewitt's days at the St John's Wood Art Schools, the other a Scottish medical student. There were other visitors who had heard of the artist camping in a field, and earnest discussions of the state of the art world took place. Sometimes the group would buy cakes in Shanklin and eat them with tea brewed up by Rayner in a billy can, Australian fashion.

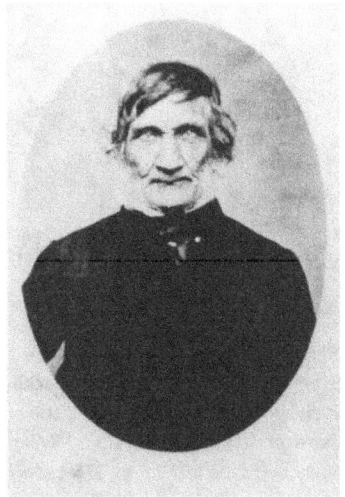

10.3 Jeremiah Rayner (1797–1870), Hewitt's paternal great grandfather and according to family tradition a successful smuggler of goods from France. sw.

They collected their post from the Post Office in Shanklin – run as it had been for many years by one of the Rayner family.

While on the island Hewitt captured in a drawing a horse-riding scene that later became one of his most successful drypoints. It came about when he was at Luccombe one day, where horses were available at the back of the Chine for people to ride over St Boniface Down. Hewitt described the picture, which depicted the horse in mid leap, as 'my best middle-period engraving'. It not only caught the attention of Princess Galitzine, but prompted the editor of *Horse Magazine* to commission an article from Hewitt on Australian point-to-point racing. Hewitt recalled that the etching was published with the article.

The account of this 'saga' to the Isle of Wight was a project Hewitt worked on intermittently over the next 20 years. Eventually it would become part of his manuscript '*Red Violet*'. Some of the information had come from his father and grandmother Selina Jane, who had told him endless childhood stories of life on the Isle of Wight. But Hewitt also succeeded in arranging meetings with a number of Rayner relatives during his 1934 visit. Among them were his cousins Maud Clark and Harriet Prouten (both grandchildren of Jeremiah Rayner). It was Harriet who told him the family smuggling stories.

Hewitt's relatives told him of Rayners getting married in Brading church in 1556. Not surprisingly there was a strong seafaring tradition. There was also French blood, through his paternal grandmother Selina, whose grandfather had been a French officer prisoner of war called Henri Gallet. He married an Isle of Wight girl, and the family anglicised its name from Gallet to Galley. This is confirmed by Selina's Australian death certificate, which records that her mother's maiden name was Galley.

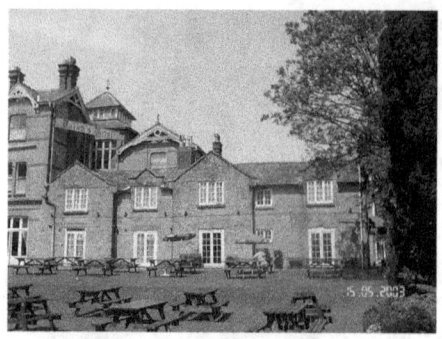

10.4 Daish's Hotel in Shanklin was built by Jeremiah Rayner in 1833 as a coaching inn. Even though much expanded, the original two-storey building put up by 'Miah' can easily be made out, some 170 years later.
PHOTO: RS.

Much of the 'Saga' is devoted to Hewitt's great grandfather Jeremiah ('Miah' for short) Rayner. He had been born in Shanklin on 12th November 1797. According to Hewitt, Miah was 'a fisherman, builder, and all-round sportsman. He was well-read, god-fearing, and a strong leader, popular with men and women alike. As a landowner and yeoman farmer, Jeremiah was one of the few people in Shanklin eligible to vote'.

Jeremiah's most lasting legacy is the large 26-room, two-storey coaching inn he built in the centre of Shanklin in 1833. Hewitt spent some time digging into the story of the hotel.

The stone-built, thatched-roof hotel, 'styled on local manor houses of the early Stuart period' according to Hewitt, was built in a field called Roaches on Shanklin Hill, opposite a tollgate. A historical illustrated book on Shanklin ['*Georgian and Victorian Shanklin, 1700–1900*', by Lindsay Boyton] shows a photograph of the hotel as it appeared around 1860, with the words 'the lodging house which became Daish's was built by Jeremiah Rayner in a field called Roaches with the profits (it is said) of the harvest of 1833'. As far as is known, Jeremiah was not a farmer, so the reference to the 'harvest of 1833' may have been a coded allusion to his smuggling activities.

Within a few years Jeremiah had sold his hotel to a man called John Daish, who had formerly been leasing the hotel from Jeremiah. The price was £1,050. The hotel was renamed Daish's, and continues under that name today.

There is a suggestion that Jeremiah may have over-reached himself with this hotel project, and lacked the funds to complete the building to the size he had originally planned. Daish considerably enlarged the premises with a big extension that dwarfed the original hotel building. However, the original building was left largely intact, so that even today the extent and style of the Jeremiah Rayner coaching inn can be easily identified. The historical importance of the original hotel building was recognised in 1992 when it was awarded Grade II Listed Building status.

Mason's Guide of 1876 mentions that in the days of four-horse coaches, on the journey from Ryde to Ventnor the coach would stop for an hour at Daish's Hotel 'to afford passengers an opportunity of visiting the Chine'.

The hotel had a flagpole in the main garden, erected by Jeremiah. This was known locally as The Smugglers' Pole. Because of the location of the hotel on top of Shanklin Hill the flag could be seen from the sea, and was used, it is said, for signalling purposes not unconnected with smuggling. Each night Jeremiah would hoist a lantern to the top of the pole for the benefit of travellers seeking the hotel. The wooden flagpole lasted until 1947 when it was blown down in a gale.

The hotel attracted many American visitors so the American flag was often flown alongside the Union Jack on the hotel's flagpole. The hotel's American Bar was evidently one of the first so-called in the UK, and the sign 'American Bar' can be seen in old photographs, behind the horse-drawn coaches collecting passengers from the hotel. There's a delightful photograph in the Francis Frith collection showing a fully-laden tourist stagecoach about to depart from the hotel in 1913.

Hewitt also looked into the story he had been told many years earlier that the young girl who would later become Queen Victoria once stayed at the hotel.

This is the story as recounted by Hewitt. In the summer of 1833 the young Princess Alexandrina Victoria was travelling with her mother (Victoria Maria Louisa of Saxe-Coburg) and an entourage that included liveried footmen and a German cook. The family were travelling from Cowes via Newport to Niton where they were planning to stay at the Crab Inn. The combination of poor roads and the frequent gates delayed the party so that as night approached they found themselves in Shanklin, where they spotted Jeremiah's newly-built hotel.

Jeremiah's wife Elizabeth welcomed them to the inn, where the party occupied the whole South East wing of the hotel. The Princess and her mother reportedly occupied room 20, where they took their meals. During Hewitt's 1934 visit to the Isle of Wight, he managed to take a look inside the room.

The Rayners made very little of the incident at the time, at least outside the family, but when John Daish took over the hotel in 1839 he had the inn's notepaper, crockery and glassware badged with the royal coat of arms. This continued until the 1950s when the Warrant Holders Association discovered that the hotel had never been officially granted a royal warrant, and stopped it from using the coat of arms. This information comes from to a letter to Hewitt from Lt. Colonel G.W. (George) Spencer, manager of Daish's hotel, 10th June 1954.

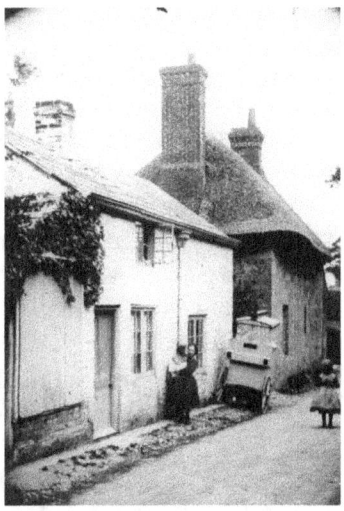

Hewitt came away from his Isle of Wight visit convinced that the story of the royal stay in the family hotel was true. There seems to be nothing in Queen Victoria's Journal for 1833 to confirm the story, but an entry for 28th July 1945 does refer to an inn she remembered from a visit to Shanklin 12 years earlier.

While in Shanklin Hewitt also explored his great grandfather's alleged smuggling activities. Evidently Jeremiah organised and made frequent crossings to France to bring back brandy, silks and tobacco from Cherbourg and Barfleur. Occasionally the men would have to play cat and mouse with the Revenue boats. Family tradition said that Jeremiah forbad any of his

10.5 Jeremiah Rayner's cottage 'The Dell' in Shanklin in the late 1800s (the thatched cottage). sw.

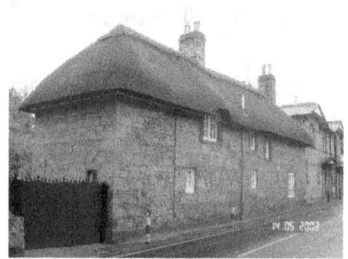

10.6 The Dell in 2005. PHOTO RS.

men from carrying guns, despite the fact that the Revenue cutters were equipped with cannons.

'Lights that flashed at night from the top window of Miah's cottage on the cliffs were not always moonlight on the glass,' wrote Hewitt. 'Not every gunshot heard in the darkness was for rabbit. Signals passed and re-passed. Jeremiah, capable seaman as he was, employed others to undertake the navigation of his fast cutters and sailing wherries. Occasionally he himself took the helm and visited the merchants of Cherbourg.'

The brandy they brought back, too strong to drink in its raw form, and colourless, would be cut back with water and flavoured with caramel that Jeremiah and his friends cooked up in huts along the Luccombe road, using copper pans. Then it would be sold to various outlets on the island.

Hewitt wrote that there were secret pathways that allowed his great grandfather Jeremiah to move 'tubs' of smuggled French brandy up Shanklin Chine and into his cottage (Dell Cottage) in Shanklin Old Village. Another chine along the coast at Luccombe was also used for the same purpose. There was a legend of a secret tunnel from a location near the waterfall in the Chine to Miah's cottage. The entrance to another secret route near Bonchurch involved squeezing through a very narrow entrance in a rockface. This pathway later became a tourist attraction called the Devil's Chimney.

According to Hewitt's notes, these chines have been used for hiding treasure for centuries, right back to the time of Elizabeth I when English ships returning loaded with Spanish gold would detour to the Isle of Wight and offload some of the booty that should have gone to the court of the Queen.

That Jeremiah was engaged in smuggling is confirmed by the fact that on 25th June 1831 he was convicted of 'carrying and conveying foreign brandy in the Parish of Brading' and sent to gaol in default of paying the £100 penalty. He was not the only member of the family to be caught smuggling. On 22nd November 1830 his brother Henry was convicted of 'concealing a quantity of foreign brandy' and fined £25. Four years later on 26th July Miah was again convicted of smuggling, fined £100 and sent to Winchester gaol when he failed to pay the fine. This information comes from the *Hampshire Telegraph* newspaper. Many dozens of Isle of Wight men and women were arrested and prosecuted for smuggling-related activities through the 1820s, 1830s and 1840s, with sentences of fines and/or gaol. Sometimes the sentence was that the guilty party should serve five years in the British navy.

It wasn't only smuggling that brought Jeremiah into conflict with the law. According to a report in the *Hampshire Telegraph and Sussex Chronicle* of 10th October 1866, Jeremiah had been careless with the pigs he kept at his cottage, and had allowed 'refuse' from them to flow into the Chine and cause 'an unpleasant and injurious smell'. At Ventnor Petty Sessions that week he was fined sixpence plus costs for 'having a nuisance on his premises'.

What stopped his grandfather's smuggling trips, Hewitt learnt from an old man called 'Didier' Kemp (real name Charles Kemp), was not the risks of being caught but a tragic accident involving three local smugglers. A wherry and its three-man crew – Tom Southcott, Crouch White and a man called Grub – were lost in a terrific gale. The story was kept from the wider public but the incident prompted the locals to call a halt to their smuggling activities.

This coast of the Isle of Wight also had literary connections going back to the 18th century, which must have added to Hewitt's fascination for the place. The poet Swinburne grew up at Bonchurch, Keats and Dickens had stayed and worked in Shanklin and Bonchurch, and many artists, poets and writers took holidays on the island.

Hewitt's research into his family background yielded information that he would often refer to in later life. The French blood that his grandmother Selina brought into the family, the seafaring traditions, the boatbuilding and other craft skills, and the artistic inclinations. He was proud of his great grandfather Jeremiah's and grandfather William's achievements. It was said that William 'could do anything with a boat, in any sea, and was a champion sculler before he was 20.'

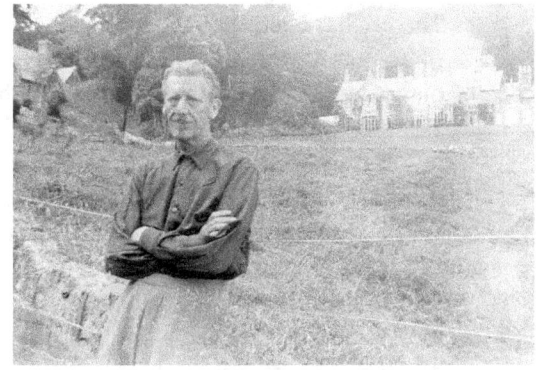

Above all, Hewitt liked the idea of being part of a family that had traditions going back centuries. An island race. He had rediscovered his people. And he had a story to tell.

The trip to the isle of Wight also seems to have helped his health. His asthma disappeared for the duration of his visit. 'I had become an asthma case that could scarcely walk,' one of his notes records. 'When I returned from Wight, the asthma had gone.'

He would make a second visit to the Isle of Wight in August 1936, and again in 1945 to regain his strength

10.7 Hewitt made further visits to the Isle of Wight. This is from a 1953 trip. He is standing in front of East Dene, Bonchurch, where the poet Swinburne grew up. sw.

after the trials of the war. There are no surviving records of this trip.

His last recorded visit was in July 1953. A letter from The Cottage, Pound Lane, Ventnor, dated 8th July, confirms receipt of his £2 deposit, and gives instructions on how to reach the property on foot from the railway station.

In April 1955 his daughter Frances went to the Isle of Wight with a friend called Anne and spent some time retracing her fathers steps. She lodged in Brading and visited various members of the Rayner family including Clifford Rayner, a longshoreman and author of *All my yesterdays* a book about the Rayner family.

11

'See as the spirit, aim high and read Keats'

On Christmas Day 1938, Hewitt finished his 200-page handwritten '*Child, when my ship comes in*' manuscript. He added a poignant note.

'The snow lies heavily on London; and I pray for strength in the coming year. The way is heavy and I have known much illness over the last ten years; my wife Theresa has been the sustaining angel.'

The 1930s were indeed tough for Henry and Theresa. The UK was in the grip of the depression, and this had badly affected the art world. Even Sickert was not exempt from its effects.

Yet the 1930s were also the most productive period of Hewitt's career. The majority of his drypoints are dated between 1930 and 1940. Selling them was another matter altogether. Sometimes he would walk the streets of London, knocking on doors and selling prints for one shilling each. A report in the *Daily Telegraph* of 21st June 1939, based on an interview with Rayner, recorded that 'he took to heart Sickert's maxim that unknown artists must sell cheap, and some of his etchings have been sold for 6d'.

Unfortunately, the 1930s are the least well documented period of Hewitt's life. From the information that does survive it is nevertheless possible to reconstruct some of the main events of the couple's lives during that period.

As the 1930s progressed, the art market continued to suffer. In his *Red Violet* manuscript Hewitt said of this period in his life: 'The bitter winds of trial were upon Theresa and me. Art lay a'bleeding. It was all we could do to find patrons for the pictures and prints I made with such painstaking labour.'

Back in London from the Isle of Wight trip, and once more in their flat at 13 Great College Street, Hewitt continued to work on his art and his writing. A densely-written notebook covering the period from 7th July to 23rd September 1933 records his deep concern with spiritual matters during that period.

At some time in 1935, he paid a visit to Sickert at the house he was renting in the small town of St Peter's, near the Kent seaside resort of Broadstairs. The imposing property, at number 15 Church Street near the junction with Hopeville Avenue, was called 'Hopeville' when Sickert arrived. Sickert had renamed the house '*Hauteville*'. This was a typical Sickert wordplay. The new name obviously appealed to his taste for the French language, and it's also appropriate as St Peters could be regarded as the high town on a hill above Broadstairs. A 1936 street directory for Broadstairs actually gives Hauteville as the name of the property. Nowadays the property is known as 'Hopeville House'.

This was the last time Hewitt saw Sickert, who he recalled was by now 'an old man with a full white beard, making him appear like a retired sea captain, and carrying a great crooked blackthorn stick.'

It was this visit that sowed the seeds of Hewitt's interest in the Ramsgate area, and two decades later would lead him to move away from London and settle on the Kent coast. 'It gave me the first idea to come to this region for health reasons,' Hewitt wrote in a 1955 letter to Andrina Schweder, Sickert's sister-in-law.

In late Spring 1935, Theresa became pregnant. Things were so bad financially that as the birth approached she was in touch with an organisation called The Friends of the Poor, at 40 Ebury Street, London SW1.

Through 1934, 1935 and into 1936 the family was receiving financial support from the Manchester Unity of Oddfellows, North London District. One Christmas they were invited to receive a food parcel from the Polytechnic Christmas Dinner Fund for the Poor (patrons their majesties the King and Queen, address 309 Regent Street, London).

The family continued to receive regular gifts of money from Hewitt's mother in Australia, and occasional parcels of food. There were also food parcels sent by other relatives and friends in Australia. His mother seems to have enclosed money with most letters she wrote to her son. She felt that he did not appreciate the sacrifices she made in order to do this – on several occasions she pointed out that each time she enclosed money it actually cost her far more in total. On one occasion when she sent him £9, she had to pay almost £3 duty on top.

In another letter from the late 1930s she wrote: 'Hal gave me a bad time this morning at breakfast because I said I was posting another £1'.

All the time she was urging him to get a job doing illustrations for newspapers or magazines, or to look for other commercial opportunities. 'Why not get into private college or public schools as drawing master or draughtsman? Most artists have to do it, to live apart from their art,' she wrote in a 1953 letter.

On 9th January 1936 Hewitt attended a meeting arranged by the 'Fellowship of the Universal Design of Life', a fringe religious organisation of the early 1930s with branches in the UK, USA and Australia. Subjects discussed at the event, in Swedenborg Hall, Hart St, WC1, included 'LIFE Evolutionary: Is there a divine

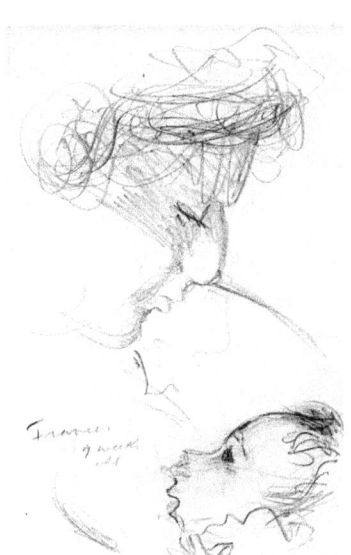

11.1 Pencil drawing of Theresa with nine-week old Frances, March 1936. 190×120mm. RS.

plan in evolution?', speaker H Montague Dobson; 'Eternal: Is immortality a present possibility?', speaker John F Fellowes; and 'Everyday: How this divine plan is applied', Speaker C A Threadgold. The Chairman was a Mrs Marian Threadgold.

His first daughter Frances Wilmett was born on 27th January, weighing in at 5lb 13oz. Hewitt sometimes called her 'Franny'. At birth Frances had jet black hair, dark blue eyes, and very long eyelashes. Over the next two or three weeks her hair lightened.

On 7th February, Theresa and the baby were moved to The Middlesex Branch Hospital in Clacton-on-Sea, travelling by train from Liverpool Street station. They stayed there until the 14th.

Hewitt told Theresa in one of his letters that he had spotted a little shop in Camden selling prams, and seen a suitable second-hand pram, but did not want to decide until Theresa has seen it. In the same letter he described meeting in the city an artist called Clarke who despite having exhibited 17 times at the Royal Academy was 'now reduced to colouring photographs for a living'. Clarke advised Hewitt 'Never work for photographers'.

It seems that Theresa did not tell her mother of the birth of her first daughter. By then she and her family were no longer on speaking terms. When Hewitt's mother heard of this she wrote: 'You mean to tell me Tess's mother knows nothing of the baby or our help? I can't believe you and don't.'

At the end of August Hewitt and Theresa took Frances on a visit to the Isle of Wight by coach.

Hewitt did numerous drawings, paintings and etchings of Frances at various ages, so there is a good record of her growing up. He sent an etching of her to his mother later in 1936. His mother replied on 24th November that she thought the lines and the shaded areas were too heavy for a portrait of a baby, but that she was 'still delighted to have an etching of her'.

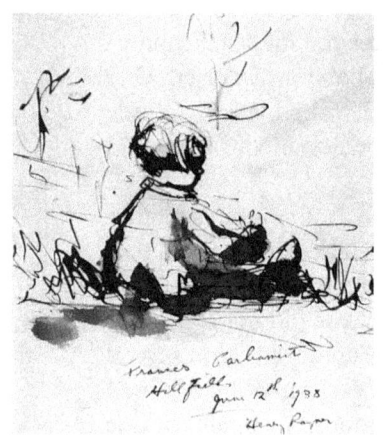

11.2 Watercolour of Frances on Parliament Hill Fields, June 12th 1938. 170×144mm. RS.

Hewitt's maternal grandmother Edwards must have still been alive in 1936 because his mother wrote in the same letter that she would have liked another copy of the etching 'to send to mother, as Frances is the first great-grandchild.'

He was also busy with other drypoints. One work in particular held special significance. It was titled '*There is no shelter*', done in 1936. 'I saw the war approaching,' he wrote, 'and made an etching – 'there is no shelter' – as a satire on English lethargy and a warning to wake up. Every manner of man bought that etching.' It was one of a series of prints he did around this time with social and political messages.

During this period he was hard at work on his '*Child, when my ship comes in*' manuscript about his childhood in Australia. He must have asked his mother for information on her own childhood and on the true history of the family home in Brighton. She referred to these matters in three different letters in November and December 1936. She took the opportunities to complain about how badly she had been treated as a child.

On 10th November, she wrote: 'It's no good my sending you any news of my girlhood. I've told you all that before. My mother kept on having children, and all my life I was just a slave, washing napkins, doing dirty work, and a baby always on my hip. I'm the eldest of seven, and if I didn't do things cleanly and well I'd get a good thrashing, until my mother never looked at me as human.'

She returned to this theme in another letter, undated but probably from the early 1940s. Talking about her grand-daughters she said: 'Babies will grow up. It's marvellous how soon they notice, and

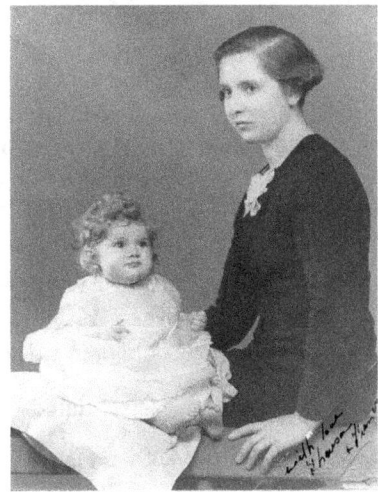

11.3 Theresa and Frances in 1936. sw.

it's now time to teach them exactly what you mean in their knowing. You are good and true and they will mimic you. I had no-one to teach me. I seemed always alone. My mother never in her life had any interest in me. I can remember from a baby.'

Then, about the Brighton building that had been Hewitt's boyhood home: 'I tell you that hall was only a bit of a place. No one knows what it was.' Nevertheless, she did go to Brighton Town Hall to try and find out more about the building. It was unsuccessful, and no written records could be found. All she found was that probably the building was by someone called Webb, and a man called Dr O'Hara had used it as a school.

Hewitt and Theresa's second daughter Kay Emily was born on 5th November 1937 at City Maternity Hospital. She weighed 6lb 15oz and had golden hair and 'really blue' eyes. The next day Theresa wrote a letter in pencil to her husband, who was looking after Frances at home.

> Dear Hewie
> Everything being over I shall now drop you a line. I feel concerned you're having to look after Frances. It's another trial but something achieved when over, and to your credit, remember that. Let Miss Osborne have Frances occasionally.
>
> Well, I brought another female into the world. A nurse described her as an elf, and not far out either. Quite at home with the world, has taken to her thumb, I was told this morning. Miss nobody is your living image, has golden hair and really blue eyes. Weight 6lb 15.
>
> I would not care to repeat that again. It was quick, but by gosh what tugging & pushing it required. I think I howled the hospital down, luckily through a gas muzzle.
>
> Visiting days are Wednesday evenings from 4 til 8 and Sundays 4 til 5. If you should find time and can manage to come along. I am without butter, sugar and eggs. Don't bring bananas. A few biscuits would not go amiss.

To save having wet washing in the room during the day, you will find it helpful to do it at night & hang it outside over the stove. However you will probably have found your own method by now.

Please don't worry. I am going to give that up. How will the germ results get on? And Frances – I pray she won't be troubling you too much.

I would also like you to get me a roll or bundle of black tape and 4 ½p stamps.

Lots of love and a hug for impy.

Your little wifie.

Theresa

PS: Children are not allowed to visit the patients.

Another letter dated 11th November

My Dear Hewie

How are you getting on? Neglecting yourself entirely, as per usual? Don't do it, it won't pay you and it worries me. I shall be so glad to get back home. My time shall be up on the 13th day and that falls on next Thursday, the day I come out.

I want a name for this little one. Try to find time & get a list ready for me. I have nothing here I can refer to. Sunday, when you come along, we can decide together what to call her.

A man called from the Registration Office today, and is calling again on Monday. The charge will be 2/7 [Two shillings and seven pence] done here now, and 3/7 later at the office. Let us have it done here: it will save, and less trouble & inconvenience.

What is little Frances thinking and doing? I expect she is at home with everyone by now.

Oh dear! A hospital full of rushed, stupid, snobby nurses and the patients at their mercy, and mothers for their convenience won't do a tad more than they are obliged to do. One night nurse to attend this ward of mothers and babies.

I must remind you to bring with you the 2/7. In amongst my cottons in the drawer there is a steel crochet hook. I would like you to bring it along, whatever you are able to find in that way. You need bring just two eggs, of everything else I have enough to carry on with. I seem to be asking you for all kinds of things, not many days, thank the good God. I am waiting for your papers, perhaps today.

Well dear, till Sunday, & please hold your head up for we shall win through yet. The race is not yet at an end.

Your loving wifie.

Theresa

By this time the Rayners were living in Gospel Oak, a small suburb of north London bounded by Hampstead Heath to the north, Kentish Town to the east, and Belsize Park to the west. This would be their home for almost 20 years, until they moved away from London in 1955.

Gospel Oak wasn't one of London's fashionable inner suburbs. But for Hewitt and his family it held some real attractions. It met his goal of getting away from the River Thames and on higher ground, for the sake of Theresa's chest. It was inexpensive, compared to its neighbouring districts. Public transport to and from central London was good. It was not far from Sickert's stamping ground of Barnsbury Park and The Angel, Islington. And it was very close to Hampstead Heath.

There was a convenient footbridge across the railway line that allowed the family to walk from their home to the Heath in five or ten minutes. This brought them to Parliament Hill, a location where Hewitt had done several watercolours when he first arrived in London from Australia.

He generally described the family as living in Hampstead. This was strictly incorrect, but was a harmless deceit, and carried the implied status of being a Hampstead resident.

The family had several addresses within Gospel Oak. When Theresa was in hospital in November 1937, having just given birth to their second daughter Kay, she wrote to Hewitt at number 5 Lismore Circus. This was a charming green circle surrounded by shops and pubs, with roads of Victorian houses radiating in all directions.

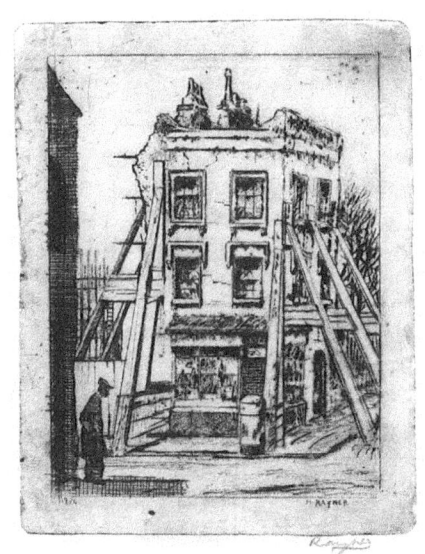

In 1938 they were living in a house in Twisden Road for a time. In October 1939 the family was living in Herbert Street. This is the address given by Hewitt when he wrote a letter to the editor of *Cavalcade*, published in the 31st October 1939 issue. When the war started, they were living at 69 Mansfield Road but were forced to move because of bomb damage. At one stage they lived at number 64. It was number 121 Mansfield Road that became their home for the longest period, from around 1943 until 1955.

11.4 *'Old St John's Wood* , This is the area where Hewitt first lived when he arrived in England. Drypoint, 170×130 mm. sw.

Through the 1930s Hewitt was working on sonnets and poems, and in 1937 submitted a collection to the publishers Hodder & Stoughton in London. There is no record of the nature of these poems but surviving hand-written drafts suggest that he was exploring Australian themes. Hodder & Stoughton wrote back on 2nd December saying that

> 'I am afraid that we could not hope to obtain sales for this work which would be satisfactory either to you or to ourselves: and under these circumstances we suggest that you should approach some other publisher who specialises more than we do in the publication of verse.

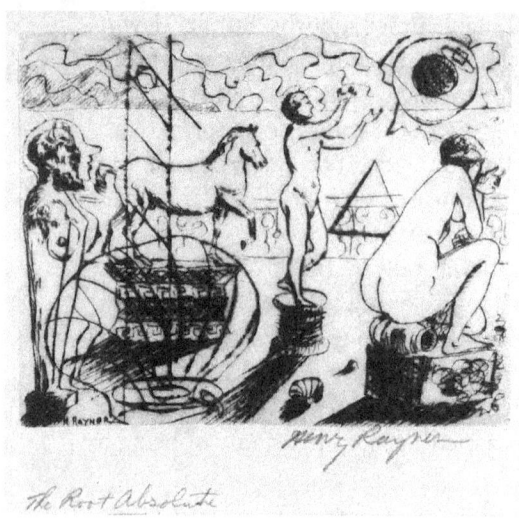

11.5 *'The root absolute'*, c1937. One of Rayner's few surrealist images. Drypoint, 95×120mm. RS.

A few days later he wrote to the noted critic and author John Middleton Murry, founder of *The Adelphi Magazine,* and former husband of Katherine Mansfield. Hewitt enclosed one of his sonnets, mentioned the proposed book and asked for Murry's opinion. On 8th December Murry replied that he had 'found something good' in the sonnet Hewitt had sent him, but that he would need to see the complete manuscript in order to offer any advice. It was a friendly letter signed 'Yours very sincerely, J Middleton Murry'.

Hewitt must have sent him a copy of his collected sonnets, possibly the same manuscript recently rejected by Hodder & Staughton, because on 24th January 1938 Murry used an old 'Adelphi' postcard to say:

> Dear Sir, I sent you a letter, some four or five days ago, to say that your MS had arrived safely. J Middleton Murry.

Then a postscript:

> I am very sorry to say that by some regrettable accident the letter was not sent. I found it unposted on my desk.

Any further correspondence on this subject has not survived.

It may be that Hewitt was inspired to write poetry by the works of Rupert Brooke. He certainly used one of his visits to the British Museum to take a look at the poet's original notebooks. He wrote a note at the time:

> 'You have never seen the actual scribbling pads used by Rupert Brooke, the English war-time poet. I have them here before me, in the British Museum. Pathetic, warm penny books. You cannot feel perhaps what I feel in looking over them. Here amongst regimental orders & directions are sad little scraps of poetry – two or three lines – crossed out, smudged or altered. Here I find a line or two from 'The Soldier' … written on the field in very pale pencil strokes, with tappings of the pencil, his terrible nervous tension revealed here.'

Later in 1938 he sent a collection of poems to Jarrolds, but they declined on the grounds that they rarely included verse in their publication programmes. The Director suggested that he try a firm specialising in poetry, such as Messrs Frederick Muller of 29 Great James Street. There is no record of whether he followed up this suggestion.

At some stage in the 1930s it looks as if Hewitt got to know a New Zealander called Douglas Glass. Born in Auckland in 1901, Glass had studied art at London's Central School of Art but later turned to photography and is nowadays remembered for his portraits for *The Sunday Times* newspaper through the 1950s. Prints of some of them are in Britain's National Portrait Gallery.

Hewitt probably had much in common with Glass – they were almost the same age and both had worked as farmhands in New Zealand before coming to Britain. In 1938 Glass was living at number 4 Albert Street,

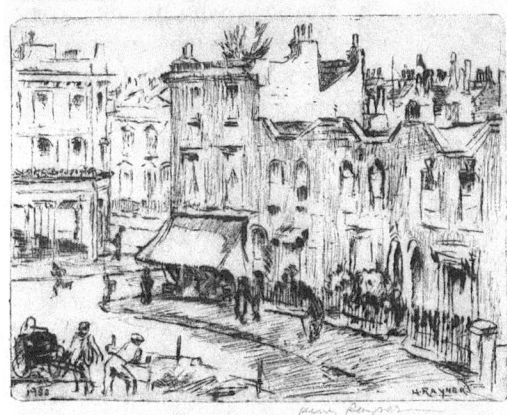

11.6 The heart of Gospel Oak was Lismore Circus. It was demolished in the 1970s to make way for a local authority residential scheme. Drypoint, first state, 1937, 116×148mm. IMAGE COURTESY ELIZABETH HARVEY- LEE.

London NW1. For some reason, in the Rayner archive is a receipt for artists watercolours purchased by Glass from Windsor & Newton, 51–52 Rathbone Place, on 25th February 1938.

Hewitt may have made a visit to see Sickert in Bath sometime in 1938. There is a drypoint titled '*RW Sickert 1938, Bath*' which shows him reclining in an armchair in his library.

In the late 1930s, Hewitt started using the term 'new romanticism' to describe not only his art but also the poetry he was increasingly interested in.

On 16th September 1937 the *Hampstead and St John's Wood News* ran a story recording that Hewitt 'believes in a new romantic movement with strong Christian precepts. His motto is 'See as the spirit; aim high and read Keats'. Hewitt had also talked to the paper about his poetry. His goal was said to be 'to free the English Sonnet to higher ends to fill it with a content worthy of the English mind and destiny'.

Around the same time another London paper published a letter to the editor from Theresa, taking issue with an earlier article about a London-based Viennese artist called George Krista who had referred to 'new romantics' as 'a new art movement that has its inspiration in the romance of Vienna itself'.

The letter appeared over the name Theresa Zecchin, but one can assume that it had actually been carefully crafted by Hewitt.

This is the main part of the letter:

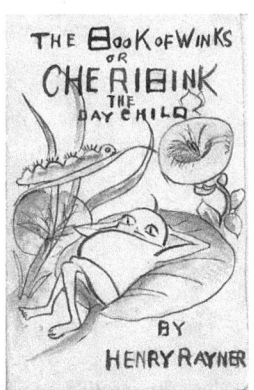

11.7 In 1934 Hewitt turned some of the stories his mother had made up about a character called Cheribinks into an illustrated children's book. It is not known whether he ever tried to get it published. sw.

'It would seem to me that the real movement had its inspiration nearer the purlieus of London than of Vienna. Its originator is Henry Rayner, the British painter-poet, who not only coined the unusual term New Romanticism, but developed the movement's principles as far back as the beginning of last year – when surrealism was yet a power. Rayner made public his aims some months ago, and has been writing and publishing new-romantic poems, which are anything but continental; and there is nothing of mawkish eroticism about them. All this man's work is lighted up by inspiration and deep sincerity.

The object of the movement according to its founder is to establish a sounder basis for modern English painting and poetry, using all that is best in our long tradition, for cleaner craftsmanship, freer and higher aesthetic expression.

Romanticism itself has been one of the most powerful forces through the ages in the building up of our island culture; it was no fleeting doctrine, but a lasting principle that would still guide the passions to finer achievements, if approached with unslovenly temper and balance; balance the Briton possessed in generous proportion; there was nothing to signify that it should cease as a theory and as an inspiration. Rayner believed that the time was ripe for such a declaration, and thus the present reaction against pseudo-classicism and the degenerate extravagences of much modern art.

The exalted romantic mind stands for creative energy, freedom and vital spirituality, as against the confines of lesser moulds.

Rayner is not bemused by the lighter implications of romance, or drawn to its grossly immoral side-sheets, or to its superficialities of style. It is the common-sense of romanticism that appeals to him; its spirit rather than its character; its grandest results rather than its low conveniences.'

Hewitt would later expand on this theme in the catalogue for the 1945 Brook Street Art Gallery exhibition, although without explicitly mentioning the term 'new romantic'.

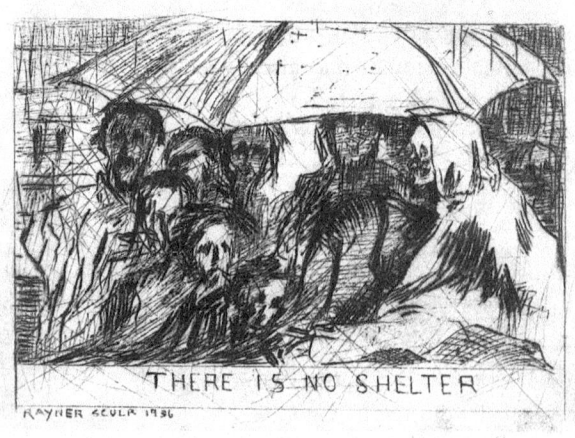

11.8 'There is no shelter', 1936, Rayner was making a point with this work – that there is no shelter from the storm approaching from Europe. Drypoint, 138×191mm. RS.

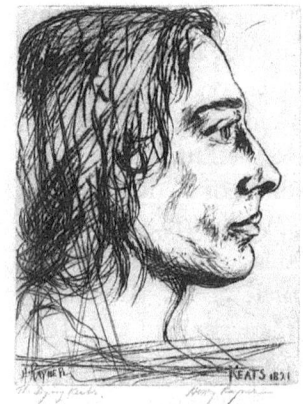

11.9 'The dying Keats', undated., limited to 10 proofs. Based on an 1821 image of the poet. Drypoint, 203×152mm. RS.

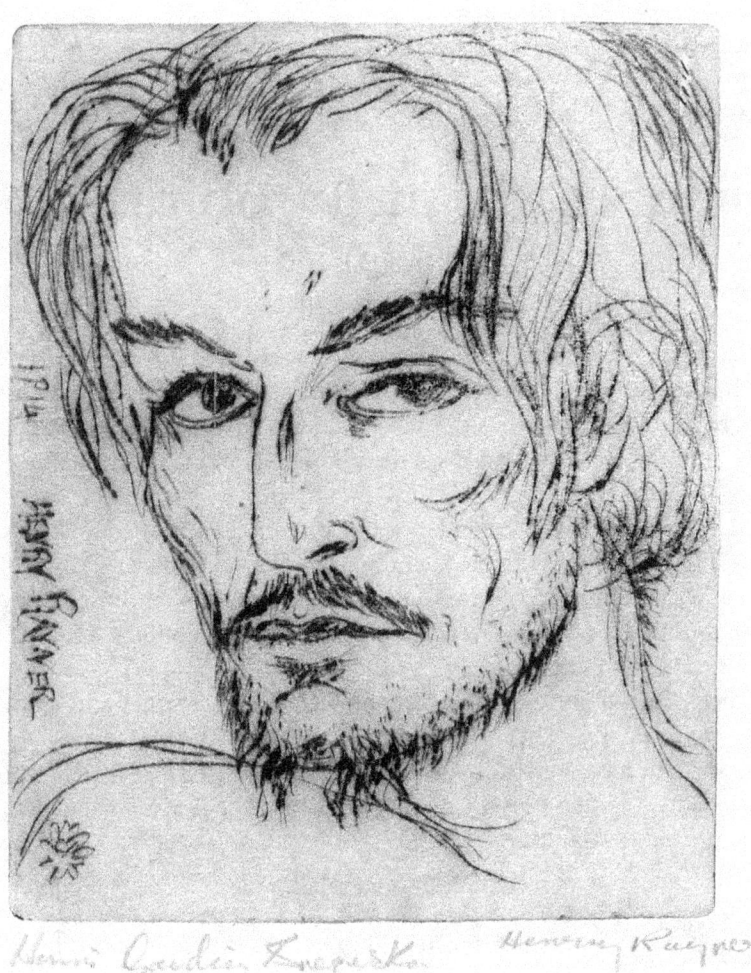

11.10 Sculptor, artist and printmaker Henri Gaudier Brzeska (1891–1915) held a special fascination for Rayner. This is one of three drypoints he did of the artist. 139×110mm. RS.

The artist notes in the exhibition catalogue included the following:

> 'His extreme sensibility, his deep feeling for everything in nature, enabled him to avoid so much of the formlessness and hypocrisy in Modern Art; and he loved all that was best in living art; and though he is in the line of best tradition, he cannot be considered to belong to any 'school'.
>
> 'Like all men of pioneering and progressive spirit he has cut new ground and has evolved a technique of his own. He took from the old what he wanted for the new and living.
>
> 'His method approaches that of the Impressionists. He does not believe in cluttering his surfaces, or indulging in grand, eloquent phrases. He wants to say something and get its said poetically, succinctly. Simplicity and purity of line is his aim.'

12
Passionate about drypoint

It was discovering the work of the Impressionists when he was living in New Zealand that triggered Rayner's interest in coming to Europe to study. In the artist biography he penned for the catalogue for his 1945 Brook Street Art Gallery exhibition, he wrote that his style of drawing and painting 'approached that of the Impressionists'.

Early in his career, Hewitt worked in watercolour, oil and pencil. Many examples have survived, showing clearly the influence that Sickert had on his painting style. Once he had launched himself as a printmaker, his output of drawings and paintings dropped sharply away. The one notable exception to this was the watercolours and oils of his children.

His choice of drypoint etching as his main creative channel and source of income was unusual. Even Sickert thought so.

'Sickert discouraged me from beginning,' Rayner wrote. 'He was a plain etcher. Indeed he, the pupil of Whistler, could boast of being a great etcher. But he never approved of drypoint.

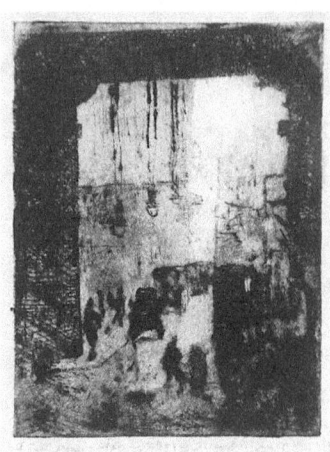

'The reason for this I could never discover. It was perhaps because so few impressions could be pulled from the plate. However, he always respected my ambitions in art, and when I made my first portrait of him at his studio at 15 Fitzroy Street in July 1925 he actually praised the drypoint, with one reservation: 'You are teaching me here, Rayner.'

Rayner's interest in drypoint etching definitely went against the trend at that time. Many artists regarded drypoint as a technique to be used occasionally in combination with acid etching, to reinforce part of the image.

With the benefit of hindsight, the timing of Hewitt's entry into the printmaking field was unfortunate. When he set out in the late 1920s to earn a living as a drypoint etcher, the 'etching revival' was in full flow, and printmakers found a ready market for their proofs, but an investment bubble was taking shape, attracting speculators. Within a couple of years the market for

12.1 One of Rayner's earliest etchings, dating from 1926 before he settled on his 'Impressionistic' style, *'Charing Cross'*, 102×76mm. sw.

original prints had evaporated, print prices had collapsed and the depression that lasted through the 1930s meant that few people had spare money for art – even prints.

His early etchings from 1926 are very different from the style that characterised his later drypoint work. They show a considerable amount of fine detail and a range of tones. At this time, Rayner was signing prints Gillard Rayner, bringing together his stepfather's name and his father's.

For subject matter, Rayner looked around the immediate vicinity of the RA schools in Piccadilly, and other locations. This resulted in etchings of Charing Cross railway station, Devonshire House (on the north side of Piccadilly facing Green Park), Limehouse Docks, and a broody night scene of an un-named London street. As ever, his attention was drawn not to the rich and famous, but to ordinary working people in everyday settings. His etching of Devonshire House, a grand private mansion that stood on Piccadilly facing Green Park, salutes the work of the men who were demolishing the property in 1926 rather than the Dukes of Devonshire who had lived there.

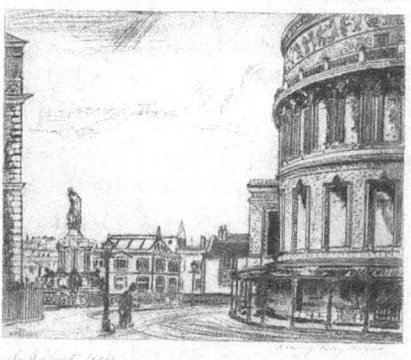

12.2 Only occasionally would Rayner choose one of London's landmark buildings as a subject. This is the Albert Hall. Drypoint, 163×195mm. RS.

These early etchings look to have been acid bitten. But it was the technique of drypoint etching that really attracted Rayner's interest. 'I wanted to create the perfect drypoint, the rarest of the engraving mediums,' he wrote in the *Red Violet* manuscript. 'Few good portraits had been created in this most difficult medium, and it had become my determination to make portraits in drypoint.'

When he left the RA Schools and moved to Chelsea, he installed a small etching press in his room. But who to learn the craft of drypoint from? 'I could find no able master to instruct me in the art of drypoint,' he wrote. 'No real masters in this medium existed in England; there were few in Europe.'

This was not strictly true. Since the 1880s, generations of artists and etchers had been learning the craft of drypoint and other techniques at the Royal College of Art (RCA) etching school in Kensington under the leadership of the legendary Frank Short. It seems unlikely that Rayner was unaware of this. Especially since Sickert himself became an Associate of the

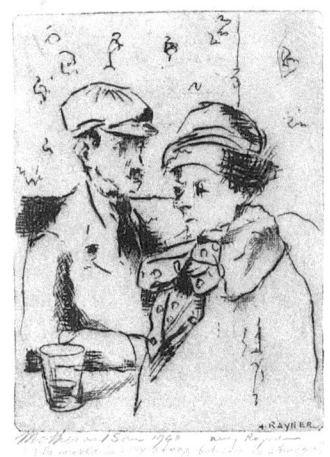

12.3 Like Sickert, Rayner saw artistic potential in ordinary people. The composition of this drypoint *'Mother and son'* is clearly influenced by Sickert's *'Mother and daughter'*. Rayner has added the words 'The world is very strong, but love is stronger' to this proof. 179×134mm. RS.

Royal Society of Painter Etchers (RE) in 1925, and Frank Short was the society's President.

Then there was the Slade school. Hewitt cannot have been ignorant of the etching skills being taught here, since his wife-to-be, Theresa, had been a model at the Slade.

But in bemoaning the lack of a 'drypoint master' Hewitt was making a valid point. There was no artist whose name was uniquely associated with drypoint printmaking. No champion for the technique. Nobody who had based their entire artistic career on drypoint printmaking.

Hewitt set out to change that. He wanted to elevate drypoint into an art form in its own right. He saw it as the perfect medium for his Impressionistic style. With his earlier experience working at a jeweller's bench and as a car mechanic he would have been completely at home with a technique involving metalwork.

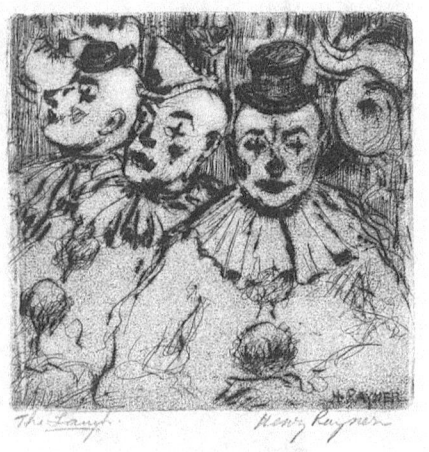

And he placed a high value on craftsmanship – something he had inherited from his father and both grandfathers.

There may also have been a practical motive behind his preference for drypoint printmaking – cost. There are no expensive paints, canvases and brushes to buy, nor acids for etching the plates. A proofing press is required, but a small table-top unit is adequate as long as the artist requires only moderate pressures. And as Hewitt demonstrated, there are ways to avoid purchasing special metal sheets and etching tools.

So, either dismissive of or unable to afford the specialised experience and training available at the RCA and other art schools, Rayner set to and taught himself drypoint, 'studying at

12.4 *'The laugh'*, one of several circus-themed etchings. Drypoint, 140×140mm. RS.

the British Museum, the Victoria and Albert Museum, and going to nature. God had blessed me with clear, sharp eyes, and I took good care of them'.

There is an interesting comment in the information Hewitt supplied for his entry in the New Zealand *Who's Who*, published in 1951. This says: 'The first drypoint etchings were made in 1926; new methods of drypoint, 1927 onwards'. This confirms 1926 as the year that he started work on drypoints, and suggests that his technique changed a year later as he refined his style of drypoint work.

The '*Red Violet*' manuscript offers some more insights into his printmaking. 'Soon I discovered that people were growing more interested in my drawings. Sales were going up and instead of just pulling off six proofs from a plate at the press I was obliged to run the plate through thirty times, until in fact the edition was through, and the plate had to be scrubbed and re-faced. Poverty had me do everything for myself.

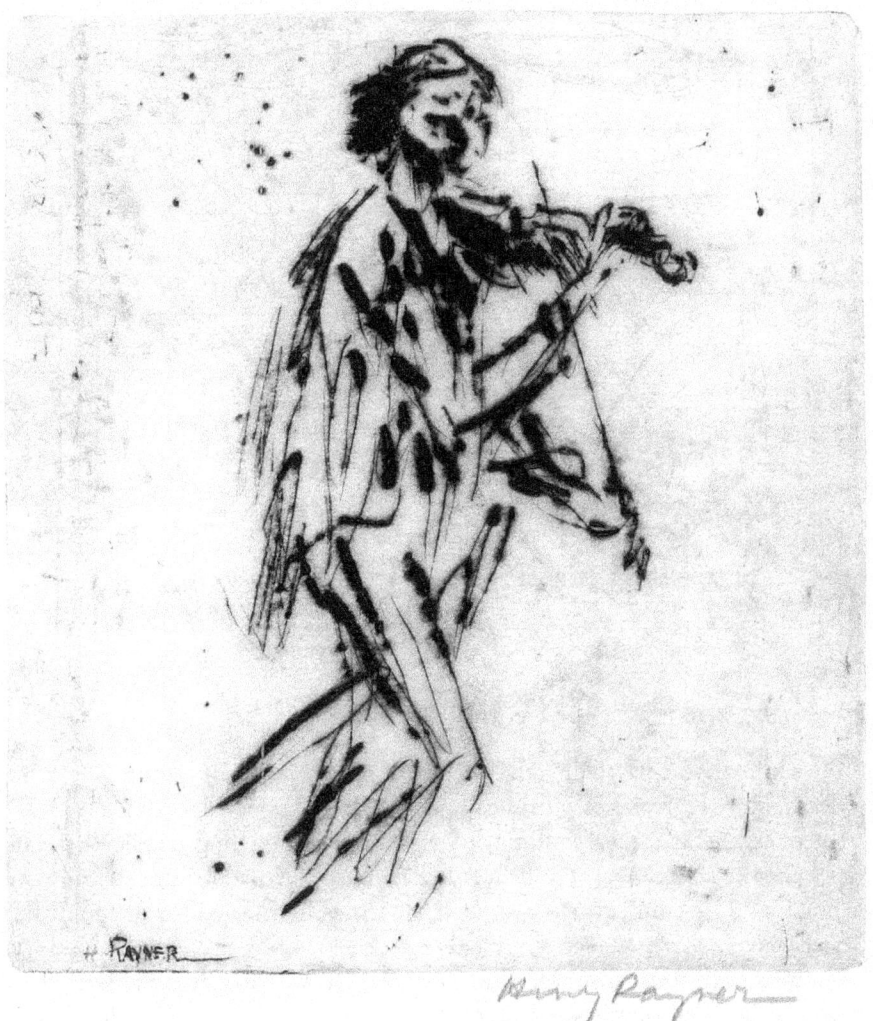

12.5 *'Passingaglia'*, also known as *'Allegro'*. Drypoint, 142×126mm. RS.

'I made my needles, cut my plates, mixed and prepared my inks, got the best paper at the lowest prices by trudging all over London to find the right men to sell it to me; introduced my own colours into the printing and soon had many secrets which are still unknown to most etchers. And what was most important, I was beginning to sell.

'The medium (drypoint) is very easy for the craftsman if he does his own printing. He knows exactly what he wants to achieve, what effects to go for. The plate, copper or zinc, is drawn on, then freely and rather quickly engraved with a needle possessing a circular point. The sharp point, cutting through the metal, throws up a burr as the ploughshare throws up a ridge of earth from the furrow.

'The ink is worked into these grooves or lines, and the burr catches a quantity which increases the rich effect of tones and shadows. Acid-bitten etching cannot

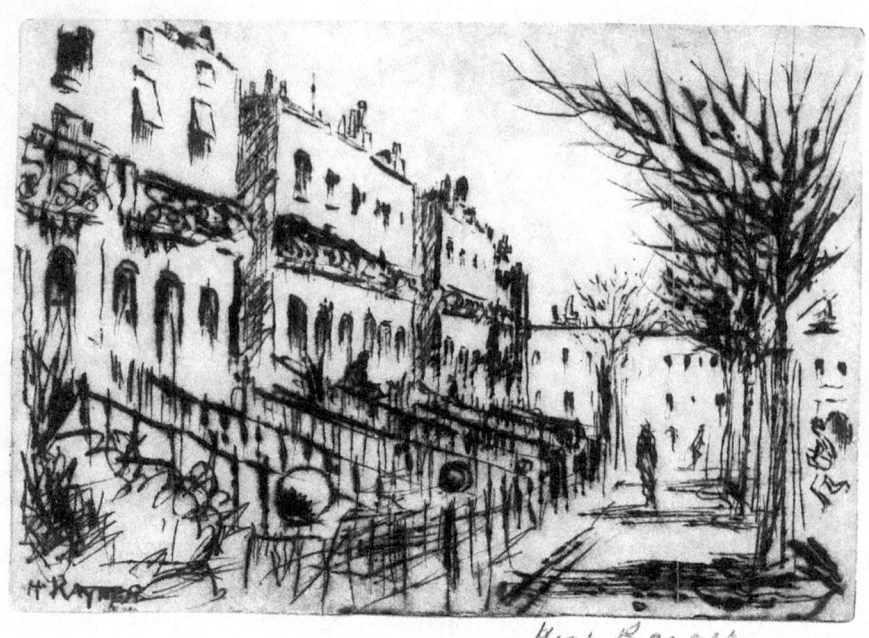

12.6 *'Kentish Town'*, c1934. Drypoint, 103×147mm. RS.

produce this, the particular velvety patina of the good drypoint. The whole process requires directness, freshness, perfect draughtsmanship.'

On one visit to Sickert's studio, he was given an etching needle that came from Whistler's studio, and had been designed by Whistler himself. However, Rayner found he couldn't use it since the needles he needed for drypoint were heavier.

About this time he discovered an inexpensive way to get suitable tools for drypoints: he used dentists' pointers, fitted into a special holder. He obtained these from his own dentist. 'For a few pence he would hand over a dozen or so of these small instruments, made of the hardest steel. They were much superior to the usually soft needles sold for etching purposes by the colourmen. And I was now able to get the rare effects I had longed for. My engineer's training helped my art.'

On a visit to see Sickert in the summer of 1926 Rayner again found himself on the receiving end of advice to abandon drypoint.

'Sickert still seemed to get as much fun out of seeing my personal impressionistic method of drypoint develop as I did myself,' wrote

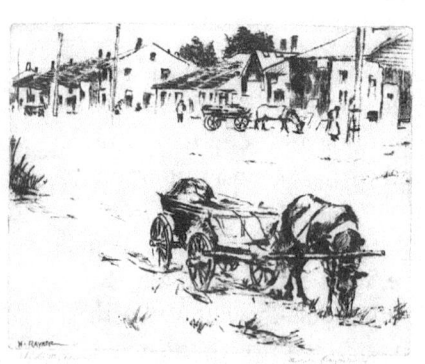

12.7 There are relatively few prints showing Australian scenes. This one is titled *'The little town'*. Drypoint, 170×205mm. SW.

Rayner. 'But he persistently continued to remark that the plates would never yield enough impressions to ensure me a living. He insisted that I should make acid-bitten plates which could be commercially handled by his dealers Brown and Phillip of the Leicester Art Gallery. Brown held some of my earlier prints, but he was more interested in seeing my painting.'

Hewitt was proud of the special ink he used for proofing his plates, which he said 'mellows as it ages with the paper to a glow and richness that drypoint 'burr' needs'. He regarded it as a secret formula that was passed down to him by Sickert, who had acquired it from Whistler. He was also choosy about the paper he used for proofing, and through the war years he carefully kept safe his stock of pre-war British-made paper. A small quantity of this yellow-toned paper has survived to this day in the archive rescued from the goatshed.

In an unpublished manuscript titled '*Black and white*', his daughter Frances wrote an intimate account of her father printing from his etched plates. It is written in the third person, but it is about Hewitt at his printing press when the family were living in Herbert Street in 1941.

> ... in the passageway of the flat, the oil lamp was on. Standing by it, the elder girl would watch her father printing. This was a familiar memory. The smell of the ink was strong.
>
> It was a very dirty and tiring job. Precision was the keynote as the artist would rush the plate through the press, taking care not to smudge the white paper to be printed on. This was always difficult when one's hands were filled with the wretched thick ink, black and penetrating. ... To stop his hair falling over his eyes at the crucial moment, the father would bring out the beret and put it on, Monty style, and resume. ...
>
> He worked terribly hard indeed and was completely devoted to the detail of the job of both engraving on the plate and the actual printing. With the very absorbing pains of asthma as a life's companion, this manual work was a strain. ...
>
> Then there were the moments when domestic issues arose at the important moment: 'I'm not calling you again,' the voice would ring out as lunch would be preparing in the kitchen. 'Come on both of you, and I shall be very angry if there is ink on my ...', and so on.

It seems that Hewitt generally didn't print a complete run of proofs from a plate in one session, but would print additional copies as they were needed. Sometimes this could be a decade or more after the plate had been etched, which led to occasional inconsistencies in titles and dates.

Most of his drypoint etched plates have survived, and it is interesting to see what materials he used. He couldn't afford to buy special-purpose plates made from copper or

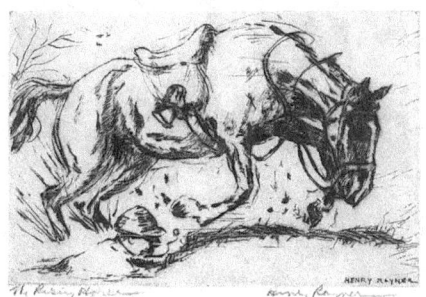

12.8 *'The rising horse'.* Drypoint, 117×174mm. RS.

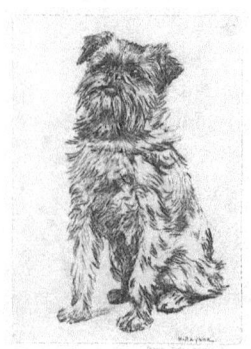

12.9 *'Griffon Bruxellois'*, one of a series of dog prints. Drypoint, 190×133mm. RS.

zinc, so he made do with virtually any kind of metal he could get hold of. Some of the plates obviously had former lives as containers for olive oil, biscuits, powdered baby milk etc. It's strange to see his striking etched images in the plates, cutting through a printed slogan for Ostermilk or Bluebird toffees.

One exception to this is the portrait he did of Neville Chamberlain, for which he used a heavy sheet of copper.

The themes he would choose for his drypoints evolved with time. Initially he concentrated on London scenes, especially in and around Chelsea. This was the area of London that held the strongest appeal for him, because of its associations with Whistler and the elder generation of artists who still lived there, and also because the images and sounds reminded him of his childhood in the coastal town of Brighton, near Melbourne.

Then there were his rural British and Australian scenes, ballet, circus and music hall scenes, and portraits. He made use of London's Regent's Park Zoo in a series of wild animal studies; and there is also a series of dog images.

He did numerous drypoints of his friend and mentor. Sickert was rarely captured in drawings, paintings and prints by his contemporaries, giving Hewitt's portraits of his mentor a rarity value. He also did drypoint portraits of other notable figures from the worlds of art and theatre. These were all portraits that

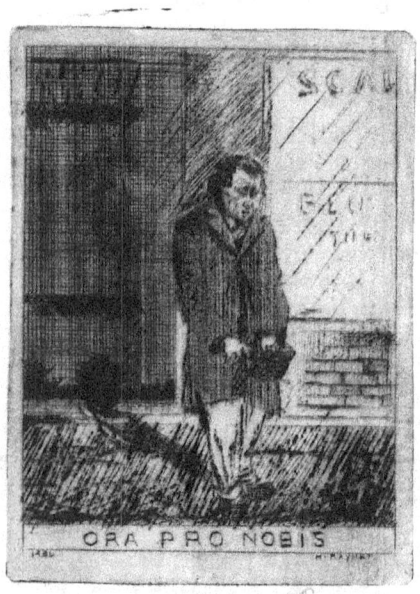

12.10 In the mid 1930s Rayner produced several prints with social and political themes. *'Ora pro nobis'* (pray for us) is from 1936. Drypoint, 150×110mm. SW.

Rayner chose to do, rather than commissions. In fact he was dead against taking commissions despite frequent urging from his mother who saw it as a route out of poverty and a way of gaining greater recognition as an artist.

Rayner was proud of his working class roots and believed that art should be for everybody, not just the wealthy. He was at home capturing everyday scenes of ordinary people and ordinary places. His many London scenes, for example, tend to show ordinary houses and streets rather than landmark buildings. His river scenes show anonymous working boats, not the yachts of the rich and famous.

There are many drawings and drypoints of his wife Theresa in domestic settings, doing the ironing, slicing the Sunday joint, washing, resting. Unsurprisingly there are also many watercolours, drawings and drypoints of his children as they grew up.

Ironically, it has been his portraits of well-known figures from the worlds of theatre,

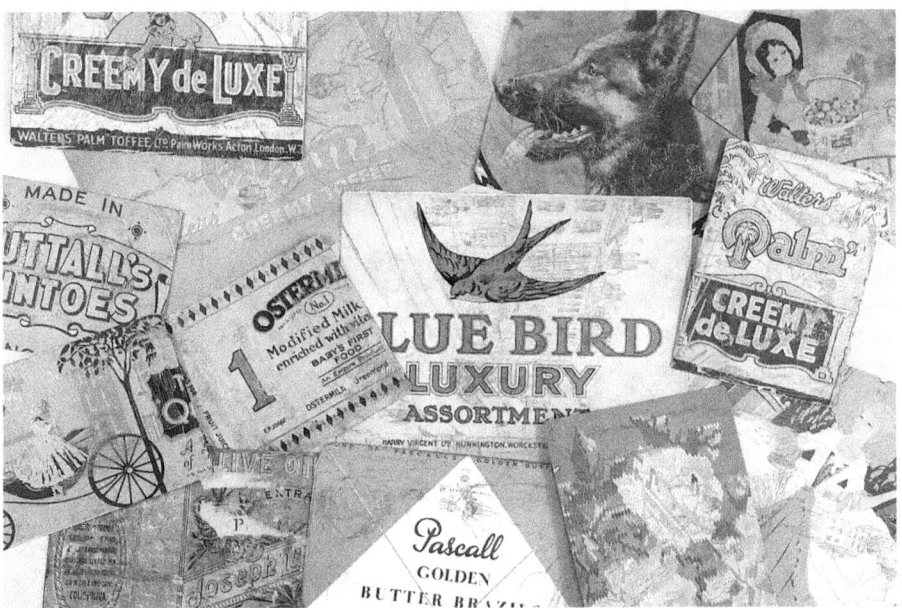

12.11 The vast majority of Rayner's original etched plates have survived. It is interesting to see that when times were really hard, and buying copper or other metal sheets was out of the question, he made do with metal salvaged from food or sweet tins, or olive oil cans. Here are some of his original drypoint plates sw.

art and politics that have attracted the most interest at auction in recent years. Subjects for his drypoint portraits included T E Lawrence ('Lawrence of Arabia') Winston Churchill, George Bernard Shaw, Augustus John, Dame Sybil Thorndike, Neville Chamberlain, Henri Gaudier Brzeska, Keats, Lytton Strachey, and the Princesses Elizabeth and Margaret. Some of the works were based on meetings with the individuals, or at least seeing them in public, others were based on photographs.

There are only two figures from the past who Rayner chose to capture in drypoints. One was the poet Keats, the other the French bohemian artist Henri Gaudier Brzeska (1891–1915). Both seem to have had particular significance for him.

In the case of Keats, there was of course the Isle of Wight connection. Hewitt was attracted by the possibility, however unlikely, that Keats and Jeremiah Rayner could have met while the poet was staying at Eglantine Cottage in Shanklin in 1817 and Jeremiah was delivering mail.

In the case of Brzeska, Hewitt wrote that he was already aware of the artist's work when he met Nina Hamnett 'one who knew both Sickert and Gaudier-Brzeska very well'. Nina had sat for Brzeska many times, and the tales she told Hewitt only enhanced his admiration for the artist. Hewitt noted in his *Red Violet* manuscript that 'this panther-like young French artist created quite a stir with his new line and original carvings. He possessed rare powers which were

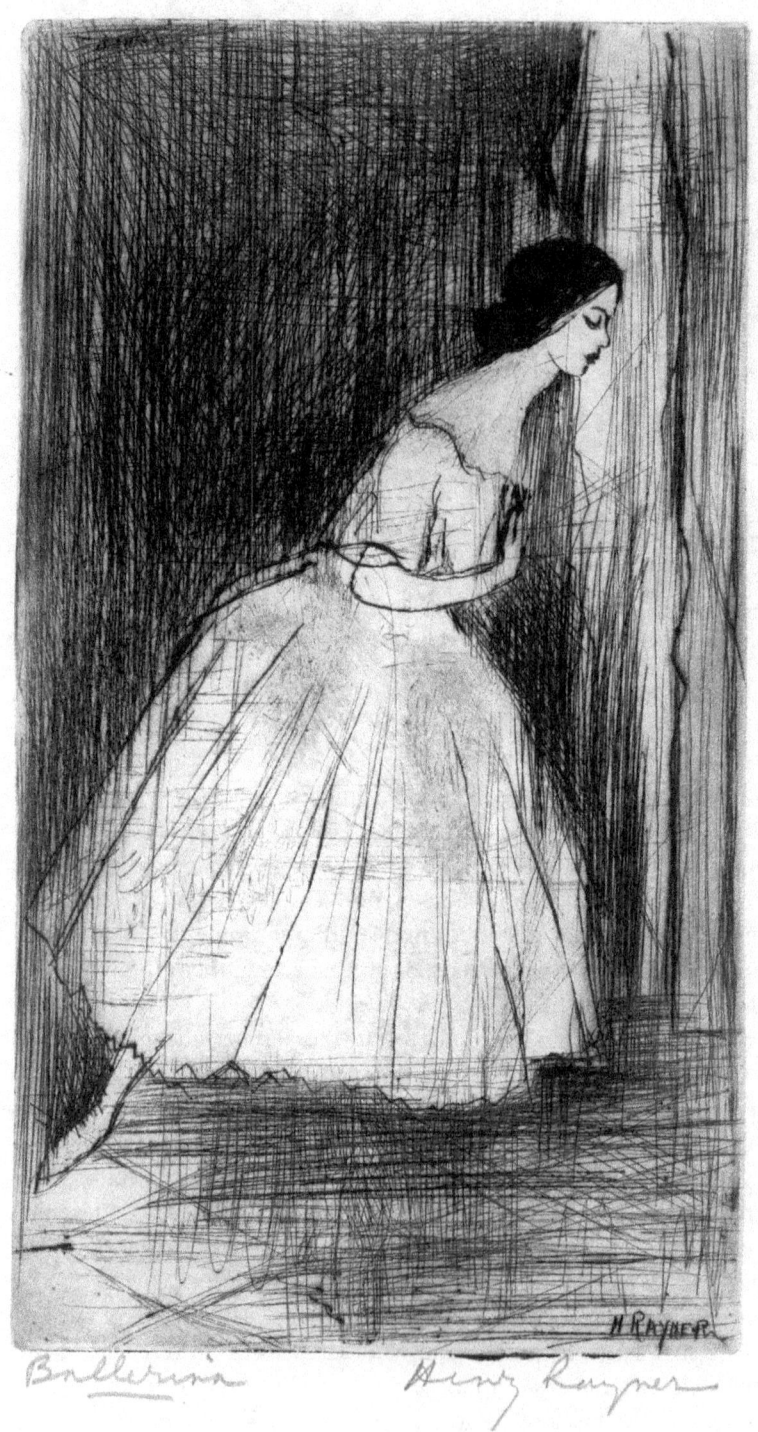

12.12 There is a large series of ballet prints, most dating from the 1930s. This is titled simply *'Ballerina'*. Limited to 5 impressions. Drypoint, 235×130mm. RS.

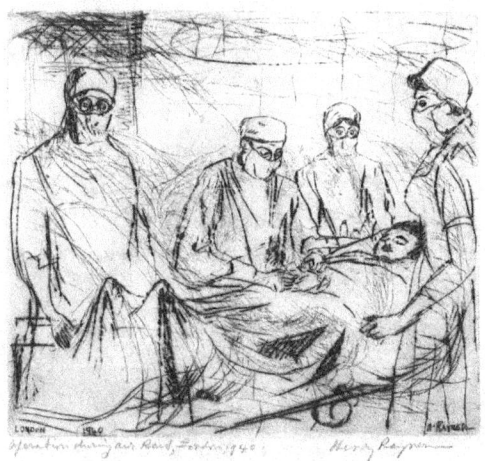

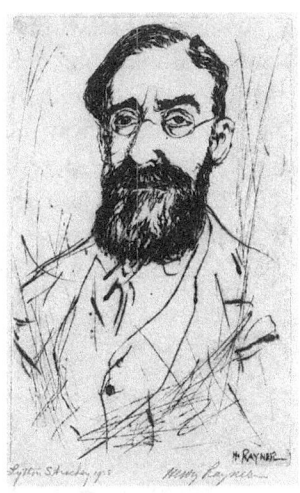

12.13 Among Rayner's 'war pictures' is a small series of hospital scenes. This is titled *'Operation during air raid London Dec 1940'*. Drypoint, 148×162mm. sw.

12.14 *'Lytton Strachey, 1928'*. Drypoint, 175×112mm. rs.

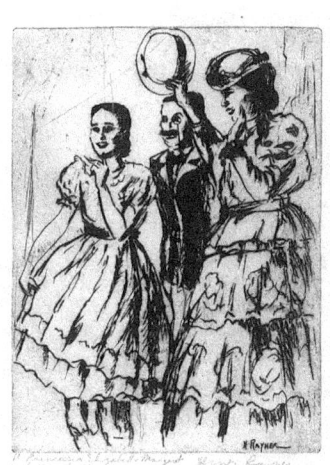

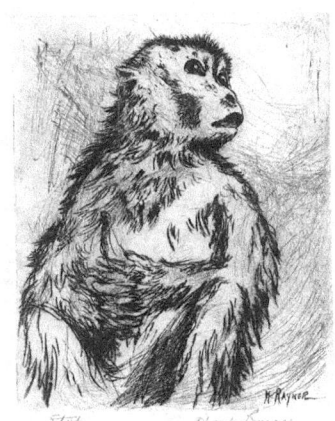

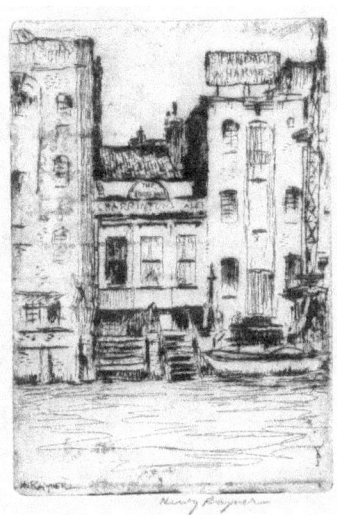

12.15 *'The Princesses Elizabeth & Margaret in the 1890 ballet'*, 1945, based on a press photograph. Drypoint, 215×158mm. rs.

12.16 *'Study'*, undated. Probably from a visit to London's Regent's Park zoo. Drypoint, 220×175mm. rs.

12.17 *'The Old Turk's Head, Wapping (demolished)'*, undated. Rayner etched this scene twice: the other version is landscape format, and shows a tall ship to the right of the pub. Drypoint, 138×94mm. rs.

just becoming fully recognised when he was killed in the trenches in that war that was to stop all wars'.

It is also known from correspondence that Hewitt and Ethel Mannin discussed Brzeska during their friendship in 1944.

It is possible that Hewitt identified with Henri Gaudier Brzeska at some level. There are certainly strong parallels in their lives. Like Brzeska Hewitt sacrificed everything for his art and lived in poverty. Like Brzeska he was an outsider, struggling to make his way in a foreign land. Like Brzeska he found his spiritual home in Chelsea. Like Brzeska he was a writer as well as an artist – although Brzeska is best known as a sculptor he was also a printmaker. And like Brzeska Hewitt produced pictures very quickly, making what he referred to as 'lighting sketches'. Sickert acknowledged this productivity when he observed in 1934

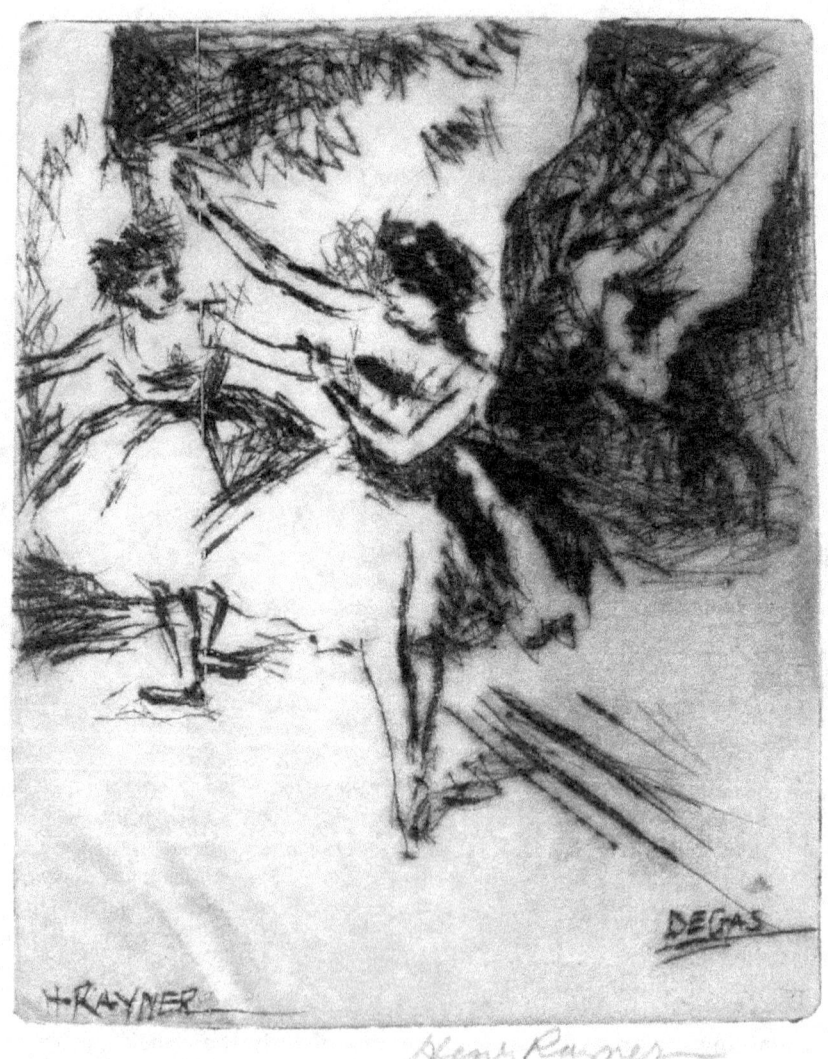

12.18 *'Degas ballet'*, 1941, 110×88mm. RS.

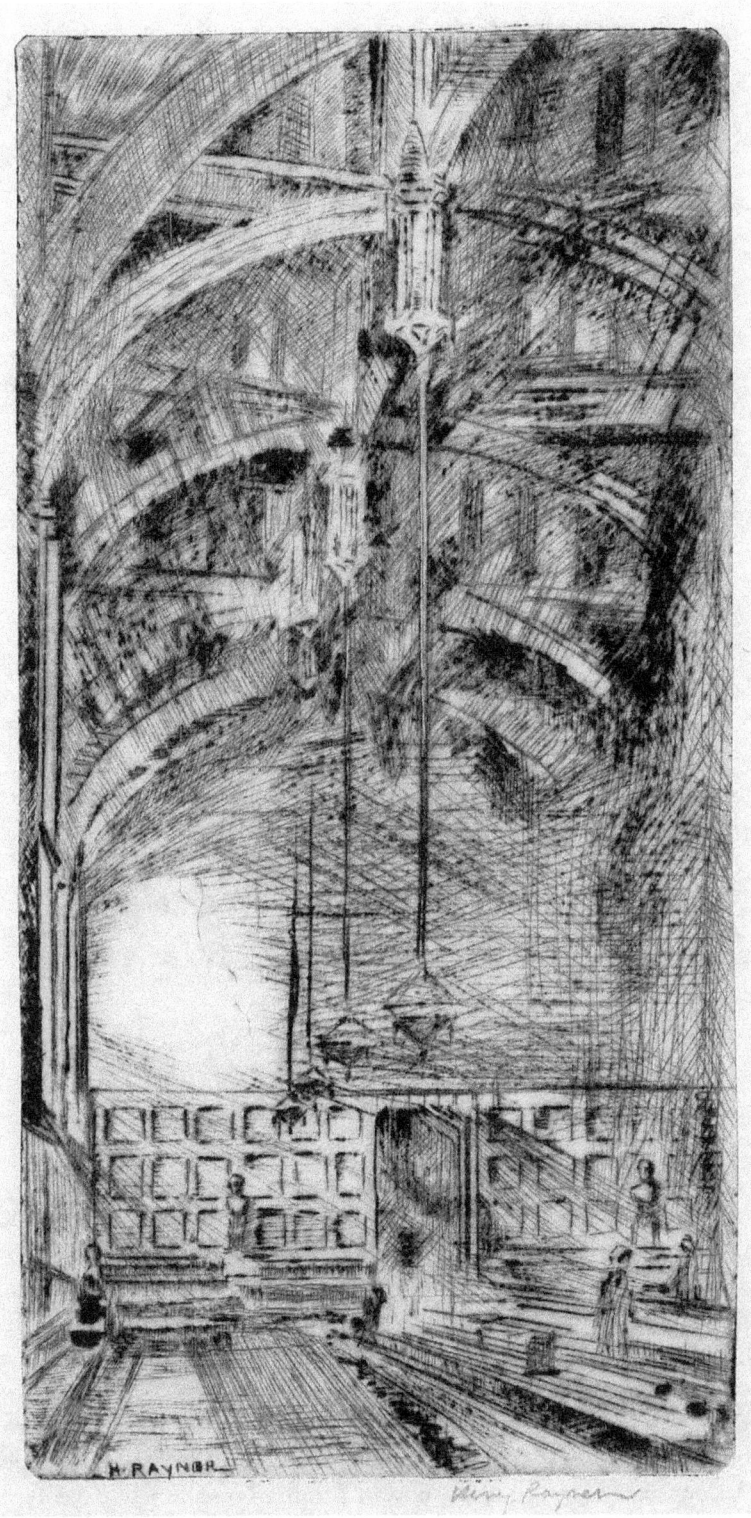

12.19 *'Great Hall, Lincoln's Inn'* c1930. It was finding this print in a charity shop in London's King's Road that triggered the author's interest in the artist, and led ultimately to this biography. Drypoint 220×110mm. RS.

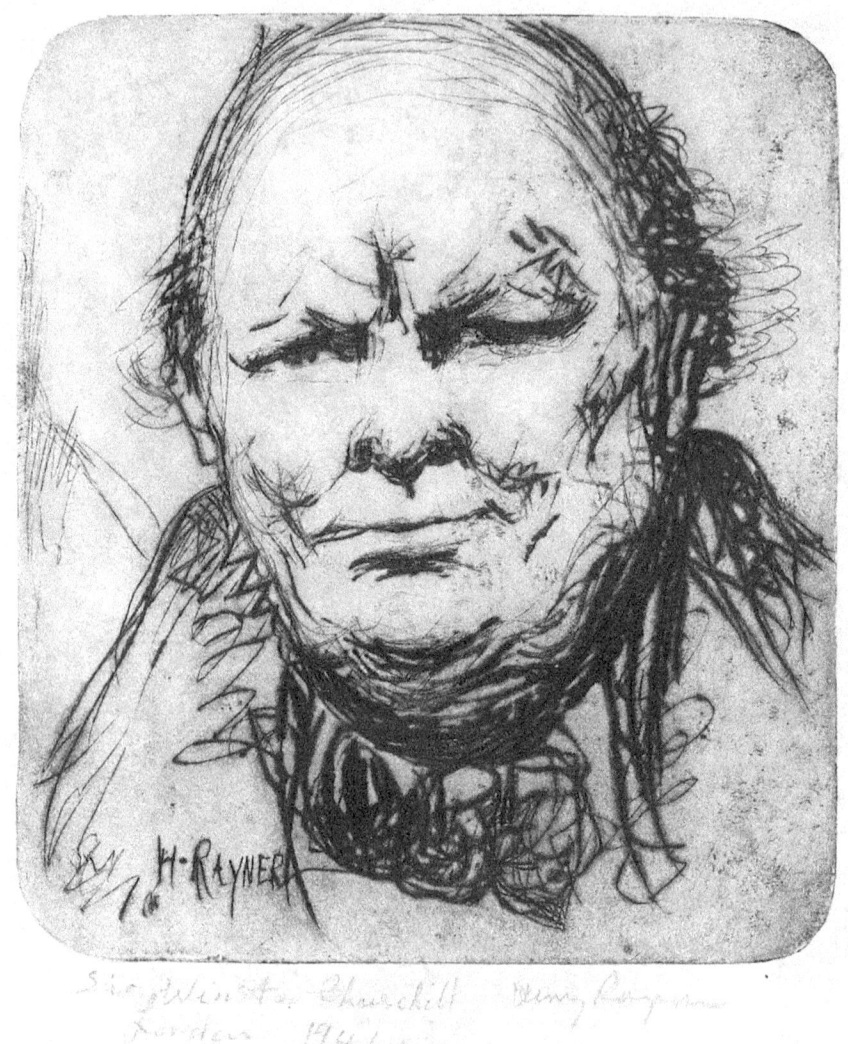

12.20 *'Sir Winston Churchill, London, 1941'*. Proofs also known dated 1940. Drypoint 187×162mm. sw.

that Hewitt's assets were 'the possession of a natural impressionism and rapid transcription.'

There is no doubt that drypoint etching suited Hewitt's temperament and personality. He was a man in a hurry – impatient, impulsive and ambitious. The drypoint technique coupled with his 'lightning sketch' approach to drawing gave him a fast means of original artistic expression.

The long-drawn-out depression of the 1930s prompted Hewitt to do several works commenting on the social problems of the day. One shows people queuing at a labour exchange. Another shows a sad man on a lonely pavement, and is captioned '*Ora pro nobis*' (pray for us). Around the same time he also tried his hand at drypoints with political/satirical themes. The work titled '*There is no shelter*' (1936) was his attempt to warn the British of the risk from the troubles gathering pace in mainland Europe.

In the 1930s he developed an interest in surrealism and mysticism, and there are a number of drypoints from that period with surrealistic themes, as well as his own personal interpretations of scenes from the New Testament. One of these works, '*The last supper*', evidently aroused some controversy because in one of the versions of his own biography, written around 1946, he referred to the work as having been publicly burnt. Frustratingly, no other references to any such event have been found in Hewitt's papers.

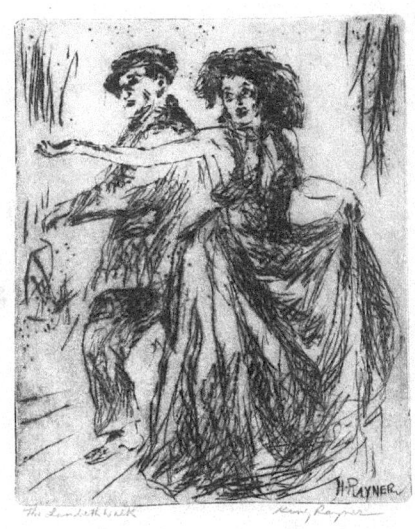

12.21 *'The Lambeth Walk'*, 1940. Drypoint 190×155mm. RS.

During the 1939–45 War he concentrated on images that showed the effects of war on people and places. His blitz scenes included a striking image of St Pauls Cathedral surrounded by bomb damaged buildings; and an incident when he witnessed an incendiary bomb that had fallen in the street near the Victoria & Albert Museum. He even devoted one drypoint to portraying the damage to his studio in Mansfield Road in the autumn of 1940 when a bomb fell next door. There is also a small series of wartime hospital scenes.

There are relatively few images of locations outside London, but the few that are known give some clues as to his occasional travel around England. His rare visits to Cambridgeshire to visit his wife and daughters during the war resulted in several drypoints of wildfowl and fenland scenes. From one visit to Leicester he produced a print of a bomb-damaged butcher's shop.

He must have travelled to Cornwall at some point, because there is a view of St Ives town and beach. A visit to France yielded a drypoint of the church in St Mamert, a tiny hamlet in France's Beaujolais region, and a vibrant oil of a Paris square.

Chelsea continued to attract him, and there are drypoints of river boats with dates of 1939 and 1947.

Most of his drypoints were completed between 1926 and 1944. In all, he etched more than 500 plates, constituting quite probably the largest output of drypoint work by a 20th century artist. Most of the original plates have survived.

13

A casualty of war.
Again and again.

In the first half of 1939 things seemed to be moving in Rayner's favour at last.

In March his etching of King George VI was included in a Royal Society of Amateur Artists exhibition at Dame Alice Godman's House. One of the visitors was HM Queen Mary (the then King's mother). Dame Alice told her that Rayner wished to present a copy of the proof to the King. She clearly liked the work, so Dame Alice offered her a second copy.

Following this, on 14th March Lady Cynthia Colville wrote to Rayner from Marlborough House to say that Queen Mary liked the portrait of her son. The letter described the proof as 'a really delightful portrait, besides being in itself a very pleasing picture'. The letter then went on to point out that the two proofs given to Her Majesty were numbered proofs 1 and 2, and she wished to check that Rayner was happy to part with these first two proofs. 'Her Majesty will not therefore frame her own, or pass the other one on to the King, until I hear from you your wishes in this respect.'

To celebrate, Hewitt took Theresa and the girls to the woods by the Chinese pagoda at Kew, and they had a picnic. 'You are beginning to justify my Academy expectations,' commented Sickert when he heard the news of the Queen's purchase.

The same year, Mrs Anthony Eden purchased a copy of Rayner's '*cold joint*' work, showing Theresa slicing a joint of meat. This work was almost certainly inspired by a Sickert print titled '*The rasher*'. Later Mrs Eden bought 12 prints of Chelsea.

The *London Evening Standard* ran the following story on Tuesday April 18 1939

> **Artist Mrs. Eden befriended gives portrait to the King**
> **Once begged in the streets of London**
>
> Evening Standard Reporter
>
> The King and Queen Mary now have proofs of a portrait etching of the King by an Australian artist who a few years ago was begging in the streets of London.

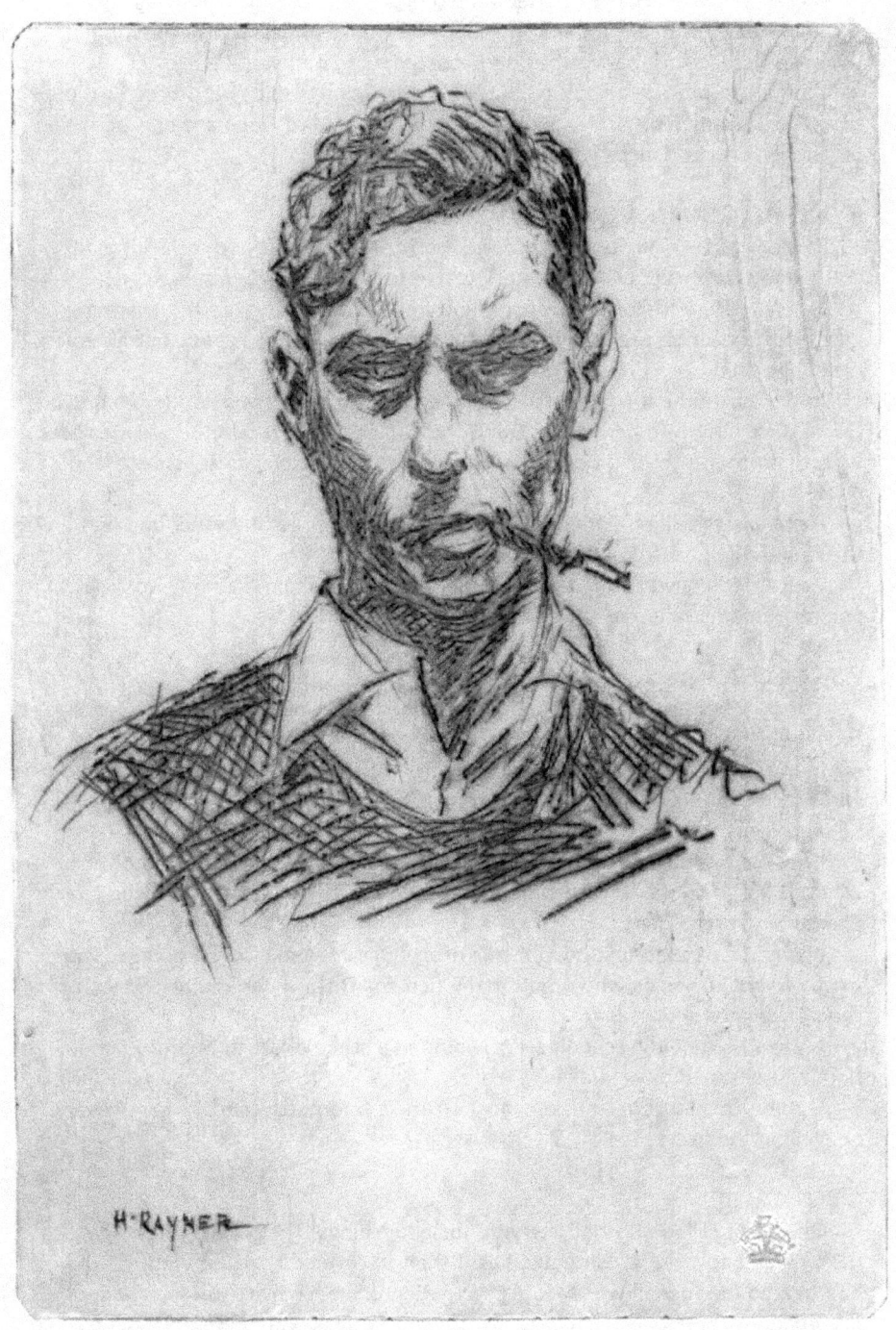

13.1 This 1939 etching of King George VI was the work that drew Hewitt to public attention when Queen Mary (the King's mother) acquired a copy. Unusually, it showed the King in informal clothes. Rayner always referred to it as his 'democratic' portrait of the King. Drypoint, 185×123mm. RS.

The artist is Mr. Henry Rayner, and the portrait, built up from lightning sketches made as the King has gone about his public duties, shows the King in the open-necked shirt he wears at his boys' camp at Southwold.

Wishing to present a copy to the King, Mr. Rayner sent two proofs to the recent Royal Amateur Art Exhibition where Dame Alice Godman, one of the organisers, pressed Queen Mary to accept them.

'DELIGHTFUL PORTRAIT'

Two days later Mr. Rayner received from Marlborough. House a letter in which Lady Cynthia Colville, Lady-in-Waiting to Queen Mary, wrote:

'Her Majesty wished me to thank you most gratefully for such a charming gift, for this etching is a really delightful portrait besides being in itself a very pleasant picture.

'In the meantime the Queen has noticed that it is proofs one and two which Dame Alice has given her Majesty, and the Queen wonders whether you really wish to part with these proofs or whether you would prefer to substitute later ones.

'Her Majesty will not, therefore, frame her own or pass the other one on to the king until I hear from you your wishes in this respect.'

Mr. Rayner replied asking that Queen Mary should retain the first two proofs and forwarded two more.

WAS MECHANIC

Today Mr Rayner, whose home and studio is in Gospel Oak, told me something of his early struggles.

'In my young days in Australia I combined earning my living as a mechanic while studying under Nuttall, a well-known Melbourne black and white artist,' he said.

'I worked my way over to England in 1924, and after a spell with a motor firm was able to go to the Royal Academy Schools, where I was taught by the late Charles Sims and Sickert.

'It was Sickert who first bought one of my pictures and who encouraged me to go on, and it was he who urged that when an artist is poor and unknown he should sell his work cheaply.

'I walked out of the schools after joining in a strike effort to improve conditions and returned to Australia.

'Coming back to England in 1930 I struck a bad patch, and in 1933 I was begging in the streets.

GIVEN A MEAL

'One day I called at a house trying to sell etchings. They asked me in, gave me a meal, and bought some pictures. I then discovered that the woman who had treated me so well was Mrs. Anthony Eden. She has since bought more of my work.

'I have always borne Sickert's advice in mind, and while I can dispose of some of my etchings at £2 or £3 each, I often sell for much less to people who can afford only a little,.

'Last year I sold 2,000 etchings at sixpence each.

'My ambition now is to establish a small school to teach and carry on the Sickert tradition.'

Mr. Rayner, who is 36 years old, is married to an English woman and has two children.

It is interesting that when talking to this journalist, Hewitt had not claimed to have led the student strike at the Royal Academy Schools, but more modestly to have 'joined in the strike effort'. Not for the first time, he had mixed up the dates of some key events in his life. To say that he had left the RA Schools and gone back to Australia, returning to England in 1930, is an accidental or deliberate distortion of the real sequence of events. In fact he stayed in London after quitting the RA Schools, newly married, and didn't go back to Australia until 1931, staying for just a few days before returning to England.

At around the same date, the following story appeared in an unidentified London newspaper.

The King's portrait

Recently, while Henry Rayner, the artist, was working on his portrait of the King, which has been accepted by the Royal Family, he was taken seriously ill, but his wife, once considered the most beautiful model in London, urged him on with 'It is going to be one of the best portraits of His Majesty.' The artist has not failed. Not only was Queen Mary highly pleased, but numerous people who have seen the work.

Mr Rayner now lays all honour to his wife, who has laboured beside him since he walked out of the Academy schools as the first mover in the student strike, which has improved conditions in that famous institution.

Mrs Rayner is a native of Marylebone, where her husband has painted and etched his best work; but as an Australian he has not always known the best studio conditions. He spent much time at his easel in the dense bushland outside Melbourne, for years – seeking nature. Once, lost in those hills, with nothing but paintbox and rifle, he was obliged to make a rough bed of gum leaves, and 'carve' his hard-won dinner (kangaroo) with a pair of scissors.

Perhaps it was the grimness of his early life that inspired him to portray the King in the open shirt of his camping attire.

These references to the King's attire in the Rayner drypoint underline the fact that at that time it was not normal to depict royalty in anything other than formal or ceremonial dress. Hewitt had taken something of a risk. But it didn't seem to deter Queen Mary or other members of the Royal Family. They liked the work.

He later referred to this particular work as the first 'democratic' portrayal of King George VI.

From this point on, various institutions acquired prints, either buying them or accepting them as gifts. In June 1939 the British Museum Department of

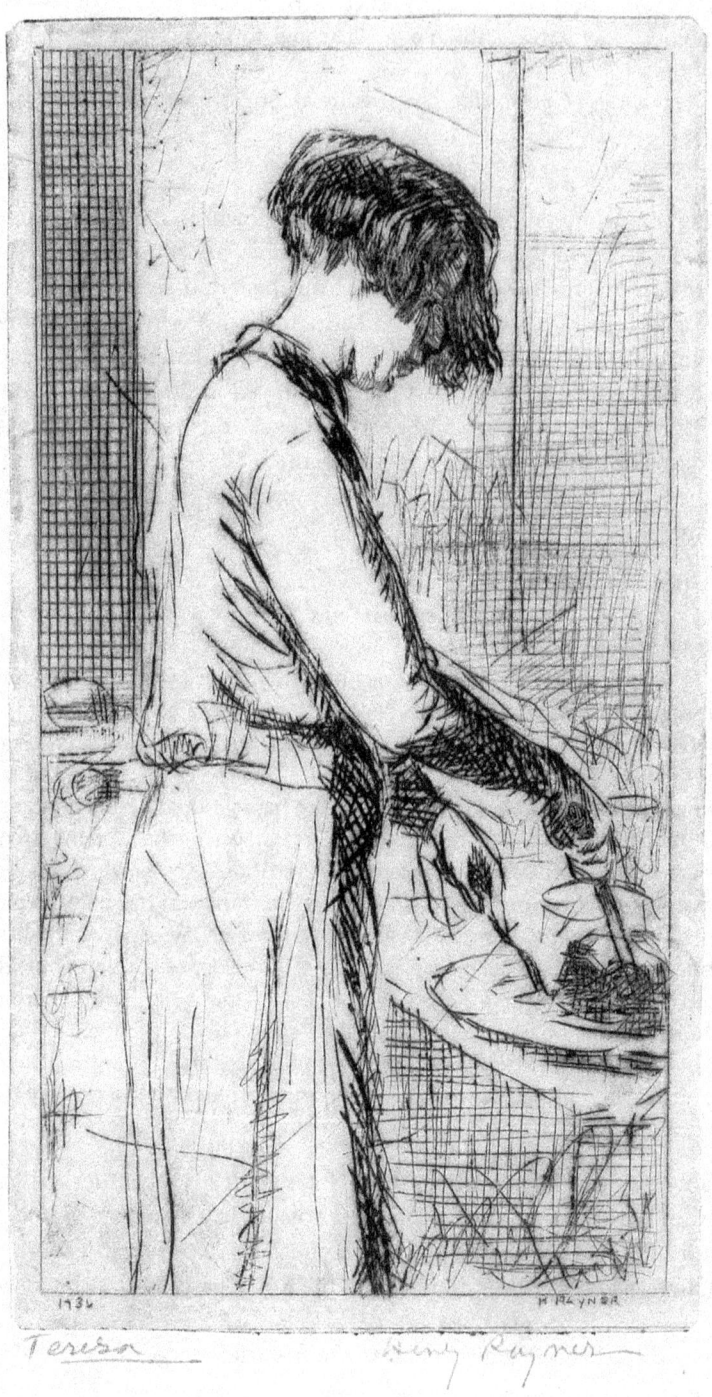

13.2 *'Teresa'* also known as *'the cold joint', 1937*. A proof of this work, which echoes a print by Walter Sickert titled *'the rasher'*, was acquired by Mrs Anthony Eden (wife of the former British Foreign Secretary) in 1939. A copy of this work was published in *The Artist*, Vol XIII No. 5, July 1937. Drypoint, 216×115mm. RS.

Prints & Drawings accepted three drypoints including one of Winston Churchill and one of Henry J Harben.

In June 1939 the Victoria & Albert Museum accepted two of the three prints Theresa had offered them – the portrait of '*King George VI*' and '*The etcher*' (trial proof). They returned the third print, '*Chelsea mangle works*', saying that 'the growing exigencies on our space make it impossible to do more than represent the work of modern artists'.

Hewitt and Theresa wasted no time in telling the press about his successes. A piece in the *Daily Telegraph's* 'London day by day' column dated 21st June 1939 and titled 'Australian potraitist's success', mentioned that Queen Mary and the V&A had copies of his '*King George VI*' print. The newspaper reproduced Rayner's '*self portrait, 1938*' drypoint.

One interesting detail to emerge from this report is that Hewitt had obviously told the newspaper that the plate of the '*King George VI*' drypoint had been destroyed. We now know that this was not the case, as the original plate (or a duplicate) still exists.

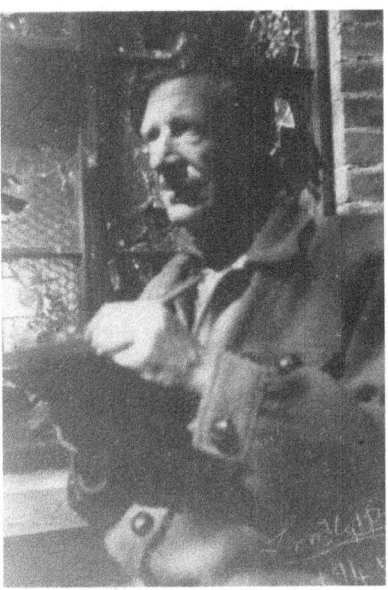

13.3 Rayner's own notes about this 1941 photo state that it was taken while he was working on a scene that would result in his drypoint work '*When we stood alone*'. SW.

At around this time, a copy of Hewitt's '*Old Lombard Café*' drypoint was presented to the librarian of Chelsea Public Library, Mr A Denton, by a group of artists to mark his retirement. The library sent him a letter on 5th July thanking him for the print. Hewitt's address at this stage was 5 Lismore Circus.

He must have really thought that he was finally beginning to make his mark in the art world. Then the war started. He always referred to it as the 'Hitler War'. It began badly for him and never really improved.

In August he had been offered his first one-man exhibition at the enterprising Wertheim Gallery at 8 Burlington Gardens. Lucy Wertheim had made it her business to open a gallery that would showcase the younger generation of artists. In 1930 she had founded the Twenties Group of English artists – the name comes not from the decade of the twenties, but from the ages of the artists, all still in their twenties. The list included Barbara Hepworth, Victor Pasmore, Christopher Wood, Mervyn Peake and Maxwell Bates.

'Mrs Wertheim had discovered Christopher Wood and was on the point of discovering me.' Rayner later wrote [although Lucy Wertheim herself always

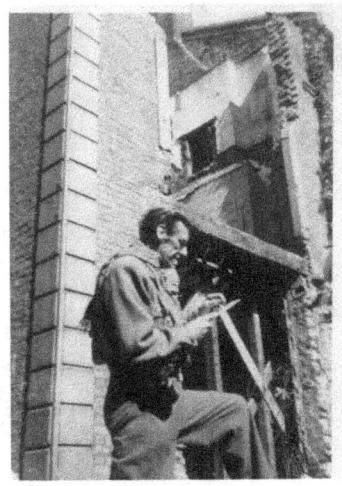

13.4 Sketching bomb damage c1941. SW.

protested that she had not 'discovered' Wood, and that 'this was hardly the appropriate word to apply to an artist who at the time I made his acquaintance was already holding his second London exhibition'].

'She offered me her sumptuous gallery, and I opened the show 'as a gesture of calmness and British confidence in the face of bluff'.

'The Royal Family allowed me to place my portrait of the King in the window, where sandbags were being piled by the ARP workers in grim preparation. It was a strange scene. Cars rushing out of the city crammed with every sort of object and valuable; small squads of pale-faced lads in ill-fitting uniforms marching in the streets; queues of enormous length waiting at the ARP centres in driving rain and sleet to be fitted for their gas masks.'

Wertheim's offer, in a letter dated 19th August, was for him to have the use of her gallery for one week starting 2nd September. The deal was that he would do the 'selling and showing' himself, and would give the gallery 33.3% of any sales made or commissions taken during the show.

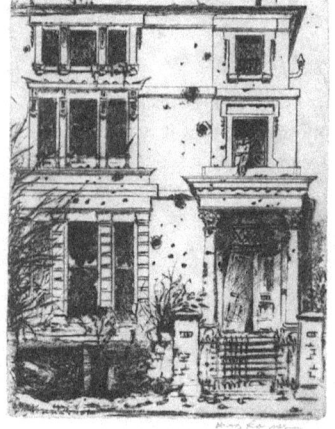

13.5 *'Last night a short alert was given'* (also known as *'the blitz begins, 1940*). Drypoint 215×163mm. sw.

Sadly, what should have been his exhibition break-through was rudely cut short by the outbreak of war. After Chamberlain's BBC radio broadcast at 11.15am on Sunday 3rd September, announcing that Britain was at war with Germany, there was a series of short official announcements. One declared that all theatres, cinemas, music halls and other places of entertainment were to be closed immediately.

'The police came and kindly closed my exhibition,' Hewitt wrote, 'and we got on with the war, but not before the painter Dunlop, following my stand, opened his show in the West End, just to let the Germans know we were still a crazy race.'

What should have been Rayner's first one-man exhibition was to be the very last exhibition ever staged at the Wertheim Gallery.

The closure of the exhibition was reported in the *Record and West London News*, 9 September 1939.

A history-making war exhibition

Henry Rayner's very interesting exhibition of art, including his successful portrait of the King, now in the Royal Collection, and at the Wertheim Gallery, came to an abrupt end this week with the outbreak of war. Rayner was the only artist in London, and Mrs Wertheim, of the famous Gallery, the only proprietor of such a gallery, determined to hold a crisis exhibition, in spite of the bombing and gas, as a gesture of calmness and goodwill on the part of British Art.

Rayner did not want it felt that Hitler could stay an artist of this Island from exhibiting the Art of this Island. The well-known papers which had promised support through it all were prevented publishing and he carried on alone with the support of the plucky members of the Gallery. But the show was ordered to close.

The exhibition represented the life work of the artist, who spent his student days in Marylebone depicting the life of London on etching plate and canvas. His latest work has been acquired by the British Museum, National Portrait Gallery, South Kensington Museum, Melbourne National Gallery, and the Royal Library of Belgium.

Considered one of the best coming men of the New School, Rayner will now drop the brush and take up the rifle.

[The 'South Kensington Museum' was what the Victoria & Albert Museum had been called prior to 1899. Hewitt tended to use the old name].

In fact, there is a degree of confusion about the closure of the show. In her own biography *Adventure in art*, published in 1947 by Nicholson and Watson, Lucy Wertheim recalled that the exhibition was closed before it had even opened:

On September 1st we hung an exhibition of drawings by a New Zealand (sic) artist. The Private View was fixed for Tuesday September 5th. We had sent out two thousand invitations.

On Sunday September 3rd war was declared.

On Monday morning September 4th the police informed us of a regulation forbidding more than 12 people to congregate in one room. The artist dismantled the walls and gave up all thought of his exhibition.

On September 5th the authorities declared they were taking over the gallery premises for an air-raid shelter. I removed all my belongings.

Notices were inscribed in the Personal Columns of *The Times* and *Daily Telegraph* requesting artists to collect their pictures.

The gallery was no more!

On the other hand, Hewitt recalled that there had been a few sales as a result of the exhibition.

Whatever the precise circumstances and timing of the closure, the cancellation of this show was a crushing blow. He had put tremendous effort into promoting the event, sending invitations to everyone he could think of.

One of them was Sir Winston Churchill. In a masterful piece of understatement, Churchill sent a message via his private secretary as follows.

Winston Churchill, The Admiralty, Whitehall 12th September 1939

Dear Sir

In reply to your letter of the 29th August, Mr Churchill has asked me to say how much he regrets it was not possible for him, for obvious reasons, to respond to your kind invitation.

Yours faithfully

B C Sudell, Private Secretary

Hewitt had as usual written to all his press contacts about the exhibition. One result was a piece in the William Hickey column in the *Daily Express*. Unfortunately, this appeared on Wednesday 6th September, by which time

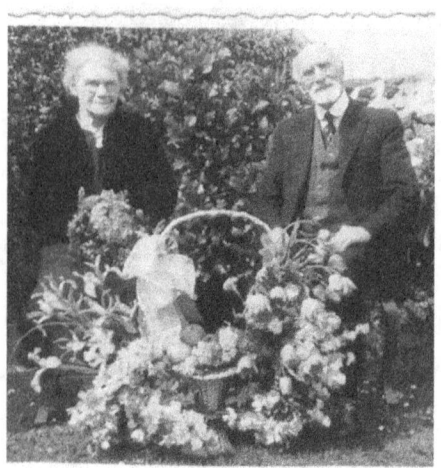

13.6 Hewitt's mother and Hal around 1940, in their garden at St Kilda near Melbourne. sw.

the show had been prematurely closed. In his letter Hewitt had evidently written: 'The show is a gesture of calmness in the face of present difficulties. I shall enlist as soon as it ends.'

The run up to war also affected another of Hewitt's friends. The Japanese artist and writer Yoshio Markino was by now living in reduced circumstances with his wife and child in a basement flat at 68A Finborough Road in Fulham. He wrote to Hewitt on 2nd July 1939 saying: 'You know, I am still the same Markino who wrote those books, but in these days the whole world has become insane through misunderstanding, misleading, unreasonable suspicions and hatred. A week ago our house agent sent us the bailiff for just £9 arrear of rent without any forewarning. It hurt me, for you know, during the [1914–18] war time I dispursed [sic] £1,200 from my small purse for the English sufferers. It is always so familiar story: honourable landlord stand on no ceremony. He think artist same as dirty commercial – pocket full moneys, and threaten the throw-out.'

13.7 On 10th October 1940 The *Millennial Star* magazine (published by the British Mission of the Church of Jesus Christ of Latter Day Saints) used Rayner's drypoint of Chelsea Old Church on its front cover. © THE CHURCH OF JESUS CHRIST OF LATTER DAY SAINTS. sw.

Hewitt had made some complimentary comments about Markino's work, in response to which Markino wrote: 'I blush to think that even in this time you are one of the very few who look at my work more than my nationality. I hope you will see my latest oil painting one day. I feel I can work far better than those early ones you have seen.'

When war was declared in 1939, Markino was evidently 'hurried away in a Japanese staff car – a little tired old man gazing at his beloved London for the last time.' Hewitt never heard from him again.

The war years were not good for Hewitt either. Theresa and the girls were evacuated from London on several occasions through the next five years. But Hewitt felt it was his duty to stay and work in central London.

A curious record from the Rayner archive is a letter dated 3rd May 1940 from the Peruvian Legation in London. This asks how long Hewitt was planning to stay in London, and what he might charge for giving tuition in art to the daughter of a Monsieur Benavides. This most likely relates to Felipe Benavides (1917–1991), best known in later years as a leading ecologist and environmentalist. He was a volunteer ambulance driver in London, so one possibility is that this is how he and Hewitt had met. No follow-up correspondence has survived, so it is a matter of speculation whether Hewitt ever did provide any painting lessons.

Life continued more or less as usual for Hewitt and his family until August 1940 and the Battle of Britain. He was so moved by the aerial battles in the skies over Southern England, and the losses, that he wrote a poem and turned it into a drypoint etching. This is his only known prose print:

Battle of Britain
He had loved who went smiling into death
For England. She with happiest fields to give,
And dear hearts worthy of that final breath;
Her song, her more profound self hard to live;
And those not lapped in old, soft Lydian airs,
Who had known, looking onto yesterday,
Seeing those flowers – garland grave which bears
That youth, her soldier, smiling from that clay.
Knowing this, and our quietly gleaming seas,
Our far-off sons, and simple force of love;
The loyalty of these dead, bringing us peace,
Triumphant calm restraint that in us frees
To deep humanity, we were above
Some bitterness to have this faith not cease.

The work is signed in the plate 'Henry Rayner, London, Sept 1940, under fire'.

By the end of September the war had entered a new and more deadly phase for the residents of London, with the commencement of bombing raids. Between the autumn of 1940 and 1944 Hewitt and his family were separated on three occasions, as Theresa and the girls were moved to safer places. The first time was in November 1940, when they left London for the city of Leicester. Then in 1941 they were evacuated to a small village called Sutton near Ely in Cambridgeshire. There was a third evacuation in July and August 1944, this time to Leicester again.

Theresa and Hewitt corresponded regularly during these periods of separation, sometimes even daily. Hewitt's letters have been lost but many of Theresa's have survived. There are three batches of her letters, covering periods in 1940, 1941 and 1944. They give moving insights into the pain of separation and the deprivation and dangers of wartime Britain.

The family was trying desperately to stay together in spirit. Money was constantly in short supply. The children were missing their daddy. Their schooling was seriously interrupted. The family were experiencing hostility from some of the locals who resented the evacuees. Theresa was constantly urging her husband to find a way for them to be together again, either near London or somewhere else.

Sometimes Hewitt was able to visit them and stay for a few days. But he was obsessed with the need to stay in London to safeguard the family's possessions – in particular his drawings, paintings, prints and manuscripts.

Leicester, 1940

Theresa, Frances and Kay departed for Leicester from the local school. Hewitt wrote of his sadness of seeing his wife and children off. 'They were tired, and could scarcely keep their eyes open after long nights of continuous bombing when we stood or slumped in the passages of our house with others, just waiting, waiting, while the roar of guns and the whistle of bombs went on, the building shaking and rocking into the early hours of the morning.

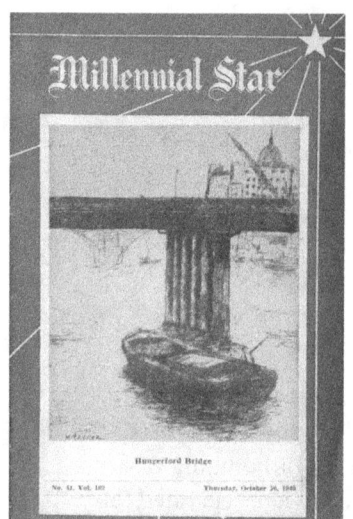

13.8 On 14th November 1940 The *Millennial Star* magazine used Rayner's drypoint of a barge near Hungerford Bridge on its front cover. © THE CHURCH OF JESUS CHRIST OF LATTER DAY SAINTS. SW.

'It was a sad farewell. Many were never to meet again. We men tried to smile it all off as the buses got into gear and the kiddies waved their handkerchiefs.'

As events turned out, Leicester would be arguably no safer than London. It was going to be heavily bombed, but when the Rayners and thousands of London families were sent there it seemed a safer place to be.

Arriving in Leicester, Theresa and the two girls were taken with many other families to the de Montfort Halls reception centre where they slept on camp beds. Then they were billeted in a house occupied by a teacher and her elderly mother, aged 98. This didn't work out, so within a day or two Theresa asked to be moved.

They were next billeted with a family called Flower, originally from London, who lived at 46 Melbourne Road. The rent for this place was high at 25 shillings (£1.25) a week. The Flower home was at the top end of the range, and Theresa was only able to afford it by asking for Welfare. In fact she had originally been asked to pay 30 shillings a week but Mrs Flower had agreed a lower rent.

This time the family seem to have fared better. Theresa described Mrs Flower as a real family woman, very thoughtful and kindly. 'The lady here is a real mother, and full of consideration. In fact the whole family is, and that is what I like. They play with the children and help them in a very good way. I consider myself fortunate in being billeted with such people. They let me do as I like – we sort of fall in with each other. I of course try to march to their tune. Everything is very orderly, and very clean and nice.'

It is difficult to date most of the letters with complete accuracy because the stamps with their Post Office franks that might have aided dating have in most cases been cut off the envelopes. In addition Theresa had the habit of dating her letters in the style 'Monday 1941'. She and Hewitt were exchanging letters often on a daily basis, so the day of the week would have been the most important reference point for them at the time.

Theresa talks of the frequent bombing raids on Leicester, and hearing the bombers overhead on what they later learnt were the massive raids on Coventry on 14th November 1940. The air raid shelter in the house where they were living in Melbourne Road was under the stairs. There was also a public shelter nearby.

The city of Leicester received some 30,000 evacuees during the second world war – more than any other city. But on the 19th and 20th November 1940 the city was on the receiving end of heavy bombing, with over 4,000 houses damaged, 550 of them seriously.

The sleepless nights and the worry caused by the raids, coupled with the separation from her husband, made life a misery for Theresa. She and the girls lived in the top floor of the house in Melbourne Road. In a letter dated November 1940 Theresa expressed her concerns about what to do for the best during a raid.

'I suppose faith is about the only shelter and strength of mind. We are supposed to get ready tonight and to go to a shelter. I don't know what to do – to remain here or not. You will think my letter panicky. The thing is, I am responsible for the safety of these children, and all this dashing about is not going to do their health any good. The billeting officer tells me it is safe nowhere, that if you get bombed, well it is one's destiny, your time is up, so to speak. I agree.'

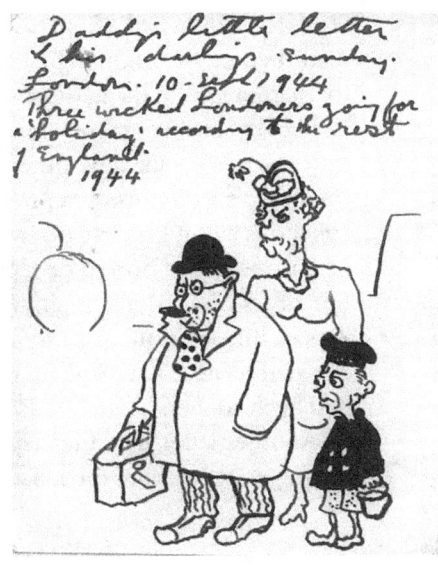

13.9 An ironic cartoon Hewitt sent to his family in 1944. They had been evacuated to Leicester for safety, and Theresa had been experiencing hostility from some locals. Ink, 115×93mm. sw.

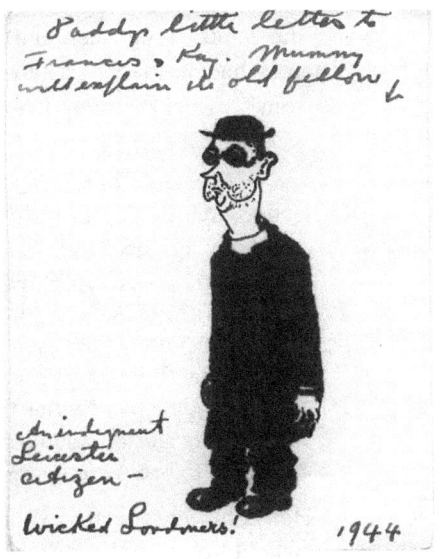

13.10 Another cartoon along the same lines, dated 1944. Ink, 115×90mm. sw.

In her letters Theresa wrote of the problems of living as evacuees, being 'billeted' on people, and not knowing how she is going to pay her weekly rent.

She was concerned about her children, as they outgrew their clothes, were disturbed by the bombing and missed their father. There are regular references to Theresa asking the authorities for money to live on.

She was also concerned about her husband's health. He seemed to get drawn into worries concerning other people, and Theresa repeatedly urges him to let the world sort out its own problems. She was constantly trying to cheer him up, solicitous about his state of health and also his state of mind.

She reminded him to drink a pint of milk regularly. 'It's food,' she points out. She urges him to take malt, buy coal for the fire, and eat regularly, and not to expose himself unnecessarily to danger. In one letter from Leicester, she says, 'I am glad to hear you have an overcoat at last, better late than never. I wished it had been sooner.'

Another letter dated Friday 20th November 1940 was written on the reverse of a typed letter from the Leicester Food Control Committee. This reads:

> Take the enclosed form (R.G.33) with your ration books and pages of coupons to any retailer in the Leicester District, who will supply you with rationed commodities during the next 14 days.
>
> When your billeting address has been definitely fixed it will be necessary for you to attend at this office during the above period of 14 days with the ration books and Identity Cards in order that the necessary change of address and re-registration with local retailers can be effected.
>
> L. McEvoy, Food Executive Officer, Leicester

The contrast between the dreadful formality of this letter and the words Theresa had written on the reverse could not have been more stark. She was obviously rather distracted. She wrote:

> Dearest Hewie
> I have your letter. Don't tell me you were out in a raid again. I don't quite understand whether the shock of your last experience or another hit from bomb splinter. I understand, I've just re-read your letter. The bombs in the road must have un-nerved you something dreadfully. I am at my wits' end to know what to do. The kiddies and you are my chief concern.
> [Here] there's the usual dashing to a surface shelter. Last night we went there in the pouring rain. The alert sounded at 7.30. I put the kiddies in the pram. Can you imagine, old Flower took the safest spot at the extreme corner. After two hours the all-clear sounded. Still pouring with rain. We dashed home. I sent the kiddies to bed. I thought 'well, they can do their damndest, I shan't move again.'

Her comments relate to the bomb-blast that damaged Hewitt's studio at 69 Mansfield Road.

There are very few references in these letters to Rayner's etching work. In one from around September 1940 Theresa says 'I must comment on your etching. It is great. Like a modern master. That's the stuff that will live.' Unfortunately there are no clues regarding which etching she was referring to.

As a postscript to one letter, Theresa talks about the etching Hewitt had made of a butcher's shop in Leicester. Evidently, the windows of the shop had been smashed during a raid.

In a letter from the autumn of 1940, Theresa criticises some sketches Hewitt has done as 'bitter'. 'Creative genius should not be so, as you yourself admit,' she points out. 'The spirit and the sight to see life in all its bright and tawdry colours is to know. And to know is to see.'

On 2nd December 1940 Theresa and the children move to a new billet in Leicester. 'She is an old lady about 65, and a daughter of 21 at business, and wants her mother to remain at home, so the billet money will help her do so. The dear soul seems to think it is too humble for us, but I assured her I like it so, and I mentioned your coming along, and she said 'the more the merrier'.

Sutton 1941

It seems that the family were reunited in London, probably in early 1941. But then, possibly in April, Theresa and the children were evacuated again; this time to a village called Sutton, hear Ely. They took the train from King's Cross station. Surviving letters have dates between August and October that year.

Life in a small rural setting was very different from Leicester, and very different from London. The first billet they were given was an unheated room in a small farmhouse. Older daughter Frances, just five and a half at the time, recalled that it smelt badly of cows. The very next day they moved into the next-door farm run by a Mrs Batchelor, and stayed there until they left Sutton.

Life in the fens had its compensations, though. Frances discovered horses, triggering a lifelong love of horse-riding (although she didn't start riding until

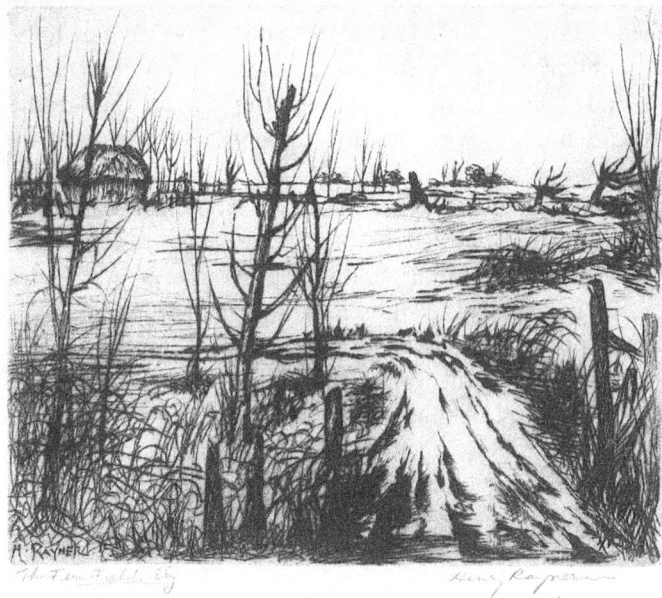

13.11 Hewitt used the opportunity of rare trips to visit his family to sketch local scenes. This is titled *'The fen field, Ely, 1942'.* Drypoint, 175×202mm. RS.

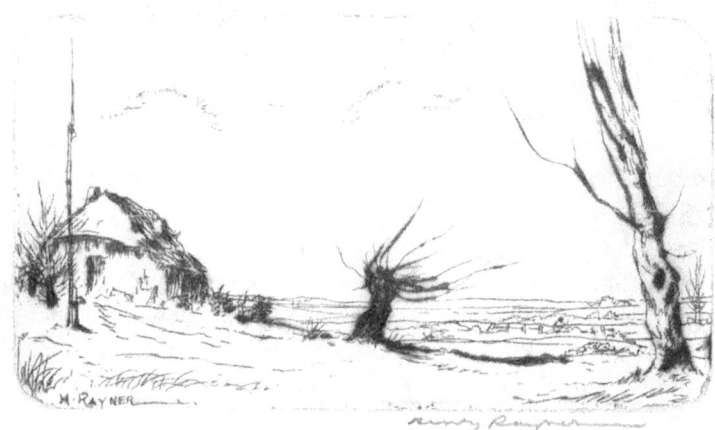

13.12 *'The flagstaff'*, also known as *'The fens of Ely'*, 1945, drypoint, 88×155mm. sw.

the age of 14). Despite the rural setting they were very aware of the continuing war. Columns of tanks would pass the front of their temporary home, and Frances would sit on the gate waving to the soldiers. In the distance they could see barrage balloons.

Financially, times continued to be tough for the Rayners. Theresa made clothes for Hewitt, and sent them by parcel. One garment was a corduroy jacket in a striking yellow colour that lasted Hewitt for the rest of his life. On one occasion Theresa posted him two apples. On another, tomatoes, potatoes and raspberry jam she had made.

He sent her parcels containing things she had asked him to buy, such as buttons, fabrics and wool for the clothes she was making. He also sent surprise items such as bacon, and on another occasion a packet of sweets. She scolded him for sacrificing his ration allowance in this way. One parcel, when Theresa and the children were in Sutton, contained a children's tea-set which they loved.

Meanwhile the two children were growing up and missing their father. Theresa sometimes included little drawings and messages from the 'kiddies' in her letters to Hewitt. Schooling was seriously disrupted – something that Frances felt gave her a lifelong disadvantage.

In October 1941, Theresa talked in a letter about a change in the rationing laws so that only children were entitled to oranges. She was experiencing what she saw as unfair treatment from one of the local shopkeepers in Sutton. Oranges are important to her, to help the children fight off colds. She is planning to return to London in the next few days. 'I hear mothers are simply streaming home,' she wrote, 'winter time, they all want to be in their own homes. … It's beginning to get quite bleak. I think that winter time here would not do the children much good.'

She also tells Hewitt that Frances is suffering from whooping cough, and the doctor said she will have it until May. 'Perhaps the London air may change that.

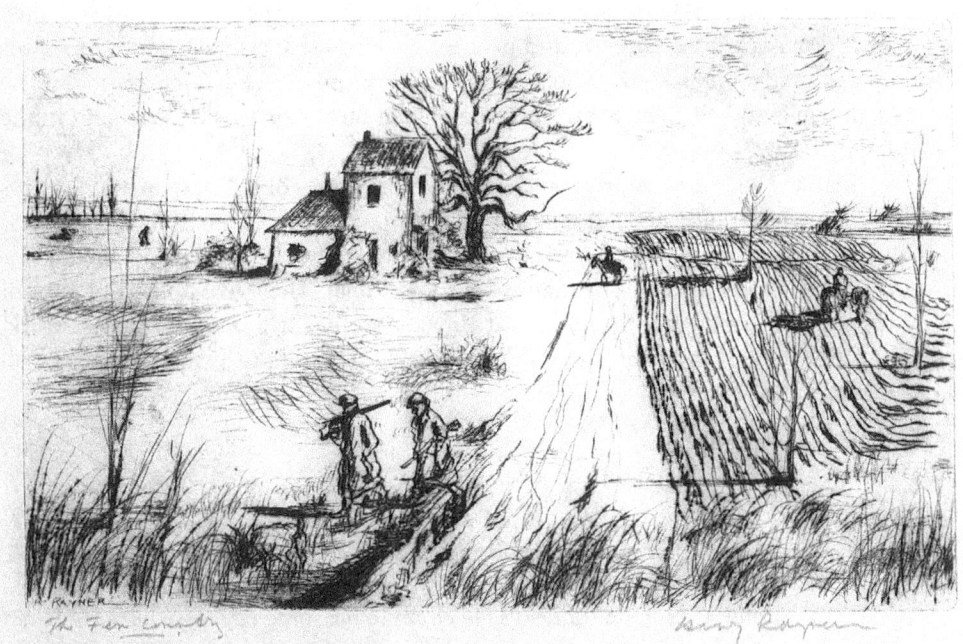

13.13 Another work inspired by a visit to Cambridgeshire, this is titled *'The fen country'*.
Drypoint, limited to 15 prints, 160×248mm. RS.

It's not a sickness to worry about. The worst thing about it is that she won't be able to attend school.'

It must have been around this time that Hewitt and Theresa realised that their younger daughter Kay was suffering from learning difficulties. The subject was carefully excluded from any of their letters, and the only documentary evidence of the matter is some correspondence from the later 1940s about Kay's special schooling needs. Kay's problems were also confirmed by Barbara Griffin in an interview in 2005.

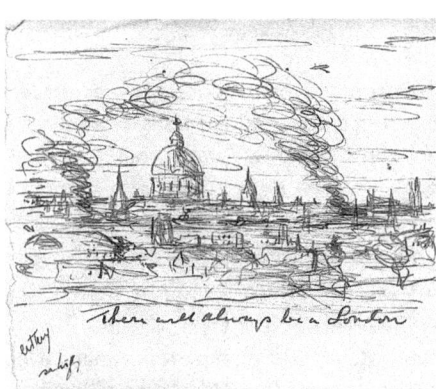

13.14 *'There will always be a London'*. A 1944 sketch from Hampstead Heath. Pen and ink, 90×150mm. SW.

Theresa and the girls did move back to London that month, and were reunited in the 18 Allcroft Road flat. They were met at King's Cross railway station by Hewitt, and Frances later wrote about keeping an eye open for 'a head that would be higher than most on the crowded platform.'

Although almost none of the letters written by Hewitt to Theresa during these war years have survived, there are some letters he wrote to his two daughters. It was his practice to write to them almost every day, right through the periods of separation. But these letters were never posted. They were done as a kind of diary, and perhaps as part of Hewitt's wish to arrange his affairs neatly, for posterity. 'Some day you may read these letters, some day,' he wrote on 23rd February 1942. 'Some day when our fields shall shine again in the happy peace.'

'Dad preserved memories, and he cared for echoes of the past,' wrote Frances in her own unpublished autobiography.

The letters themselves have not survived but Rayner himself included a few from early 1942 in his draft manuscript *Red Violet*. They give a vivid picture of his state of mind (and body) at that time, as well as insights into his art work, and the state of the war. The references in these letters to his painful arm will become clear shortly.

London, 23rd January 1942

My dearest Frances and Kay

My Children

Sickert died yesterday. News has just come through from St George's Hill, Bathampton, Bath, where he lived. He was eighty one years of age. He worked to the end. Dies quite suddenly. He wrote to me some days ago, but I could not understand his writing.

We are still braving the threats of a harsh enemy in a new year. The milk-man dragged his sledge, or, rather, soapbox, filled with milk bottles, down our street this morning. The place is piled high with hard and glistening snow. The dead cold has chilled us for days. Coal is so scarce; my room has been at a lower temperature than it should have been; but this evening a sudden change in the wind has caused a quick thaw; and the loosening snow drips, drips, drips from every roof and window. Only the sound of dripping water. All else is silent.

I have been home for some days now, fighting the cold in my chest and endeavouring to get back the use of my shattered arm. One finger after another is reclaiming its nervous strength, but the arm itself remains stiff. One has faith. Just enough freedom of hand has been left me to slowly draw and paint, and no more! I am making the best of my experience and trying to convert it into grand thought and useful action.

Today the market was empty … able to buy a ham bone that was placed in the casserole and made into soup, much rice being added later as a filling. I try out five more etching plates, and draw in the motifs (war scenes), the first drawing work I have made since the smash. The best design is the new Lambeth Walk, a dance drypoint.

But who will want art now? The Germans are thrusting at us in the east; and the Japs threaten my own land, Australia, which is without protection; and every day we receive less food, less clothing. Shall we survive?

At the moment, one sits by the kerosene stove, etching a plate … Shall I ever have the strength to print it? Mummy has promised all aid. And you are too young to read my letters yet.

God bless you. Daddy Rayner.

London, January 28th 1942

My Dears

Churchill has spoken in the Commons. London is silent, isolated, alone. All through last night enemy planes circled over the city, in a chill windy sky. Searchlights played softly into the cold spaces. I lay prepared, gazing through the curtains. Could not sleep at all. Arm painful. It was your birthday yesterday, Frances dear. I did not forget you, and have sent some pastry. Snow has fallen again. The Battleship Barham sunk, 1000 dead! Arm is very stiff. I look at my dusty printing press. Hope to try to pull twenty or thirty proofs Saturday with outside help.

God bless you, Daddy

London, 14th Feb 1942

Dears

Enemy planes over the city all last night, little bombing. Today I visited Miss Sylvia Gosse, the great British woman painter, at her studio in Belsize Park Gardens (where she had moved from Camden Road). We talked about Sickert, who had been her very close friend for many years. She tells me that Therese Lessore, his wife, is remaining in Bath, and greatly laments his passing. She has given me an introduction to Mr. Wright of Colnaghi's, Bond Street.

Her charming little basement sitting room is strongly reminiscent of the '90s. I felt that she was very lonely. She said that Robert Emmons in his book on Sickert had captured in time so many of those little facts that might easily have slipped into oblivion. That is right; he was very thorough, and had a great esteem for Walter. She was amazed at the number of my prints that had been sold in the last six years … I am waiting for you …

Daddy

London, Feb 22nd 1942

My Dears

Snow lies thick everywhere. The Japanese take everything before them! We still breast the storm.

This morning I saw a notice outside a shop in Camden Town: HORSEFLESH SOLD HERE FOR HUMAN CONSUMPTION. Have not had meat for days.

I am in mourning for Sickert. I feel a void now he is gone. Strange, but I feel exactly as if my own father had died … only his favourite paper *The Times* gave his death much notice. I feel lonelier, more isolated … I attempted to visit him before he passed, and was on the point of departing for Bath when the fateful smash came …

Your latest Shakespeare song UNDER THE GREENWOOD TREE you sing very prettily, Frances, Mummy tells me.

God bless you both, Daddy Rayner.

Leicester 1944

In September 1944 he sent his daughters two little cartoons he had drawn, to cheer them up. The ironic tone of the cartoons says a lot about the treatment his wife and daughters were receiving from some people in Leicester, where they were billeted. He obviously thought his daughters would not really understand the irony, judging by his comment on the card: 'Mummy will explain'.

At around this time he also sent them a little sketch of central London, probably done from Hampstead Heath, showing the smoke from fires, and aeroplanes circling. He called this 'There will always be a London'. On the back of the scrap of paper he had written a rather odd message to send to two young children:

> Daddy's little letter to his darlings Frances & Kay
>
> Daddy wants you to be ever so bright & happy. He is very glad you have begun school. I wish I were able to go to school, too.
>
> You must tell me all about it when I visit you, as I hope to do shortly. I shall come to see Mumma and you as soon as health & circumstances permit. But my thoughts are always with you. I always want to see you.
>
> As the years go on you shall realise what it has all meant to Mumma and me, this most frightful war. Yesterday I saw women, Mummas and little children all cut to pieces by bomb and glass; & poor men like grey dead ghosts, carried out of masses of debris, their faces & bodies gashed by timber & glass.
>
> Soon all this shall pass. You shall live to make the better world & make men understand one another, your loving daddy xxxxx

Meanwhile, in London

Throughout the war years Rayner refused to leave London or to go into hospital. He never used the air raid shelters. He carried on etching and painting. And he sorted and labelled his possessions. 'I packed my papers and prints away into neat packages with my paintings and other precious belongings, each numbered and named, a readiness for death.

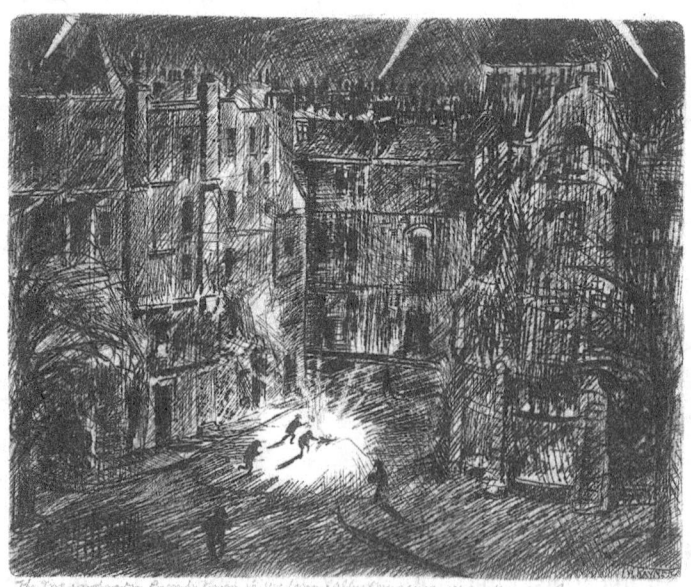

13.15 *'The incendiary bomb, from the Victoria & Albert Museum, 1940'.* Also known as *'The incendiary bomb, from the South Kensington Museum'* (the former name of the V&A). Drypoint, 180×214mm. RS.

'I went through my old diaries to while away the hours, for I would never use the air raid shelters. The old yellowed documents and photographs and letters were brought out, my first synopsis of the 1934 trek to the Isle of Wight.'

By 1940 the family had moved from Herbert Street to nearby Mansfield Road, number 69. Frances recalled the relocation from to Mansfield Road, with a van carrying most of their possessions but her father carefully carrying his important papers and art.

In November 1940 when his family were in Leicester, during the first heavy raids on London a landmine fell behind the basement studio at 69 Mansfield Road while he was working there. The blast blew out all the windows and knocked him over. He was cut by flying glass. At the time he was working on some etchings commissioned by the Leicester Municipal Art Gallery, so despite the damage he carried on working by candlelight to get them finished.

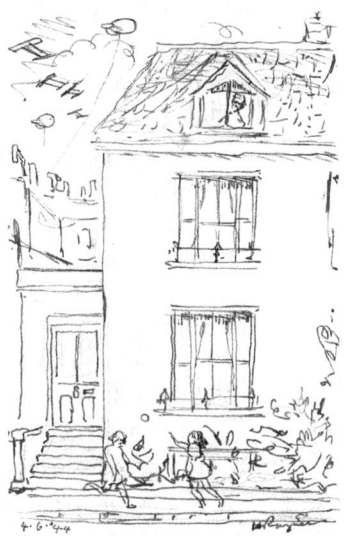

But, as Theresa explained in an interview given to the *Evening Standard* (7th January 1943), 'He had been more affected by the blast than he realised. He has never been well since.' Later in the war, on 6th February 1944, Hewitt wrote in a letter to the curator of the Merthyr Art Gallery that 'My chest was injured … and I coughed blood for nine weeks.' He was treated in Hampstead Hospital.

Even before the war Hewitt's lungs were not in great shape. He suffered badly from asthma and hay fever, ailments that were little understood and for which there were limited treatments. Experiencing bomb blast was the last thing he needed.

13.16 From one of Hewitt's wartime sketchbooks. This is the only pictorial record of the family's home at 121 Mansfield Road, Gospel Oak, on the corner of oak Village. June 1944. The family occupied the first floor and attic. sw.

Never a person to let a picture opportunity slip by, Hewitt did a drypoint etching of the devastation in his studio after the bomb blast.

In the days that followed he stayed put in his basement studio, every night listening to the 'nagging drone of enemy planes and the burst of anti-aircraft fire from Primrose Hill. … The shattered windows of the studio were still only covered with light pieces of cardboard and sheeting'. He wrote of the silver balloons that hung over an embattled city.

He recalled one very bad night when 'hell on earth began. The guns opened up, as, at the same time, the sound of planes sweeping in from the north filled the air around me, plane after plane diving, with heavy zoom of engines following on, and the sickening immediacy of exploding bombs and the familiar crash of broken glass. The blast of a distant bomb bursts the outside door open, and icy air came streaming in.'

The bombing on this area of London was heavy, which at first sight seems strange as there were no major factories or other obvious targets in the vicinity. The locals believed that the bombers' target was the main railway line that passed between Gospel Oak and Hampstead Heath. By the end of the war there were many bombsites where houses had previously stood. But the railway line escaped unscathed.

Hewitt was very conscious that his studio was in the basement of the house. Every day he saw houses that had been bombed, causing the entire building to collapse into the basement. So he moved, just a few hundred metres to a house at 18 Allcroft Road. Letters from Theresa in Cambridgeshire from July, August and October 1941 carry this address. He continued to live there through into early 1943, and it was given as the family's address in an article in the *London Evening Standard* in January that year.

During this period he met a watercolourist called Thomas Hennell, whose work impressed him. He described Hennell as a lanky bohemian but abstemious, with the gift of the gab. 'He painted in crisp pearly grey-green light morning airiness; country scenes of unsurpassing beauty. He came to London to sell his wares from a large portfolio he carried under a long arm. He wore his trousers a little short, and as he hastened through the city he attracted considerable attention.

'He would bring a bouquet of flowers to dealers, if they happened to be women; and he handed them over with a charm of old-time courtesy that captured their hearts immediately.

'He wanted me to join up with the different art societies he belonged to, and never tired of speaking of the 'new blood' that was needed in the art world of Great Britain. He said that he had discovered an unknown artist whose works had surely inspired Sickert's early and best painting, but I never learnt who that unknown man was'.

Hennell later became an official war artist, and survived the D-Day landings but was killed in Burma during an uprising in 1945. His watercolours have received growing interest, especially since the publication of a biography in 1988. In May 1948 Hennell would contribute some of his wartime photographs to a small exhibition Hewitt set up in his studio/home.

Hewitt was eager to do his bit for the war effort, but on 18th July 1941 his military medical examination by Holloway Medical Board resulted in a Grade III classification. His health problems made him unfit for military duties. 'The army refused me,' he later wrote.

Undeterred, he worked as a volunteer on stretcher parties dealing with the results of the nightly bombing. 'I joined up with the stretcher party in Allcroft Road, hoping to do my bit, but was one of the first bomb victims.' Thereafter, he concentrated on his art: 'Only my art could sustain me, and only this I possessed to give to the world.'

On 27th December 1943 he received a letter from the Regional Commissioners for the number 5 (London) region, certifying that he was exempt from all duties under arrangements in force under the Fire Guard (Business and Government Premises) Order 1943; and all duties under the Fire Guard (Local Authority Services) Order 1943. The letter was sent to him at 18 Allcroft Road, and redirected because by then he had moved to 121 Mansfield Road.

Despite the evacuation separations, Hewitt did manage to visit his wife and children from time to time. A visit to Leicester in 1940 resulted in the '*butcher's shop*' etching. He was in Leicester again on 2nd December 1940, when he purchased a small oil painting by G. Boswell, a potteries painter, at the Potteries Museum.

Visits to Cambridgeshire in the autumn of 1941 resulted in several etchings of local scenes, including '*the fishing contest*', '*Fen field, Ely*', '*Fenland*', '*Fen cattle*', *Ely Cathedral* and the series of wildfowl etchings.

During one of these visits he took a doll's pram for the children, which he had purchased second-hand in Camden Town. Frances and Kay loved the little pram, since the travelling around during evacuation did not allow much in the way of toys.

While his wife and children were away in Sutton in November 1941, Hewitt was again injured badly. This time, there were no bombs involved. At least, not directly. He slipped while sketching in the ruins of a bombed building and shattered the elbow of his working arm – he was left handed. 'He became very ill indeed and was unable to do any work at all for over a year,' Theresa would later tell a journalist (*Evening Standard*, 7 January 1943). This was a slight exaggeration. Hewitt's own account of this period refers to the drypoints he made and printed during 1942.

His left arm and hand were practically useless. He underwent a major operation called an 'excision of radius' in the Mount Vernon Military Annexe of the Middlesex Hospital. Hewitt always held the surgeon who had carried out the work in very high esteem. And so he might: it was Arthur Sydney Blundell Bankart, one of the great names in orthopedic surgery, neurosurgery, and paediatric surgery. By then he was close to retiring, but working as hard as ever.

While Hewitt was in hospital, on 7th December his stepfather Harry Gillard died, and was buried in Boroondara cemetery, Brighton, alongside his first wife.

On 18th December 1941, Theresa wrote to Hewitt, still in hospital. She had taken the children with their skipping ropes to the circus (this reference is to Lismore Circus, originally a small park, but newly disfigured with air raid shelters). She is planning to visit him next on Boxing Day, taking advantage of the fact that on that day patients can have two visitors. She evidently found Hewitt looking relaxed on her last visit, and elder daughter Frances had said 'Doesn't daddy look lovely, in bed there?'

The operation was followed by physiotherapy and ray treatment designed to recover the use of muscles and nerves. His foot had also been damaged, and he found himself doing exercises alongside crippled sailors.

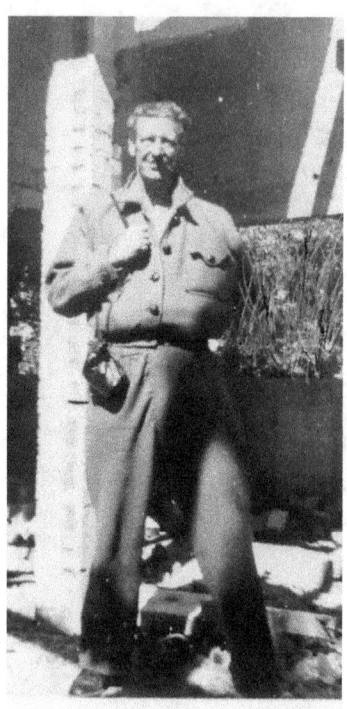

13.17 In the Spring of 1942 Hewitt's left arm (his drawing arm) was still in a sling from the fall he took in November the previous year. sw.

This must have been a traumatic time for an artist. He wrote: 'in the long nights, in my studio, I would say to myself 'your line is gone, you will never paint and draw again'. My artist's touch had indeed gone.'

He was discharged from hospital in mid-January 1942, in the middle of an extremely cold spell in London. Milkmen were using improvised sledges to deliver the milk. Snow was piled high in the streets. Coal was scarce. As well as his damaged left arm, Rayner was suffering from a chest cold.

On 23rd January he wrote one of his never-to-be-posted letters to his daughters. In addition to his state of health, the cold, the food shortages, and his worries about his future ability to draw and paint, Rayner had just received yet more bad news. The previous day, his friend and mentor, Walter Sickert, had died.

He missed Sickert. 'It seems strange and even morbid to say it but I sorely missed the presence of Walter. His magnetic and pervading personality had become almost part of myself. Most of all, I missed his criticism. Not that I ever relied on him for my 'grip', but his words had been ever a solace to my doubting.'

Hewitt must have been especially upset by the fact that in November the previous year when his accident happened he had been planning a trip to Bath to see Sickert. It never happened, of course, and now it was too late.

Hewitt's low spirits are evident in the letter to his daughters. 'One finger after another is reclaiming its nervous strength, but the arm itself remains stiff', he wrote. 'One has faith. Just enough freedom of hand has been left me to slowly draw and paint, and no more!'

He bought a tennis ball, and started bouncing it with his crippled hand. This speeded his recovery, and within a week he found that he was able once more to hold an etching needle firmly, and 'turn it to my will with steady driving force and cut sweetly into the metal plates, throwing up the same rich old burr that used to bring me the praise of Walter.'

But the arm itself remained stiff and useless for other work. 'This old left arm is a bit too stiff to be any good for painting any more, but it's all right for etching and that's my favourite medium anyway,' he would later tell a journalist.

It seems that Hewitt's painting skills did recover further, since there are some watercolours and oils that date from later periods. But most of his work as a painter was done prior to the accident.

As the days went on, he regained the strength in his left hand, and was able to increase his output of etchings. He started etching blitz scenes, without official authority as he later admitted, and also making new '*Les Sylphides*' plates, 'to help cheer people up and take their minds off the war.' Another new work was '*The Lambeth Walk*', proofed a day or two before 27th February. He described this work as a great success. He also printed the first proofs of his drypoint from 1941, showing St Paul's cathedral after bombing.

In early 1942 he was selling prints door to door. One of the people who admired his work and purchased four prints on her doorstep was Stella Morris, then living in Hampstead at 21 West Heath Close. As a nurse with experience of looking after wounded soldiers, Mrs Morris took pity on Hewitt who had his damaged arm buttoned up inside his blouson jacket. Her son Leslie told the author in 2012 that his mother had mistakenly assumed that Hewitt had lost his arm in the Great War. He also recalled his mother saying that she had paid £5 for the prints, although whether this was per print or for all of them is uncertain. The sum of £5 for each print would have been a lot of money in those days.

The four prints she purchased were '*The blitz begins 1940*' (the work also known as '*Last night a short alert was given*'); '*Chelsea Old Church*'; '*Westminster Abbey, 1941*'; and '*Augustus John and the Blue Cockatoo, Chelsea 1937*'.

In early 1942 Hewitt met up one evening with Philip Wilson Steer in Chelsea, during one of the worst periods of bombing. The two of them had walked along the Embankment from Cheyne Walk to the Suspension Bridge. 'Steer moved very slowly, his gas mask in its square black case dangling in front of him like a beggar's collection box,' wrote Rayner. 'He would never stir abroad without this case.'

As they reached the head of Pier Street, Steer (who was blind by then) turned his head towards the golden evening light at the head of the Reach. Despite the planes droning and circling overhead he said quietly, lifting his hat from his head: 'I always think the river is at its best at this hour.'

The Germans were during this period trying to bomb the Lots Road Power Station, which provided electrical power for the London Underground. The power station was only a few hundred yards from where Steer lived. 'It disturbed him not,' Rayner recalled, 'he seemed to be unmoved by the bombing almost every night, this man who might be considered the greatest in paint after Sickert.

'A couple of weeks after this meeting, Steer died', says Hewitt. It is a matter of fact that Steer died on 21st March 1942, so this meeting on the Embankment would therefore have been in February or March.

In September 1942, a copy of Rayner's portrait of King George VI was accepted by the Castle Art Gallery & Museum in Nottingham.

Ironically, it was just at this time, when Hewitt was trying to recover from his injuries, that his commercial success gathered pace. In the winter of 1942 a letter arrived from the Palace, commanding Rayner to send a selection of his latest works. 'Now was the test of the latest endeavours with my crippled hand,' he recalled. 'So many of my old works were sold, or destroyed by enemy activity. I was compelled to supply new ones. The Queen inspected them while the bombs dropped on London.' Following this inspection, she purchased another portrait of the King, as well as a drypoint of '*Chelsea Old Church*' (largely destroyed by bombing in 1941).

In February 1943, the Aberdeen Art Gallery paid £3.3.0 for a copy of his '*Cheyne Walk, Chelsea*', drypoint. Four years later, the gallery would also acquire copies of the '*Augustus John*' drypoint, and the '*Lambeth Walk No. 2*' work, for a total cost of £11.11.0. In April he received a cheque for £5.5.0 from the librarian at Windsor castle in payment for three drypoints, although Hewitt's copy of the hand-written receipt doesn't record the titles.

Commercial success continued. The Belgian Minister of Finance purchased a proof of '*When we stood alone*'. 'The term caught on,' said Hewitt. 'One heard it repeated in the press.' The '*Lambeth Walk*' was acquired by the Aberdeen Industrial Museum. Albert Einstein purchased a proof of '*Les Sylphides No. 5*'.

In early 1942 he approached the British Museum to see if they would be interested in acquiring some of his drypoints. On 19th March he heard back from A M Hind, Keeper of Prints & Drawings, inviting him to send in a selection of prints, but pointing out that even when they had funds available, the trustees practically never approved the purchase of contemporary prints. There was, however, a tiny glimmer of hope in Hind's letter, when he mentioned the small prints & drawings fund of the Contemporary Art Society.

The Russell-Coates Museum & Art Gallery in Bournemouth acquired a copy of one of the Barnsbury Park prints of Sickert wearing his fez and reading *The Times* newspaper, dating from 1931 or 1932. In one of his letters to the museum director, a Mr Silvester, dated 4th July 1943 Hewitt noted: 'In this drypoint [Sickert] is talking about 'the silly Academy banquets, which do not attract me. I shall not be intimidated into going!' Hewitt recalled that day eating boiled eggs fresh from The Angel, Islington, and drinking delicious coffee, before going for a walk with Sickert 'down Park Street to his shed studio, he wearing Wellingtons, a red scarf and large straw hat, and talking French to the huge interest of dawdling cockneys.'

This reference going down Park Street to a 'shed studio' is a bit of a puzzle. This was the period when Sickert had his big studio at Highbury Corner – hardly a 'shed'. So this 'shed studio' reference could indicate some other unrecorded premises that Sickert rented nearby. If so, it must have been near his home, as he was not noted for walking any great distance. The street name could be shorthand for Barnsbury Park itself.

By January 1943 Hewitt and his family were reunited, at least temporarily, and living at 18 Allcroft Road. Hewitt and Theresa were photographed for an article in the *Evening Standard* on 7 January 1943. Hewitt is in bed. Only his right arm is visible. The two of them are looking at some of his etchings. He is described in the accompanying article as 'ill but cheerful'.

At about this time Hewitt returned to the Cheribink fairy stories he remembered from his childhood, and compiled a new hand-written book of stories for his daughters.

He and Theresa were obviously still working hard to interest the press in his work. On Friday 1st January 1943, the *Daily Express* William Hickey Column ran a piece about Rayner. It mentioned the usual information about the artist, and ended with:

> 'This artist seems to thrive on difficulties. His studio was blitzed; his painting arm was broken. He is at work again – facing the future, says his wife, 'with high old British serenity.
> 'Certainly he has my warmest New Year wishes'

A further comment appeared on 28th January in the Beachcomber column, without any accompanying explanation:

> Motto for ambitious artist SIMPLY ETCHING TO SUCCEED

It seems that Hewitt and Theresa must have contacted William Hickey and invited him to visit them at their home in Allcroft Road, because he wrote them a note on 21 February:

> Dear Mr Rayner
> Many thanks for your welcome invitation. I should like very much to come and see your work, and try your coffee. For the next week or so I am absolutely overwhelmed with work and engagements, but I will keep your address by me and get in touch with you again as soon as I can find a spare morning.
> Yours sincerely
> William Hickey

It is not known whether anyone from the William Hickey column ever visited the Rayners, but something happened that incurred Hewitt's wrath, because he wrote a letter of complaint to Lord Beaverbrook, owner of the Daily Express, about what had been published.

On 28th March the newspaper's editor wrote back:

> Dear Sir
> Lord Beaverbrook has forwarded your letter to me.
> I have examined the cuttings of the comments made by William Hickey on your art exhibition, and on yourself, and I confess I cannot see that he has done anything but present you in a proper light. His comments seem to me to be entirely in praise of your great work, despite the difficulties of war-time.
> I regret that you have interpreted these comments in another way. There was never, I can assure you, any wish to print anything that would be hurtful to you.
> I will convey your feelings to Mr Hickey, and if there is any way in which we can help you, we will gladly do it.
> Yours faithfully
> H. S. Gunn
> Managing Editor

The comments in the William Hickey column had one unexpected result when a journalist called Guy Innes wrote to Hewitt in January. He had seen the pieces in the *Daily Express* and *Standard*, and as a result was planning an article for the *Melbourne Herald and Sydney Sun*. He asked Hewitt to answer a list of questions for the article.

In April that year, Hewitt was in contact with Dr Karl Parker, Keeper of the Department of Fine Art of the Ashmolean Museum in Oxford. Dr Parker was evidently receptive to acquiring some of his drypoints, so Hewitt posted off a selection including several of the Chelsea works. Dr Parker selected six for the museum's collection. They were the '*Old Lombard Café*', '*Cheyne Walk*' (a version dated 1925 showing the view from across the river, with Chelsea Old Church on the right), '*Chelsea Reach*' (both from the Chelsea set), '*The Etcher, 1938*' (one of Hewitt's self-portraits), '*T E Lawrence*' and '*The presentation at the Temple*'.

All six prints are today in the Ashmolean Western Art archive, together with two letters Hewitt sent to Dr Parker. These reveal some interesting insights into how Rayner himself viewed the works. In a letter dated 28th April 1943 he wrote: 'I think '*The presentation…*' is considered my best subject drypoint next to '*The Last Supper*' which is in the Royal Library, Windsor.'

This comment if his about '*The presentation…*' is interesting, in that there is only one other reference to in his papers – in a list drawn up by Theresa, which notes that Portsmouth Museum acquired a copy in October 1943.

A few weeks later, on 16th May, he wrote again to correct the date of the '*T E Lawrence*' work, which should have been dated 1929 and not 1928. He wrote: '… Lawrence arrived in London January 1929 if I remember rightly, & I saw him about the 16th in Barton Street, London.'

He concluded by saying: 'I am pleased to be among the Contemporary Collection – your collection, Mr Parker. It will be your heart's pride. I gave a few of the best I've done, & feel very happy about it.'

It is worth noting in passing that the Ashmolean's print collection at that time was almost entirely devoted to work by the Old Masters. There was no publicly-stated intention to build up a contemporary collection, but presumably Dr Parker must have said something unofficially to Rayner about his future plans in this respect.

After several years of moving home within Gospel Oak, including a short period at 45 Herbert Street, in early 1943 the family settled into number 121 Mansfield Road. This would be their home until 1955. As he had done with their earlier homes, Hewitt always gave his address as 'The Studio'.

The house is no longer there. It was pulled down in the 1960s, together with most other properties on the south side of the road to make way for a large local authority housing development. There are no surviving photographs of the house but a childhood drawing by Frances and a sketch by Hewitt both show an end-of-terrace property with steps going up to the front door. Their home was probably on the corner of Mansfield Road and a road called Oak Village which ceased to exist when the whole area was redeveloped.

The Rayners occupied the first floor flat. This gave them a large living room, a kitchen, and two bedrooms in the attic. The girls slept in the front bedroom. Evidently these attic rooms were uncomfortably hot in summer, and cold in winter – and when it rained the roof leaked. The weekly rent for this unfurnished flat was 17/6 at first. On 5th April 1954 it rose to £1–0–3, said by their landlord to be necessary as a result of an increase in local council rates.

According to Barbara Griffin, a school-friend of Frances, there were two large oil paintings by Hewitt on the walls of the main room. One was a view of Kensington in the rain. The other was a nude Theresa, reclining. Some visitors evidently found this an unusual subject for the wall of a lounge, but the family seemed unaware of any embarrassment.

There was a small balcony at the back of the house where they kept a tin bath containing coal for the fire. From this balcony it was just possible to see St Paul's Cathedral.

Hewitt had an ambition to become an Official War Artist, but his first application had been turned down. One day in June 1943 he visited Augustus John at his Tite Street studio to ask if John could help him. He probably knew the older artist through John's son Edwin – a fellow-student of Hewitt's at the Royal Academy Schools.

A plan was hatched for a batch of ten Rayner drawings and drypoints to be put before the War Artists' Advisory Committee by Augustus John himself, aided by his wife Dorelia. On 6th September Hewitt received a letter from Sir Kenneth Clark, informing him that the etchings would be shown to the War Committee at their next meeting. However, the letter also pointed out that there were no vacancies for full-time War Artists, and the committee was reluctant to commission etchings as they had no means of using a number of impressions.

Four days later the committee wrote Hewitt a letter advising him that they had looked at the prints he had submitted, but they 'could not recommend purchase'.

He was bitterly disappointed. He jumped to the conclusion that this was another example of the art establishment closing ranks to exclude him, all because of the allegations against him in 1926 at the Royal Academy Schools. In pursuit of this suspicion, he went as far as to write to the War Artists' Advisory Committee, asking to see what Augustus John had said about him in his letter of recommendation. Their reply was that John's letter had been written in confidence, and he could not see a copy.

To the end of his life, Hewitt remained suspicious about this incident.

However, the dealings with Augustus John did have two benefits. The first was that perhaps to soften the blow of a second refusal the British Council included work by Rayner in its art exhibitions that travelled the world for the next two years.

The second was that Hewitt used the meetings to do some sketches that led to a close-up portrait of Augustus John dated 13th July 1943. Proofs of this were later acquired by the National Portrait Gallery in March 1945 and Bristol's Museum and Art Gallery. There are two other Rayner drypoints of Augustus John: one showing him in front of his house at 33 Tite Street, Chelsea, and the other of him standing in front of the Blue Cockatoo restaurant in Chelsea.

Although Hewitt never was appointed an Official War Artist, in later years he ingeniously described himself as an 'Unofficial War Artist'. His drypoints of blitz scenes were popular.

In March 1944 Hewitt was in Highgate Hospital. While there, he received a surprising visitor – the man who would later become Prime Minister of New Zealand, Walter Nash, accompanied by Dr Campbell, Secretary to the High Commissioner for New Zealand. When a nurse warned him of the impending VIP visit, with the advice to 'spruce himself up', he at first assumed it was a practical joke. It wasn't. Hewitt was told by his visitors that some of his works had been bought for New Zealand and they want him to approve their choice.

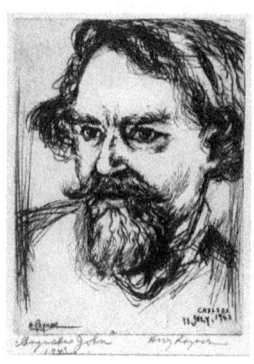

13.18 In late 1943 Hewitt visited Augustus John to seek his help in securing a position as an official war artist. He did some sketches during the visit, resulting in this print. Drypoint, 228×160mm. sw.

'Nash sat on the visitor's chair by my bed, his hat stuck on my stomach,' recalled Hewitt. 'The big handsome Campbell sat on my toes, on the end of the bed. In the semi-darkness of the night-lights the rest of the ward looked on, silent. It must have constituted a strange and unusual scene in a public hospital at that period.'

Before visiting the hospital Nash had dropped in on Hewitt's family at their home. The next day (31st March) he wrote to them from the Offices of the War Cabinet, offering to increase the amount he should pay for seven of Hewitt's prints. He had already paid ten guineas, and he proposed increasing this by £2.

This all came about because Walter Nash had spotted some of Hewitt's drypoints in the office of his colleague Dr Campbell, and written to Theresa asking if she could send him some prints to look at and make a selection from.

It's not clear how long Hewitt stayed in hospital on that occasion, but by the 3rd April he must have been back at home, because the letter from Nash addressed to him at the hospital was forwarded to his home address.

On 26th May he received a letter from Australia House about the purchase of two etchings – '*When we stood alone*' and '*London hospltal during air raid*' – for £2.15.0 and £3.10.0 respectively.

On 28th June 1944 a letter from the New Zealand Government offices at 415 Strand, London discussed the purchase of six drypoints totalling 12 gns. Hewitt later noted on the letter that Peter Fraser, Premier, acquired three of them. An earlier letter dated 11th May thanked Hewitt for the gift of a print titled '*Dunvegan Castle*'.

In July 1944 Hewitt was yet again in hospital: in Ward 1 at Highgate Hospital. He was suffering from blast shock after another bombing incident, this time the result of flying bomb raids on London. This incident was at 2.55pm on 11th July, in St Pancras Way. Theresa wasn't around to comfort him, because she and the girls were in Leicester again, and would be there through August and September.

Leicester again

Initially, Theresa was billeted with a Mrs Terry at 8 Hilders Road, which cost her £2 a week. There wasn't room there for both children, so Kay volunteered to stay with a family who lived across the road. Both host families had children of their own, and Frances and Kay were happy. From early August, Theresa was billeted at 'The Beaches', 123 Letchworth Road. She and Hewitt wrote to each other almost daily, and Hewitt managed to make some visits to Leicester. Theresa was trying to find some accommodation that would allow Hewitt to join them but this never happened.

She had taken a quantity of Hewitt's etchings with her and from time to time reported that she had sold some of them. On 27th July, for example, her letter card to Hewitt reported that she had sold etchings worth three guineas to a Mrs Renwick. In another undated letter she told him she had sold etchings worth five guineas that morning, and this had enabled her to pay off all her debts. In the same letter she wrote of her worries that Hewitt was voluntarily working in stretcher parties. 'I shall worry if you continue to assist in getting these poor people out of debris', she wrote.

On 8th August after seeing Hewitt off on a bus back to London she wrote urging him to 'say less to the ordinary people, for their mental outlook bars them from hearing you. It is a waste of time and good material. You have a remarkable brain. Keep it for your work.'

Throughout the war years the family were receiving food parcels from Hewitt's mother in Australia. These would add things like sultanas, chocolate, tinned bacon, buttered toffee, sugar and fruit cake to their rationed diet.

Theresa was also working hard to bring in money, having a salaried position during the daytime then coming home and working on dressmaking on her own account. Her home-made invoices carried the slogan 'Theresa Rayner, *Haute Couture, modèles originaux*, gowns, day dresses.

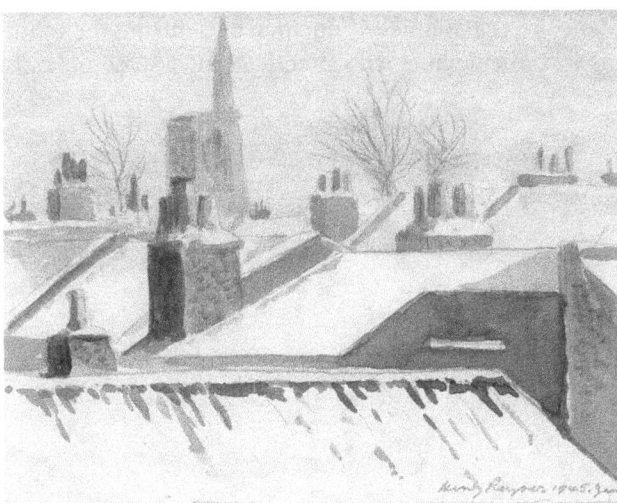

13.19 In January 1945, with the war almost over, Hewitt captured this scene from the family home, looking across snow-covered rooftops in Gospel Oak to the spire of St Martin's Church. Watercolour, 21st January 1945, 140×177mm. sw.

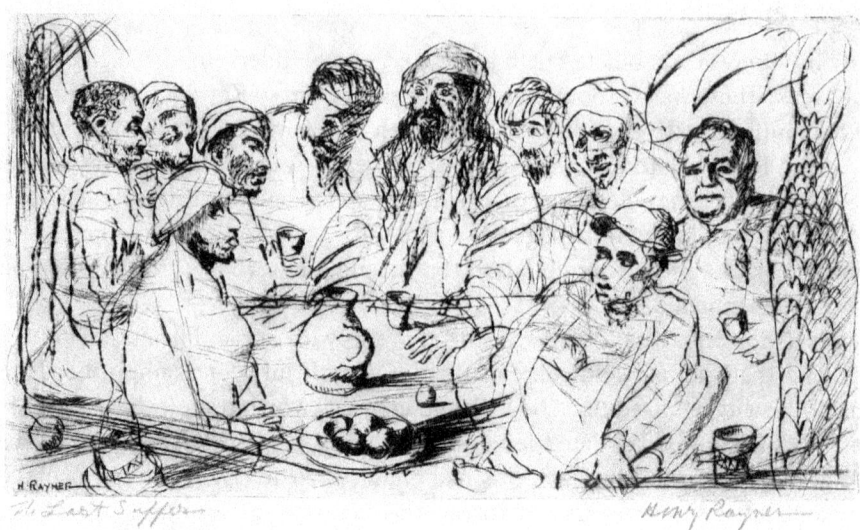

13.20 During the dark days of 1941 when he was alone in London, perhaps as an antidote to the grim reality of the blitz scenes he was sketching, Rayner turned his attention to religious themes, producing a series of drypoints of New Testament scenes. This is a study for '*The Last Supper*', 1941, 133×233mm. He has annotated this particular proof in pencil: *Study for the Royal Collection Last Supper, Windsor castle, 1942*. RS

Hewitt's physical condition remained poor. Any emotional strain such as an argument would trigger an asthma attack. When that happened he would send Frances along to the local chemists for the drugs he needed. Frances and her mother both became adept at administering the drugs with a hypodermic syringe.

Frances noted in her own unpublished autobiography that lime trees are a menace to hay fever, 'and we had two prize specimens of these in the back garden overlooking father's room.'

Rayner had little confidence in the abilities of doctors, and during the 1940s there were fierce arguments with the doctors who attended him, and complaints to the Health Authority.

14

The Ethel Mannin episode

In late 1944 Hewitt was involved in an intense but short-lived friendship with Ethel Mannin, a well-known novelist, journalist, libertarian and anarchist. He met her through Gwen Otter.

'During my convalescence she visited me, sometimes bringing eggs from her Wimbledon home, and flowers. 'A handful of hours', as she expressed it, in which we discussed the problems facing literature and the arts in general after the war.'

It was a friendship conducted mostly through correspondence. It lasted through an eight-week period. Only the letters and cards sent by Ethel to Hewitt have survived, but even reading just one side of the correspondence it is possible to follow the evolving relationship and see how quickly things progressed. And how quickly it all went wrong. Largely, it seems, because of the way Hewitt behaved, and Ethel's growing doubts about what she might be getting into by encouraging him.

From start to finish their friendship lasted from early November 1944 to early January 1945. Reading between the lines, it seems that the relationship meant a lot more to Hewitt than it did to her.

Judging by Ethel's letters, reproduced here with kind permission of her daughter, it is doubtful if the relationship was ever an affair in the modern sense of the word, despite Hewitt's strong feelings. But however far the relationship went, the correspondence makes it clear that the two of them found in each other a kindred spirit. At least to begin with.

Three years later, Hewitt wrote about this episode in a letter to his mother.

> The story of Ethel Mannin's and my own love was very tragic, and I came off worse. It was a love based on deep intellectual knowledge and feeling and sympathy. Our backgrounds were different and our minds apart. She was a Hedon, I a mystic. There we differed.
>
> As she said (you will read it in *Proud Heaven*) it was a fight of the starry forces and the earthy ones. In the book she inscribed to me, she wrote that; and it is a very ancient difference.
>
> Her devotion in soul was to the artist, the creator, the poet, but her passion tore the love to pieces … it was a strange and refting love. But the mystic cannot suffer the pangs of the world to shatter him, so the fight becomes a veritable physical campaign. And the two; the male and the female, are not a whole, but

> a contesting force flying to each other for destruction … mutual destruction … determined destruction … intellectual destruction.
>
> And if the contesting forces are not aware of the social and personal implications, all the worse for those they have to love them

What on earth his mother made of this letter can only be guessed at.

All Ethel's cards and letters to Hewitt are typewritten, usually in red ink, with the occasional edit in red pen. She probably used the red half of the fabric ribbons, which would otherwise be wasted, for correspondence to friends. She uses frequent shorthand devices as one might expect of a journalist and author. So 'your' gets shortened to 'yr', 'about' to 'abt', 'would' to 'wd' and so on.

When Ethel Mannin's daughter Jean read these letters for the first time in 2010, she commented 'Henry Rayner should have come with a health warning – 'Fragile: handle with care''.

The letters from Ethel to Hewitt are reproduced here in their entirety, with only the lightest of editing, and the omission of some comments unconnected to their friendship.

The first contact between them seems to have been when Hewitt wrote to her out of the blue, asking for a copy of one of her books. Her reply, the first of what became a steady stream of letters and cards from Oak Cottage to 121 Mansfield Road was written on 1st November. It was quite a guarded response.

> *Confessions* is an early work; it was written in 1929 & it is now 1944; both I and the world are older. The book you refer to as *Tattered Banners* is *Ragged Banners* & this is also a fairly early work. I don't know which book you mean when you say *Rose*. There is *Red Rose*, which is a novel based on the life of the veteran anarchist Emma Goldman, & there is *Rose & Sylvie* which is a study of child delinquency.
>
> I should be happy to give you one of my books without anything in exchange. But I have no idea what you would be interested in. My last novel, *Proud Heaven*, has a musical theme; *Rolling in the Dew* is a satire; *The Blossoming Bough* is an Irish novel, and so on. They are all different. If you will indicate your preference I will see what I can do.
>
> Sincerely Ethel Mannin.

The tone of her next communication, typed in red ink on a postcard dated 6th November, was very different. In the meantime, Hewitt had sent her three of his drypoints.

> Just a note to say that the pictures have arrived. It's extremely sweet and generous of you. They are lovely! I shall give the horse one to my daughter I think, as she loves horses and has great artistic appreciation. Les Sylphides & the self portrait I shall have framed for my study. Bless you and thank you. It's lovely delicate work.
>
> I am intensely interested in pictures – don't know if you know. I wish to God Picasso would paint as he used to paint (or does that seem reactionary to you? I hope not. I like craftsmanship, you see, & in all this modern stuff, all this

formlessness, there seems to be none, no technique. The Old Masters knew their job.)

Today, for you to be going on with, I've sent you my *Morality* book; I don't think it was amongst those you listed, (but the sequel to Confessions, Priv. Spec. was, wasn't it?).

I am ordering *Proud Heaven* from Jarrolds for you, also my satire *Rolling in the Dew*, also my Irish novel *The Blossoming Bough*, its comments on modern so-called art may interest you. I do hope you'll get as much pleasure from them as I do from your lovely drawings. Are you better? We must meet, if you could bear, with a pacifist anarchist (unrepentant).

Sincerely Ethel Mannin

PS: If you're not better is there anything I could bring or send you? Flowers? Eggs?

Three days later, on 9th November, Ethel sends him a typed letter on headed notepaper:

Dear Henry Rayner

I would like you to have some flowers from me to brighten your studio & you should get some tomorrow – the day you get this. I wish I could send some from the garden, but it's more or less finished now. The books are on order for you, but I don't suppose they will arrive till next week – everything takes such a time these days, and if I am to come and see you I might as well bring them. If you want me to come it had better be soon for any day now I may go to Ireland (O wild and lovely dream! It's crazy of me to count on it – I've had two applications for a permit refused these last two years, but I have a better 'excuse' for going this time, and I know in my heart I am counting on it … I've got a wee cottage out in Connemara, where all is wild and bare and as old as God; I've been over twice since the war, but my last applications were refused, the regulations having tightened up. Other people can get over – but they are all good patriotic citizens who deplore Ireland's neutrality and have no dossier at Scotland Yard, as I have). Well, as I was saying, if I am to come it had better be soon – 'in case'. I can come, let me see, not Tuesday, as I have then, God help me, to appear at the Conway Hall in the evening to speak on behalf of Indian Freedom and I shall be in a state of nerves all that day, nor can I come Monday, but I could come any other afternoon that week, i.e. Wed, Thurs or Fri. So it's up to you. Tell me how to get to you if I'm to come, what station and how to proceed from there, and don't for God's sake draw a map, for though I like maps when climbing and walking, I hate the sort of local maps people draw when it's so much easier to say turn right, turn left …

But perhaps you would rather wait till you are fit and about again before we meet? Perhaps at the Studio there is some fierce Lady of the House who frowns and says 'Who is this woman?' or merely exclaims 'That woman!' (as some do). Well, you will tell me. I'd like to come to the studio, whether I come now or later, though (if there's no fierce Lady to object – though I could make her like me even if she starts off hostile; I've done it before!) because I'd like to see more of your work. If I do come you've not got to do anything about me, no fussing with tea or anything: I will just come and look at some of your pictures and talk of this and that and go away within a couple of hours. I'm usually rather shy meeting strangers – but it soon wears off, particularly if they themselves are easy, as I think you will be.

I am wondering what you mean about the 'decision of Nature' – your health or your work?

Best wishes, Sincerely Ethel Mannin

PS: That picture in *Morality* is not really 'me'. I've less glamour but more personality! Only people who are very sentimental about me think that picture like me. I am fair, incidentally, not dark. Get so tired of people exclaiming when they first meet me 'Oh I always thought you were dark.'

In a separate note found in the Rayner archive, it is apparent that Ethel Mannin had suggested he leave London and take her cottage in Connemara.

Three days later, 12th November, she sends a postcard.

Sunday

Thanks for yrs. Yr family sounds v. nice. I am sure I shall like them & hope they'll like me. How about next Friday? (That gives you good long notice for hair brushing and washing behind the ears…)

Hope the flowers came and that they were nice. I'll bring more when I come. Also some eggs if my hens do their duty … and the books, I hope. Will keep yr instructions.

Hope you have had a better night by now? One is too busy not to be fit – has too much to do. I must go. I must go. A thousand things to do.

A bientot.

Ethel

The next day, Monday 13th November, she sends another postcard, this time hand-written in red ink, in response to a letter from Hewitt that seems to have been written on the back of one of his drypoints.

Yr lovely drypoint used as a piece of stationery! How generous you are! I love generosity. Yours crossed with mine suggesting I come Friday. I hope I may. I agree that one mustn't defer anything one wants to do – life goes so quickly & is so terribly uncertain.

Yr ill health & pain troubles me – are you receiving the best attention?

I'm afraid my translation of dreams is largely Freudian. I'm a materialist, not a mystic. I wonder what a lion cub symbolises for you!

A bientot

E

It's interesting to see the rapid change in tone of her letters to Hewitt. In just two weeks she has progressed from signing her letters and cards 'Sincerely Ethel Mannin', to simply '*a bientot*, E'. Rayner's next letter to her must clearly have indicated that he interpreted her solicitous comments about his health as 'pity'. It provokes a strong response:

Nov 14th 1944

Hell, why should I pity you? You have yr art, you have a zest for life (it seems) you have a good wife, lovely children – and a new friendship which is perhaps a little exciting and is anyhow full of promise – why should I pity you? I am always sorry to hear of ill health, particularly when accompanied by pain, particularly when it's someone with zest for living and work to do, but that's not what I mean by pity, & not, I think, what you mean when you shrink from it. That kind of compassion doesn't wound one's pride, but is a little healing – surely, surely? The gentle hand on the brow, full of tenderness …?

As to being full of confusion for a few humble gifts – hell, again. Myself I love to give, and I love receiving. I will take anything from anyone always – gladly, gratefully, as happy with the thought as with the gift. But I shall give the eggs to yr wife, who will be glad of them, being a woman and knowing that eggs are as precious jewels these days, and a dam' sight more useful – in fact I shall give anything I am able to bring to her (except the books) & then you will be spared the embarrassment (???) of having to thank me … (Damn you!)

You _have_ made me handsome presents already – your lovely pictures. And I am happy to have them, because they are beautiful in themselves and because it was dear and generous of you to give them – and because it made you happy to give them.

I like your self-portrait (there's a self-portrait in yr letters too) and unless you've grossly flattered yourself it's a good face. I like yr letters too, but oddly (or isn't it?) I didn't much like yr first – I thought I would send a book (one only) and be done with you … but it seems it wasn't to be, for yr pictures came and I said My God, he can draw (which from me is a helluva compliment; I myself would ask no more than that someone I respected should say My God, she can write!)

I wrote you a postcard in a Post Office yesterday saying I will come Friday & briefly answering your last (lioncub) letter. I hope you could read it … To this end I would now add that I shall probably arrive about 3.30. I don't really know how long it will take on the tube, but I shall leave here around about two I expect. But if it should take me longer than expect so that I arrive later you'll know I'm on the way. I'll come all right, short of being killed on the way. And I'll leave you, I think, about 5.30 and keep an appointment in town about 6. But if it's a bad day and you feel ill you must send me away before then (but I shall see, I hope, whether I tire you or not. I can't forget you're ill if you are, dammit! But it's fine news that you are working again & feeling better).

Blessings. _A bientot._

E.

Her next postcard, typed in red ink and posted the following day, is clearly in response to something Rayner wrote.

Nov 15th 1944

Please no, not as a great artist or a great person, but simply as a friendly human being who is a little shy, but full of goodwill & trust. I am horribly aware of my shortcomings both as a writer & person; I take pains & I write sincerely, but I am incurably careless – the Irish in me no doubt. As a person I mean well

& <u>want</u> to be 'good', but get so angry at times (again, the Irish I expect) & find it hard to live according to the Christian tenet of loving your enemy in which I believe (it's very hard to 'love' Mr Bevin, *par example!*). I'll be happy in your home & meeting you & yours; don't worry – & for God's sake don't fuss in any way. The thing I most dislike in people is affectation – an affected intellectualism, an affected Bohemianism – affectation & pretentiousness – ugh! I love simplicity in people & believe you have this quality, & now I positively will not write you again this week!

This resolve didn't last long.

Thursday 16th Nov 1944

My Dear

I said I positively will not write again, but your letter I received this morning compels me, for I can't determine from it whether you are angry or hurt – or merely laughing. I hope the latter. And I'd far rather have you angry than hurt – though I don't want you to be either … and there's no need. Ah, please, there's no need! (This is me taking your hand, beseeching you …)

It ought to mean something to you – it ought to mean everything – that though I didn't much like your first letter the moment I saw your work I said 'Let's meet!' It's a great tribute to you both as artist and as a person. And that I've liked your subsequent letters is self-evident, in my response to them. Of <u>course</u> there's a self portrait in letters – in everyone's! I'm not going to 'sit and analyse you'. I hope to get to know you – that's all. I am already in the process of doing so, surely? (as you are in the process of getting to know me; though you have an advantage over me in this respect in that you've got my books and can study my mental and emotional make-up at leisure and in detail). And in this way is friendship built up.

You must bear with me over my first card or cards to you. If you knew the number of people who write wanting to meet me – I've even got printed cards which I had done in desperation to send out saying how impossible it is to meet everyone. I'll enclose one! But I didn't send <u>you</u> one, did I? A writer <u>has</u> to be on the defensive – to be 'sure' before 'going out' to the stranger. As it is, being cautious, one still makes an occasional mistake, and the cost is in time, and a nervous and mental and emotional giving-out, that one can't spare. Surely you see? But I've 'gone out' to you freely, and I feel quite 'sure'. You do fine delicate work that has sensitivity and strength, and fine craftsmanship; and you have a good face; and your letters are all sincerity … <u>I have no misgivings</u>. Please believe.

I shall come empty-handed. You have quite unnerved me. I don't understand this resistance to taking what is generously offered. But I will come empty-handed, and then all the indebtedness will be on my side, and perhaps that is the way you wanted. I don't mind. I want you to be happy in knowing me. Perhaps later you will let me give to you. (But I am giving to you all the time, even in writing this, my spirit flows out to you…).

You mustn't think of trying to meet me, as I can't give you a time at which I shall arrive at Camden Town. I imagine that by reaching Waterloo at 2.30 I shall be at C.T. about 3 and *chez vous* some ten or 15 minutes later. But I don't know.

And you are 'convalescent' and the winds are cold. If it's not too cold you could perhaps come a little part of the way with me back to the bus or tube when I leave so that I can have a few minutes alone with you. I think it's difficult to get to know people with others around, however much one may like the others (and that I shall like your wife and children I am sure), But if there's a treacherous cold wind you mustn't consider it. There will be other occasions my dear, I've already come to your 'good heart'. What am I going to do about it? Exactly what I _am_ doing – give you my loving friendship.

   E.

Ethel Mannin's first visit to the Rayner's home took place as planned on Friday 17th November. The next day, she wrote him her longest letter so far.

Sat. night 18th Nov

My Dear

That I _did_ like you, you will know. That I had to go when I did was a pity for we were beginning to know each other, the initial strangeness and (in me at least) shyness having worn off. But I want to come again – perhaps sooner than you had expected. I would like to come on Wednesday if I may. I have to be in town on the evening to take a young friend to the ballet. If convenient to you and your wife I would like to come to you again at about 3, leaving in time to reach the Café Royal by 6. Please write and tell me I may come.

This time I hope I may without offence bring one or two things – some sweets to fill the children's little jars (such lovely children. I want to know them better, too, but more of this later) as I always reckon to use my sweet ration on kids, not being a sweet-eater myself (except for chocolate when I go walking and climbing with Jean) and some eggs, because now I know the nature of your illness I realise (none better) all the dietary difficulties, especially in these days, & I do want you to take care of yourself – you are valuable, not merely to your sweet wife and dear children, but to the world – and to me, your new-found friend. Also I now, at long last, have two books to bring you, and I much want you to have them – one is my Irish novel, _The Blossoming Bough_, and I think you'll like it, because it's about an artist – not a painter but a young poet; and I want you to have my last novel, _Proud Heaven_, because it too is about an artist, a young violinist, and also because I want you to see how I can get into the male mind. This book is written in the first person, as a man … and if it wasn't overburdening you I'd like to lend you the American edition of a novel I wrote back in the twenties, _Pilgrims_, which is primarily about painters. I was going the rounds of the Paris studios at the time, and living amongst painters. I expect it's 'young' and immature as to writing, but it will show you the feeling I have for painters and their dreams and their struggles (their struggles both as to work and living). I can only _lend_ you _Pilgrims_ from my files, but the other two I would like you to keep – you said we would 'exchange' our works, and I have 3 of your lovely pictures, and if you have these two books you will have (with _Morality_) 3 of _my_ works…

I meant it when I said I'd like the children to come out here. I'm sure they'd enjoy it. It's a good place for kids – a sort of 'fairy house' with old beams, and a garden full of little secret paths, and a little wood, and a pond with a fountain and fish ... I wondered if you'd all come out on Boxing Day, Tues the 26th, when I shall have a little Xmas tree. I have it every year. .... I was thinking that this year there will be no children for the tree, but if you will come with yours it would give point to it again; give point to the otherwise rather meaningless business of Xmas. There would only be me here on the 28th, and I thought maybe if you felt up to it you would come with the children and their mother (if you don't feel up to it perhaps she would bring them without you, but that would be a little sad for us all) coming out in the early afternoon ... You can tell me Wed (if I may come then). It would be a sad little tree with no children.

We only touched the edges of everything, didn't we? It was good of your wife to give us a little chance to talk *à deux* – it made it easier, I think, though she is so sweet, and intelligent, and I hope in time to know her too. I liked her very much. I like her quiet beauty, and the feeling of quietness about her. I love quietness in people – the feeling of inner stillness. Perhaps because there's so much unrest and vehemence in myself.

I am excited that you think I can make a novel of the life of Gaudier. It's exciting and, for me, 'strange', because as I told you, after letting the idea lie fallow, on Sunday I suddenly reverted to it and got out the big life of Gaudier that I have (it's the same text as *Savage Messiah*, but in this edition is called *The life of G.B.* and contains plates of his work, sculpture and drawings). I would like to go through it with you sometime – when you come here... (Ah, when! Lovely thought!)

But first I must do the idea which has been working in me for the last few months – it's an important idea, a big idea ... perhaps it's too big for me. I don't know. I only know I must do it.

Sometime you must meet sweet Reginald Reynolds, to whom I am married. We don't live together – never have – we merely legalised our relationship after four years (we've been together 10 years, 6 of them legal) mainly to please his mother and continued to live as before. I'm not to be lived with – like to be alone – <u>need</u> to be... He is a fine person. If you have *Privileged Spectator* (have you? I believe you said you have, or have read it) there's so much about him in it and a picture of him. He is an impassioned fighter for the cause of freedom – and a very good writer and poet. But there's no hurry on your meeting him. When you first come here I'd like for there to be only me. One thing at a time. Yes?

In your last letter you said that love is rare. I know. I know. Have I not often quoted that it is 'the miracle that happens to one in thousands'? Have I not said that the word is used too lightly ...That Keats greatly loved his Fanny is indicated in his letters, but whether she loved him is debatable; she seems a little trivial for his poet's fire of flesh and spirit.

When I come Wed. (as I so much hope I may) I'd like to look at your etchings. I have asked my librarian friend to get me that Japanese artist's book.

I got home quite easily (I had cancelled my evening appointment as I wanted to work) and thought of you a great deal, hoping (oh so much!) that my visit to you had been all that you hoped of it, had left you happy, and full of hope for the friendship in the making... Thank you for coming through the rain to the bus with me. And for the strength and warmth of your handclasp.

Bless you, and once again – *à bientot*

E. And after all this, I realise I haven't said Thank You for your hospitality. But I do, I do! And for so much more!

The comment about 'that Japanese artist's book' probably refers to Yoshio Markino's book *A Japanese artist in London*.

On the Monday morning 20th November Ethel Mannin received a letter from Rayner. This is her reply:

Nov 20th 1944

My Dear

I hope you had my letter today, and that it made you as happy as yours (Bless you) made me? I've left it too late now to write you all that I would – the post goes at 4 and it's already 3.30. (Ah, how little time there is always for the things one wants to do!)

I'm glad my visit seemed a gift to you. You gave, also, to me. For which, again, bless you.

No, nothing shall destroy our friendship, and it will grow, and flower, and bear fruit. It will bear fruit in the book you want me to write (confirming my own desire) and perhaps it will bear fruit in your work too, or in your spirit. In mine, certainly.

Odd your saying about no woman ever having written the Life of Jesus, because I was the woman who wanted to do it. Jesus the Man. Only I felt it was too Big – that I was not big enough. Not nearly big enough in stature either as a writer or as a person. I want to see your '*Last Supper*'. May I please? You know I'll understand. We speak the same language.

There's nothing symbolic in my dedicating the book about Brzeska to you – it belongs to you, in every way. To whom else could I dedicate it? Before a line is written it is already, in my heart and mind, inscribed to you, my Dear.

You must live! Ah, you must live! I need you, now. (I had to be ready for you, it seems. I had to discover Brzeska. I had to get other things out of the way. The 'pattern in the carpet' had to be worked out slowly, through the years …)

Why does your letter make me want to cry a little? I don't know. But it does. Though it makes me happy, too.

You'll know by the letters you already have from me how much I 'liked' you (which is an inadequate way of expressing the flow of response to a kindred spirit – so I put it in inverted commas. I felt sympathy and a flow of affection – caring – tenderness – friendship, all these things) and that I want to come again, on Wed. Soon, the day after you read this.

I must go now.

May I, without being misunderstood, send you my love?

E.

What'd you like to be called – by me? Do your friends use the name your wife uses? I don't want to 'intrude'.

This last comment was added as a footnote in Ethel's distinctive red ink. She had noticed that Theresa called her husband 'Hewie'.

Two days later, on 22nd November, Ethel writes to Theresa.

Nov 22nd 1944

Dear Teresa (if I may make so bold – in friendliness – to use your lovely name!) I feel I must write and thank you for yr great sweetness to me on these last two occasions. Not merely for the excellent tea you have on each occasion provided (I did enjoy those sandwiches this afternoon; I was hungry, having had only an egg for lunch, in the rush to get out … I do all my own housework and there's so much to do before one can get out, as you know) but for so sweetly allowing your husband and me to talk *à deux* – which is so much easier than with anyone else about, however sympathetic, in the early days of friendship. I am a little shy, and I've been grateful for yr sympathetic tact. Only in time I wd like to get to know you, too, if I may.

I thought your husband seemed v much better in every way today, much less nervy, and looking better physically, and if my friendship has helped at all (and I think perhaps it has) I am very glad. If, when he feels equal to the journey, he wd like to come out here I wd like it very much – but only if you had no objection. I would never want to do anything to hurt or worry you (but, in fact, you need not worry. However I don't think you would. Yr husband told me that you and he had complete confidence in each other, and that is how it is between my husband and myself. We regard each other as each other's Best Friend. I think perhaps yr husband wd relax here (he's such a restless person, isn't he?) where there are trees and birds – and everywhere, books! (And I wd see that he had the right things to eat, and return him to you before dark!)   I expect he told you I wd like you all to come out on the day after Xmas. I agree that one can't plan ahead these days, but I wd like it very much if you could and would come. I shall have a tree anyhow, but children give a tree (and Xmas itself) 'point'. A woman artist friend of mine is making them a doll each – but don't tell them. They are lovely children – and I have always maintained that children are the loveliest people in the world. (I should have had more … but it was an unhappy marriage, and by the time I'd made my present happy marriage it was too late.)

Now I must write a few lines to Frances …

My love to all, and grateful, appreciative thanks to you, dear Teresa.

Please believe me to be

Very Sincerely

There must have been another meeting on 23rd November, because late that night Ethel wrote a long letter.

Wed night 23rd Nov

Hewie, my dear, listen. It's midnight; I've just got in and I'm v. tired, but I must write to you now because in the morning I won't have time, as I have to go out early & be in town all day, and there are things I want to say. There are things to be got straight-

And the first, my Dear, is that you mustn't, mustn't MUSTN'T just say things that you can't possibly believe to be true – such as that I am bored looking at yr work. Oh I know you say them because of a certain self-consciousness & shyness you still feel with me, but they are like a wound in me … and part of me fills with tears, and another part of me wants to cry 'Damn you!' half-way between exasperation & crying ... because I feel you ought to know, that you MUST know, that anything of you is of interest to me. All yr etchings interested me, & some of them moved me. I <u>had</u> to say 'Give me yr hand' when we left the house because I felt that somehow in the few moments that remained I had to get close to you ... and being a very simple person, of the earth earthy (as you are of the stars starry, bless you!) I made my appeal in the only way I really know, by the physical contact ... And when the bus came (so promptly!) I didn't want to get on it! I hadn't any thought when I turned to you; only the blind impulse.

And then I want to say, you must write to me always and as often as you want! <u>Please!</u> How can I make you believe that I love yr letters? Doesn't it say anything to you that I go through the pile looking for one from you & when there is I take it out and read it first as I told you – doesn't that say anything to you? Oh it must, it must! You will write to me when you want to do so – and when you don't want to write you will be silent. And I will always answer yr letters. If I can't answer at once, nevertheless I will answer them eventually – and not so late. And unless you want to break my heart you won't say any disparaging things abt your letters, or about Henry Rayner as artist or man, for I respect Henry Rayner, both artist and man, and admire him.... And I want him to be well, and I want (so much) that he shall be happy.

I thought about you v. much during Les Sylphides tonight. I thought of how you'd tried to reach me in those other years & failed, & how it was a good thing, for you'd not have liked the woman I was then – I hadn't suffered; it had all been too easy, as I told you, & I had no sobering responsibilities as now. And I thought how yr first letter this time didn't 'reach' me – and then you sent your pictures & my response was immediate; then you reached me; through yr art – wouldn't you sooner have it that way? You cld have evoked my pity because you were sick, but how much better you should evoke my respect & admiration through yr work, Dear my Dear!

If you wd like it (and only if you wd) & feel equal to the journey perhaps you will come here & we will spend the day quietly. It is peaceful here, with birds & trees & an illusion of the country. The birds sing & there are many books. Wd you like to come? If Teresa wdn't mind. I don't want to do anything that wd hurt or worry or distress her. She has sweetness and goodness. If it's something that wd worry or hurt her, we must think no more about it. But if you wd like to come & cd do so without pain to her, then it is something I wd like v. much ... and I have an idea that you wd relax here. You are restless, restless.

I hope it made you happy coming today. I wd like you to tell me that it did. It's true that only great tiredness and the fact that it was already 1am prevented me from writing you last night. I wanted to send you a poem of my great friend the late W B Yeats, 'the uncrowned king of Ireland', & the last of the great poets. I will send you the poem now – because in yr letter before the last you referred to the Most Perfect Rose in the World ... which again is strange for I have often used that poetic phrase, Rose of all the World. Here's the poem. I wd that I had written it – for you. But here it is, for You, from Me – It is called 'The Rose of Battle'.

After the words of the poem, Ethel went on ...

'You who have sought more than is in rain or dew – you who have been washed up on 'the wharves of sorrow' – you 'the sad, the lonely, the insatiable', as all artists are whether they write or sing or paint…Well, I have said, that is from me to you. And now you will never again put up that barrier of unmeant words between us, will you, because, as I told you, there is no need (and this is me saying to you again, 'Give me your hand').

Well, you will read this – when? Perhaps on Friday if I go out and post it now (and 'now' is gone one! [o'clock]). I may or may not go to Ireland Sat. If I don't go perhaps next week you will come here for a handful of quiet hours. I will write again at the weekend if I am still here. If not from Dublin.

Bless you, Dear. Ethel.

On Friday, Ethel wrote again, proposing a day for Hewitt's visit:

Friday

My Dear; the permit hasn't come through yet. It seems as though it may next week, so if you are to come here it had better be soon. Monday is no good, so the first day is <u>Tuesday</u> – but don't arrive before 12 as I have to go to the shops and I'd hate you to arrive whilst I was out! (I'll go early in order to be back early, but I say 12 in order to give myself an outside amt of time). You won't mind my asking you to go at 5, will you, as Jean comes in for tea at 5.30 and looks forward to an intimate chat. But you mustn't come at all unless Teresa is perfectly happy about it – <u>please</u>. I like and respect her, and her devotion to you, and I wd not wish to make her unhappy or to worry her in any way. If Teresa has the slightest feeling abt yr coming here I will come to you instead on Tues – if I may.

But if you can come without anyone being hurt or worried, then you come as follows – Camden Town to Waterloo on the tube, and then on the Southern Rly to WIMBLEDON. It's quick – about 20 mins. Only three stations, Vauxhall, Clapham Junction, Earlsfield, and trains every few minutes. They go from plat-forms 1, 2, 3, and 4. But you'll see the big indicator up at that end.

At Wimbledon station you get the 93 bus which stops on the bridge. You come out of the yard and crossing the road and turning to the left see the bus stop. You get the bus up to the Rose and Crown (which was Swinburn's pub and is now EM's!!) Just past the R&C on the same side is MARRYAT RD. You go down this long straight boring middle-class road to the cross-roads, and turn left, and then in the dip, with a huge oak tree towering over, you find a small white cottage with a white gate, and that's where you turn in. … And you do NOT go in at the imposing drive labelled 'Oak Lodge', for that is nothing to do with the humble place next door … And you will forgive the neighbourhood because of Oak Cottage with its oak trees and its squirrels and its shut-awayness … or so I hope.

Please, I wasn't 'perplexed' by yr etchings. They're not at all that obscure! Some I liked v. much and some not so much and a few (only) not at all. I didn't feel called upon to comment on each one, and I can only repeat that I enjoyed looking at them and was interested – in both the artist (expressed in them) and the man in the artist.

You say you don't want to be a great artist, but in an early letter you wrote that we must be 'great or nothing'. I suggest that every artist, whether in words or wood or stone or paint or any other medium, wants to be a first-rate artist, a great artist, and that's why we all go on (those of us who are sincere) striving, and being dissatisfied and going on again.

Yr journey here will take you about 1½ hours from door to door. Just send a line when you get this to say whether you will come on Tues. or whether I should come again to you (only I can't keep on being yr guest and eating Teresa's teas! It's not right, dammit). My love to you (but we mustn't fall in love, must we? Somehow we must avoid it – so that no-one gets hurt. Not us, but others. That's important).

The planned Tuesday meeting never took place. On Saturday Hewitt received a telegram from Ethel.

Fear must disappoint re Tuesday. Reg here ill with old kidney trouble. Very worried. Writing. Ethel.

As promised, Ethel followed up with a letter, dated Sunday 26th November.

My Dear: I wired you last night. I got in about nine from a day in the country with Jean and found poor Reg here and wracked with pain – renal colic, 'the greatest pain known to surgery'. I rang the dr and he came and gave morphia. Reg had an operation for stones in the kidneys back in 1940 but they cld only get 3 out of 5 out. The other two give trouble from time to time. He was bad back in the summer. He passed a stone today and is now much better. It's a good thing I didn't leave for Dublin Sat. night or he'd have had to be all alone in his room at Chelsea. I don't know when he will be about again – it's impossible to say; another stone may be on the move too. He has to stay quiet for a bit.

I'm terribly sorry about Tuesday, Dear, but quite helpless. It just wasn't to be, it seems. But you will come here eventually, to be quietly alone in 'friendship building' with me – of that I am quite sure. Only – only – no-one else must get hurt in the process.

My love to you

I write in great haste to get the post. Have had so much to do in all day, and little time left now.

Monday night (27th November)

Hewie, my Dear. I had yr letters this morning but I have had no time to write till now. I wrote you following my wire Sunday & you shld have had this today. I blessed you for yr sweet letter about poor R's illness. These are bad, black days. He was rather better after passing a stone Sunday, but collapsed later in the a/noon and had a temp of 103 by evening & I was very frightened. This morning his temp. was down to 101, but its up again to 102 tonight, and he has been terribly ill all day; he has eaten nothing, and done nothing but lie with a cold cloth on his forehead. And there's nothing I can do except keep filling up the hot water bottle, wringing out the cold cloth, filling up the drinking water bottle, making barley water (good for kidney cases), empty the jerry, and all such small trivial things, and all the time I long so terribly to be able to relieve his dreadful pain. I phoned the dr Sunday night when his temp was so high; he thought then it might be a 'hang-over' from the morphia, as it's not unusual to run a fever with renal colic. This morning he seemed to suspect complications, but after examining him thoroughly seemed to think there was nothing abnormal, but that the stone had set up some inflammation… It's all terribly worrying and upsetting. In desperation when I was out today I spent ten bob on a small bunch of grapes for him, but he doesn't want them – not yet anyhow. One longs so terribly to be able to do something! It's been such a long history of illness, R's and my life together. He was in hospital four times in the first five years! But all this suffering has bound us together; we've been through so much together … I expect you know how it is. Or Teresa will know, anyhow, I expect. It's the bad times that really 'marry' people to each other, don't you think?

Isn't it a good thing the permits didn't come through for Ireland for Sat. night? (The sailing tickets were for then). I'd have been on the Irish sea, and poor R. lying alone with his dreadful pain in his basement room in Chelsea … talking of Chelsea, reminds me that I saw Clifford Hall in the town this morning. He is art teacher at the local public school – King's College School. I came across a reproduction of a painting in a new literary paper (oh <u>ever</u> so literary – the way I can't bear it) and I thought Hullo, a blue period Picasso – but oh dear no, it was master Clifford Hall imitating Picasso instead of Sickert, for a change. God, how I detest 'derivative' painters! One is influenced, yes, of course, but need one slavishly <u>copy</u> the master?

My Dear, my Dear. How are you? You write of a bad night again. Oh dear, I did so hope you would stay, exultantly, on the upward grade. I did so want it! We will meet just as soon as I am out of this dark wood – and how I hope I will find you with that lighted look you had in yr face last time, Dear my Dear. In the meantime you have me in my books.

I must go now, Dear. This is really only just me reaching out from the dark wood to take your hands again and assure you that I am still here, and still holding you in my heart. Bless you

Hewitt of course also knew Clifford Hall, as the two had started at the RA Schools at the same time.

The next day Ethel is less stressed by her husband's illness.

Tuesday

Hewie dear: I wrote you y/day, but it's no burden to me to write again today, to thank you for yr sweet letter, bless you. I know all the 'drill' of renal colic (alas). Reg had an operation for stones (following an attack of renal colic) in 1940; the surgeon cld only get 3 out of the 5 stones (shown by the x-ray) out he thought the other two might settle down & give no more trouble, and they didn't till this summer when he had another attack, but we got a second opinion & the spec. said he didn't think a major operation was called for, though stones were shown in the x-ray again. He too said they wd 'settle down' … and now this lot. This time he has passed a stone, but whether it's one of the 1940 lot or a fresh growth we can't know. Anyhow his temp was 102 last night, which was an improvement on Sunday, & is down to 100 this morning. His raging headache is much better & though he still feels ill (and looks awful) it's definitely an improvement, though the dr is bothered abt the continued temperature.

Well, that's the bulletin to date. I don't feel so overwrought myself today. In view of the slight improvement; y/day I cld have cried my heart out. It seems so awful that someone like Reg must suffer so, he who is so fine and self-less & generous – as you say you can count good men on yr fingers! Thugs like Churchill live to be 70 and even when they get pneumonia they survive … It's disgusting.

Dear, no one can be hurt by the flow of gentle love twixt thee and me; what I am afraid of is that we might fall in love, that we might become lovers or want to be, & then pain wd enter in for us, and for Teresa, and for someone else, & things wd be pain & conflict all round. Well, you know my definition of morality and immorality – it's all in my book. I try to stand by it. It's not always easy (by God it's not).

Oh it does mean something that you are better, my Dear; I wrote to you only y/day now much I hoped you were.

Yes, yes, only good will come of our loving friendship, if we handle it right, and I think we will – I think we will – There's the 'good heart' in us both that <u>means</u> well, anyhow!

Bless you, Dear: I can't stop for more now. This comes to you mainly to bring you news of the poor patient, and my love – my gentlest love.

The next day, a postcard

Wed.

No time for more than a hurried pc today as I've had to go out & had a lot to do & the post goes in half an hr & I've other letters wh ought to be dealt with. But it's to thank you for yr sweet letter – particularly for the little flower of Frances – I wd always rather have a compliment from a child than from anyone. Reginald is much better today, no more temp. & going to get up for a little while. He has eaten the grapes! Also, a piece of turbot a neighbour gave me for him!

I must go. I wish you hadn't any pain – that is v. grievous, and disappointing. My love to you and yours.

Then on 1st December there was a picture postcard sent by Ethel to Frances, which led to all sorts of misunderstandings and problems. It was a black and white photo of a statue in Cordoba of Saint Teresa. Ethel wrote on it:

Thursday night. Frances dear, thank you for your new letter. I hope your Daddy is much better. My Reginald has been up all day today & is now getting well fast. I hope you like this card which shows your lady mother reading a book & talking to a pigeon at the same time. You can see by the name it is your mother & by the sweet face. Love Ethel Mannin. XXXXXXX.

Things took a turn for the worse. On 2nd December Ethel felt it necessary to send Hewitt a telegram:

Grieved by your letter which was unnecessary. Friendship surely not dependent on letters. But will write Sunday. Affectionately, Ethel.

The next day she wrote a letter.

My Dear. I wired you y/day, not having time to write you, yr last letter grieved me – it seemed unreasonable, as you had several times told me there was no need to write in reply to all yr letters, and then when, rather than not write at all, I send a PC just to report progress on my patient & acknowledge yrs, you write me that it 'seems cold' and you are 'heartbroken'. It is also not fair of you dear to need so many reassurances of friendship, and that I will see you again. I have said you have my friendship , I have said I will see you again – I can't keep on saying yes I am yr friend, yes I will see you again … For one thing I am too busy, and for another it ought not to be necessary, and it wouldn't be if only you'd have a little faith and trust in this friendship which you so desire!

Now listen, my dear. Reg returns to work on Monday, the day (I hope) you read this. I am not free the rest of that day, but I <u>am</u> free on <u>Tuesday</u> – it was Tues you were to have come before, wasn't it? If you are free on Tues. and want to come, then do – about 12. And tell me if you can eat eggs, otherwise I must think again about what to feed you on. If you write by return I should get it Tues. morning.

About going back to Australia, it is of Teresa and the children & yr work & health you must think of, not of me, because I maintain that friendships, if they are real, can be sustained with a world between and do not depend on meetings. But we can talk of this. I must go now or I'll miss the post.

My love to you, and do please try to believe in me a little more – or what's the use?

Ethel was obviously getting a little worried about the intensity of Hewitt's 'friendship'. In the event, the Tuesday visit didn't take place. On Monday 4th December she sent him a telegram:

This morning's mail makes Tuesday difficult. Can you come Thursday instead. Ethel.

A letter posted the same day as the telegram confirms the change of day, but is mostly devoted to her concerns about a letter she had received from Frances.

Monday

My Dear: After writing you y/day that Tues wd be allright for me for you to come here I had to wire you today to make it THURSDAY. This I hope you can do. I am a bit cluttered up this week owing to having got behind in things owing to Reg's illness, but Thurs. is quite free, so I hope it's all right for you. I'll be here all Tues. and Wed. but with so many things to do, and by Thurs. I'll have got them out of the way. For one thing I have to go out Tues. whereas I am 'all clear' in that respect Thurs.

I had F's letter this morning and have sent the child a pc in reply. But Hewie that you dictated that letter – or that Teresa did – stands out a mile! No child of 9, left to itself, says 'I don't care for Saints'. A child of 9 is much more likely not to have any idea of what a Saint is!! (come to that not many grown-up people have!) A child of 9, also, doesn't say (of its own volition) 'Perhaps we may be friends' – that sounds very like Daddy! If the child wants to write me a letter let her, bless her, and help her with the spelling if you like, but let the child say what is natural to her to say. Mostly kids haven't much to say to adults… You said in one letter that Frances is 'taught to be sincere'. This is something that <u>can't</u> be taught. You cannot make a child sincere or kind or any of the adult virtues. You can only make the kid a little artificial hypocrite. Children, left to themselves, are <u>naturally</u> sincere. They say, with simple candour, You look funny, Bring me some sweets … but if a child starts saying I love my Mummy, I love my Daddy, then I begin at once to doubt the sincerity of the child, because the child doesn't think of love in those conscious terms; you can't teach a child these things; but that's another matter … Well, but I've written books on all this, so has A S Neill, who is to me what Sickert was to you, and of Neill I am only the pale shadow, but a little I learned from him, and am still learning. 'No child can love,' Neill writes in *The Problem Parent*, 'He can only want to be loved. No child can be grateful, for his interest is in the thing given, not in the giver.' A child is all egotist, a bundle of egotistical nervous energy. Ah, let little Frances alone; let her write out of her childish self, Dear Miss Mannin I am quite well, I hope you will bring me some sweets when you come, I cannot think of any more to say … I hope you like my drawing … But leave her alone & I doubt if she'd want to write me at all, bless her. This letter probably outrages you. I can't help it. You want the kid to be sincere & it seems to me you're doing yr best to make her a little hypocrite, & loving kids as I do, I rebel – and protest!

    Love, *à bientot*
    Ethel

A S Neill was progressive educationalist and founder of Summerhill School in Suffolk, where Ethel Mannin sent her daughter Jean. Neill contributed a foreword to Mannin's book *Common Sense and the Child : A Plea for Freedom* (1930)

Despite her suspicions about the card from Frances, the same day she sent her a card back, addressing the matter of St Teresa.

> Frances dear, thank you for your nice letter, also for the very nice painting, which I like very much. I am very glad your daddy is getting quite well. I hope to see him soon, and then I shall see you all again at Xmas I hope.
>
> A Saint is only a person who has been good and kind and then when he or she dies hundreds of years later far away in Rome the Pope says 'I will make that person a Saint'. Of course, a lot of very good people never get made Saints. It's a kind of special honour that just happens to a few. The lady on the postcard was a Spanish lady and she was very brave and strong, like your Daddy. Of course, she never knew they made her a Saint.
>
> Love from Ethel Mannin xxxxxxxxx
> PS: Don't bother to answer this. Writing letters is a bore.

Hewitt must have written a letter proposing that he would bring some food when he visited Wimbledon on the Thursday, because on Wednesday Ethel sent him this postcard:

> Wed. For heaven's sake don't bring butter or sugar – I can give <u>you</u> some! (Have pounds of sugar in the cupboard although I make jam & often send fats to my mother!) I don't need <u>anything</u>, & it wd be a fag for you to take it all

back again! Thanks for the thoughtfulness, though. It's appreciated. All right, we'll just have boiled eggs & b. & butter & tea, unless you prefer stout which I have, & that will save cooking & we can have it in our laps beside the sitting room fire. Re. F – much simpler if when you found she was taking my adult humour with a child's literalness you'd said 'Miss M. doesn't <u>really</u> think that's a picture of Mummy – she's just pretending.' <u>Please</u> for the Lord's sake – I didn't write a book about 'training' children! God forbid! I wrote a book about leaving 'em alone! I didn't train Jean in Pacifism – ghastly thought. She'd probably have joined the ATS if I had! Until she brought in the calling up form I'd no idea she intended registering as a C.O.! I'd often wondered what her views were. Wd much rather have Kay's cuss word than any pretty speech from any child. A child of 9 who says I love you to a parent is highly suspect – emotionally! Yr kids are sweet – & I can only repeat be damned to all this training & guidance & what not; leave 'em <u>alone</u>.

But you won't; you won't… *à bientot.*

Ethel must have torn her hair out when that same week Frances sent her a little gift. This is her reply, as usual on a postcard, dated 11th December.

Monday. Frances Dear, this is to thank you for your nice letter, also for the lovely card, and the very useful milk jug cover which I like very much and is just what I wanted. I think you have done it very nicely. I have put your card with other Xmas cards I have received on my bookshelf in my workroom. I also have your cut-outs pinned up there.

Please thank Daddy for his two letters, but tell him I can't write just yet as I am very busy with the proofs of a book which is being re-printed, so haven't much time for letter (this week).

Of course I didn't <u>really</u> mean that the postcard Saint lady was your Mummy. I was only pretending, because the name was the same and she had a nice face. I think your mummy is much nicer.

Love to you all from Ethel Mannin. XXXXXX

Despite being busy with the proof-reading, Ethel did write to Hewitt that same day.

Oak Cottage. Monday.
Dear Hewie, I don't know, really, what to write to you (and strictly speaking I've no time for I have an endless accumulation of letters, and all the proofs of my reprinting *Commonsense and the Adolescent*), but I have letters of yours and must send you something. But the problem is to match my simplicity against yr complexity; my transparency against yr obscurity. But I'll try.

So-

I am glad you were happy in that afternoon. I wanted you to be.

I am very glad indeed you are working again and pray that it may continue to go well. It's always a good feeling to feel that one is helping someone to be creatively happy and well, mentally and physically. I do very much want you to be well, in all ways, to have physical health and to be able to work as you wish.

I am not (replying to your letter) separated from someone I care for. I don't know what gave you this impression. The particular person I referred to I see at fairly frequent intervals. He was 3 years in prison under 18b but was released last August. He has a deep need of me. My life is very complicated and I shrink from complicating it further. In fact I don't think I cld stand the strain of further complications and worries. (Sometimes I feel I can hardly stand the strain of those I already have!)

Of course I liked you after our first real *tête-à-tête*. But why shouldn't I? Though it irritates me when you accuse me of being 'bitter' and 'cynical', when I'm not, nor is there any trace of either in any of my work. If you maintain there is it's up to you to show me.

Your sonnet seems to me to have flashes of poetry in it but I don't pretend to understand modern poetry – or painting, or music. I don't understand obscure imagery. I am very simple. Pity my simplicity (if you like).

As to when we shall meet again I don't know. We are due to meet, *en famille*, on Boxing Day, Tues. the 26th. I doubt if we shall meet before then. I have so much to do – and other claims on my so limited time (I am at my desk most nights till midnight as it is, to get everything into the 24 hrs) … my life, I repeat, is very complicated, and with all my heart, therefore, I pray that we may keep our friendship clear of emotional complications, because there is a limit to how much emotional wear and tear one can stand …

Now I must work. I may not write again for a bit, but friendship, as I said before, should not (doesn't, if it's the real thing) depend on letters, or even on meeting.

With all my heart I hope you continue to stay well and happy and do good work.

Please believe me, Ethel.

The reference to '18b' is to the controversial defence regulation introduced by the British government during the 1939–45 war. It enabled them to arrest and intern people suspected of Nazi sympathies.

It is unclear from this correspondence whether Hewitt ever did visit her home in Wimbledon. His own autobiographical notes state categorically that he did. He wrote about going to see her 'one mellow autumn afternoon when V2 rockets were falling to the North of the city'. He recounted how, during the visit, she had encouraged him to finish the draft of his saga (the trip to the Isle of Wight). This had been in progress since the trip itself in 1934. In fact the draft manuscript had to survive the war years, including a soaking from firemen's hoses, before Hewitt would get it finished in 1954.

He must have written another tiresome letter to Ethel, because on Saturday 16th December she had to put him right on what friendship meant. And she raised the matter of the outstanding invitation to Hewitt and his family to visit her on Boxing Day.

Hewie dear: Yr letter makes me sad, and a little it puzzles me. For why should 'the curtain descend' and why should I forget you and yr good heart? You wanted my friendship – and you have it. More than a loving friendship I cannot give. I am not free to give it – and even if I were, you are not free to receive it. I am not capable of being in love with two people at the same time, and even if I were, if you were still living with Teresa (or any other woman who loved you) I wd still say we can only be friends. But this friendship is something special and something you sought, so why suggest I came and saw and went away? I did, and have done, nothing of the kind! I am still here, holding out the friendly hand …

Will you discuss with Teresa as to whether you will all come here on Boxing Day? Teresa wd not commit herself when the matter was first mentioned. If she has something else to do nearer home I shall understand. I shall understand if she considers the journey too far to make with the children, or if she just doesn't 'feel like it', but if she wd like to come, I shd like it very much – and I hope you will come with them. I wd like to know soon (right away if possible) as if you are not all coming here I wd like to post the dolls I am having made (by a woman artist friend) for the children. I wd like you to come – but only if you and Teresa wd like it. Reg will be here, as he has had to change his C.D. shift. There will also be a friend who works in our bookshop, a nice kid. A young Italian girl may also be here. Please don't be sad (me, taking your hands) I want so much that you shall be happy, dear, my dear.

I send you my gentlest love, as always.

Ethel

If you are coming Boxing Day I wd suggest arriving earlyish in the afternoon, three-ish rather than four-ish, as no doubt you will want to leave not too late in the evening, on account of the children.

The Boxing Day plan was still unresolved two days later, but further complicated, it seems, by a letter Ethel received from Theresa. This is her reply. From Theresa's letter Ethel had realised the correct spelling of her name, and the letter 'h' was added in red pen:

Monday Dec. 18th 1944

Dear Theresa, Your letter to me crosses with one I sent Hewie y/day asking him to let me know definitely whether I am to expect you all on Boxing Day, as you had rather left it open – and I'd said I'd ask you again nearer the time.

As I wrote Hewie y/day, he wanted my friendship and he has it. If he chooses to throw it away because it is not perhaps along precisely the lines he had hoped, that is his affair! I am in an intolerably false position because I cannot speak openly to you – if he doesn't.

I am still glad to see you all if you care to come – this also I wrote to him. If he doesn't want to come and you don't feel like making the rather long journey alone with the children I shall understand and will post the dolls I am getting for them. Or leave them at your house. Wd perhaps be rather sad (for all of us) if you came without him, but if you care to you are very welcome. Reginald will be here. He is a nice person and you could hardly fail to like him – or he you and the children. It seems very strange to me that you should say you don't know what sort of reception you wd get from me coming alone. I liked you and I liked the children (I love all children) and I thought you realised it. I have utterly no quarrel with you, and I have none with Hewie, nor any 'estrangement', even – unless he chooses to make it that way.

You are entirely free to show him this letter – in fact I think it would be a good thing if you did.

I couldn't come to you as I have other people here over Christmas – one or two of them staying in the house. But it is extremely sweet of you to ask me.

Perhaps you would let me know your feeling about Boxing day, and whether you will come alone with the children, or all of you, or not at all ... if I could know quickly it wd help, so that I can make my plans accordingly.

The best to you all

Ethel Mannin

Thank Frances for the cutout Hewie enclosed in his last. It is on my mantel-piece tell her, and looks very smart.

It looks as if the Rayners didn't turn up at Ethel's house on Boxing Day. On 28th December, Ethel sent this postcard to Theresa:

> [no salutation]
> I didn't really expect you on such an evil a/noon. I am v. sorry you have the entire family down with coughs and colds & hope they soon recover – & that you yourself don't go down also. I will post the dolls off on Sat. when I am out shopping. Hewie, in a note, says that they shall be 'put away & kept fresh', but please I don't want this at all; I wd like the children to have the dolls to <u>play</u> with ... Thank the children for the lovely cards & Hewie for doing them; also thank him for the fine drypoint, & his verses. I like particularly his one in the John Clare manner & wonder if he knows the work of that 18th century agricultural worker poet. It's grievous that the children had to be disappointed, but perhaps they will be able to come when the weather is better & the flowers are out & they can enjoy the garden. Meanwhile the very best to you all.
> E.
> Forgive card. Have enormous arrears of mail to make up.

The final milestone in their deteriorating relationship was when Hewitt wrote asking for his drypoint etchings back, and enclosing a £1 note in payment for the gifts Ethel had given him. She was insulted ... and incensed. The exact date of this letter was sent is not known, as Ethel's reply is not dated, other than 'Wednesday'.

> Dear Hewie
> It seems to me very odd to ask for gifts to be returned. Even more so, in this case, in which the gifts were to be made a matter of 'exchange' at yr own suggestion. I am at a loss when you speak of my forcing 'unwanted gifts' upon you; when you first suggested this exchange I wrote that I should be happy to give you a book or two but wanted nothing in return – as you promptly sent the etchings (which I much liked) if anyone did any forcing of unwanted gifts it wd be truer to say it of you, though I liked the generosity of yr gesture as much as I liked yr fine craftsmanship.

For the rest, I sent you a few flowers when you were ill, refrained from bringing you anything when I first came to see you as you had some curious complex about gifts, and brought a few eggs the second time because eggs are good for sick people and difficult to procure these days.

I return your £ as I felt – very strongly – that yr wife and children had greater need of it. I will post the etchings to you Friday when I go out shopping. Some of them are inscribed, which makes it odder still asking for them back! But – *comme vous voulez*!

I certainly don't want my books back – if you don't want them you can always put them in the dustbin or give them away.

There is no need to send the postage of the etchings. It will be only a matter of a few pence; but if you feel you MUST send it the amt wd be most useful to me in stamps, of which I am always running short.

But all this emotional 'flap' and melodrama in the midst of a world-war, full of unimaginable horrors, and people dying all the time, and when we may all of us be rubbed out without warning at any moment, strikes me as quite simply silly!

And oh, so boring!

As ever, E.

One thing I would like back and had intended asking you for, as it (or they –forget which) was (were) only on loan, is that Irish magazine *The Bell* I brought you. I forget if there were one or two copies, I think only one …

PS: As R. is still ill in bed, it's possible I may not be able to get out Fri. In that case I will send when I am able to get out.

The last communication from Ethel to Hewitt is dated Tuesday 23rd January 1945, when she sent him a card to acknowledge receipt of the Irish magazine.

Tues. Thanks for returning the *Bells*.
Hope you are better. Reg continues to be ill, alas (though is improving).
The best, as always.
E

No 'Hewie, Dear'. Not even a 'Dear Hewie'. Their friendship was, it seems, over for good.

15
Recognition at last

As the end of the war approached the sun suddenly shone a little on Hewitt. He was given the opportunity of a one-man exhibition at the respected Brook Street Art Gallery. It opened on 14th June and was initially planned for a two-week run, but proved to be so successful that it was extended for another week. Prints worth more than £110 were sold and the event was favourably reviewed by critics.

Here at last was the recognition that he had been fighting for. *The Times* newspaper ran a small item on the opening, and there was a good volume of press coverage in British and Australian publications.

Arranged with the help of Hewitt's friend Henry Harben, the exhibition was opened by Mr W J Jordan, New Zealand's High Commissioner in London. Jordan originally came from Ramsgate in Kent. Also present at the opening was a Mr Keys, representing the High Commissioner of Australia, Lady Freyberg, Gwen Otter, Mrs Quinn [wife of Australian portrait painter James Quinn, and mother of Hewitt's fellow-student René, who had died in 1934], James Laver and others.

Theresa noted in a typewritten note about the exhibition that 'Jack Lindsay was present'. Jack Lindsay (1900–1990) was the son of famous Australian artist Norman Lindsay, and a publisher, poet, artist, translator and author of over 150 books. He had come to London in 1925 or 1926, and set up the specialist publishing company Fanfrolico Press. Lindsay asked Hewitt if he would send an invitation to artist James Boswell, now working alongside him in the Army.

As usual, Hewitt and Theresa put tremendous effort into promoting the event, alerting journalists and sending invitations to a wide circle of contacts. Handwritten draft letters to the *London Evening Standard* and the *Associated Press* news agency have survived, each over Theresa's name but almost certainly

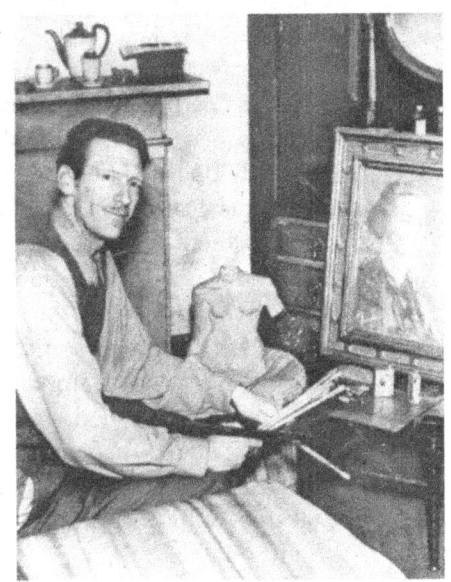

15.1 Cutting from *Tatler*, 20th June 1945, around the time of the Brook Street Art Gallery exhibition. © TATLER MAGAZINE. SW.

197

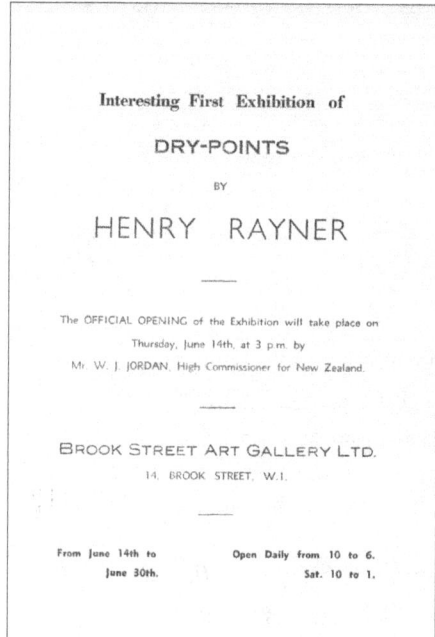

Interesting First Exhibition of

DRY-POINTS

BY

HENRY RAYNER

The OFFICIAL OPENING of the Exhibition will take place on
Thursday, June 14th, at 3 p.m. by
Mr W. J. JORDAN, High Commissioner for New Zealand.

BROOK STREET ART GALLERY LTD.
14, BROOK STREET, W.1.

From June 14th to   Open Daily from 10 to 6.
June 30th.   Sat. 10 to 1.

15.2 His one-man exhibition at the Brook Street Art Gallery in 1945 was opened by Mr W J Jordan, High Commissioner for New Zealand. sw.

drafted by Hewitt. Publications listed on a copy of the exhibition programme, probably indicating that they attended, include *Consolidated Press*, *Cavalcade*, the *London News Agency* and *Picture Post*.

A handwritten reply from James Laver, Keeper of prints at the V&A Museum, dated 7th June, gave Hewitt a useful hint. Laver suggested that he send some tickets to Lt-Col Lascelles, National Savings Committee, Smith Street, SW1, as this man was in touch with organisations including the American League, so could distribute some tickets. He also said that he would try to get to Hewitt's exhibition but they were rather busy trying to get their own exhibition open.

Other replies came from Cecily Binyon (widow of author and poet Lawrence Binyon, best remembered for his poem 'For the fallen'), A P Herbert, Field Marshall Smuts, John Winant (US Ambassador to Britain), and writer Sheila Kaye-Smith.

The whole family visited the exhibition, and a press photograph shows the three of them admiring Hewitt's work. While in town they went to the St Paul's area. Frances later remembered it as full of smoke, dust and falling debris.

Curiously, at the time Hewitt was preparing for the Brook Street exhibition he was also getting ready an exhibition of war etchings and photographs at his home. His idea for this was to show recent works that depicted London buildings and streets that had been changed by the war. The charming Lismore Circus, for example, had been spoiled by tarmac and bomb shelters. Together with the drypoints there was a series of photographs of Hewitt at work in a variety of bombed-out London locations [some of these photographs are reproduced in Chapter 13].

The Times newspaper ran a second item about the Brook Street Gallery exhibition a few days later, announcing that it was being extended to 7th July.

Hewitt had assembled some 160 works for the show, a mix of early and recent drypoints. Some from before his serious accident; a few from after. He was especially proud that of the works purchased during the show many were destined to be taken back to Australia and New Zealand.

Some or all of the prints needed for the exhibition were framed in Chelsea. A receipt from J Middleton, T & A Heaney & Sons at 231 King's Road, dated 26th April 1945, shows it cost £17–5–0 to 'mount 20 drawings in thick cream cartoon cut-out mounts and frame in half-inch beech'.

It looks as though he also had to arrange the printing of the tickets for the exhibition. The 200 tickets cost 10 shillings from The Grafton Press, 84 Grafton Road, NW5, as the bill dated 15th May shows.

The exhibition catalogue shows a list of 96 etchings, grouped into sets as follows: Religious, Ballet and circus, Chelsea scenes, Sickert memories, Portraits, Landscape, Australian scenes, War scenes, and miscellaneous. The first two etchings in the catalogue – '*A soldier of New Zealand*' and '*To New Zealand*' – are set apart, as though Rayner assigned special importance to them.

Prices are shown against all the etchings. They range from 20gns (£21) for '*The last supper, 1941*' to 5gns for '*The fish*' and others. Most of the prints are priced in the range 6 to 10gns. It is interesting to note the ones that Rayner considered most valuable, with prices above 10gns. These include the two New Zealand prints, all the religious subjects, one or two of the ballet subjects, the portraits of Sickert, G B Shaw and Rayner's mother, '*Old Regent's Park*', '*Turks Head, Wapping*', '*When we stood alone*' and '*Anton Dolin*'. (There is an amusing typographical error in this last entry. It refers to the Bluebeard ballet rather than Bluebird).

The full text of the Brook Street Art Gallery exhibition catalogue can be found in Appendix 6. Hewitt's own copy of the catalogue carries annotations he made during the event, including who had purchased various of the works. This also shows that there were additional prints on show, not mentioned in the printed catalogue. These were: '*Spring interior*', '*Les Sylphides*', '*Castel San Angelo*', '*The little path*' and '*Jesus heals the earth proud*'.

Interestingly, although in the 1930s he produced several drypoints with a surrealist theme, none of these was exhibited at the Brook Street Art Gallery show. Perhaps the organisers took the view that the subject matter was altogether too strange for a public that was exhausted by the war and wanted to see uplifting images.

He was very proud of the opening speech made by William Jordan, and he kept a transcript. It concludes: 'In war as in peace, this artist did his bit. In years to come, the pictures we are looking at today will tell the story of the great period of struggle through which we have passed, and of this brave and worthy artist.'

Among the visitors during the three-week run of the exhibition were Lord and Lady Vansittart, Lord Norman (governor of the Bank of England, whose portrait had been painted by Augustus John), Sir Arthur Bliss (composer, later to be Master of the Queen's Music), Commander Battine of His Majesty's Fleet, the ex-mistress of Mussolini, and Lord Methuen (a former pupil at Sickert's art school in Islington). Lord Methuen evidently purchased the 1925 Sickert drypoint, and the '*Old Turk's Head, Wapping*' proof.

Ironically, Hewitt himself almost didn't make it to the event. He had been confined to bed but with the help of some special injections was able to attend. He spent his days there observing the visitors, talking to them, and clearly enjoying the limelight.

The exhibition created a lot of press coverage, undoubtedly to a large extent the results of Hewitt and Theresa's efforts in sending out press information. Eric Newton, writing in *The Sunday Times* on 24th June 1945, described the exhibition as: 'A fine set of drypoints by Henry Rayner, a friend and worthy disciple of Sickert. They have strength, economy of means and a delightful humanity.'

Maurice Collis gave the exhibition a mention in an art review for *Time and Tide* magazine, in which he summarised Rayner's subjects as landscape, portraits, genre and interpretations of the New Testament, adding: 'These last are very expressive and personal creations, in which he seems quite free from influences noticeable in some of this other work. They are among his latest, and I have no doubt that, if he can pursue this vein, and possibly illustrate some text for publication, he will become much sought after.'

An item in *Cavalcade* about this 'tall, gaunt, 55-year-old Australian artist' went on: 'His early life as a cow hand and a motor mechanic gives his etchings a solid, down-to-earth realism, together with a remarkable breadth of outlook, while his later drypoints, especially those of his Chelsea period, show the superb draughtsmanship and taught technique he evolved under the guidance of his friend and master Walter Sickert. Notable are his impressive, nightmarish pictures of the 'blitz'. [Giving Hewitt's age as 55 was an error. He was only 42 at the time of the exhibition. What he thought of the error is not recorded].

Hewitt sent his mother a copy of the exhibition catalogue, and enclosed hand-written copies he had made of the best press reports in British and Australian publications.

While the exhibition was still running he received a letter dated 2nd July from his former fellow student at the RA Schools, Clifford Hall. Then living at 8 Trafalgar Studios, Manresa Road in Chelsea, Clifford complimented him on the event and invited him to drop in. A letter from Lord Methuen dated 19 September refers to the proof of a Sickert etching for which he included the sum of £7.7.0. 'Not much money, I know, but cash is short these days!'

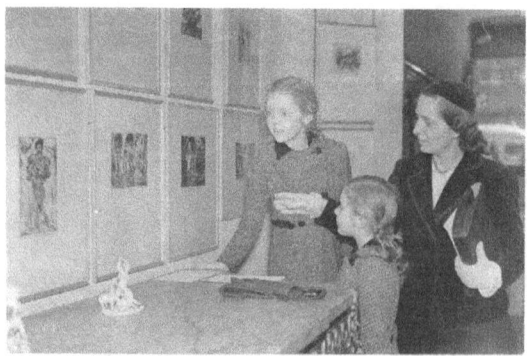

15.3 (Left to right) Frances, Kay and Theresa at the Brook Street Art Gallery exhibition in 1945, admiring some of Hewitt's drypoints. SW.

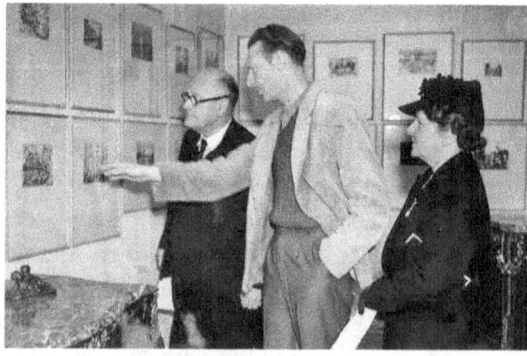

15.4 Hewitt with William Jordan, New Zealand's High Commissioner in London, and Mrs Jordan, at the Brook Street exhibition. PHOTO COURTESY PETER ZECCHIN.

Although the Brook Street exhibition was the highlight of the war years, in fact since 1939 there had been a steady trickle of sales to individuals, museums and galleries. Theresa had even taken some prints with her to Leicester, and made a few sales.

In 1945 Hewitt produced several oil paintings with an Australian theme. Now in private hands in Australia, these pictures depict in vibrant colours Luna Park (St Kilda), the Melbourne Regatta of 1913, the road to Walhalla, the 1903 sea baths in St Kilda, and a stockman among gumtrees.

Hewitt was still receiving regular letters from his mother. Theresa's Catholicism was still a really big issue for her. She mentioned it frequently in her letters, but rarely with so much vehemence as in an airmail letter dated 3rd October 1945.

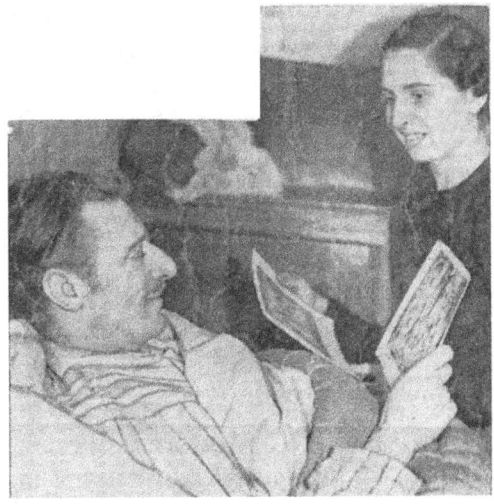

15.5 Cutting from the *London Evening Standard*, 7th January 1945, when Hewitt was in poor health. © LONDON EVENING STANDARD. SW.

She had been ill, was in pain, and was worried about the future. She was obviously thinking about what happens if she should die. The letter is rather garbled, but her concerns about the religion issue are very strong; even to the point of threatening to cut her son and his family out of her will unless her grandchildren took an oath to follow a protestant religion. The first part of the letter has already been reproduced (see page 102). It goes on ...

'I may live for years but I don't think so, and I'd love to see Tess and the children free and happy, and I could make it so for them. I've been talking to my solicitor Bert again. I say it will have to go to protestants. We have brains and know the way to heaven is only in our own hearts. There's no such thing as Mary or purgatory or any of those awful things to make people unhappy and get their money. Look at the grand churches with poverty & wretchedness all round them.

'Are you sending the children to the W Ellis Grammar School, as you said you would? They must mix with intelligent children, not cowed down children doing penance. It is a worry to me, for I must beg Hal. It is his darned money, and I do not want to die and not help you.

'You must give me, & Tess, your word of honour & your bond. I must fix everything at once if you will promise. If you came out here I am afraid Tess would go to that awful church and then I would not give Hal's money away to you.

'So hard to explain. Love Mother.'

Barbara Griffin, a childhood friend of Frances, talked about the situation regarding religion in the Rayner household in 2004. She summed it up simply as follows: 'Theresa was catholic, Frances was catholic but non-practising, and Hewitt had his own religion'.

Hewitt's mother expressed her religious concerns again in another letter. When she saw a photograph of Frances with her friend Barbara, she said only: 'She seems a nice girl. Is she a protestant?'

In 1946 the Royal Society of British Artists acquired for their Council Room at Suffolk Street, Pall Mall, a copy of one of Rayner's drypoints of Sickert. This was the square plate titled '*Richard Sickert 1932*'. The society received the ninth proof. Hewitt offered them a special price reduction of 50%, so the Society paid only four guineas. He sent out a press release that resulted in a story in *The British Australian* magazine dated 11th January 1947.

Royal Society Of British Artists To Have Portrait By Henry Rayner

A PORTRAIT of the late Richard Waiter Sickert, one of England's greatest painters and teachers, by Henry Rayner, Australian artist, is to be bought by the Royal Society of British Artists, the Society's council decided last month.

The portrait will be hung in the Council room. Sickert was a past president of the Society and was, at that time, one of the most vigorous personalities in British art.

'This is a crowning achievement for any country and me,' Mr. Rayner writes. 'The honour is indeed a high one for any living artist, but for me it is much greater because the portrait was the one thing I wanted to do for Sickert when he died.

'He was my friend and teacher for so many happy years.

'I had not thought that the Council of leading artists would choose me as they have done. I may also say that the decision had the strong recommendation of Lord Methuen, my friend and colleague.

'I met Sickert in 1925, when I was a raw young man from Melbourne. He took me, a pupil from the Academy Schools, and we painted together in Kensington Gardens and his studio in Fitzroy Street.

'It was Sickert who, about 1939, told Wilson Steer he considered me one of 'the best living draughtsmen' another honour that to me was beyond gold.

'The Council by their unanimous approval have given me one of the highest honours that any Australian could hope to come by, and I think of it as something done for my country.'

Despite illness due to war injury, Mr. Rayner has recently painted portraits of June, daughter of John Tilt, the pianist; Nina Hammett, celebrated Bohemian authoress, Irene Vanbrugh, Kay Hammond, and the Sickert portrait. Other Rayner portraits are Augustus John (1943), FieldMarshal Montgomery (1944), the Princesses Elizabeth and Margaret (1945).

The Queen bought a Rayner portrait of the King in 1943 and commended Mr. Rayner for his bravery during the blitz on London when he was a Civil Defence worker.

Mr. Rayner is represented in the galleries of the British Museum, the Victoria and Albert Museum, the Library of Congress, Washington, USA, Melbourne Art Gallery, Cardiff, the Royal Library at Windsor, Buckingham Palace, Manchester and the Ashmolean Museum, Oxford.

He has recently been very ill and declared he owes his life to his wife, who nursed him.

The war years had certainly taken a heavy toll on Hewitt's health. His older daughter Frances wrote later that he had lost a lung in the war. His lungs were certainly damaged by bomb blast, although there is no evidence that he lost a lung. He certainly suffered badly from asthma, and in later years emphysema. And his mental health was not good.

Hewitt wrote that after the war he suffered a complete breakdown, and this is borne out by a note from a Doctor Stocks, dated 27th October 1948. This states that he was suffering from asthma and emphysema following blitz injury, and also a nervous breakdown due to worry. The doctor wrote that '… in my opinion his health would be much improved by a rest, especially in clean air'.

Once the war was over, and the family reunited, they were able to relax a little. They went on picnics at Kenwood House, Hampstead Heath, taking egg and bacon sandwiches and cakes. Some of Rayner's woodland drypoints are of scenes at Kenwood. There was often a heavy price to pay for these interludes as Hewitt frequently suffered a hayfever attack as a result. He discovered that blue sunglasses helped ease the symptoms.

They also went to Hampstead Heath to play tennis. Areas of the Heath had been taken over by allotments for vegetable growing during the war but were now being returned to their former use as a leisure resource. Hewitt was a good tennis player and the whole family enjoyed the game. Another regular destination was Richmond, taking an LMR train that ran directly from Gospel Oak station.

Through 1946 Hewitt suffered several acute asthma attacks, and was a regular visitor to the Hampstead General Hospital. He attended as an outpatient on 21st March, and again on 22nd June and 4th July.

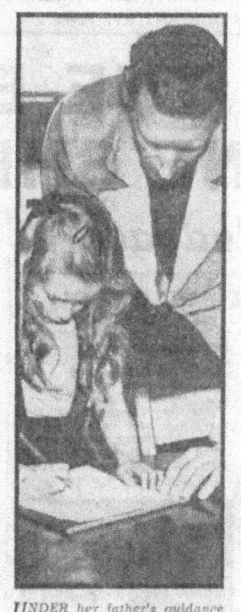

UNDER *her father's guidance*

15.6 Cutting from the *London Evening News*, Hewitt with his elder daughter Frances, 27th February 1945. © LONDON EVENING STANDARD. SW.

In June 1946 Theresa took the girls away on two weeks' holiday in Southend-on-Sea. It was also a business trip: Theresa was trying to get people interested in Rayner's art, and set up an art exhibition in the town. Why Southend was selected for this project is not known.

As usual when they were separated Theresa and Hewitt wrote to each other almost daily. Only Theresa's letters have survived, but they provide some interesting information.

This was the girls' first holiday and their first sight of the sea. They stayed at 238 York Road with a Mrs Baker ('Bed & breakfast, furnished apartments & attendance, terms moderate, 3 minutes sea, 5 minutes bandstand, 5 minutes station, bus stop outside'). Theresa got on well with Mrs Baker who she described

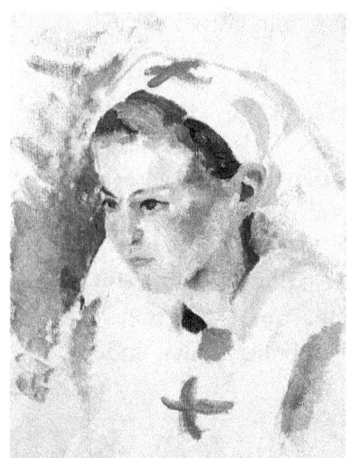

15.7 Oil painting by Hewitt of his elder daughter Frances, c1945. RS.

as 'very motherly towards the kiddies'. In a very rare reference to Kay's learning difficulties Theresa wrote that 'She [Mrs Baker] thinks Kay a lovely kid and a very normal child, and Frances is the right sister for her; she is very understanding.'

In Theresa's first letter to Hewitt (a letter card that she wrote in the Post Office), dated 15th June, she commented on the high price of lunches – 2/6d each for lunch with a sweet. 'So to cut down on expenses we can eat lunch well at Woolworths'. The high cost of living in Southend was a recurrent theme in her letters. In one she wrote: '… You will weep when I tell you I paid 4/6 for a basket of strawberries. I keep saying it's their holiday, and I don't suppose they will see any in London.' Theresa noted that they didn't go bathing because the cost of a bathing machine would have been two shillings.

On 16th June she wrote a letter while the family was on the beach. Hewitt was going through a bad patch with his asthma, and most of the letter was devoted to her concerns that he was getting some sleep, and that the spasms were not too severe. He was evidently taking a drug called Helsol, and Theresa wondered whether the drug had affected the tone of one letter he wrote. She queried 'did you have anything when you wrote this …?'

She repeatedly urged Hewitt to look after himself, and to join her and the children in Southend. She had checked with her landlady that this would be OK. She said that Southend could be crowded, but there were always quiet spots to be found.

One of her letters is largely devoted to the practical issue of the family's weekly egg ration back home in Gospel Oak. Eggs were still rationed in this immediate post-war period, and she was concerned not to lose the week's ration because she was away and not there to collect them.

Five days into their stay in Southend, Theresa started putting feelers out to try and find some customers for Hewitt's work. She started with the librarian who put her in touch with two people known to be interested in art. But no luck. 'One was a really dried-up solicitor who, he tells me, helps his own friends' she wrote in her letter of 21st June. 'It was like casting pearls before swine. How English!' Theresa's next plan was to visit the principal of the art school, a Dr Venables. The librarian had advised her that he was the person who had the power to arrange an exhibition of Rayner's work.

She was obviously also worrying about Hewitt's business dealings; in particular she was worried about the motives of one of Hewitt's uncles. He had evidently taken Hewitt on a day trip to Windsor and Eton, but Theresa was of the opinion that what her husband really needed was 'a real respite by the sea air.'

On 24th June 1946 she wrote: 'What's happened to Uncle calling on you so frequent? Now, you let me do the business part of disposing of any work to him. I've had no luck here. It is awkward here with the children. I can't leave them too often. They must be kept quiet. I keep reminding myself that it's their first holiday. I think they are disappointed you are not sharing it with us. If only you could spend the latter part of the week with us. Don't let this uncle of yours put you out or excite you. Think of yourself first. I feel that Windsor trip must have upset you. Do call on Dr. Dean. I think he will understand you. Now, don't keep postponing this holiday of yours, making money. Come now, while we are here. … I appreciate your daily letter. … '

In the same letter she responded to something Hewitt had evidently mentioned in one of his letters to her. It's difficult to make out the exact details, but it seems to relate to his drypoint of the King. She wrote: 'You are certainly doing great stunts with this King of yours. What a brilliant idea! But as I said, let me do the business part. Perhaps this King will give you the golden touch after all. Make him gold, that lovely gold. I should say you are the most original artist of this age, when history writes of you. Your stunts are so original.'

Hewitt was also in contact with Walter Nash, New Zealand's Deputy prime Minister, and Theresa noted: 'I hope Nash will do something for you.'

Hewitt's poor health was a constant theme in her letters. He had visited the hospital against her wishes, and she was urging him to go instead to a local doctor, Dr Dean, who had a practice in Mulden Road. But whatever treatment he received from the hospital had worked. Reassured by the news, in her letter of 25th June Theresa told him that she had decided to stay another week in Southend, and asked Hewitt to send her £7.

Unfortunately, Theresa's letters covering the second half of their stay in Southend have not survived, so it is not known whether Hewitt did ever join his family by the sea, and whether she was able to stimulate interest in her husband's art in the town.

The contact with Walter Nash did, however, yield a result. He took Rayner's 1946 painting titled '*The Unknown Soldier*' for hanging in one of New Zealand's galleries. This painting was based on a real person, but his identity was not known, even to Hewitt. 'I found him in a London Services' Club,' he explained in a press interview published in *The Star* on Thursday 6th June that year. 'He was a typical bushman type whom I considered symbolised the New Zealand fighting man. I didn't even know his name – I just painted him.'

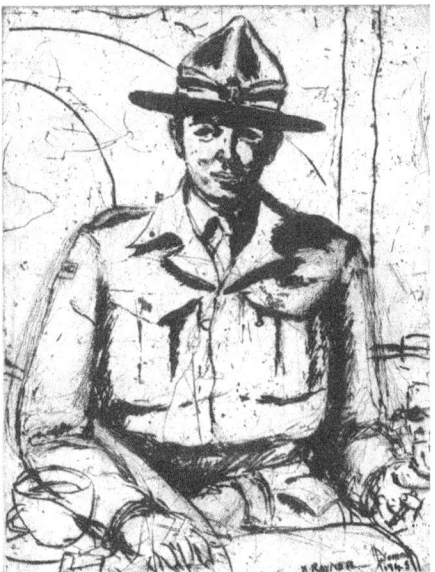

15.8 '*A soldier of New* Zealand', also known as '*the unknown soldier*'. Drypoint, 280×217mm. Restrike print from the original plate. sw.

Hewitt later did a drypoint with the same title. It is unusually large for a Rayner drypoint, measuring 28 x 21.7cms. He sent a copy to Walter Nash in June 1947, and in August that year it was accepted by the trustees of New Zealand's National Art Gallery and Dominion Museum in Wellington for the national collection.

In August 1946, a copy of the 'King George VI' portrait was presented to the Auckland Art Gallery in New Zealand, and reported in the *Auckland Star* of 30th August. Perhaps this was the 'brilliant idea' mentioned by Theresa in one of her letters from Southend.

In January 1947 Hewitt was advised by the British Council that three of his drypoints – '*Old Regent Street*', '*Chelsea 1941*' and '*W R Sickert 1930*' – were to be included in an exhibition that would visit Austria, Czechoslovakia and Poland.

Money continued to be tight. In 1947 Theresa and Hewitt hatched the idea of writing to the management of British companies in an attempt to get them interested in buying drypoints. Several draft letters have survived, and this is a typical example:

> Dear Sir
> I hope that you may be able to give my letter some serious attention. I am the wife of Henry Rayner, the well-known etcher-painter who was seriously injured in the Blitz. In between nursing him and helping my young family, I endeavour to make contact with some of the famous firms in the British Isles with the object of interesting those of them who have art-loving managers & directors. I am determined, and always have been, to bring the work of this gifted artist to the notice of discriminating men & women, and to try to help us over this very difficult period.
> Henry Rayner has been considered one of the leading etchers. He has Royal patronage, and works in numerous galleries & museums, including the British Museum, the Ashmolean, Oxford, & Glasgow Art Gallery (etchings) & Aberdeen Industrial (Prints).
> I would be very glad if you would allow me to send a selection of his early and late etchings – a very beautiful collection of which I possess in first proofs. He was unofficial war artist during the war, and after his injury the Queen commended him for his bravery.
> I hope that you may feel like seeing his work.
> Yours …

It looks as though this marketing effort did yield some results, because in May 1947 they came to an arrangement with Mr E J W Stanley, a director of Pye Ltd, to accept a Pye Model 47A radio as payment for six drypoints.

In early March 1947 Theresa offered London's National Portrait Gallery a copy of the drypoint of Augustus John based on drawings at 33 Tite Street in July 1943. The assistant keeper of the gallery wrote back to say that 'portraits of living persons are not exhibited, but if you are willing to present the portrait for our reference portfolios, it will be very acceptable.' This is what happened and the gallery confirmed receipt of the etching in a letter dated 12th March 1947.

The Belfast Museum and Art Gallery purchased copies of 'The Lambeth Walk' and 'The Farm, Ely' on 9th June 1947. The same year, a proof of Hewitt's 'My mother' drypoint was presented to the National Gallery of Victoria by Theresa.

On 20th Dec 1947 the Reuters news agency reported that Sir Ralph Richardson had acquired Henry Rayner's study of the famous ballet Les Sylphides 'in the new form the artist has adopted since the War'.

Throughout this period, in addition to their efforts to promote Hewitt's art there was the constant worry over their daughters' education. The schooling arrangements for Kay were even more complex, on account of her serious learning difficulties. Finding a suitable school was a constant struggle for Hewitt and Theresa, not only through the war years.

This matter was never mentioned by Hewitt's mother in any of the letters she wrote to her son, so it is likely that she was never told of her younger grand-daughter's problems.

The years of war had serious effects on their schooling. Frances, born in 1936, had attended seven different schools by the time she was 12 years old. The exigencies of war also led to very large classes. When she was 11 years old, she recalled, there were 45 children in her class. She always put her academic weakness down to this interrupted schooling, although there was another factor – she suffered from bronchitis. Each attack kept her away from school for three weeks or so. 'Being ill in January was always a blow to me as a child, because I was without fail in bed for my birthday,' she later wrote.

More seriously, illness also caused her to miss the '11 plus' examination that should have decided how her schooling would continue after the age of 11. This resulted in her being treated as though she had failed, and she ended up at New End School the following September. Only the receipt of a money gift from Hewitt's mother in Australia enabled the family to move her to a private school where she mixed with a very different set of pupils. Then at the age of 13, in the summer of 1949, she moved to Camden Grammar School for girls, in Prince of Wales Road, having passed an examination. Hewitt sketched the school and sent the sketch to his mother in Australia, noting on the reverse: 'Frances's dining hall [is] the room on the ground floor just above the main gate in the drawing'.

This was Frances's ninth and final school. Here, she discovered tennis and chess. She also took up writing and drawing, undoubtedly encouraged by her father. Despite the early educational challenges Frances ended up as a teacher, teaching art and other subjects, and running chess classes.

Kay attended a special school in Islington but in 1947 was transferred to a convent boarding school in Uxbridge where she stayed for two years. Then in 1948 when she was 12 years old, new problems arose. She had been attending Offord Road Special school (a council school for children with special needs) but distressed by her daughter's treatment there Theresa had moved her to Savernake Preparatory School, a private school near their home. After an examination by London County Council's School Medical Officer, Kay was recommended for schooling in a special school for educationally subnormal pupils. Theresa took the initiative and placed Kay in All Soul's School, Hillingdon, a Catholic school for girls with learning difficulties.

Worried that the education authorities might remove Kay from this school Theresa did what the Rayners did in times of stress. She wrote a letter. This time to His Majesty the King. The King's Lord in Waiting passed her letter of 5th December 1947 to the Ministry of Education. Theresa must also have written to the London County Council about the matter, because they re-assessed Kay's case and decided to normalise the situation by accepting financial responsibility for her place at All Soul's School.

Letters from Kay to her parents in 1951 and 1953 show that she was still at the school, by then known as Pield Heath House School.

At the end of May 1948 Hewitt set up an exhibition at his home, showcasing mainly works that were executed between 1939 and 1945 although not necessarily all depicting war images. Some of the prints on show were works that had been displayed at the Brook Street Art gallery exhibition three years earlier – these included the Augustus John portrait, and ballet scenes including 'Les Sylphides No. 5'. The exhibition also included wartime photographs by Thomas Hennell and Bly.

He billed it as the Henry Rayner Anniversary exhibition, but his press release dated 28th May failed to reveal what the anniversary was. Perhaps the third anniversary of the Brook Street exhibition itself. The press release did give the opening times – between 10.00am and 5.00pm every day.

The family continued to receive occasional money and food parcels from Hewitt's mother in Australia. A letter from Hewitt to his mother dated March 1949 records that recent parcels had contained pears, apricots, tomato soup, chocolate and puddings, as well as mittens and handkerchiefs for him. This same letter contains references to a family falling-out, involving the repayment of a debt owed to Rayner by 'Hewitt' – probably Hewitt Edwards, the relative of his mother's who had taken some of his pictures in order to try and sell them in New Zealand.

As Britain entered the 1950s, Hewitt was not facing the future with confidence. In a long essay-like letter to his mother in October 1951 he commented: 'Now a new era begins and I must find where I stand, for the old friends are nearly all dead. At fifty I must begin all over again, and only with God's good help may I be enabled to do it.'

Through most of 1950 he was receiving sickness benefit, on account of dermatitis and asthma. Towards the end of the year he was also suffering from nervous collapse and exhaustion. During a period when Theresa and Frances were also ill, the family fell out with two doctors. The situation escalated to the point where Hewitt complained first to the Executive Council of the National Health Service, and then in April 1951 to the Prime Minister's Office. The Prime Minister considered himself 'unable to intervene personally in an individual case of this kind.'

Either Hewitt was a difficult patient when ill, or he was unlucky with his choice of doctors.

Through the early 1950s Hewitt was battling with asthma, emphysema, bronchitis, seasonal hay fever (April to July) and other problems including diverticulosis and an ear abscess. Getting a good night's sleep was a constant challenge. He kept a diary of his daily symptoms and the treatments he tried, and it's clear he was using a whole range of medications. These included calcium gluconate, valerian, paraldehyde, glucodine, Thymol (for nasal douches), sodium nitrite, salicylate of soda, sodium bromide (for headaches), salol (for urinary tract and intestinal problems), iron plastules (for anaemia), potassium acetate (acidity control) and birch tar. Some of these medications were prescribed by doctors, some were self-prescribed. He was an early adopter of colonic irrigation.

It's also clear from the diaries that the whole family were big users of medicines. Whether they would have taken so many medications without his urging is not clear. Theresa suffered from arthritis, and this was affecting her spine is well as other joints. Hewitt prescribed sodium salicylate, which he described as 'my discovery', and recorded that this provided some relief. Hewitt himself was at one point concerned about an intestinal obtrusion, and the possibility of an absess.

Surviving notebooks contain a daily record of his and his family's medical conditions, and the medicines they were taking, between 1952 and 1955. As he entered his fifties, his medical conditions had become a preoccupation. Some of the notes provide insights into health issues that were never mentioned elsewhere. For example on 10th January 1952 he noted that the little finger on Frances's right hand was badly mis-shapen as a result of rickets.

As if he didn't have enough challenges, in 1950 the Rayners had reached breaking point with regard to the other residents of 121 Mansfield Road. There was a man called Basil Blake living in the basement flat with his wife, and a family called Tilleys living on the ground floor. In June 1950 Theresa wrote a very strong letter to the Parliamentary Secretary at the Home Office about the behaviour of their neighbours. Blake, she alleged, was mentally unstable, and 'has frequent drunken bouts, shrieking foul language through the house, and slashing and banging all night.' She described Hewitt in the letter as 'a man with high artistic honours, a gentle person, and one not capable of handling this slime that fills the house, for I cannot think of a better term after years of persecution and imposed filth'. Two years earlier, the Rayners had won a court order against Blake following an attempted assault. There is no surviving correspondence to suggest what the outcome of this dispute was.

Perhaps the stress of all his problems led Hewitt to dream of going somewhere far away. In May 1950 he wrote to Government House in The Falkland Islands asking for information on travel and accommodation on the islands. He was, he wrote, planning a visit with his wife and family.

The 1951 edition of *Who's who in New Zealand* included a profile of Hewitt Rayner on page 195. It read:

Rayner, Hewitt Henry (Henry Rayner), painter-etcher. Born near Hawthorn, Melbourne, 19.9.1902, son of Henry Redstone Rayner and Emily Ellen Edwards (of New Zealand); married 1926 Theresa Mary Charlotte, daughter of Joseph, of Udine; two daughters.

Educated Prahran Technical School, Melbourne, and Royal Academy Schools, London; pupil of Richard Walter Sickert, L.L.D.; '24–26. First painted in Waikato; a member of the First Waikato Reg (Cadets) '20, Cambridge; painted in Auckland 1921; Gippsland 1923 as student mechanic; Royal Academy Schools, 1925; Sickert bought the first large works; first drypoint etchings made 1926; new methods of drypoint, 1927 onwards. Chelsea set (drypoint) made from 1927–39. Portraits of Sickert; Wilson Steer; McEvoy etc made in this period.

Etched portrait of the King ('39 in Queen Mary collection, and proof in Royal Collection, Windsor 1939); drypoints in British Museum, Library of Congress, USA; R. Riksmuseum, Amsterdam; Academy des Beaux Arts, Paris; and royal and national collections in many countries. Unofficial war artist World War II '40–45. Commended by Queen for works made under blitz conditions '40–43; author of articles on point-to-point racing in 'Horse' magazine '39. Recreation: tennis.

Private address: Studio, 121 Mansfield Road, Hampstead, London NW3.

In March 1951 Theresa was engaged in sorting out with her brother Severino, by then living in Edinburgh at 28 Salisbury Street, the terms of her late father's will. There was a property that Theresa and her two brothers had inherited from their mother, but Theresa was angered by what she saw as an unfair split between the three of them.

Later that year, Hewitt told his mother about a visit the family had made to Hampton Court on 28th July. It was evidently the day of a British Pageant with medieval jousting. This delighted Frances who at the age of 15 'had a mania for horses'.

In 1952 Hewitt was collecting postage stamps as a hobby. There is a long letter from a philatelist in New Zealand, about exchanging stamps. In the course of the letter, the writer mentions that he has just seen the two articles on Hewitt's life in the *Waikato Times*. This is the account of Hewitt's early life in New Zealand.

On 13th Feb 1952, he went to pay his respects at the Lying in State of King George VI. Snow had fallen, but this did not deter the crowds queuing to pay their respects. Standing in the cold gave him a chill, so that evening he took salicylate of soda.

A startling revelation from his medical diary for 19th April 1952 notes that his daughter Kay had a thorough medical examination at her school, and was declared to be suffering from malnutrition and general medical and dental neglect.

That month, *Life Magazine* published a feature on Rayner, illustrated with three of his drypoints.

Later that Spring he was the subject of a large feature in *The Australian Women's Weekly*, dated 23rd April 1952. There was nothing in the article that adds to the information already covered in this biography, so there is little point reproducing it here. It was a full-page spread, illustrated with four of his drypoints: 'Les Sylphides No. 3', 'Self portrait', 'Walter Sickert 1932' and 'King George VI'

In the summer of 1952 Hewitt took his wife and daughters to Canterbury for a week. They travelled by coach from Victoria on 5th August and lodged in Hillmead Guest House in St. Stephens, on the north side of the Stour valley and run by Olive Keeley. Hewitt described it as 'an old rambling house on a meadow. Our windows hold one of the most magnificent views you could imagine. We are having our best respite and relaxation since 1945. This is England in the 18th and 19th centuries.'

The week's full board accommodation for the four of them cost 16 guineas.

During the trip Hewitt took a photograph of his daughters in front of a castle. On the reverse of the print he sent to his mother he wrote a poem. The photo itself has not survived, but Hewitt kept a copy of the poem:

> Two ladies of old England, her beauty to adorn;
> The castle and the green mead, the river and the lawn.
> And wind that comes from Dover way;
> And all the scented hay.
> The straight and noble ladies in a Canterbury day:
> Frances Rayner, Kay Rayner, all beautiful as May

When his mother heard that the family had taken this holiday, she encouraged them to visit France next summer.

In January 1953 Hewitt at last won some recognition from his homeland, when the Australian Embassy at Victoria House in London's Aldwych staged a display of his work in one of its windows. Coming some nine months after the story in the *Australian Woman's Weekly* it may be that the story had some effect in Australian government circles. Equally, letters from his mother around this time suggest that she had played a role by introducing her son to an Australian connected to the Embassy.

Whatever the background, she certainly played a practical role in the exhibition. Hewitt asked her for money to help with the framing, and she sent him £60.

The exhibition ran from 12th to 30th January. The invitation described it as 'An official winter exhibition of the paintings and drypoint etchings of Henry Rayner', describing him as 'Henry Rayner, the Victorian artist' [i.e. from the Australian State of Victoria]. It was held under the auspices of the Australian Government at its embassy in The Strand. The invitation states that 'The artist's portrait of King George VI has been lent for this exhibition by Her Majesty Queen Elizabeth the Queen Mother.'

The story behind the loan back of this print is interesting, as correspondence in the Royal Archives at Windsor Castle shows. Information from those letters between Hewitt and Buckingham Palace through October 1952 is reproduced here with permission.

Hewitt first wrote to the Palace in October 1952 stating that an exhibition of his work, arranged by Australia's Agent General Sir John Lienhop, was due to be staged in Australia House, London. He wanted to include a proof of his 1939 drypoint of the late King George VI who had died earlier in the year. However he had no proofs left, so he asked if he could borrow one of the proofs acquired two years earlier by Her Majesty Queen Elizabeth (the Queen Mother).

It proved to be an awkward request as Her Majesty was at the time in the process of moving to Clarence House. Most of her possessions were packed away for the move, and although a search had been made, the Rayner prints had not been located. Then a solution to the problem unexpectedly arrived in the form of an early proof of the King George VI drypoint that Hewitt's mother had sent back to Hewitt from Australia. Hewitt was quick to see a way around the difficulty. He offered to give Her Majesty this print as a gift, then borrow it back for the duration of the exhibition and return it after the exhibition. This allowed him to say quite correctly that the print of King George VI on display in Australia House had been loaned by Her Majesty.

Arthur Penn, Treasurer to Queen Elizabeth the Queen Mother, accepted the suggestion but stressed that Her Majesty would not want to keep the print after the exhibition if there was a chance that Hewitt's mother would like it returning. In passing, Mr Penn described the drypoint as 'an outstanding likeness of His Majesty'

So nobody ever knew that the Rayner print with pride of place in the Australia House window in January 1953 had travelled from the UK to Australia and back before being given to Queen Elizabeth the Queen Mother only a few weeks earlier, and then given back to Hewitt. Whether he did actually return the print to the Palace is not recorded.

Photographs from January 1953 show Hewitt standing in front of the window at Australia House where his paintings and drypoints are on display, with the King George VI work in pride of place at the front. The arrangement of his paintings and prints in the window followed a plan designed by Hewitt.

It was not primarily a selling exhibition, although Hewitt did make a list of the paintings on show in the window, with prices:

Oils

The old Melbourne regatta 1912	80 guineas
When we stood alone; the blitz on London	50 guineas
Old Bloomsbury	60 guineas
Les Sylphides, ballet rehearsal	40 guineas
Brighton 1933	70 guineas
Old Montmartre	50 guineas
The little wood (France)	60 guineas
Chelsea Reach, London, 1937	50 guineas
The artist's daughter Frances 1945	40 guineas

Watercolour

The Lambeth Walk	20 guineas
Pastel	
Mary	17 guineas
Drypoint	
The King	Not for sale; one or two copies left for sale at £20

The list records that one of the paintings – *Brighton 1933* – was sold. No list of the drypoints on show has survived, but the photos taken by Hewitt and Frances show that the display included one of the Gaudier Breszka prints, the harlequin drypoint and a drypoint of Frances.

The *Daily Express* of 15th January mentioned the exhibition.

In 1953 Hewitt seems to have experienced a renewal of interest in sailing. He was regularly taking out one of the small sailing boats on Regent's Park Lake, and he kept a log of these sessions. In October he illustrated and assembled a little book for his daughter Frances, titled *'Henry Rayner's Sailing Book: a small manual on the art of handling a sailing boat for beginners by Henry H. Rayner, 1953'.* In it he added a dedication to his daughter Frances, 'who brought me back to sailing after many years of landlubbering.'

In August that year, problems with the neighbours were worrying him again. On 27th August 1953 he wrote a long letter to the landlord, a Mr E Bennett, about

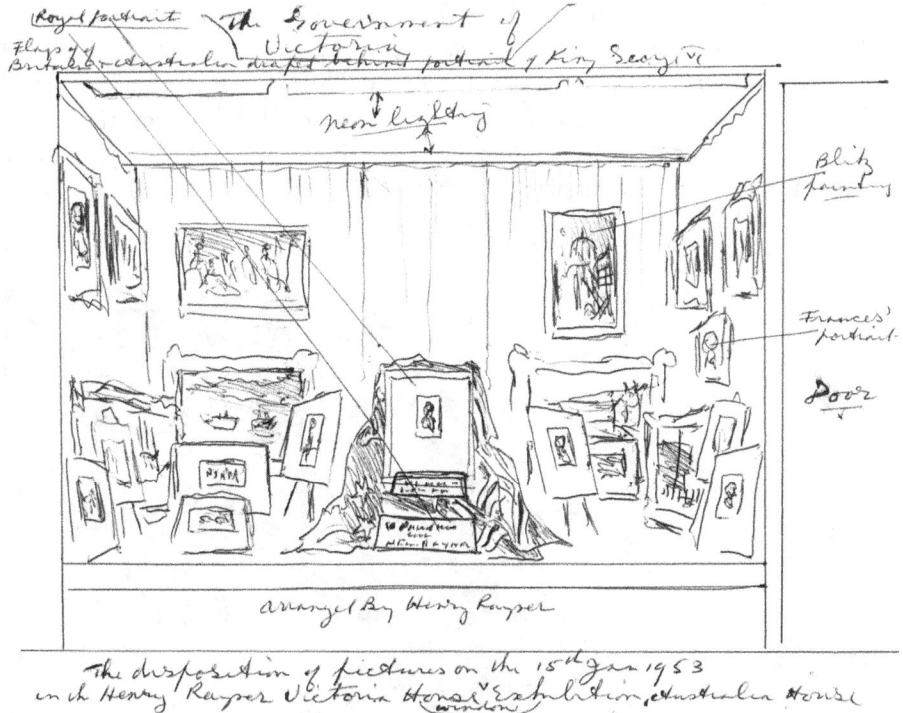

15.9 Hewitt's plan for how he wanted the window display arranging for his January 1953 exhibition at London's Australia House. sw.

the rowdy behaviour of the tenants of the ground floor flat and his suspicions that it was being used as a brothel. Evidently the problems continued because on 5th September he wrote again saying 'all through the summer I was ill and under my doctor for asthma, nerve and heart trouble. … The house has assumed the character of a brothel rather than a respectable house.'

Towards the end of 1953 Hewitt was in touch with celebrated boat designer Uffa Fox. He had proposed that Uffa should sit for him for a drypoint portrait, and the idea was well-received by Fox, although he pointed out that he was under considerable financial pressure following the unsuccessful sale of his Cowes boatyard. On 9th November Fox wrote: 'It is jolly kind of you to want to do a drypoint etching, but my trouble is that I am in no state to pay for anything these days.' In a later letter, he wrote: '…I cannot afford to come to London unless it is fairly urgent work'.

Hewitt was also angling for a chance to sail with Uffa and had initially offered to travel to Cowes to work on the drypoint. Fox's view was that at this time of year (November) there was little point in Rayner travelling to Cowes as most of the boats had been laid up for the winter, and anyway the sailing conditions were not good.

It is possible that Hewitt had exaggerated his own sailing experience when he first wrote to Fox, because in a letter dated 13th November he came clean and revealed that 'I blush to own it, and I can see your smile, but the noblest efforts I am seen to make are in the face of mighty uncomfortable puffs over Regent's Park lake.' He went on to recount his Isle of Wight pedigree, and the experience he gained sailing his father's yacht in Port Phillip Bay.

This admission doesn't seem to have put Uffa Fox off, however, for a couple of weeks later he wrote to Hewitt, still willing to sit for the portrait. It is not known whether the sitting ever took place, or whether Hewitt ever produced a drypoint of Fox.

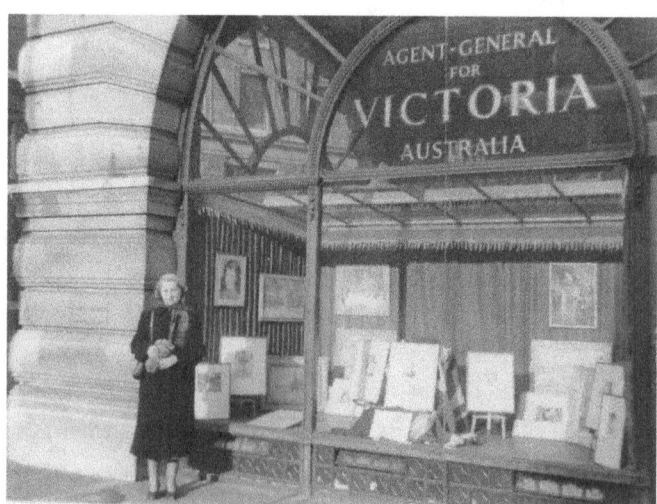

15.10 Theresa in front of the window display at Australia House in London, January 1953. sw.

In May 1954, completely out of the blue Hewitt received a letter from R M Campbell at the New Zealand Commission, 415 The Strand, London. Campbell's reason for writing was to enquire whether he could purchase a proof of Rayner's '*Old Chelsea Church*' drypoint as a wedding present for a friend's daughter who was going to be married in the church ('or what remains of it'). Hewitt not only supplied a copy of the print Campbell wanted but went with his daughter to deliver it personally a week later.

By the 1950s, Hewitt's health was poor. His wartime injuries still affected

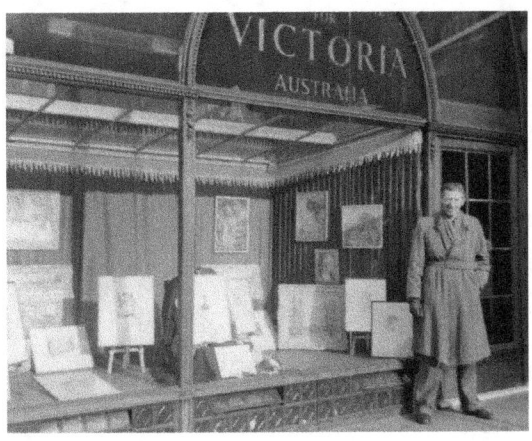

15.11 Hewitt in front of the window display at Australia House in London, January 1953. sw.

his chest, and there were the regular bouts of asthma, and hay fever every Spring. Added to that, the air quality in London had deteriorated, threatening the life of anyone with a respiratory problem. The winter of 1952 had been exceptionally bad, when very cold weather encouraged Londoners to heap even more coal onto their fires. This combined with a high-pressure zone and very light winds to create what became known as the Great Smog – responsible for an increase in crime and the deaths of 4,000 people.

Bad weather … poor health … problems with noisy neighbours … after nearly 30 years, London had lost its appeal to Hewitt. He had a big idea that involved moving somewhere else. And for the first time in his life he would soon have the money to pursue it.

IV

One final effort

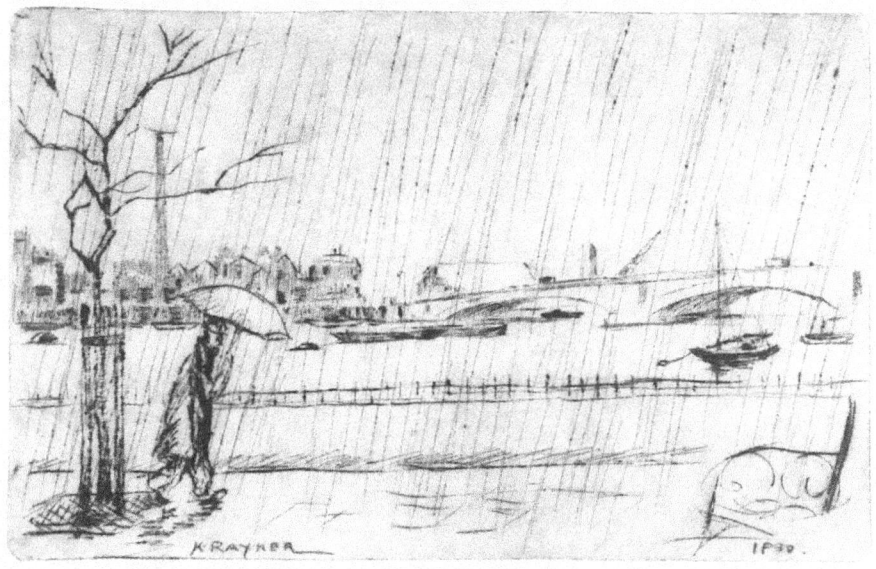

Fig IV Untitled, a wet day on the Thames Embankment at Chelsea, 1938, drypoint, 127 by 198mm. RS

16
The Ramsgate project

On 27th September 1954 Hewitt's mother died in Australia at the age of 75. She left her son a legacy of £1,000 from the sale of her home at 238 Richardson Street, Albert Park. There was also a cabin trunk full of papers which was shipped to Hewitt (he had to pay £6, which he asked to be deducted from his legacy).

The family used the money to implement one of his dreams – the setting up of a school of art in the Sickert style. This had been an idea of Hewitt's since the 1930s. The earliest reference to the idea comes from a news report published in the *London Evening Standard* of 18th April 1939.

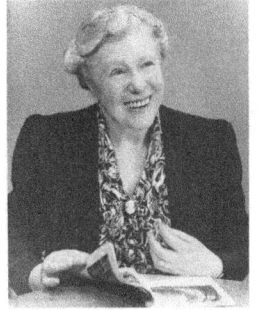

16.1 Hewitt's mother in 1950 at the age of 71. SW.

The Kent coast appealed to him because of its climate and the historic links with artists such as Turner. But above all because Sickert himself had lived and taught in the area in the 1930s. 'It was with his [Sickert's] wife that I first visited Ramsgate, where Sickert taught for a few weeks in 1934, and I came to love the place,' he wrote in one of the letters explaining his plan. 'I told Sickert that I would probably settle there in time. He was all for it and he set the germ of art in this part of the coast in his particular brand of poetic Impressionism.'

Hewitt would undoubtedly have liked to set up his home and the art centre in St Peters, the historic village near Broadstairs where Sickert had lived. But probably for financial reasons he chose nearby Ramsgate. On 7th June he deposited the cheque for £1,000 in his account at the Commonwealth Savings Bank of Australia in London. On Saturday 25th June Theresa took a trip to Ramsgate 'to see a £600 house'. Hewitt wasn't fit to travel.

On 3rd August as the family were getting ready for the move to Ramsgate, Hewitt was laid up with diverticulosis. He was beginning to realise the magnitude of the family's relocation to Ramsgate. He noted in his medical diary: 'God help my venture, and help my dear wife and children. I have tried to be strong, and full of a spiritual and physical courage and power'.

Hewitt was desperate for some peace and quiet. His hayfever and asthma attacks meant it was rare for him to get a good night's sleep, and the noisy neighbours were an added problem that earplugs didn't adequately deal with. On 13th

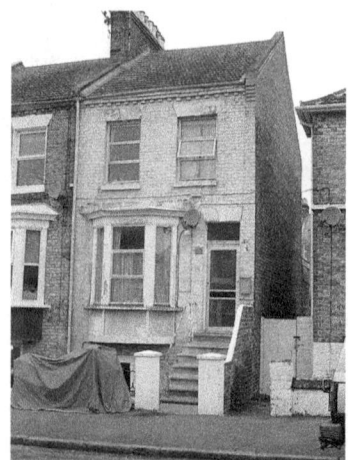

16.2 Number 39 Duncan Road, Ramsgate, the house the Rayners purchased in 1955 for £600. PHOTO RS.

August, a Doctor Silverman gave him a sick note that referred to 'nervous depression the result of lack of sleep caused by noisy neighbours'. He was prescribed Nembutal to help him sleep.

On 30th August he, Theresa, Frances and Kay moved into the house they had purchased at 39 Duncan Road. The removal company was Smiths Removers (Ramsgate) Ltd, of 95 King Street, Ramsgate. The cost was £16. Hewitt would never see London again.

A visit to Duncan Road, a few blocks away from the seafront and harbour, reveals a very strong clue as to why the family chose this particular house. It is part of a terrace of four Victorian properties collectively named Ventnor Villas. Ventnor is an Isle of Wight coastal town on the same stretch of coast as Shanklin, where the Rayners had lived for generations. This must have held a special attraction for Hewitt.

But the relocation did not turn out the way Hewitt had hoped. Initially the whole family moved to Ramsgate, but Frances did not stay long. In November she moved back to London to live in South Hill Park, Hampstead – initially at number 51A and then a few weeks later at number 45. This was the same street where her great friend Barbara lived. She wrote several letters a week to her parents, and travelled back to Ramsgate for weekends.

In October 1955 Hewitt started laying the groundwork for his proposed Sickert Group Art Centre in Ramsgate. He wrote to many people asking if they would lend their name to the project. Many of the letters, and the replies he received, are in the Rayner archive.

A typical example of his approach is letter one dated 31st October 1955 to Lord Methuen (a former pupil of Sickert from the Highbury Place school).

> My Lord
> I have begun an art centre dedicated to our mutual friend and Master Walter Sickert, here in Thanet. This little school sets out to teach those who desire to master the craft of painting, drawing and engraving; and I shall lecture and speak of Sickert, and collect what I am able of his writings and teachings, other than what he gave me.
> I have come to this Royal Harbour town to retire and find health in some further measure, and the school is my pleasure; each pupil receiving close personal attention.
> It is known that you admired Sickert for his many great qualities. He taught near here for some years, and I wish to carry on the work humbly and well.
> For the sake of those days when we all knew him so closely, and enjoyed so much of the wit and inimitable humour, and the perfect manner of the whole man as an artist and gentleman and helper, I ask if you would honour us by

becoming honorary member to the Group, there being no further appeal than this.

I have the honour to remain, my lord, your lordship's obedient servant,
Henry Rayner

By and large, he received positive replies from the people he approached. Many were handwritten, such as this one from Sylvia Gosse.

335 Old London Road, Ore, Hastings, Sussex

Dear Mr Rayner
Thank you very much for your letter and for what you kindly say about my work.

I hope that the art centre will prove a great success and will inspire Ramsgate to a love of the arts. I shall feel honoured at having my name included among those of the other honorary members.

With all good wishes,
I remain your sincerely
Sylvia Gosse

Mrs Andrina Schweder, Sickert's sister-in-law, wrote that she had once visited Walter at Broadstairs and was quite charmed by the lovely climate. 'I hope you will collect a nice school of pupils. I fancy Walter actually taught in one of the prep schools there in spite of his great age'.

The letter also mentions that she had attended a recent auction at Christies where a small collection of works by Sickert had fetched over £5,000.

She said she had recently purchased a small Sickert painting of the fountains in Kensington Gardens looking up the Serpentine, and she wondered if Hewitt had been with Sickert when this was done.

In Hewitt's reply he provided some extra information regarding the Serpentine painting.

Yes, I was with Walter when he painted the Serpentine.... He did not paint on this first day, but made washes and two or three drawings. I had to do the same. Later, at Fitzroy Street he had me fill in a ground in two colours, and this was dried and the monochrome taken by him to the Schools to show the students there how to form a two-colour base for painting. Later he painted over the surface quickly. There should be about five washes of that scene (reproduced in Lillian Browse's [book] *Walter Sickert*), some small drawings and two or three paintings, one large one. I would like to know which of them you possess. Mrs Rowland Bristow owns one painting, I know. I made about three drawings, two of which Walter kept and paid for.... Your painting should have a large tree in the left corner.

In fact, it turned out that the painting Andrina owned was not the one he described. But the exchange still adds a little more detail to Hewitt's Kensington Gardens meetings with Sickert.

Another Sickert acquaintance approached by Hewitt was novelist Enid Bagnold, who had attended Sickert's school in Bloomsbury. She had just returned from three weeks in America where she had 'managed to get my new play 'The Chalk Garden' through the gunfire of the critics'. She accepted immediately, and in her letter of 21st November 1955 she recounted the amusing story of how she came to join Sickert's school in the first place.

> 'I joined his school in the most absurd way. My mother told me I could never go to London without a maid. But we hadn't got a maid to spare. (Her remark was a remark passed on from her mother, who had plenty). So, in order to regularise myself, feeling that an art student had permissions of freedom, I looked down the advertisement column of the *New Age*.
>
> 'Why a girl of 19 and the daughter of an Army Officer took the *New Age* I can't now imagine. I found Sickert's advertisement of his school in Bloomsbury.
>
> 'Also, again by some strange way of life which I can't now remember, I also knew Lovat Fraser. We were both 19. We went together.
>
> 'I so remember Sickert opening my huge portfolio of drawings. I had been to a drawing school at Blackheath. Looking in silence at one great pencilled nude after another, so badly placed on the pages that often the head came out of the top. After he had seen every one he looked up at me with that ravishing smile and movement of the cheekbone (which the wretched beard so often afterwards hid) and said: 'But perhaps you paint?'
>
> 'Lovat he sent away altogether. He said he had a tiny and fully developed talent to which he could add nothing. It wasn't in his genre.
>
> 'Afterwards I knew Sickert well, and when he moved to Red Lion Square I used to prepare his plates for him with wax and smoked candle, and he gave me the first pull of so many – which I have here.
>
> 'I like 'Sickert gave me a letter to teach' in your letter. I am sure this is an expression he got from the Italian painters. He used to talk in terms of 'school of' very often.'
>

The letter Rayner wrote to Sir William Jordan contains some very interesting comments on his motives for the Sickert centre. 'I shall speak and lecture about him [Sickert] and teach painting and drawing and engraving in the tradition he set. The centre will set out to help working men and women pupils of talent, to assist them in mastering the craft of painting and engraving, and to teach any who possess sufficient gifts. It is not a profit-making effort, as I have come here to retire and to find pleasure in devoting my time to each pupil, my wife helping me.'

Hewitt's plan was to convert part of the family home in Duncan Road on West Cliff, a place he said was famous for its wonderfully bracing air. 'Artists and students will be invited to come here to stay and to paint and draw,' he wrote in one of the letters, in November 1955. 'So far, the winter here is marvellous. It is a veritable sun trap.

'I am getting the large front room prepared for meetings and exhibitions, but I think the ideal place for larger showings will be the West Cliff Hall, which is an underground pavilion girt with blossoms, gnomes, and large illuminated frogs, all animated to the sound of surf and sea birds.'

In the same letter he revealingly commented: 'I sadly miss London, but I think I am here to stay.'

Having gathered enough honorary members, he officially launched the Sickert Group in December 1955. The brochures were printed for him by the *East Kent Times* at 85 High Street, Ramsgate (cost £2.8.0) and he started sending brochures out on 16th December. A local art shop, Lovelly's, showed copies of the brochure.

While these moves to establish his Sickert Art Group were going on, Hewitt was also putting out feelers towards the Art community in the Ramsgate area.

Sir William Jordan (who had been born in Ramsgate) wrote from his home in Auckland, New Zealand to say that he had been in touch with 'a very important public man in Ramsgate' on Hewitt's behalf. Jordan also says in the letter that he bought one of Hewitt's etchings at the Brook Street exhibition, and that 'it is with other of my valued possessions still in London, I hope to gather them up next year and return them to my home.'

The 'very important public man' was the Mayor of Ramsgate, the Rev. Harcourt Samuel. He got in touch with John Moody, Principal of the City of Canterbury College of Art, on Rayner's behalf, concerning possible openings for art teachers.

In a letter of 3rd January 1956, Moody cautioned Hewitt not to be too optimistic: 'I think I should warn you that opportunities for employing teachers of drawing and painting in the East Kent Art Schools are few and far between.'

Moody and Rayner met in January, and Moody offered to propose Hewitt for membership of the East Kent Art Society. He put him in touch with the society's honorary secretary Miss Honor Bacon. He was elected a member at the committee meeting of the Society on 17th February, having submitted several examples of his work.

The Sickert Art Group

Hewitt wrote and published a four-page leaflet announcing the Sickert Art Group. The group's aims were stated as 'discussions, talks, lectures, indoor and outdoor painting classes, art therapy, annual meetings and dinner, and exhibitions'.

Membership conditions and fees were available on application. The prices for separate art lessons were given as 3/6 for children and 4/6 for adults, with reductions for talented students at work. Studio and Centre was at the Rayner's home, 39 Duncan Road. He made a small card nameplate for the front door of his home, stating: 'The Sickert Art Centre. Two knocks.'

In the little leaflet Hewitt included the names of all the people who had agreed to lend their names to the project. Listed under Senior group members and associates of the late Walter Richard Sickert BA, LLD, are the following: The Right

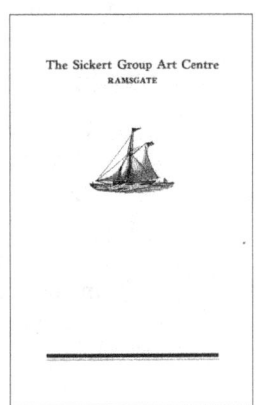

The Sickert Group Art Centre
RAMSGATE

16.3 The leaflet Hewitt had printed to promote his art school. sw.

Hon. Lord Methuen MA, ARA, RWS, FSA, Miss Sylvia Gosse, BBA, FRSA, Miss Enid Bagnold, Lady Jones, Theresa Charlotte Zecchin, Henry Rayner, Andrina Schweder (sister-in-law to Sickert).

In a typically creative Rayner move, he added for good measure several 'Members defunct' – Wilson Steer QM, Dame Ethel Walker DBE, ARA, James Quinn RP, ROI, and Therese Lessore.

His own role was stated to be Founder and Secretary, Instructor (painting, engraving and drawing), describing himself as 'Holder of the Sickert Teaching Certificate and Royal Academy Schools Ivory, Art Advisor and Critic'. This is followed by a list of the galleries and museums where his work could be found, the main exhibitions of his work that had been staged, the famous people who owned copies of his drypoints, and various achievements he considered noteworthy.

Hewitt's elder daughter Frances was given the title of Visiting Teacher (especially children).

Clearly Hewitt had used in the promotional material every scrap of information he felt would help his cause. To some extent he stretched the facts to the very limit – the 'Sickert teaching certificate' in all probability refers to the reference letter Sickert wrote on his behalf before his trip to Australia (see page 100).

The individuals named as members and members defunct are mostly friends from the past. Lord Methuen, he had met while attending art classes at Sickert's 1927 art school in Highbury Fields, when he left the Royal Academy Schools. Theresa Charlotte Zecchin was of course his own wife. James Quinn was the Australian artist and father of Rayner's friend from the RA Schools. Therese Lessore had been married to Sickert. Wilson Steer, the artist, was an old friend of Sickert, and someone Hewitt knew – he had drawn his portrait more than once.

In usual Rayner style, he gave press interviews to publicise the Sickert Group Art Centre. *The East Kent Times and Broadstairs Mail* of 21st March 1956 ran the following story:

He aims to make Ramsgate a Mecca of art

Maintaining Sickert tradition

A man who sees Ramsgate as a 'future Mecca of art' is Australian artist Henry Rayner, of 39 Duncan Road, the founder and secretary of the Sickert Group Art Centre at his home.

Mr Rayner, who has lived in Thanet for six months, is the latest fully elected member of the East Kent Arts Society, as a painter and etcher. He has come here to carry on the tradition of his great friend and teacher Walter Sickert, who lived at St Peter's.

After their first meeting in 1925, Mr Rayner became a great admirer of Sickert, and he says of him: 'He educated me in the art of real impressionism and colour tone.' He describes him as 'the first modern old master we have'.

It was Sickert who first told Mr Rayner of the beauty of this part of the world. 'He said it had never been exploited,' says Mr Rayner, who shares Sickert's opinion of Thanet.

'The harbour has not been exploited enough,' he told me. 'It is really lovely. It is going to be a future Mecca of art. Ramsgate is not far from London and such a place can become highly cultured if the traditions started by Sickert can be carried on.'

Mr Rayner, a former freelance medical student at Waikato, New Zealand, describes himself as 'an artist of the people', adding with characteristic 'Aussie' candour 'I have had to live with the ordinary people from an early age. I have had to work hard – I didn't have my 'daddy' to keep me all my life – and as a craftsman I intend to live here with the people and pay my rates willingly and happily.'

He is a great believer in art therapy. 'To be able to create is one of the greatest assets in the world,' he says, 'and I have always said that patients in the medical world would have far less need of doctors if they would use their creative faculties.'

Sickert, he points out, scorned the attention of the medical profession upon himself. 'His only doctor was myself; I had on occasions to give him sleeping draughts, and then very much against his will.'

....

Mr Rayner was blown up three times during the war when he refused to leave London, and is a sick man. He intends to stay in Ramsgate with his wife – who is also a Chelsea artist – and two daughters.

He maintains 'Sickert was the greatest art teacher England ever had. He asked me to carry on the tradition which I intend to do while I live. I should like to work for the people of Kent to the best of my ability.'

With his usual enthusiasm, here was Hewitt retelling the Rayner/Sickert story, but with a new twist – carrying on the Sickert teaching tradition. The 'art therapy' theme may well have reflected Hewitt's own experience recovering from the injuries he sustained during the war. What Sickert would have thought of the claim that Rayner was his only doctor is open to speculation.

There are some interesting clues to what any students at the Sickert Group Art Centre would have heard, in a long letter (one of several) Hewitt wrote to a friend called Ron in New Zealand. This Ron had evidently asked Hewitt for some advice. Hewitt passes on the advice he received at the St Johns Wood and Royal Academy Schools, so the ideas expressed in the letter presumably reflect Hewitt's own guiding principles.

'Have you, at your art school, been taught anything about human anatomy? If not, then you must begin. Half your first drawings should be from the figure and the bones. ... If you can draw the figure, you can paint a landscape with more confidence. ... Try to draw your own head from life in a simple light, study the proportions, and do not worry about likeness so much, that all comes later on. Draw the head with a heavy pencil or charcoal, going for proportions only, not worrying too much about the sentiment of the thing. Picture-making comes later. ...

'Please forget any sentimental picture-making – I want you to seek the form in the picture. You will probably be able to get hold of some of the great modern etcher Segonzac's work in reproduction. I recommend this as a real guide to landscape. ... Do not worry about following some vague sentimental preconceptions in art, or some other man's view. Study to make your own pictures, and go at it as if you meant it. You are you and nobody else, remember that.

'I am against too much copying, it is liable to get one into bad habits, lazy habits, and an artist cannot afford to be a lazy man. ... Study nature day and night, the rich interplay of shadow and light, the wonderful merging of colour in the simplest little scenes, and the simple scenes are the best. ... Do not worry much about that thing called technique. Technique comes from your use of the brush naturally. You gain your own style by hard application and the natural placing down of colour as you feel it.

'I have suggested to you the free use of colour, plenty of it on your brush in oils, drawing it richly over the canvas or board, the canvas should, as the board, be primed first of all with a base of white, and it needn't be too smooth. ...

'Do not choose pretty scenes, but those which contain something fine you have seen, and try to arrange your own composition. But eschew the pretty. It may seem very hard at first to dig the beauty out of nature, but it comes very quickly with serious application. You will live to thank me for this advice. ... I have been very fortunate in knowing the greatest painters of my time, and I tried to follow what they taught me, and I am giving you the benefit of the united teaching'.

Hewitt's Art Centre project can be seen as the culmination of a lifelong dream. In his teenage years in New Zealand, he felt acutely the lack of art tuition available to people in rural locations. He had always highly regarded Sickert's teaching skills. Sickert had encouraged him to take up teaching, and Hewitt knew that Sickert had had a dream of starting up an art school on the south coast. The project also fitted in with Hewitt's lifelong vision of making art more accessible to ordinary working people.

Sadly, it never came to anything, only attracting one person to the school. Frances wrote that the Sickert art school project was the last thing her father ever tried to get moving.

17

A terrible winter

Hewitt's health was deteriorating. The winter of 1955/56 was hard. In 1956 he spent several weeks in hospital in Canterbury. His weight had dropped to just eight stone – very low for someone of Rayner's 6' 2' height. In April 1956 his daughter Frances recorded in her diary that her father had been ill in bed for two months and was very weak.

It wasn't just the weather that was affecting Hewitt. 'I could see that life was not working out,' wrote Frances in her own unpublished autobiography. 'Mother was working locally and Kay was set up in her centre. Father was alone in the house and it was a lonely place too. It was a terrible winter of burst pipes and sickness.'

In her diary several months later, Frances described her father as 'feeling hemmed in by circumstances, unable to move out of it.'

Barbara Griffin believes that Hewitt and his family found it difficult to be accepted in Ramsgate, and this contributed to Hewitt's depression. On 20th Nov 1956 Graham Cumming Ltd, church publishers, of Chapel Place, Ramsgate, Kent, offered Theresa a job in the Post Room at a wage of £3.10.0 weekly, subject to a month's trial. This seems to have added to her husband's anxieties.

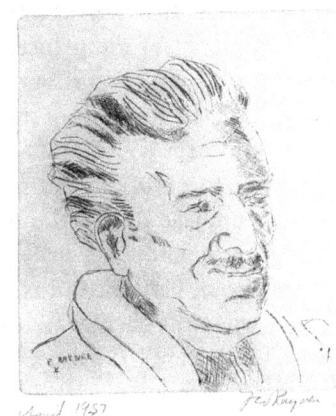

17.1 This drypoint by his daughter Frances shows Hewitt in April 1957, exhausted by illness, lack of sleep and depression. Drypoint, 171×145mm. sw.

Meanwhile, Frances had given up her job in London, and moved back in with her parents, getting a job with the company where her mother worked. In the winter of 1956/7 she was struck down with an attack of influenza that lasted several weeks. While she was ill she was sacked from her job. Recovery from the influenza was slow, and even walking the 100 yards to the nearby shop exhausted her.

Hewitt himself was in poor shape that winter. He recorded that through February and April he was regularly receiving Persomnin and Codeine from the doctor. Persomnin is a now-obsolete drug containing bromide, used at that time to treat psychological excitement or anxiety, and induce sleep.

Some good news came in February when Her Majesty Queen Elizabeth purchased a copy of Hewitt's 1939 etching of her father, King George VI, for £15.15.0 (15 guineas).

He wrote a press release about it for the newspapers in the Ramsgate area. 'Before the Queen left for Portugal last week she purchased for her private collection a portrait of her father, the late King George VI, from the British artist Henry Rayner, whose home is at 39 Duncan Road, Ramsgate. On the 7th February the artist received a command letter from the Queen requesting him to send the work to the palace.

'Rayner already has four works in the royal collection, Windsor, and Queen Mary and the Queen Mother became his patrons during the Hitler War in which he was injured when a parachute landmine fell near his studio in Hampstead, 1940. Later his painting arm was smashed.'

The *East Kent Times & Mail* treated it as a front page story, under the heading 'Queen buys work of local artist'. The sale came about after Hewitt had written to the Queen offering to send her a copy of the etching of her late father. When the offer was accepted, Rayner actually sent several etchings to Buckingham Palace. There were four proofs of the portrait of King George VI, using different coloured inks. One was a two-colour version in sienna and blue. Hewitt explained that he had only pulled two proofs in this particular colour mix.

He also sent for inspection a portrait of himself at his etching table, the portrait of the princesses Elizabeth and Margaret in the ballet of 1945, a copy of '*Ballet 48*', and one of '*The Lambeth Walk*'. He commented that he had only done four proofs of the portrait of the princesses, one of which was in the Queen Mother's collection.

The Queen communicated through a Lady-in-Waiting that she wished to purchase one of the portraits of her late father. Despite Hewitt's invitation for her to name her price, she chose to pay the full price marked on the back of the proof. He sent in his bill on 16th February. He was so thrilled by the sale that when the cheque arrived from the Privy Purse, drawn on Coutts Bank and dated 26th March, he drew a copy of the cheque before banking it.

A month later, on Wednesday 24th April, spirits in the Rayner household were low. 'I had had so much of the sickness, and we were all tired,' Frances wrote in her autobiography. 'That night he [father] was not himself. When I said goodnight to him I said it three or four times as he sat at the fireplace while mother ironed on the board. He looked up at last as if he did not recognise me.'

Frances climbed the two flights to her bedroom but could not sleep. Her father later knocked on her bedroom door, hoping to talk with her, but she pretended to be asleep to avoid getting drawn into a conversation.

The next thing she knew was being woken by the sound of weeping from the kitchen downstairs. It was her mother. During the night, her father had taken his own life by turning on the gas tap in his bedroom. He left two suicide notes, which were taken away by the police.

The next day, Friday 26th April, his death was reported in the *East Kent Times* and the *Thanet Gazette*, and *The Times*. They all said more or less the same thing: that 54-year-old Rayner had been found dead in a gas-filled room at his home early on the previous day, with some additional information about the Queen recently buying one of his prints. The inquest was set for the following Monday, 31st April.

There were longer press reports after the inquest.

The Coroner, Mr W R Mowill, asked Theresa about the background to her husband's death. She recounted the story of their relocation from London to Ramsgate, which she said was to try to mend her husband's health. She made no mention of the plan to set up a school of art. This omission was undoubtedly in order to protect Hewitt's reputation. If she had talked about the art school plan she would have been forced to reveal that it had been a failure.

In her comments she explained that Hewitt had suffered from asthma and bomb blast since 1940, and that after the damage to his drawing arm, despite a 'marvellous operation' he never recovered his real touch .... never regained the full range he used to have. Since the accident, she said, he had worked only sporadically.

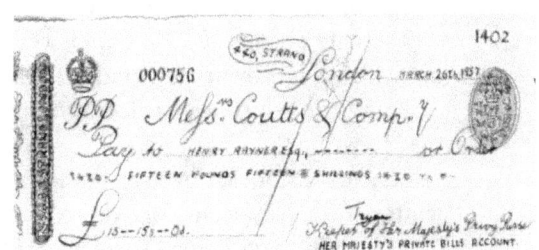

17.2 Hewitt's drawing of the cheque he received from Her Majesty Queen Elizabeth II in March 1957 as payment for a proof of the 1939 drypoint of her father, King George VI. sw.

When asked whether he might have taken his life because of general depression or because he could no longer further his professional career, Theresa stated that she thought it was a combination of both. She said that he slept very badly because of his asthma and that sleeping pills did not help, however many he took. She also mentioned that the noise of jet aircraft seemed to worry him. She stated that he had often mentioned that he found life hard and had talked about taking his own life. One of the phrases reported in several of the press reports was that he 'felt inadequate to be the head of the household.'

On the facts of the night Hewitt died, Theresa said that he had wanted to talk to her at 3am. This was evidently not an uncommon event. She heard no more, and then at about 7.30am she went to his room and found him lying on the floor, and the room full of gas. She forced the door open, which had been difficult because of a pillow that was blocking it, turned off the gas supply and opened the window.

The policeman who attended the house in response to the emergency call stated that he found Hewitt's body lying on the floor in a first-floor bedroom. The room was full of gas fumes. His head was on a pillow and the pillow was on a gas ring that had been connected to a supply pipe on the wall. The policeman had attempted to revive Hewitt, with no success.

The consultant pathologist from Kent and Canterbury Hospital stated that the cause of death was coal gas poisoning.

The inquest returned a verdict of suicide while the balance of his mind was disturbed. The death certificate records: 'Coal gas poisoning through inhaling gas from a gas ring, killing himself whilst the balance of his mind was disturbed'.

One puzzle is the suicide note that was discovered in the Rayner archive. It was written on the reverse of a quotation for fencing panels from the Advance Wood Company of 347 Margate Road, Ramsgate. It reads:

> 19.3.56
> 11pm. Gas on.
> Dear Frances and my Kay & Theresa
> You will be happier now, & Radcliffe will do everything for you. I tried to love you both & your mother so much in my silly way, & always will in Eternity.
> I've been very ill for nine days now having had two strokes.

Radcliffe was the Rayner's lawyer.

The date on this suicide note is very strange. It is the wrong year, the wrong month and the wrong day. Had there been a previous suicide attempt 13 months earlier? Or one month earlier? Or was Hewitt simply in such a confused state that he wrote the wrong date?

Hewitt was buried on 1st May 1957 at Ramsgate cemetery. After a long, hard winter and a grey spring, the day of the funeral was bright, sunny and warm.

It was four days before Theresa's birthday.

18
Back to London

The value of Hewitt's estate was £1,175 gross, £1,125 net. At the time of his death, his late mother's estate in Australia was still being wound up, leaving Theresa to attend to some final matters.

Letters of condolence arrived from Sylvia Gosse, New Zealand Commissioner R W Campbell and others. There was also a letter from Severino Zecchin, Theresa's younger brother, who lived in Wood Green, London. 'Sever' had only found out about Hewitt's death by reading a story in the *Daily Express*.

Theresa had been in touch with Ailsa Craig, the highly-regarded journalist who in 1957 was a London-based correspondent for the Sydney Morning Herald, shortly to move to the Australian magazine *Woman's Day*. This resulted in a feature article in *Woman's Day* about Henry Rayner under the heading 'Unhappy artist wished for death – Henry Rayner came so close to success, but circumstances always beat him'.

It told the Rayner story from his wife's point of view. Much of the factual information in the article is well-known from other sources, but the writer had clearly met and interviewed Theresa (whom she described as 'attractive and youthful looking').

Theresa had told Ailsa that for her husband Ramsgate had been a little hell where he deteriorated rapidly, couldn't sleep at night and took too many sleeping pills. She had lived in dread that Hewitt might take his own life, and it seemed that when she took the job in the church publishing firm her husband's disenchantment was complete. She said that he felt hopeless and a burden to his family.

In a memorable comment Theresa said that 'Henry was a great artist who died of neglect. Just another genius on the scrapheap.'

A year after his death, on Friday April 25th 1958, the family inserted this *In Memoriam* notice in *The Times*:

> Rayner, Henry Hewitt – to the memory of an artist, husband and father, who left this world on the 25th April 1957. We pay tribute to his courage and genius, the fruits of which he gave freely to mankind. We, his family, are left to mourn the loss of one so loved by us – Theresa, Frances and Kay.

With Hewitt gone, the family found Ramsgate held little appeal, and in October 1958 they moved back to London. But not central London. They wanted

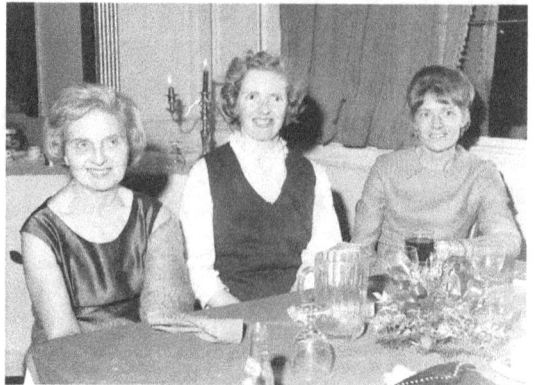

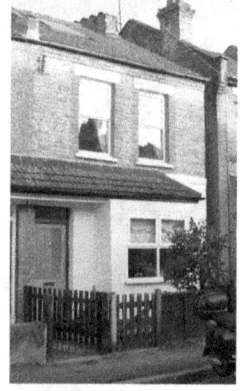

18.2 Number 22 Crane Road, Twickenham, where Theresa, Frances and Kay lived from 1958 until their deaths in the late 1990s. PHOTO RS.

18.1 Theresa, Kay and Frances c.1970. PHOTO COURTESY PETER ZECCHIN.

somewhere where they could breathe. So after several research trips from Ramsgate, they decided on Twickenham, and purchased a house at 22 Crane Road.

The family used a little (£200) of the money they had inherited from Hewitt's mother to purchase a plot at Highgate Cemetery, and had Hewitt's remains re-buried there. It seems that at the time they actually purchased two plots at Highgate. The second plot was never used by the family, and according to Barbara Griffin was part of Frances's estate when she died in 1999.

The grave is at the southern end of Highgate Cemetery East, close to the Chester Road gates (which are kept locked). The foot of the gravestone carries the words: 'Artist – Mystic'. Along the west side are the words 'Made the famous drypoints during the Blitz of 1940. Protégé of W R Sickert.'

The grave caught the attention of Judi Culbertson and Tom Randall, who included a brief item on Rayner in their 1991 book 'Permanent Londoners: an illustrated guide to the cemeteries of London'.

Theresa continued to work at promoting Hewitt's reputation. One initiative she pursued was to offer a large collection of his works to New Zealand, to form a travelling exhibition. In April 1960 she wrote to Mr A T Campbell, the Public Relations Officer at New Zealand House in the Strand, proposing the idea and offering a collection of Rayner's works.

This idea of a travelling exhibition of his prints was clearly one that Hewitt himself had dreamt of. Theresa described it in one letter as 'a dream he cherished, and one that he had hopes of realising, to return spiritually.'

There was an exchange of letters lasting until August. In the correspondence, Theresa states that she has 'over 100 prints, apart from the framed ones.'

Mr Campbell sounded out the Internal Affairs Department in New Zealand, asking them to take up the matter with the leading galleries in the country. In the event, no-one was prepared to take up the idea of a travelling exhibition of Rayner's drypoints, and manage it.

The high point of Theresa's campaign was in March 1960, when a retrospective exhibition of her husband's work was held at the Richmond Hill Gallery in Richmond. It was Sickert's centenary year.

The exhibition received a brief mention in *The Times* newspaper of 22nd March, and there were two longish articles in the *Richmond & Twickenham Times* on Saturdays March 12 and March 26 1960.

Unique art show at Richmond gallery

A unique opportunity is provided by the Richmond Hill Gallery, 47 Hill Rise, Richmond, in a show that is open now and for the next two weeks, to see no less than three quarters of the total life's work of a celebrated artist.

The work is that of the drypoint artist Henry Rayner. About 70 of his total published output of just over 90 prints are in the show.

Apart from the importance of the show as an artistic event, the range of prints shown is full of delight and variety.

Rayner came to this country from Australia and New Zealand as a young man, to study at the Royal Academy.

He became a pupil and friend of the painter Sickert, whose centenary is being celebrated this year, and he knew a host of the most celebrated people in this country.

Identical prints

Many of them sat for him, and the results are to be seen in the present exhibition, in the form of drypoint prints of such people as King George VI, Sir Winston Churchill, Walter Richard Sickert, Augustus John, George Bernard Shaw, Lawrence of Arabia and Anton Dolin.

Identical prints from the same plates are in the Royal collection at Windsor, the British Museum, the Ashmolean Museum, the National Portrait Gallery, and the Queen Mary collection.

Though Rayner was supreme in this specialist branch of pictorial art, he suffered from depression about his work and ill-health.

He died in 1956, and his widow and two daughters live at Crane Road, Twickenham.

City scenes

Into these small prints, all of them technically exquisite, and none of them more than a few square inches in size, Rayner has concentrated a visionary's whole world of faces, scenes, allegory, religion, mysticism, happiness, misery and social criticism.

The London street scenes, of which a number are shown, lend themselves particularly well to this medium. The portraits of celebrities are of course intensely interesting.

But perhaps most enjoyable of all are several pictures of children, realised with incredible economy and delicacy of line.

© RICHMOND & TWICKENHAM TIMES, 12TH MARCH 1960

An artist's widow fights to win his place in posterity

An exhibition now at the Richmond Hill Gallery is the first since his death in 1956 by his own hand, of the works of Henry Rayner, the celebrated drypoint artist.

But his widow, Mrs Theresa Rayner, of Crane Road, Twickenham, is determined that it shall be remembered in years to come as the first step in a new wave of recognition and acclaim for Rayner's works.

Although pictures by her husband are in the National Portrait Gallery, the Ashmolean Museum, the Royal Collection at Windsor, and leading collections abroad, Mrs Rayner considers that her husband was never accorded the fame his talent deserved.

'There are so few people with such great gifts as my husband,' Mrs Rayner told me. 'He should have been encouraged, and nursed along by the state. If he had had the recognition he should, he would not have died as he did.'

Australia

Mrs Rayner is hoping that one of the first moves in her crusade will be an exhibition of Henry Rayner's works in Australia, the country of his birth.

Life with the dedicated artist, as portrayed by his widow, emerges as a combination of great happiness with his family, and extreme depression about his work and ill health.

Early days were troublefree. The artist arrived from New Zealand and worked as a motor mechanic ('He knew a car engine Inside out') and then realised that this would have to be given up for full-time art training.

His friend

It was at the Royal Academy that Henry Rayner became the pupil of famous Walter Sickert, whom Mrs Rayner remembers with gratitude as the man who not only encouraged her husband with his faith in what he called 'your unusual powers' but also became his friend.

Rayner's 24 year-old daughter, Frances, is at a similar position as her father when he stood at the crossroads before deciding whether to continue both his job and his art, or to abandon everything else for his pictures.

Like her father again, Frances has decided for art, and in the words that Rayner might have used 'I have little choice really, when it comes to art. Art is like that'. Again like her father, Frances is combing the galleries and studying incessantly. She is hoping for an art scholarship, and though she prefers painting on canvas, she also works in drypoint.

Lost Tradition

'To an extent, the tradition of drypoint has been lost,' she says. 'It is a craft that must be learned, and instilled into you. My father did not teach me. I did not ask him to, but I worked by his side, even as a child, and in this way I learned from him.'

Henry Rayner's talent has obviously lived through his daughter, as a drypoint portrait of Prince Charles that Frances produced after one glimpse of the boy has been accepted by the Queen.

The exhibition catalogue listed 65 drypoints by Rayner. Prints worth £44 were sold, and after the gallery's commission and transport costs Theresa received just short of £33. The last picture sold at the exhibition, noted Theresa, was a portrait of Sickert at Fitzroy Street, purchased by Sickert's sister-in-law Andrena Schweder.

Theresa, Frances and Kay continued to live at 22 Crane Street until the 1990s. What happened to them over the following three decades is outside the scope of this biography, and in any case there is very little information available. In 1961 and 1962 Frances was living and studying in Australia, in the Melbourne area where her father grew up. A few surviving letters show that on 19th Dec 1961 she was living at 2 Sydney Street East Prahran. The letter had been forwarded from 209 Spring Street. In Dec 1961 she had been studying at the Prahran Technical School, 142 High Street, and gained a certificate of Art, 1st year group, achieving a score of 605 out of 1000, and was accepted for the second year. In March the following year she was at 131 High Street, Prahran.

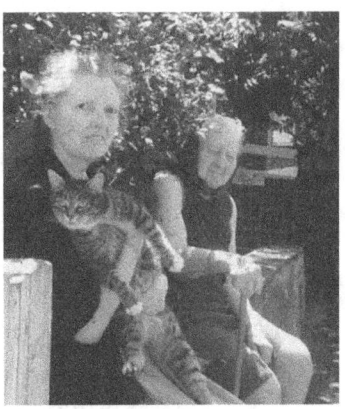

18.3 Theresa Rayner and younger daughter Kay in the 1990s. PHOTO COURTESY BARBARA GRIFFIN.

The next significant date is 5th May 1997, when Theresa died in West Middlesex hospital. It was one day after her 92nd birthday. The death certificate showed the cause of death as pneumonia, but also noted that she was suffering from dementia.

Everything of Theresa's, including all of her husband's plates, prints, paintings, manuscripts and other archive documents, the family home at 22 Crane Road and her part share in the family property in northern Italy passed to older daughter Frances. It seems that Theresa had lost or destroyed very few of her husband's possessions. They had both been hoarders. His day passes to the Reading Room of the British Museum survived, along with examples of his work from the Royal Academy Schools in 1926 and 1927. Even the receipt for his and Theresa's ticket to Australia in 1931 had been carefully kept.

Barbara Griffin recalled that Frances also found cupboards full of fabrics, linen, soap and all manner of things that had been carefully hoarded over the years by her mother. The privations of her parents' early life together had never been forgotten.

The matter of the property in Fanna, Italy in which Theresa had inherited a share along with her brothers Richard and Severino, was a continuing problem for Frances – and in fact was not resolved by the time she died. Theresa had always assumed that she had inherited a one-third share, but upon investigation it turned out that the brothers had each inherited a 7/18ths share, while Theresa received only a 4/18ths share. This was evidently the result of Italian inheritance law at the time the will was drawn up, prior to the 1930s. There is a rather terse letter from Theresa to Sever dated 2nd March 1951 in the Rayner archive, in which she is raising questions about her inheritance. A further complication in this long-running matter was that Theresa's older brother Richard had passed away in 1995.

After Theresa's death, events unfolded rapidly.

Younger daughter Kay died one month later on 6th June in the family home in Crane Road, Twickenham. She was 59. At the time, she was wheelchair bound, and suffering from undiagnosed cancer that had spread. Barbara Griffin recounted how Frances and Kay were at home in Crane Road one evening, and Kay suddenly said to Frances 'I need to talk to you.' Frances was working on school papers, and said she needed to finish what she was doing. Suddenly Kay said 'Frances', let out a long breath, and died.

'Frances blamed herself again, feeling that this was the second time the same thing had happened,' said Barbara. 'First, her father. Then her sister.'

Frances had a stone plaque added to Hewitt's grave in Highgate Cemetery, in memory of her parents and sister. It carried a quote from Francois Duc de la Rochefoncauld (1613–1680):

> There is a kind of dignity which does not depend upon fortune; it is a certain manner which distinguishes us and which seems to destine us for greater things, it is the value we insensibly set upon ourselves.'

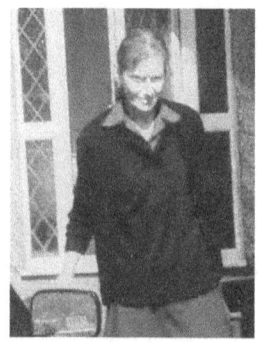

18.4 Frances Rayner in the 1990s. PHOTO COURTESY BARBARA GRIFFIN.

Frances made a will on 24th December 1997. She herself died two years later on 6th December 1999, at the Memorial Hospital, Teddington. She was 63, and suffering from a lung abcess.

Theresa's nephew Peter Zecchin said in 2012 that his aunt always harboured a sense of grievance that her husband had not been recognised. This carried through to Frances, who in Peter's words 'railed against the world and its unfairness until the day she died'.

He told a bitter-sweet story about Frances's burial in December 1999. He and his sister Christina went to Highgate Cemetery to pay their respects. As they entered the cemetery they encountered a good friend of Frances who was carrying flowers, a prayer book and three Tesco carrier bags.

'She was completely laden down,' said Peter, 'So I offered to help. She accepted gratefully, and gave me two of the bags, saying 'This one is your Aunt Theresa, this one is Kay, and I'll carry Frances'.

Theresa's and Kay's ashes had been kept at the family home in Twickenham since their deaths, and they were all to be interred at the same time. Peter, Christina and the friend solemnly walked down the hill to the grave, and improvised their own funeral service. 'It was sad and funny at the same time', Peter recalled. 'There were lots of bizarre stories like that, and I miss that eccentric part of the family.'

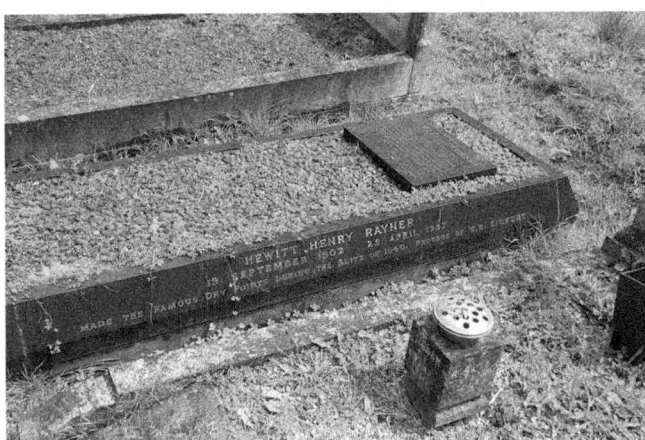

18.5 Hewitt Rayner's grave at London's Highgate Cemetery East. His wife and both daughters are also buried here. The gravestone carries several inscriptions including 'Made the famous drypoints of the Blitz during 1940. Protégé of WR Sickert'. PHOTO RS.

According to the terms of Frances's will, a substantial cash sum went to two of her friends: Barbara Griffin, who had known Frances since the 1940s, and Atiya Khan. There was a £3,000 bequest to the London Borough of Camden for maintenance of the family plot at Highgate Cemetery. At the time of Frances's death, the matter of the inherited house in Italy was still unresolved. It was only cleared up in 2004, and the money released by the lawyers.

Frances's will stipulated that the prints made by her father were to be offered to New Zealand in the hope that a permanent home could be found to display them. There was another substantial amount of money allocated to finance the shipping of the plates to New Zealand, and for framing them, in the event that the country accepted the offer.

Likewise, all her father's papers and other memorabilia, as well as her own writings, were to be offered to New Zealand.

In the event a representative of the New Zealand government did take a look at all the material. A few proofs of Rayner's wartime drypoints were chosen, but the offer of all the prints for a permanent exhibition was declined. So all the material became part of the residue that passed to Frances's old schoolfriend Barbara Griffin.

Many of the drawings, paintings and prints from this archive were subsequently put up for auction through Bonhams of London in 2000 and 2002. This was the source of most of the Rayner pictures that appeared for sale via print dealers and auction rooms in the years that followed. Several oil paintings subsequently found their way to Australia and New Zealand.

The remaining material, including many of Hewitt's original notes, autobiographical writings and other personal mementos, all his drypoint plates, and some drawings and paintings, was stored in a goat shed in Lincolnshire.

Fortunately, it was discovered and rescued by art teacher Sheilagh Wilford. It is this archive that has provided much of the factual information about Hewitt Rayner for this biography.

19

An untouchable rebel?

Hewitt Rayner always believed that his involvement in the student protest at the Royal Academy Schools in 1926 tarnished his reputation for ever, marking him out as an 'untouchable rebel'.

Was this true? Did Britain's art establishment gang up against him? Or was he being paranoid?

Physically, Hewitt was a striking figure, with his 6ft 2in height, blond hair and grey eyes. Photos from the 1930s and 1940s show a man with a slim face, perhaps even gaunt. All the photographs and drawings of him, going back to 1922, show him with a moustache.

He was fit, except when suffering one of his hay fever or asthma attacks which happened with increasing frequency after 1940. He walked everywhere in London, rarely taking public transport. He enjoyed playing tennis, preferring grass rather than hard courts, and regularly took his family to the public tennis courts on Parliament Hill, Hampstead. After the war they would picnic in front of Kenwood House.

Barbara Griffin was a schoolfriend of Frances who knew the family from the mid-1940s onwards, and was a frequent visitor to their home at 121 Mansfield Road, on the edge of Hampstead. Talking in February 2005 she said 'He wasn't what I'd call good looking. But he had a lot of charm.

'The way he spoke, the interest he took in everybody … he was so interested in people and life. Unless you wanted to know something about him and his life, he was more interested in finding out about your life, and what you were doing. He was able to enter your world. He made you feel interesting. He wanted to look into people's characters as well. But once he got talking about Australia and the outback and various experiences, he was well away. And he was very interesting, and he had wide experience of different things.'

Family life at 121 Mansfield Road was occasionally fraught. 'Theresa was very Italian, always up and down,' said Barbara. 'She and Hewitt would have furious arguments, often the result of her jealousy when he seemed to be flirting with a woman.

'This happened on one occasion when I was at the Rayners, and he had been telling me stories about Australia. Frances and I went out, and when we returned it was clear there had been a furious row. Hewitt came up to me and asked 'Was I flirting with you?'

[What went on in the Rayner household during Hewitt's short-lived friendship with Ethel Mannin in 1944 can only be guessed at].

'It was dangerous when Hewitt got angry, because it could start an asthma attack. It was ghastly. It happened whenever he was made upset by Theresa. Once he got emotional, it would come on. I don't know how often it happened. Frances went in fear of it. She once said to me: 'He could die'.

'There weren't any inhalers to help in those days. He would be gasping for air, and would say to Frances 'You know what to get'. I would be left on the doorstep, with 'you can take yourself home'. Frances used to get something from the chemist. I don't know if they used to burn it or pour boiling water on, so he could inhale.

'The family knew grinding poverty. But Theresa was a very good cook. Frances told me they always had something to eat. Being a good cook, her mother could always make something out of nothing. There was always food. The only thing I remember is they used to smell of garlic most of the time.'

Theresa was a top quality seamstress. Barbara Griffin recalled that she had an enormous sewing machine at the family home in Mansfield Road, and she could turn her hand to any type of clothing. She made all her daughters' school uniforms, and when Frances needed a pair of jodhpurs for her horse riding Theresa borrowed a pair, made a pattern from them, and made a pair.

Even when Theresa had a salaried job she was still taking on dressmaking at home. A surviving invoice from 1956 shows that she made one of her clients a black lace blouse, silk brassiere, plaid dress with cape, and printed seersucker dress with appliqué, for a total cost of £6.5.0.

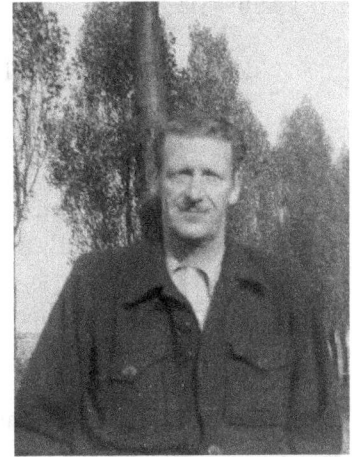

19.1 Hewitt in Parliament Hill Fields, October 1947. sw.

Hewitt's mother clearly didn't understand the quality of clothes her daughter-in-law was capable of making. In an airmail letter dated 19th May 1953 she says she is sending her son £40, of which £20 is 'for a suit and for shirts and socks. I wish it to be used for you, Hew, to go to a tailor and have a proper tailor-made suit, for your own appearance's sake, and for your girls. You cannot always be seen in home-made clothes; they are good enough for your work or your bike. Frances is to see you go to a tailor, and do as I ask – clothes speak your way of thinking. This is my order. I will send no more if this is not obeyed.'

Barbara remembered Hewitt as very practical, and good with his hands. 'He could turn his hands to anything,' she recalled. 'He taught Frances to be practical. In that household it was probably a good thing. Frances had her own bike, a Raleigh. Her father taught her to look after it. Mend punctures. Take the whole thing to bits every weekend and oil everything.

'He was a casual dresser. But then I don't think he had the money to spend on buying anything very decent. I remember him in sloppy clothes, looking to my mind like an artist should look'.

Usually, he wore clothes that had been made for him by Theresa. These included the striking yellow corduroy jacket she made for him during one of their forced separations during the 1939–45 war. He also had an army-style battle-dress jacket he wore, most likely also made by Theresa. This proved to be useful when his left arm was in a sling in the winter of 1941/2, as he was able to button up the jacket around his damaged arm.

He was not particularly aware of fashion. In a letter to Frances in 1936 he commented: 'I begin to feel rather fashionable in my suede shoes. I find they are worn by the students and *literati* of Bloomsbury. I am very slow at discovering such things – fashion and the like.'

He often wore a beret which also served a useful purpose indoors when he was working at the etching press by preventing his long hair from falling over his eyes.

Writing in the 1960s in an unpublished manuscript, his daughter Frances described him as 'A tall man, thin but possessing inward strength. He surveyed one intently with grey eyes and never lack of interest. In former years his sense of humour and a good singing voice were often his saviour. A quick man, he worked long and fervently, when ill and when well, and on his own. He was always studying and reading.'

He was evidently a good cook, and was very interested in home remedies for ailments.

Barbara remembered that if anyone suggested that he should use his skills to teach, he was horrified. 'But I think he would have been a good teacher,' she said. 'He taught Frances, after all. He made her draw lots of perfect circles, lots of 'O's. He said: 'If you can make a perfect circle, you can draw.'

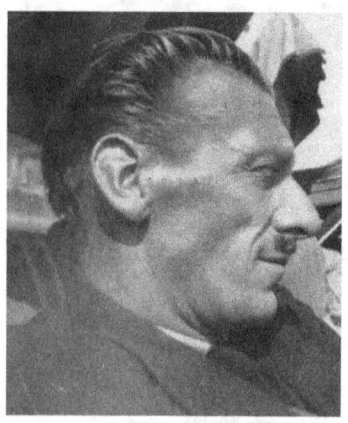

19.2 Hewitt looked relaxed and fit during his 1934 trip to the Isle of Wight. He even managed without his injections for asthma. sw.

Throughout his life Hewitt was worrying about the causes of his poor health. Strangely, perhaps, for someone suffering from asthma and hay fever, he smoked. Sometimes he used the discarded cigarette packets as an impromptu notepad for jotting down thoughts that had popped into his mind. This reveals that he smoked Kensitas Extra Size cigarettes. One such note carries the cryptic wording 'Pyrotechnics. Limn, limning and a youthful exuberance.'

It is notable when reading through the letters written to him by friends and family, how many times people say they are sorry to hear he is not well. His state of health was obviously widely known.

Hewitt Rayner was an only child. His mother doted on him. Perhaps too much. Later in life he wrote 'My

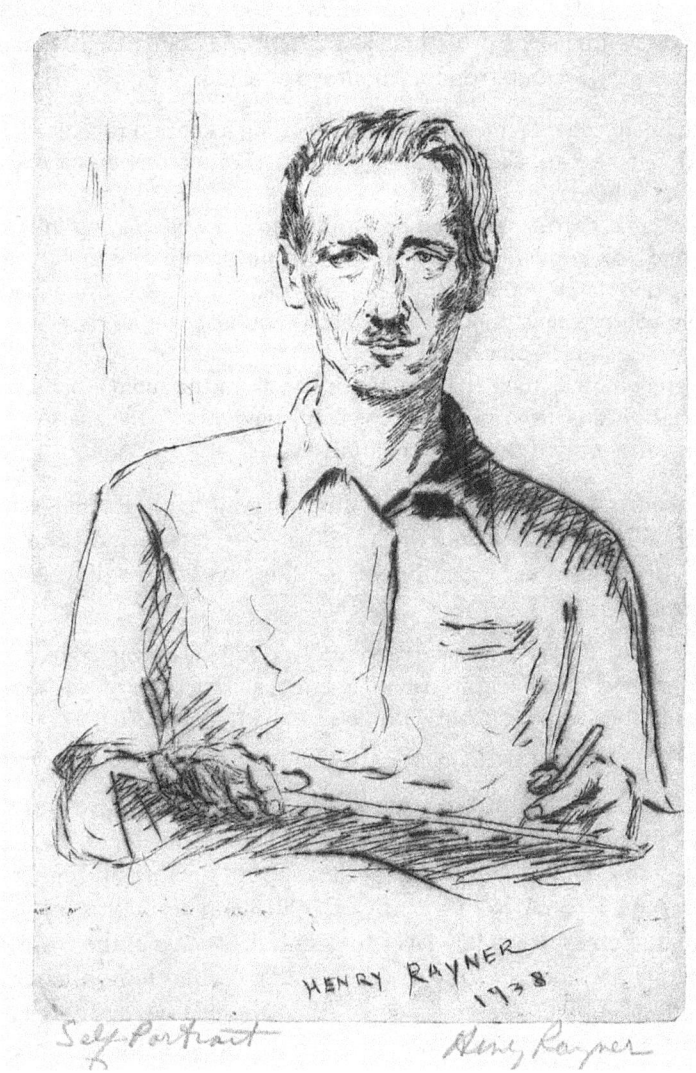

HENRY RAYNER 1938

Self Portrait

Henry Rayner

19.3 'Self portrait' 1938. Carries the added pencil wording: '*That is forever England. This proof exhibited to Queen Mary, Badminton House, Nov. 1942*'. On another proof of this plate Hewitt wrote: '*Rebel of Royal Academy schools against old conventions. Brought first cheap art prints to the British Public 1937–1940. Made first democratic portrait of the King. Had first British War Exhibition London. 'A peddler of dreams'*'. This work appeared in the *Daily Telegraph*, 21st June 1939, in the London Day by Day column, together with an item about the drypoint of the King being acquired by HM Queen Mary. Drypoint, 195×130mm. RS.

mother thought I was too good for the world, I think, and tried to keep me to herself.'

He was a sickly child, and believed that his parents were disappointed in him. His father had been strong and very physical – one of his Saturday afternoon recreations was to engage in wrestling matches with his workmates.

Not long after he left the RA Schools and became a full-time artist in Chelsea, he had consulted a doctor, who said: 'You are burning the midnight oil, old man. Be careful or it will burn you. Eat one bloody steak a day.' That last comment must have been painful for Hewitt, who was penniless. 'No man may tempt an empty pocket,' he wrote.

In 1945 Hewitt wrote to his mother to ask whether his head had ever been injured when he was a child. Here is what his mother replied in her airmail letter dated 26th November 1945, written from her home in St Kilda:

> You ask me to tell you if I remember you ever getting a knock on the head. I don't know why you ask to rake up misery of the past. Your father was always banging you on the head.
>
> When we were at Carrum, and you and a little cousin were playing in the dining room, and you both were tumbling about, your grandmother told you both to stop. Like children you started again, and your father, as you tumbled near him, gave you a terrific punch on the head that sent you all of a heap against the opposite wall, terribly hurt.
>
> Your dear grandmother took the cousin and ran from the room. That's all I ever remember getting from her – mischief. Anyhow what's the matter? I thought it was your stomach. Surely after all these years.

Judging by a letter from his mother in November 1945, though, Rayner was less considerate of other people's health. His mother was recovering from a bout of Erysipelas. Also known as St Anthony's Fire, this was a feared disease in pre-antibiotic days. She wrote

> I haven't any news. If I tell you I have been sick, you will say as you did before you don't want to hear my whining. I had no-one to make me a cup of tea: they all got frightened they would catch it. Erysipelas in my face. It has gone down, but left both my eyes sore.

Factual information about Hewitt's health comes from various letters from doctors and consultants. One referral letter written in 1953 by his doctor to the Royal Free Hospital states that he had been experiencing chest pains, and suffering from an anxiety state, asthma, hay fever, diverticulitis, and dermatitis.

He attributed his susceptibility to hay fever to his mother's side of the family. But he believed that he had found a cure. 'I had been exploring the substances that are charged into the blood, affecting people who are sensitive responders,' he wrote. 'I had studied the action of adrenalin, as one of the glandular secretions that issue into the blood under certain conditions. From these studies I must have been one of the first to use consciously and with clinical precision Calcium Gluconate to stay hay fever.

'As the season of grass pollens approached I began by taking half teaspoonfuls of the powder once a day, and it worked. In medical text books Calcium Gluconate became listed as a specific, which is almost saying that it is a certain cure. But at that time I did not know that it was best absorbed with Vitamin D.'

One of Hewitt's relatives from the Edwards side of the family was his Uncle Hewitt. In 1946 he was working for London-based Pocock Bros – slogan: 'Pocock bros, the boot people'. [This was a highly successful firm of leather-tanners and boot- and shoe-makers founded in 1815 by Thomas Pocock, who also founded the Royal Blind Society.] A letter from Hewitt senior, dated 11th June 1946, includes the following:

Your condition worried me very much. I am sending on to Hilda today the paper you gave me on Saturday for the asthma powders. ... I do hope your health is improving, Hughie (sic), and will contact you immediately I return to London.

In 1949 he was in St Mark's Hospital where he had some sort of bowel operation. A year later he described it as an 'unnecessary operation' that had affected his health to a serious degree.

Among the material from the Rayner archive, and a study of his signed prints, there are some hints that Hewitt could become mixed-up, perhaps when he was suffering one of his asthma attacks. One example is the strange affair of the three prints the British Museum acquired in 1939. Hewitt must have given his name as Henry Redstone Rayner, because this is who the reply from A M Hind was addressed to. This is, of course, Hewitt's father's name rather than his own. Some eight years later on 29th March 1947 a Mr Popham of the British Museum wrote to Theresa asking her to clarify Hewitt's name for their records. He asked: 'Is it Hewitt Henry Rayner or Henry Redstone'.

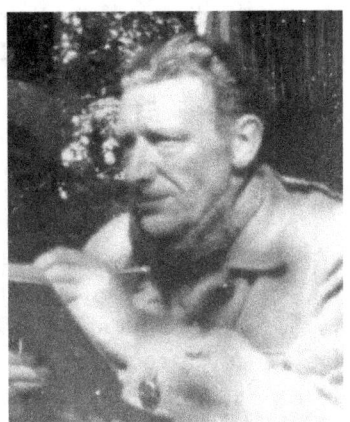

Then there is the drypoint etching of his wife during the six-week voyage to Melbourne in 1931. It shows her reclining on a bed on the ship. The title, written in pencil in Hewitt's distinctive handwriting, is 'Kay going east'. Clearly this is nonsense. Kay had not yet been born.

There are quite a few inconsistencies in the titling and dating of his proofs. This could be down to simple carelessness, as some proofs were taken many years after the plate had been etched. But it is difficult to imagine the conditions under which a person would accidentally give his father's name rather than his own.

19.4 At work during a daylight raid in 1941. Hewitt was just 39 years old, but looked older. Years of poor health, poverty and the stress of the war show in his face. Later that year he smashed the elbow of his drawing arm in an accident when out sketching on a bombed-out building. How bad could things get? sw.

Hewitt and Theresa worked hard to get the newspapers interested in his art and achievements, and they regularly sent out press releases on significant developments. They achieved a considerable amount of press coverage, in British, Australian and New Zealand newspapers.

Along with mentions of famous people who had acquired his drypoints, the press information Hewitt prepared always included references to his wartime injuries and his general poor health. It's almost as though he took a perverse pride in the personal sacrifices he had made in order to stay true to his art, and the challenges he had overcome.

Equally, it gave journalists an interesting angle for their stories, so the health and poverty issues were duly included by most journalists when they wrote about him. A small piece in the *Canberra Times* in April 1939, for example, recorded that the King and Queen Mary had accepted his drypoint portrait of the King, and carried a title 'Portrait of King: Australian artist's success'.

But half the story was about his health and poverty: 'Rayner came to England in 1924, and was almost bedridden for several years. He struck a bad patch in 1933 and was reduced to street begging, trying to sell his etchings.'

In January 1943 the *London Evening Standard* ran a story about him with the heading 'Artist knocked down by bomb – But he went on working'. It included a photo of Rayner in bed, and reported that: 'Today he lies, ill but cheerful, at his home in Allcroft Road'. When *The Times* newspaper reported Rayner's death in April 1957 one paragraph of the report was about his illnesses and poverty.

The 'artist beats illness, injury and poverty' angle in press reports seemed to stick. In more recent times, whenever one of his pictures appeared for sale after the dispersal of paintings and prints from his estate in 2000 and 2002 the same message came across. In 2008 Wikipedia had just this to say about the artist:

> Henry Rayner was born in Australia and trained as an artist in Britain. He worked with Walter Sickert & was a friend of Augustus John. He was injured during the London blitz and thereafter became something of a recluse.

When Hewitt met journalists face to face, he was evidently not always impressive. The London correspondent of the *Argus,* a Melbourne paper, met him at the Brook Street Art Gallery exhibition in 1945, and in the resulting article described him as 'dour and shy'. To be fair, Hewitt had left his sick bed to attend the event, so this could explain why he seemed subdued. In the same article the writer described Hewitt as 'one of the most interesting figures in modern British art.'

Another journalist writing for the *London Evening Standard* gained a different impression of Rayner, writing: 'Over six feet tall, with thick sandy hair, Mr Rayner strikes you as a man who would overcome anything by sheer willpower'.

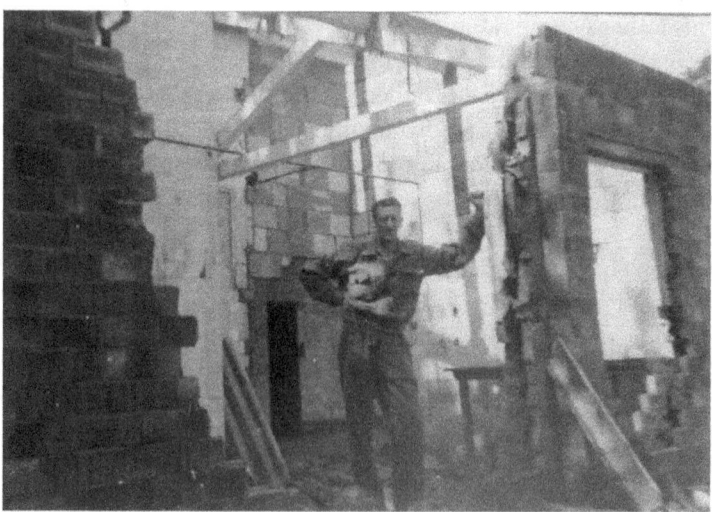

19.5 Hewitt's own caption for this 1941 photo says it all – 'Ruins of studio number 2'. sw.

When his mother saw some of the photographs taken at the exhibition, she commented that he looked strained. She strongly believed that his personality underwent a change sometime in the mid 1920s when he was at the Royal Academy Schools. She said as much in a letter to him a few years later:

> I have all your letters Hew, from the day you landed in London, and how full of hope and ambition. You loved the schools. All at once your letters alter, and you start to despise everything.

In 1939 she returned to this theme.

> 'I was going over some of your first letters last night. So different, so full of the Academy, and how you liked it and everyone there. All at once you leave it, and go and live almost in the slums, and never seem to have altered in ten years.'

Hewitt's background and upbringing in Australia and New Zealand would certainly have made him different from most of the aspiring artists who enrolled at the Royal Academy Schools in the 1920s. He knew how to survive in the outback, killing animals for food and using the bushcraft skills taught him by his father.

Even by the pioneering standards of Australia, Hewitt regarded himself as something of a rebel. A comment from one of his 1920s notebooks is revealing: 'I was a child with a fund of rebellion, deep-seated rebellion.'

It is easy to imagine the likely conflicts when a young man with this kind of background entered the stuffy atmosphere of the RA Schools. In the 1920s the RA Schools hadn't adapted to the changes that were sweeping through British society after the Great War, and were struggling to find their own purpose in this changed world.

It is not surprising that Hewitt and the RA Schools fell out. His new-world, 'can-do' attitude and his relentless ambition made it almost inevitable that he would become caught up in the student strike of 1926, which was triggered by the frustration of students in a teaching institution that was still working on Victorian lines. He was blamed for things he always claimed he hadn't done. It turned him away from the RA. It made him suspicious of everything and everyone.

Almost 20 years after the 'student strike' events, he clearly still harboured a simmering resentment that he had been cold-shouldered by the British art establishment, and that it was all traceable back to the reputation he had acquired as a result of events at the RA Schools in 1926.

He said so in no uncertain terms in the biography he wrote for his 1945 Brook Street Art Gallery exhibition catalogue. It says this about his time at the RA Schools:

> '... with his earnest, impassioned nature and his modern, progressive outlook he led the student strike, and was for some years after regarded as an untouchable rebel by the authorities.'

Of course, whether Hewitt actually led the student strike or whether he was simply caught up in the situation is not entirely clear.

His older daughter Frances recalled that her father had once said 'I was born in the wrong period of time'. He certainly felt out of place in Britain and at odds with the British art community. He had come to Britain in 1923 burning with ambition to make his reputation as an artist. He was captivated by the stories he had read about the French and British artists of the late 19th and early 20th centuries. Especially the Impressionists.

But he was too late. The art world had moved on. And most of the artists had moved on. Chelsea was no longer the artists' colony it had been 50 years earlier.

Chelsea, originally just a small fisherman's village, had been colonised by artists in the second half of the 19th century. But by the 1920s Chelsea was becoming expensive, and Camden became the centre of gravity for a newer generation of young artists. Then in the 1930s, Hampstead beckoned. According to the London Museum, Hampstead's residents in the 1930s included 'intellectuals, writers and a group of fiercely committed modernist artists such as Ben Nicholson, Barbara Hepworth and Henry Moore. Their presence turned Hampstead into the headquarters for avant-garde art in England.'

Hewitt did live on the fringes of Hampstead for almost two decades, but his heart was in Chelsea. He went back there at every opportunity. He did many drypoints of Chelsea scenes. And he sought out and got to know some of the older generation of artists who could talk about Chelsea in the good old days. People like Philip Wilson Steer who still lived in Chelsea until his death in 1942.

If Hewitt was a generation too late to experience Chelsea in its artistic heyday, he was probably a generation too early for the Royal Academy Schools, yet to move on from their Victorian values and teaching methods.

To compound all this Rayner launched his career as a drypoint artist at precisely the wrong time. Public interest in etchings collapsed in 1929, prices plunged, and the entire economy went into a recession that lasted ten years. The 1930s were not a good time to be trying to earn a living as an artist. Especially a black and white artist.

Another factor that stood in the way of Hewitt's ambitions was his vision of bringing art to the people, concentrating on depicting everyday people and places rather than the rich and famous and refusing to seek or accept commissions. He took pride in his endeavours to make art affordable. A pencil note on a proof of his 1938 self-portrait states simply: 'Brought first cheap art prints to the British Public 1937–1940.'

In a hand-written 1944 briefing note for the press, he described himself as 'a self-made man of Australian working class parents, a people's artist'. In a different press briefing note he wrote: 'He [Rayner] represents the vanguard of the young worker artists, and believes passionately in art for the people. The people are the craftsmen and workers of the world of tomorrow – a cultured civilisation believing consciously in truth, beauty and sincerity to self'.

In another pencil note on that 1938 self-portrait he described himself as 'a peddler of dreams'.

In one of the notebooks in which he recorded ideas that would eventually surface in his '*Child*' manuscript, he wrote: 'I have never laid claim to exceptional gifts, have never achieved anything of magnitude in the world. I am a common fellow, a slow reasoner with a love of nature and mankind.'

Further thoughts along the same lines come from a 1944 letter he wrote to the then curator of Merthyr Art Gallery: 'I believed that art should come nearer to the ordinary man, and that artists should seek the counties and organise exhibitions everywhere. CEMA [Council for the Encouragement of Music and the Arts, part of the Arts Council] later adopted my methods. I believed in the East End group that Sickert had commenced for artisans and public. As the son of simple folk I knew that the people loved art, and want it.'

Hewitt's mother frequently offered advice on making more money from his art. This is from a letter of November 1945:

> You are known, you say. Why not get commissions in oils. People only like their own pictures or of their families. Couldn't you look out for one of the new houses I read they are building about London. I sent you enough money … to pay a few weeks in advance.
>
> I'm glad Kay got a new dress. I can't knit or sew. Surely you don't always look for charity, and your children surely don't. I can't think of you like that. Love Mother.

It seems that she may even have blamed Theresa for her son's poor health. In April 1953 in one of her letters she wrote: 'You say you are still ill. I don't know what to say. It has been your one topic ever since you married, and it has darkened my whole life.'

It seems to be in his dealings with officialdom that he experienced particular problems. These often brought out a prickly, impatient side to his nature, resulting in frequent conflicts. Any perceived slight or injustice could provoke an angry response.

The medical profession came in for the full force of Hewitt's wrath. His poor health ensured that he came into frequent contact with doctors. On several occasions he and Theresa complained to the medical authorities, alleging misconduct by his and the family's doctor, and insisting on changing doctors.

In early 1948 he stormed out of a meeting with a Frank d'Abreu of 82 Harley Street when the doctor suggested he attend the Hampstead Hospital for further tests on his chest, even though the doctor had told him he would not have to pay for it. D'Abreu had to write to Theresa to put her mind at rest, saying 'I never intended to charge Mr Rayner in view of your circumstances.'

He was still falling out with doctors in 1956 when the family had moved to Ramsgate. A letter from the National Health Service Kent and Canterbury Executive Council dated 23rd March 1956 supplies details of the steps the Rayners need to take to lodge a formal complaint against their doctor, but points out that the Council 'would not normally be in a position to investigate a complaint which related solely to an allegation of rudeness by a doctor'.

The only doctor for whom Hewitt had high praise was Bankart, the famous surgeon who rebuilt his seriously damaged left elbow after the bad fall in 1941.

Neighbours weren't safe either. He wrote to the police about the behaviour of the ground floor residents in 121 Mansfield Road, who he was convinced were gangsters. He complained to the education authorities about school-related matters. On one occasion he even wrote to the Prime Minister. He wrote to the Queen to ask her to intervene in the special schooling arrangements for his younger daughter Kay.

If he wrote to somebody and didn't receive a reply quickly, he tended to write them a terse follow-up letter asking why not. This behaviour can't have endeared him to the people whose help he was often trying to obtain.

The letters from him haven't survived, but among his papers there are enough replies to make the general picture clear.

On 18th August 1943 Augustus John's wife Dorelia wrote: 'Dear Sir, Mr John is sorry he has not replied to your letter, but he has been away,…

On July 18th 1944 Augustus John wrote: Dear Mr Rayner, I was not aware that three of your prints were left at my studio as I thought Sir Kenneth Clarke had returned them all…'

Augustus John again, from August 1943: Dear Mr Rayner, Sorry to keep your prints so long …'

On 10th June 1954, Sylvia Gosse wrote from Hastings: 'Dear Mr Rayner, I am sorry that your most kind letter should have remained unanswered for so long, but…'

By no means all the surviving correspondence is in this vein. But enough to make it clear that Hewitt could be very demanding of people. Even though the letters he wrote to Ethel Mannin during the period in 1943 have not survived, her letters to him provide some insights into how his personality and behaviour basically destroyed their blossoming friendship.

Particularly evident is the way he fell out with family members. There is no evidence that he communicated with his father's family in Australia after his parent's marriage broke down. This is possibly not surprising, as his mother was bitter about the treatment she felt she had received from her husband's family, and never missed an opportunity to remind her son about it.

In 1947 Hewitt Edwards (a relative on his mother's side) wrote a pained letter from Auckland. 'Dear Hewie, I am extremely sorry that so much misunderstanding has come about since I left England, and insinuations which to me are very hurtful.'

The letter seems to be about what happened to some etchings of Rayner's that Hewitt Edwards had taken back to New Zealand with him after a visit to England in 1946. There was also an issue regarding some prints Hewitt had sent for members of the Edwards family, and problems (as perceived by Rayner) with some articles published about him in the Auckland press. Hewitt Edwards points out in the letter that he had sent Rayner a total of £200 – a large sum of money in 1947.

The letter ends with this: 'Unless we can have pleasanter exchanges of correspondence with each other I feel that after this letter, writing would be just a waste of time.'

Another series of exchanges in a similar vein were between Hewitt and an old school friend called Alleyne Monkhouse, still living in Brighton in 1950. It was Alleyne who put Hewitt back in touch with his old schoolteacher 'Daisy' Thomas.

In a letter that starts 'Dear Hubert' (possibly deliberately to annoy Rayner, but perhaps referring back to a schoolpals nickname) Alleyne goes on to say: 'I did all in my power to assist you as a pal, and without any reason at all you just went WONKY.... I can't understand why you took the attitude you did. ... I happen to know the temperament of artists pretty well, and I am sorry that your wife has to put up with it ... Now if this note doesn't bring you to earth and to your senses, then I don't want to be bothered with you again.'

This all seems to be because Alleyne had taken some steps to get people in Brighton interested in Henry Rayner. It backfired badly when Rayner took exception to to Alleyn's initiative. It prompted him to fire off letters to all and sundry in the Brighton area, disassociating himself from Alleyne.

On 30th March 1951, for example, he wrote to a man called Arthur Francis who ran the grocery stores in Middle Brighton.

> Dear Mr Francis
> I have been informed in an ungrammatical letter from My Alleyne Monkhouse, who insinuated himself upon me during a correspondence I had with the Mayor some months ago, that you claim to have been a great friend of mine during my term at the Middle Brighton School. I want to make it very plain that I have little recollection of you, and I would have been pleased had Monkhouse not written it.
> Yours etc
> Henry Rayner
> British Artist

Even more puzzling was Hewitt's ire whenever a newspaper or magazine got some facts wrong in an article. His reaction was sometimes hopelessly out of all proportion to the error. In early 1949, for example, he wrote a very strong letter to the editor of the *New Zealand Herald*, alleging that an article by a reporter called Harvey Blanks published in January 1947 had contained 'misrepresentations and false statements made against the Queen and Mr Henry Rayner'.

The actual offence the newspaper committed seems rather harmless. It seems that it mistakenly stated that in 1943 The Queen 'found Mr Henry Rayner's picture in the street.' Hewitt was enraged. He wrote to The Queen, he wrote to the New Zealand Ambassador to Britain, and he wrote to numerous friends and relatives in New Zealand.

The outcome of this episode is not recorded. At the very least, Hewitt had ensured that the *New Zealand Herald* would not be writing about him again.

There is no evidence at all to suggest that he was ever violent. On the contrary, he seems to have had a gentle demeanour. But there are several clues that suggest he liked to feel in control. It is noticeable, for example, that many of the letters and press information sent out were over Theresa's name but were clearly drafted by Hewitt. Then there was the Ethel Mannin episode, where she spotted instantly that the messages written by his daughters had obviously been dictated by him.

His mother believed that his personality was a major obstacle to gaining the recognition he deserved. She was constantly urging him to get out and mix with people; and to keep his thoughts to himself. This echoes Sickert's advice as far back as 1925, when he cautioned Hewitt against wearing his heart on his sleeve.

He certainly seemed to acquire an unerring ability to rub people up the wrong way, even when they had extended the hand of friendship. He kept looking for ulterior motives in their behaviour.

His mother recommended that when he wanted to get something out of his system he should write it down on paper, and then throw the paper away. In one very telling letter from 1935 she wrote: 'You must get out of that accusing everyone you meet of some imaginary saying or doing. No-one on earth will stand such madness, for to anyone who lives decently it is – and looks like – mad ways, and people only pass you by'.

Hewitt believed until the day he died that the reason he had failed to make it as a commercially successful and recognised artist in Britain was the reputation he had acquired in 1926 as a rebel.

But was there any truth in this? Was he really viewed as an untouchable rebel?

His conspiracy theory about events at the RA Schools undoubtedly seemed very real to him, and it made him increasingly bitter as the years rolled by and he tried to understand why his career hadn't worked out the way he hoped. Yet nothing at all was found in the archive of papers he left to corroborate these suspicions. Nor was anything relevant found in the Royal Academy archives or any other sources.

His physical condition, however, was not imagined, and that may be a big factor in his changing personality and behaviour. Asthma, hay fever, emphysema, intestinal problems and the legacy of his wartime injuries made each day and night a painful challenge. And who can guess at the emotional impact on an artist of losing the full use of his drawing arm?

In a 1957 interview with Australian journalist Ailsa Craig, after her husband's death, Theresa said that her husband saw his shattered left arm as a symbol of a shattered career.

Is it too surprising that over the years he became more tetchy, more suspicious of people's motives, and more easily aroused to angry letter writing? This was anger borne out of two decades of disappointment, disillusionment and illness. The feeling that however hard he had worked, he just couldn't improve things for himself and his family.

20
Postscript

Half a century after Hewitt's death, there are signs that his work is attracting serious worldwide interest.

In 2001 three oil paintings were sold at auction in New Zealand. '*An English beach*' sold for 1,700 NZD, '*My last portrait of Walter Sickert*' sold for 3250 NZD and '*Brighton Beach*' sold for 1,600 NZD. [Thanks to the Blouin Art Sales Index for this information].

Works by Rayner are also attracting growing attention in the UK. In October 2005 four drypoint portraits of Sickert and a pen and ink portrait of D H

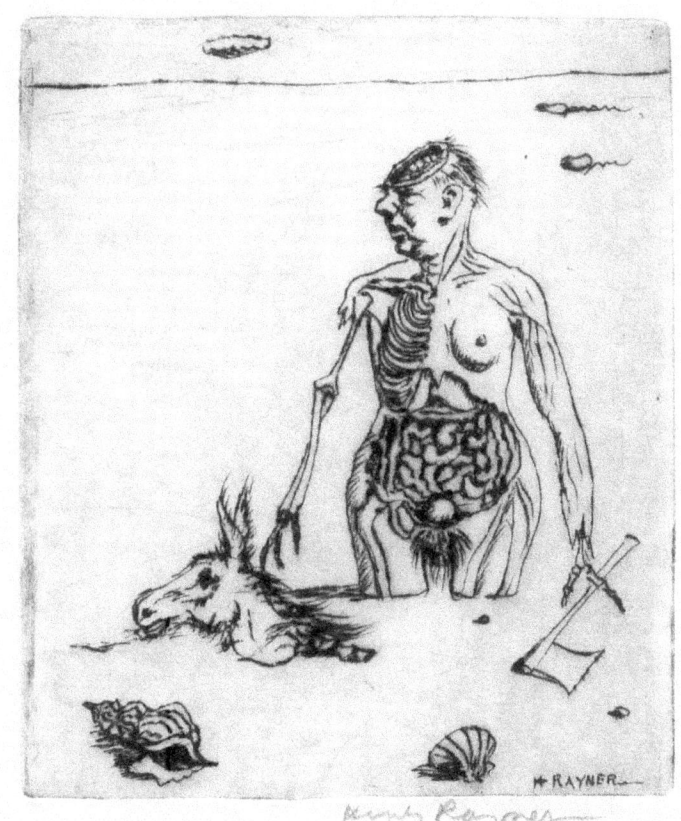

20.1 *'The man with the ass's head',* 1935. Leeds Museum in the UK has a copy of this work. The proof is dated 1935 on the front, but on the rear Rayner has noted 'Series Surreal, Paris 1929'. Drypoint, 105×83mm. RS.

Lawrence from the collection of Roy Davids sold for a total of more than £3,300 (including buyer's premium).

In the country of his birth, four of his drypoints were selected for inclusion in an important exhibition at the National Gallery of Australia in Canberra in February 2008. Titled *Australian Surrealism, the Agapitos/Wilson collection*, it celebrated the acquisition by the gallery of 285 'surrealist paintings, prints, collages, drawings, photographs and sculptures in a collection built up by James Agapitos and Ray Wilson, two Sydney-based collectors, over the preceding decade and a half.

The four Rayner drypoints were all from 1938, and had been purchased by the collectors in the 1990s from London dealer England and Co

The works were: 'The eternal stream', 'The sensitive plant (series Surreal)', 'The man with the ass's head', and 'My path is a rose, even as this plain'.

At last, a glimmer of recognition for the artist in his home country.

Appendices

A1: A Brighton childhood

In his semi-autobiographical story *'Child, when my ship comes in'* Hewitt recounted many tales of the children and adults he knew as he was growing up in Brighton. Many, or perhaps most, of the names were changed, for unknown reasons. Locations were also sometimes changed.

There are enough of these anecdotes to make an interesting book about Brighton in the years running up to the First World War; but there isn't room to include them all in this biography. For the benefit of anyone with a wider interest in Hewitt's Brighton childhood, here are some of the references omitted from the main story.

Of special importance to Hewitt was a man called 'Frederick Chappy' (a local carpenter who was also a healer, he had a strong and lasting influence on the young Hewitt). Chappy's cottage was at Brighton Beach, and Hewitt wrote that it was one of the original farm allotments sold by Dendy in 1843. The true identity of 'Chappy' has not so far been established.

An old lady called 'Granny Day' also crops up frequently, and was evidently a regular visitor to the Rayner home. She ran a small shop at the junction of Carpenter Street and Wilson Street, not far from the railway line. It is likely that this is the building that had a brief role in Brighton's administration in 1859 when it was rented by the council for meetings. It consisted of a weatherboard shop with adjacent four-roomed cottage.

Research carried out by the author suggests that 'Granny Day' may have been a shopkeeper called Rose McKillop (1874–1953, maiden name Lawrence) who had married Henry Duncan McKillop in 1897, and been widowed in 1908, after which she took over the shop. However, this lady was only 40 years old at the outbreak of the Great war, so she hardly qualifies to be called 'Granny'.

Numerous other figures get a passing mention from Hewitt in his autobiography. There is Harry Hawkes, an aviator who built his plane in Brighton. Rayner remembers him flying low over the state school, and waving to the boys. This may be a pseudonym for the real-life Basil Watson, a Brighton resident who built his own plane, and was killed in 1917 when the plane broke up in mid-air.

'Yunker' Watson's father was a bootmaker, and had a small shop. Another member of Hewitt's gang at one point was called Billy Pebbles.

A lady known locally as 'Tramway Jane' would chase the trams, dressed in a large matinee hat and wearing a piece of rope around her neck.

The Sunday School at St Andrews Church, just across the road from the Rayner family home, was run by a Miss O'Connor.

Then there was Old John, one of the Chinese market gardeners who worked in the Chinese gardens 'over the railway line, near Elsternwick'. He would bring a basket of his fruit and vegetables, all carefully arranged for maximum appeal, round to people's homes.

One of his father's workers, a man called Mr Ayler comes across as an unpleasant character. Another of his father's helpers, Jack Dupont, was liked by the young Hewitt. Jack was a hod carrier who also worked nights in a brewery in Richmond.

Hewitt noted there was a local belief that the ghost of Adam Lindsay Gordon, the bush poet who had shot himself years earlier, could be seen walking near the spot where he died.

A Mr Gittens ran the beach refreshment shop where he had an Edison-Bell phonograph on which he would play cylinders by artists such as Billy Williams. The chemist where Hewitt took Tweedie when he thought he had been bitten by a black snake was run by a Mr Rawlings.

For amusement, the children (at about 14 years old) would wear holes in the ends of apricot stones, on the concrete, and use them as whistles. They sat in the open drains and gutters and told each other scary stories about the days when aborigines lived in the area. They went down to the Marine Hotel to watch the potboys 'brawny men in aprons and shirtsleeves' fight, throw empty packing cases at each other and ride round the yard on horses. On one occasion a potboy threw one of Hewitt's friends over his head into a heap of dung.

It was Hewitt's friend 'Tweedie' who revealed that there was money to be made from the empty lemonade bottles found on the seashore, and by gathering manure for keen gardeners. The money was spent on Kola beer and popcorn, and on trips to the old Drill Hall to watch moving pictures. Trips to Granny Day's shop on Carpenter Street yielded vermilion Chinese kites and tops.

The first time Hewitt met Tweedie, he was impressed by Tweedie's demonstration of how to mesmerise animals. He stood in front of a cow in Grady's field and made complicated passes at it. Tweedie was 'a 14-year old friend to all radicals'. He had an old canvas canoe hidden in the bushes at South Brighton. He and Hewitt would drag it from its hiding place, walk down to the shore with the canoe upturned over their heads, then paddle out and dive for mud oysters.

Hewitt and his friends had other ways of making a little extra pocket money. One was to rent out to visitors the little dinghy that belonged to his father's boat. Another was to collect blue mussels from under the pier, and sell them to the fishmonger. With the proceeds, they would buy books and eat steak and oysters at a local restaurant in Church Street. Hewitt wrote that it was called Pasquale Marassi's, but this may be another invented name.

Another close friend was Yunker Watson (again, most likely a Rayner-invented pseudonym). Yunker had a novel way of defying ridicule or a hostile gang, according to Rayner. He would 'stand on his head, showing the ragged lining of his coat and unwashed shirt.' Hewitt, Tweedie-wee and Yunker went on expeditions to pick apples and other fruit from local orchards.

Yunker joined the army during the 1914–1918 war, despite being only 16 years old and technically under age. He never returned. The last time Hewitt saw his friend was at a grand fete in Brighton's Drill Hall, in aid of the Red Cross.

A2: The Rayners of Shanklin, Isle of Wight

Hewitt was descended from an old-established family in the Shanklin and Bonchurch areas of the Isle of Wight. There have been Rayners there for centuries, and it is still a common name on the island. The 2013 telephone directory shows five Rayners in Shanklin alone. The Rayners were interlinked by marriage with other old Shanklin families – in particular the Proutens and Colenutts.

Within the Rayner families, boatbuilding, seafaring, carpentry, housebuilding and hospitality are recurrent themes. In common with many other Isle of Wight families through the 19th century, the Rayners were strong-willed, independent-minded and capable. Hewitt noted that there were generations of sailors and soldiers in the family, and that a great uncle had fought with Nelson.

Hewitt's father was Henry Redstone Rayner. His family generally called him Harry. His middle name, Redstone, was his mother's family name. He was born in Shanklin in 1871. He had two older brothers, two older sisters, and three younger sisters.

Going back one more generation, Hewitt's paternal grandparents were William Charles Rayner (b. 6 Nov 1836) and Selina Jane (nee Redstone, b. 30 July 1839 in Bermondsey, Surrey).

Going back another generation, Hewitt's paternal great grandparents were Jeremiah Rayner (1797–1870) and Elizabeth (nee Hawkins). His great grandfather Jeremiah was known as 'Miah'. His exploits held a special fascination for Hewitt, especially the whispered association with smuggling French brandy across the English Channel.

Great grandfather Jeremiah ('Miah')

Jeremiah Rayner, Hewitt's great grandfather, deserves a book in his own right. He was born in Brading, one of six children born to William and Mary (nee Smith) Rayner. His siblings were Henry (b.1795), William (b.1802), Benjamin (b.1793), Charles (b.1811) and Elizabeth (b.1808). There is a possibility that there was also an older brother James, born in 1790, who emigrated to the USA in 1817.

Jeremiah and his wife Elizabeth (nee Hawkins) had a large family, with nine children born between 1821 and 1838. They were Eliza (b.1821), James (b.1824), Charlotte (1826), Ann (b.1827), Elizabeth (b.1830), Harriett (b.1832), John (b.1834), William (b.1836) and Catherine (b. 1838). It was the last son – William – who took his family to Australia in 1886, and who was Hewitt's grandfather.

Jeremiah became something of a legend in the Shanklin area, amassing considerable wealth. His most visible legacy today is the large hotel called Daish's, occupying a central position in Shanklin town. It is much bigger than when Jeremiah built it as a large 26-room, two-storey coaching inn in 1833. Shanklin was then little more than a fishing village. The building of Daish's was rumoured to have been financed by the proceeds of smuggling.

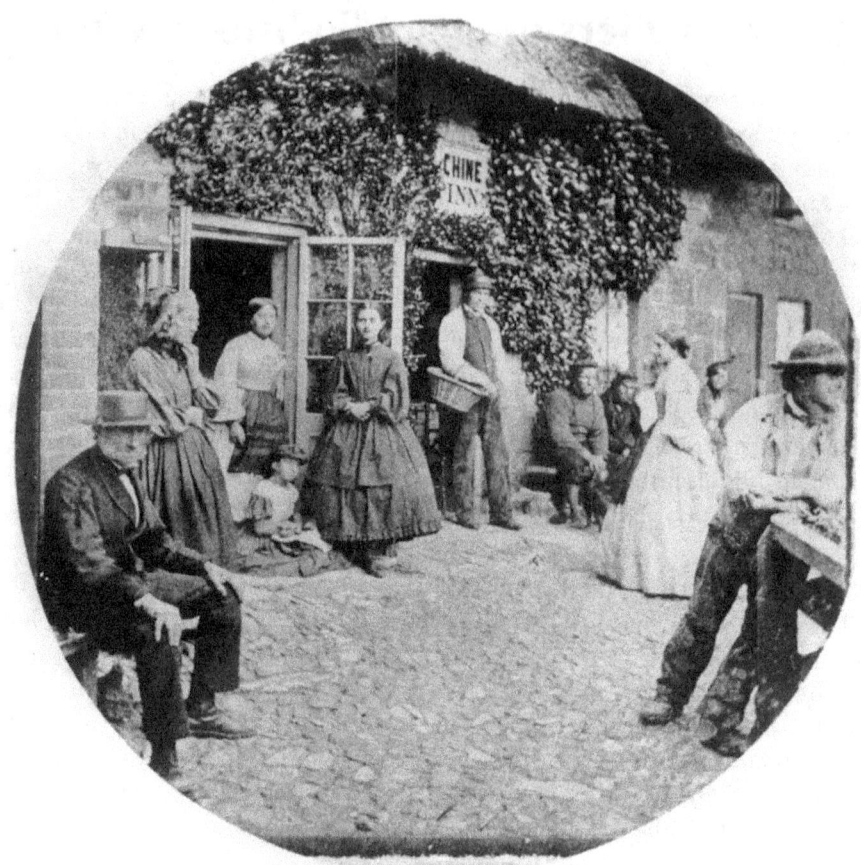

A2.1 The Chine Inn, Shanklin, 1858. This historic image underlines the extent of intermarriage between the Rayner and Prouten families in Shanklin. The Proutens had run the Chine Inn for generations. Hewitt discovered he was related to almost everybody in this photo by blood or marriage, when Harriet Prouten (his cousin once removed) identified them during his 1934 visit to the Isle of Wight. Harriet was the young girl sitting in front of the doorway in the photo. Her mother Charlotte (one of Jeremiah Rayner's daughters, and therefore a great aunt to Hewitt) was married to John Prouten. In the photo Charlotte is the lady in white, facing the inn. The lady standing in the doorway is Eliza, another of Jeremiah Rayner's daughters, who had married Tom Prouten. The man with the lobster basket is William Rayner (son of William, Jeremiah's brother), who was married to Polly Prouten, the lady in the grey dress standing in front of the glass door. The innkeeper, William Prouten, is seated on the left. The lady standing between him and the doorway is his wife. sw.

There exists an engraving of the hotel not long after it was completed by Jeremiah. This work, by Dobell, shows clearly the flagpole said by Hewitt to have been for signalling to vessels engaged in smuggling. Hewitt wrote that this engraving had been commissioned by Jeremiah.

Hewitt had an old price list from the hotel. In Jeremiah's day a bedroom cost 2/- upwards, plain breakfast was 1/-, and the table d'hote dinner was 3/-. Tallow dressing candles could be provided for 9d a pair, fires cost 1/- in the sitting room and 6d in a bedroom, and a sponge bath was priced at 4d. A sea bath could be arranged for 6d. Servants could be accommodated for 3/- per day, dogs for 6d per day, and horses for 1/- per day.

Jeremiah also owned several cottages, benefitting from the increasing number of visitors to the island. One was Culver Cottage in Bonchurch. But his main residence was a cottage called The Dell on Shanklin's main street, which he ran as a boarding house. The cottage backs onto the top of Shanklin Chine – the fracture in the cliff that goes down to the beach, said to be one of the routes by which Jeremiah and his gang would carry barrels of brandy and other smuggled French goods into the village. His brother William had a cottage across the other side of the main road.

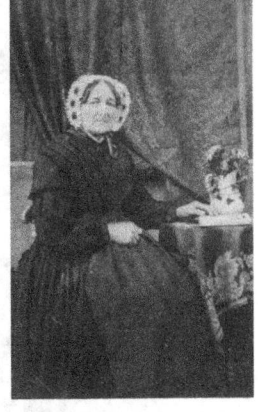

A2.2 Elizabeth Hawkins, wife of Jeremiah Rayner and Hewitt's paternal great grandmother, in 1864. sw.

There is a certain amount of confusion regarding the names and locations of the homes of Jeremiah and his brother William. In the 1851 census Jeremiah's address is given as Rose Cottage. William's is un-named.

In his 1978 book *All my yesterdays*, Clifford T. Rayner (great grandson of William) wrote that Jeremiah and his brother William lived in cottages on opposite sides of the road. That ties in with the census data. But he states that Jeremiah lived in Myrtle Cottage and William in The Dell. It's likely that this was a simple mix-up, because he also attributed the building of Daish's Hotel to the wrong brother.

One thing is sure – by 1861 Jeremiah and his family were living in what was known then and now as The Dell. Two old photos in the Rayner archive show this house clearly. It is the cottage backing onto the Chine.

It was speculated by Hewitt that his great grandfather could have met the poet Keats, visiting the island in 1817, at a time when the 20-year-old Jeremiah was delivering the post. The story was that while Keats was staying at nearby Eglantine cottage, he sat and worked in the field where Jeremiah's hotel would later be built. According to Lindsay Boynton's book *Georgian and Victorian Shanklin: a pictorial history 1700–1900*, in the early 1800s before the first hotel was built, Rose Cottage and Eglantine Cottage were the only lodging houses in Shanklin.

Jeremiah Rayner died on 16th March 1870 and is buried alongside his wife Elizabeth in the churchyard of St Blasius's, a short walk through Shanklin village from the cottage where he lived.

Grandfather William

Jeremiah's son William (Hewitt's grandfather) married Selina Jane Redstone. She was descended from an isle of Wight family with an interesting background. Selina Jane's mother, Jane Galley, was the daughter of a Frenchman called Henri

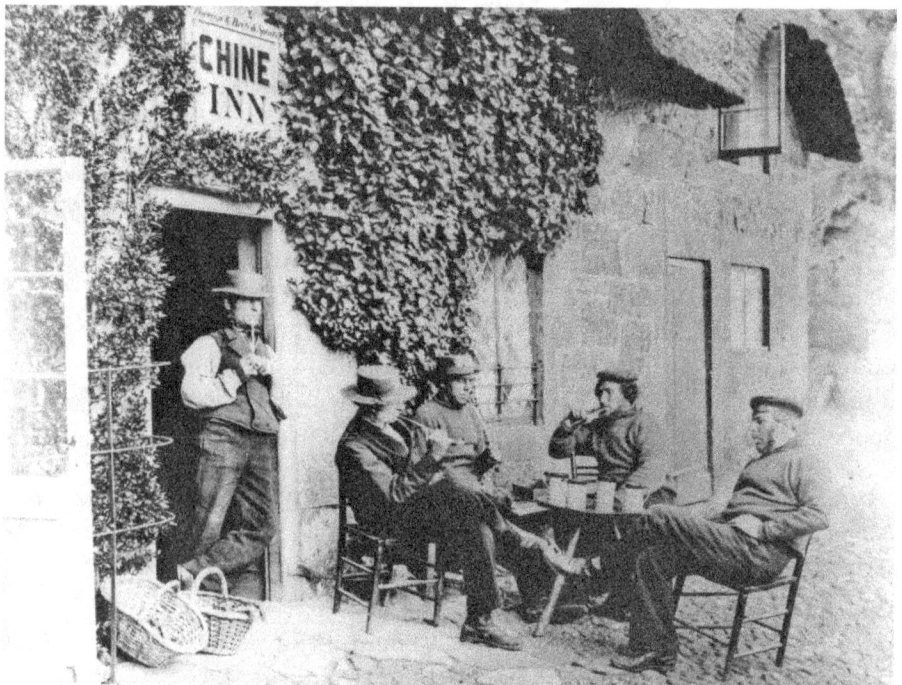

A2.3 The Chine Inn in 1860. This picture by local photographer Edward Pike, was turned into a postcard with the caption 'Quiet enjoyment, Chine Inn'. The seated figure with the straw hat is William Prouten, the innkeeper. He was a close friend of Jeremiah, Hewitt's great grandfather. The man standing in the doorway is John Prouten, the innkeeper's son. The Chine Inn was evidently known locally as 'The Smugglers', which makes the identity of the man sitting next to the innkeeper especially interesting. He was called Long, and was a coastguard.
Note that the sign above the inn doorway says 'Foreign and British spirits'. Was this a coded reference to the alleged smuggling onto the island of French brandies by locals including Jeremiah Rayner ? sw.

Gallet, who had been a prisoner of war on the Isle of Wight and never returned to France. The family name was Anglicised from Gallet to Galley. Henri's daughter Jane married James Redstone, a carpenter from the Isle of Wight. This is how the French blood that Hewitt occasionally referred to entered his family line.

William and Selina Jane had a large family, with eight children born between 1865 and 1882. They lived in a house called Marlborough House, on Queens Road, Shanklin. It may be that it was William who designed and built the property, which they ran as a lodging house. The house is still there (2006), although now part of a hotel called the Marlborough Hotel.

Hewitt recorded some amusing anecdotes about his grandfather William, based on what he learnt from his 1934 research trip to the Isle of Wight. He learnt that his grandfather's nickname within the family, when young, was 'slow William'. He apparently had a very careful, deliberate way of approaching matters. But nobody doubted his skills handling boats in any sort of weather.

Another tale relates to a workshop William rented in Victoria Avenue, Shanklin, in the 1860s and 1870s. This was evidently a large, rambling place that he used for building boats and canoes, joinery and wood storage. In 1871 the sailing ship *Waverley* was outbound from England and caught in a violent storm off Luccombe. When it foundered, the people of Shanklin and nearby villages helped save lives and cargo. For his pains, William received two casks of damp gunpowder. For many months after the event he would entertain the local boys by making and setting off fireworks in the workshop. Soon after the family emigrated to Australia, the workshop was pulled down and a large Methodist chapel built on the site.

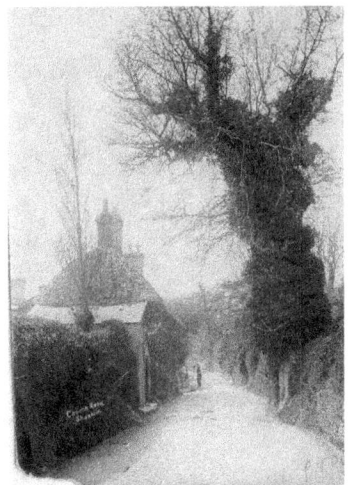

A2.4 The Dell, in Church Road, Shanklin, as it was in the 1860s. sw.

Hewitt already knew that his grandfather William had been a crack shot, from seeing him hunt in the Carrum area. But from Rayner family members in Shanklin he also learnt that William's habit of firing from the hip rather than from the shoulder, when out hunting, was something he had inherited from Jeremiah.

Hewit also collected a story about his own father's childhood on the island. This has not been verified, and is reproduced here exactly in Hewitt's own words:

'Father had to leave the Isle of Wight because he had been wild, associating with unruly lads. It came to a head when one of the lads was accidentally killed

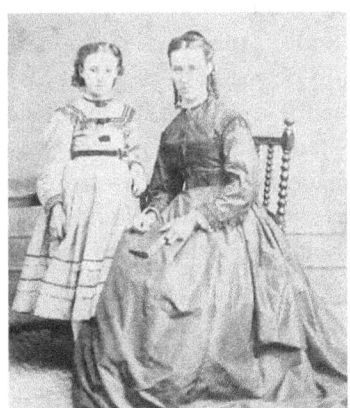

A2.5 Selina Jane Rayner (née Redstone), right, was Hewitt's paternal grandmother. She and William took their family to Australia in 1886. Hewitt's father was given Redstone as his middle name. By Photo Boquet, Wednesbury. sw.

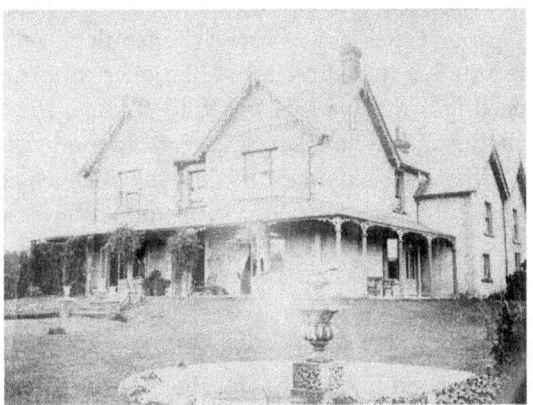

A2.6 Before the Rayners emigrated to Australia in 1886, this was their home on Queens Road, Shanklin. Marlborough House was run as a boarding house. PHOTO COURTESY DOROTHY CAREY.

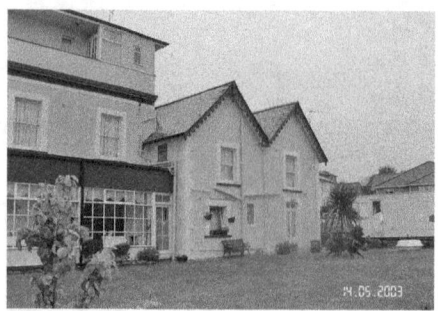

A2.7 Marlborough House as it is today, still a hotel, but much expanded. William Rayner's original house can still be identified, on the right in this photo from 2003. PHOTO: RS.

by a bullet from a pistol they were in the habit of carrying about with them on their jaunts along the coast. So father went to work at a large cloth warehouse in a street near St Paul's. He found life entirely lacking in adventure. The employer had a habit of leaving money lying about, to discover if the lads were dishonest. Father proved them wrong by one night fighting away burglars in his long night-gown.'

If true, these events may have contributed to the Rayner family's decision to leave the Isle of Wight and start a new life in Australia.

A3: An Australian adventure

In 1886 William and Selina Rayner (Hewitt Rayner's paternal grandparents) set off from England to Australia, taking seven of their children and Selina's 74-year-old mother with them. It seems that one of the children, 17-year-old Frederick W. C. Rayner, travelled to Australia the previous year.

William and Selina were not, however, the first Rayners to set sail for the new world, tempted by the gold rush. According to Hewitt's notes, a cousin of his grandfather, called James, went to Sydney and joined the *Morning Herald* as a reporter. Another uncle joined the rush, went into the mountains, and was never heard from again. A family friend from Shanklin, Henrietta Prouten, had taken the 100-day trip by sailing ship, and become a writer.

In 1886, Selina had urged the family to sell up and try their luck in the new world. She was attracted by the tales of fortunes to be made from gold prospecting. Australia was the 'gold colony'. They sailed to Australia, taking their children and Selina Jane's 74-year-old mother Jane Redstone.

They travelled on the *SS Orient*, which usually made two trips each year from England to Australia. This 5400-tonne ship, with its two funnels and four masts, was the largest vessel plying the UK-Australia route, and held the record for the London-to-Adelaide trip of 27 days 22 hours.

The family travelled as unassisted passengers, meaning that they received no financial help from the Australian government. Selina insisted the family wear their second-best clothes for the departure and the voyage. The best clothes were to be kept for the arrival in Australia.

They arrived in Melbourne in May 1886. The 14-year-old Henry Redstone Rayner (youngest of the boys) was listed in the passenger manifest as Hewey R Rayner. His mother called him Harry. The 'Hewey' of the passenger list may be a simple mis-reading of the handwritten 'Harry'. Another possible explanation is that he was called Hewitt or Hewey within the family. His siblings, as recorded in the passenger list, were Catherine Mary (age 21), William Edward James (age

19), Everilda Selina Jane (age 15), Daisy Lucy Rosa (age 12), Amy Elizabeth Lily (age 11), and Violet Maud Marian (age 9).

Harry was especially fond of his sister Daisy, one year his junior. He was deeply upset when she died at the age of 22 in 1896, and she figured in some of the stories he would later tell to the young Hewitt.

Upon arrival in Melbourne, William and Selina moved to the coastal settlement of Carrum, further south than Brighton, where they set up and ran a campsite and guest house in their bungalow by the beach, near Carrum railway station. One of Hewitt's notes records that 'people came for fresh fish, fowl – and flirtation. Grandma charged 12/- a week for the tents and hot water, and 6d for oil lamps if they were needed.'

Hewitt recorded that his grandfather William was a dead shot with a rifle, and devoted a lot of time to hunting and fishing, according to the season. He discovered that the skin of a shark, suitably cured, made good leather for repairing shoes. He was also a boatbuilder, and on rollers alongside the house at Carrum there was a white-painted rowing boat he had built, modelled on a lifeboat. This was used for fishing trips.

The young Hewitt stayed with his grandparents one Spring when he was convalescing from an illness. This was a time of year when the boarding house had few visitors. He recalled that a typical meal at Carrum would consists of schnapper (snapper), or flathead fried in butter, barracuda with boiled potatoes, jugged hare, or roasted rabbit stuffed with onions and sage. This would be followed by college pudding with egg custard. For special occasions there might be flounder, regarded as a luxury.

William Rayner died in 1909 at the age of 73 in Frankston, near Carrum (PROV reg no. 12508). His wife Selina died in April 1916 at the age of 76 in Fitzroy North, Melbourne (Reg no. 5764). A newspaper item from *The Argus* of Friday 28th April 1916 provides some useful information concerning the whereabouts of their sons and daughters by then. Hewitt's uncles and aunts were dispersed across the Australian continent.

> *A patient sufferer at rest.*
>   Rayner. On the 27th April. 1916. at her residence, 34 Scotchmer Street, North Fitzroy, Selina Jane, widow of the late William Rayner of Carrum, and formerly of Shanklin, Isle of Wight, loved mother of Mrs. Katherine Butler, William Rayner (West Australia), Frederick Rayner, Mrs. Everilda O'Sullivan, Henry Rayner, Mrs. Amy Pepper (Adelaide, S.A.), and Mrs. Violet Rawson (Adelaide, S.A.), aged 76 years.

The 'Henry Rayner' listed here would be Hewitt's father Henry Redstone Rayner. Violet Maud had been married in Adelaide on the 7th December 1907, to Thomas Rawson, eldest son of Edwin Thomas Rawson of Cheshire, England.

Following Selina Jane's death, the family had no interest in continuing the boarding house business, so the property at Carrum was put up for sale. The advertisement in the Melbourne *Argus* of 18th November and 2nd December

1916 provides some details of what it was like, and confirms Hewitt's own description of the location. Described as a 'bungalow boarding establishment', the property for sale consisted of four buildings on a plot 80 by 316 feet, right at the edge of the sea and close to Carrum railway station. The largest bungalow had eight rooms, two of the others had four rooms, and the smallest had three rooms.

Presumably William and Selina had occupied the largest bungalow, and rented out the other three to paying guests. The agents had put an asking price of £950 on the complete collection of bungalows, adding 'If you built the bungalows today and had to buy the land, the lot would cost you £2000.'

Hewitt's father's story

Little is known about Henry Redstone Rayner's movements over the 16 years after his arrival in Australia as a 14-year-old. The story told by Hewitt many years later is that his father travelled to Western Australia in pursuit of gold. Buying a licence in Perth, he set out with all his belongings in a wheelbarrow, spending time in Coolgardie, Kalgoorlie and Menzies. Hewitt wrote that he had seen an album containing a photo of his father with a long beard and frayed trousers, standing on his gold claim. This photo was not in the Rayner archive, but it is possible it still survives somewhere in the family.

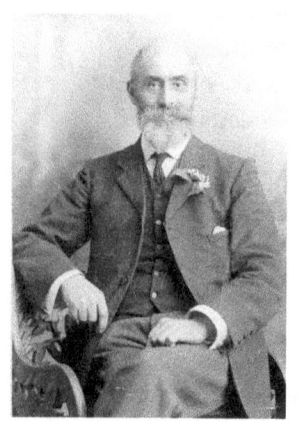

During this time he had many adventures and misadventures, which he recounted to his young son. Some of them were included in Hewitt's unpublished '*Child, when my boat comes in*' manuscript. It seems he never struck lucky, and ended up working for other people. It was probably during this period that he acquired plastering skills. Official records show that he married in Western Australia and had two sons, but both children and his wife died.

A3.1 Jabez Edwards, Hewitt's maternal grandfather. sw.

On 30th April 1901, back in the Melbourne area, Henry married again. His new bride was 21-year-old Emily Ellen Edwards, one of seven surviving children born to a family that had emigrated from Birmingham, England, in the 1870s.

Emily's father Jabez was a saddle-tree maker by trade, as were the two brothers who emigrated to Australia at around the same time. All three went into saddle-tree making in and around Melbourne, although by 1903, Emily Ellen's father had relocated his own business away from Melbourne, first to Sydney and then to Auckland, New Zealand. The *Auckland Star* of 23rd December 1919 carried an article about the Edwards' family firm, which was finding business tough in the face of competition from imports. It seems that in addition to making high-quality saddle-trees, the firm also offered a patented cast-iron stirrup bar said to be far superior to cheaper products that had riveted joints and were more likely to fracture.

Henry and Emily were married at the Christian Chapel, Church of Christ, in Hawthorn, Melbourne. The witnesses were Henry's older brother Frederick Walter Charles, and younger sister Violet Maud. It is not recorded whether Emily's parents Jabez and Emily Ellen (nee Powell) had travelled from New Zealand to attend the wedding. According to the marriage certificate, Emily had been born in Fitzroy, Melbourne, although Hewitt's birth certificate gives his mother's place of birth as Collingwood, Victoria.

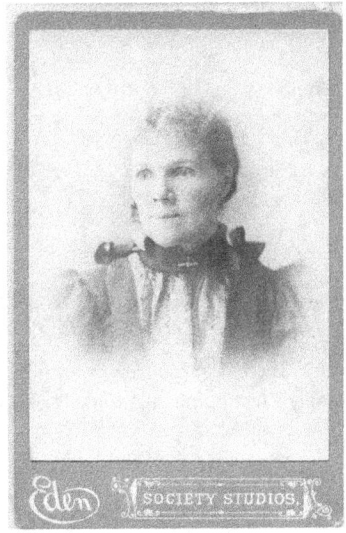

The newly-weds honeymooned in Fern Tree Gully, a popular country destination to the East of Melbourne, and nowadays part of the Dandenong Ranges National Park.

Their first home was at 26 Rathmines Street, Hawthorn, which Henry owned. The property is no longer there. It was demolished decades ago, along with the adjacent houses, to make way for commercial premises. In 2004 it was a garden centre.

A3.2 Hewitt's maternal grandmother Edwards in 1896. sw.

In 1902 they had their first and only child – a son they named Hewitt Henry. The choice of the rather unusual first name 'Hewitt' for their son may have come from Emily's side of the family. One of the Edwards, involved in the saddle tree business in Auckland, was called Hewitt.

But many years later in a letter to her son, Hewitt's mother gave a completely different reason for the choice of his name. She said that Hewitt was really a surname, and had been chosen because his father's older sister had become a Hewitt by marriage. According to Hewitt's mother, she spent her life back in England, working for the poor in the slums of Birmingham. This claim has not been researched or verified.

Whatever the reason behind the choice of name, it seems that in practice his parents and other members of the family called him Hewitt, or Hewie. There are a few instances where they referred to him as Harry or 'Young Harry' (presumably to differentiate him from his father) and sometimes Hal for short.

The family had various homes in the Melbourne area over the next few years, and in 1907 or thereabouts Hewitt's father had the idea of going to New Zealand try his chances. Hewitt's mother's family, the Edwards, lived and worked in Auckland, where they ran a saddle-tree factory. Hewitt wrote that his parents and he sailed on the *SS Old Hobart*, although this may be a name of his own invention. Many years later, he still remembered the scene as they approached Auckland, with the sea getting shallower, and the engines being cut. The trip to Auckland had taken a week. His mother suffered badly from seasickness, and hadn't moved from her bunk for the whole crossing.

The family stayed with Hewitt's maternal grandparents, and he remembered visiting his grandfather Edwards' saddle-tree factory. This was a period when

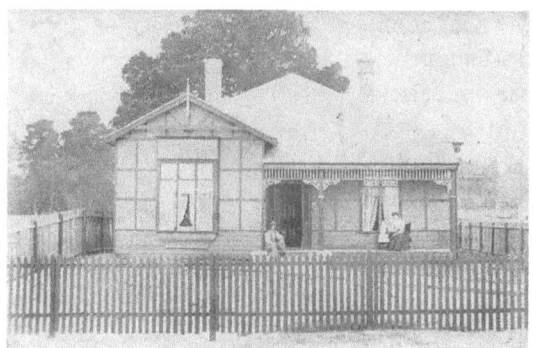

A3.3 Three-year-old Hewitt with his parents at the family's first home in St Kilda, 1905. sw.

demand for saddle trees was declining, and the factory had diversified into making shoe heels. Pat Northey, great grand-daughter of Jabez Edwards, told the author that the family's saddle-tree business had been at its busiest during the Franco Prussian and Boer wars, to meet the needs of the cavalry. Through the late 1800s, the business had been in Melbourne, probably in Charles Street, Collingwood, but after Australia's House of Representatives reduced the import tax on saddle trees from 25% to zero in April 1902 it became uneconomic. The *Adelaide Advertiser* of 21 February 1906 reported Arthur Edwards of Edwards & Co, Melbourne, saying that the abolition of the import tax had resulted in his business shrinking from 40 employees to 14, and machinery lying idle.

Years later, Hewitt described the Edwards factory as being in Grey Street, but in reality it was in Union Street. He recalled standing knee deep in wood shavings. In a dusty corner there were valuable richly-carved Maori pipes, Karri carved spear heads, and other items.

While they were in Auckland, his father had taken him down to the wharf to see Jack London's yacht, the Snark. This confirms the likely date as 1908. Jack London spent 1907 and 1908 sailing his 45-foot schooner from San Francisco to Australasia, later described in his 1911 book '*The Cruise of the Snark*'. The planned seven-year voyage was cut short and the boat sold in Sydney.

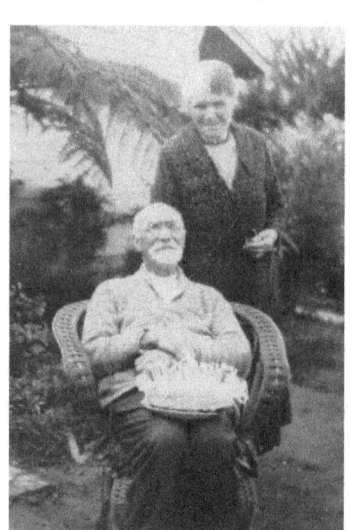

A3.4 Hewitt's mother Emily and her second husband Harry ('Hal') Gillard at their home in West Beach, St Kilda, in the late 1930s. sw.

Another of Hewitt's memories was of the crowds and soldiers in Auckland's main street when the American fleet was in.

The trip to New Zealand evidently didn't meet Hewitt's father's expectations, so the family returned to Australia, and the Melbourne area. They settled in the up-and-coming coastal town of Brighton. This is where Hewitt spent most of his childhood. His father developed a successful business building new houses on land that became available as some of the large estates were sub-divided.

After the breakup of their marriage in 1917 or 1918, Hewitt's mother, Emily, returned to New Zealand to stay with her parents in Auckland, and took Hewitt with her.

Henry Redstone Rayner, suffering from a wasting disease and wheelchair-bound, died in 1921 aged 49.

He left property and savings totalling more than £1600 to the Rayners. He left nothing to his wife and son, and chose to be buried alongside his first wife in Boroondara cemetery in Kew.

Hewitt's mother remarried on 1st June 1923. Her new husband was Harry ('Hal') Gillard, age 50, a widower and a solicitor's office manager. The marriage was at Christ Church, South Yarra. The couple lived in St Kilda. Hal died on 7th December 1941 aged 72 (ref. 12283). Emily died on 29th September 1953 (ref. 47300). She and Hal are buried in the same grave at Boroondara Cemetery in Brighton, together with Hal's first wife.

A4: Hewitt Rayner's London

Hewitt Rayner arrived in the UK in late 1923, and from then until the family relocated to the Kent coast in August 1955 London was his chosen home.

Initially he lived in the Regent's Park and St Johns Wood areas – convenient for the St Johns Wood School of Art, which he attended when he was preparing to apply for a position at the Royal Academy Schools.

In 1926 when he quit the RA Schools he moved to a room in Chelsea, and later that year, newly married, he moved into a flat in the World's End area of the Kings Road. When his wife developed TB a year or two later they migrated away from the River Thames to higher and drier ground.

Initially they lived in the Paddington area, and then in the late 1930s moved further north to Gospel Oak. This was not a wealthy or famous area of London, but had the great advantage of location and a strong community spirit. Gospel Oak is not far from the city centre, and is bounded on the north by Hampstead Heath, on the West by Belsize Park, and to the East by Kentish Town. The family had several addresses in Gospel Oak until they moved out of London to the Kent coast in 1955.

Even though the Rayners moved home numerous times, they were never far from the green, open spaces of Regent's Park and Hampstead Heath. Taking out a rented sailing dinghy on Regent's Park boating lake reminded him of sailing his father's boat off Brighton, Victoria.

He not only lived in these areas, but he also drew inspiration from them. You can almost trace his homes and haunts around London from the street scenes he chose to depict in drypoints.

It is noticeable that many of the houses in which Hewitt rented rooms are no longer there. With very little money, they were drawn to properties in less desirable parts of London – and some of these run-down locations were later targeted for redevelopment.

1924/5
3 Alma Square. This is the first recorded London address for Hewitt, in September 1924. This square is to the north of Paddington station and west of

Regent's Park, in St John's Wood. The property is a large three-storey house with basement, and backs onto a private garden. He was attending the St John's Wood Schools of Art at nearby 29 Elm Tree Road.

1925

18 Culworth Street. By the time Hewitt started at the RA Schools in May 1925 he had moved to this address, a few blocks away from Alma Square, nearer to Regent's Park and the Regent Canal. This house was later demolished to make way for a mansion block.

1926

Wellington Square, off the King's Road, Chelsea. When Rayner left the RA Schools in 1926 he immediately took a room here, drawn to Chelsea by its historic art connections. When Sickert visited the damp room, he advised Hewitt to 'move to a drier place'. There is no record of the exact address.

1926–7

28 Whiteheads Grove, Chelsea. This is probably the 'little flat in The World's End, King's Road, Chelsea' that Hewitt wrote about as their first home together. The south-facing house on a street to the north of the King's Road is no longer there, but a terrace of houses further down the street give a good idea of what number 28 would have looked like, with its characteristic cobweb-style balcony rail at the first-floor window. It is only a few blocks away from Wellington Square.

Hewitt gave this as his address for his marriage certificate, 4th October 1926. Theresa gave her parents' address at 20 Tottenham Street.

1929

20 Princess Road, Regent's Park, near Primrose Hill. A letter to Hewitt from the private secretary to Dame Nellie Melba, dated 13th February 1929, is the only known reference to this address, so it may have been a short stay.

1932

20 Tottenham Street. When Hewitt and Theresa returned from their Australian trip they lived with Theresa's parents at 20 Tottenham Street for a short while. They had to leave when Theresa's older brother – who had disapproved of the match from the start – persuaded the family that Hewitt and Theresa were taking advantage of their hospitality. Tottenham Street is a turning off Tottenham Court Road near Goodge Street underground station. The Zecchin home was at the eastern end of the street, on the north side, one of a terrace of houses with four floors and a basement, dating from the 1700s. The Zecchin family took in paying guests to help pay for the place. It and the adjacent properties were pulled down and replaced by an office building in recent times.

In November 1932, after they were forced to leave the Zecchin home, Theresa and Hewitt lived for a while in the charity-run 'House of St. Barnabas' hostel at **1 Greek Street**, Soho.

c.1934 onwards
13 Great College Street. Nowadays the road is known as Royal College Street. It's in Camden Town, near Euston and St Pancras stations. Their apartment was on the west side of the street, across the road from the Veterinary College. Theresa referred to 'our neat little back room'. The choice of Camden Town may well have been influenced by Sickert, since this was a favourite part of London for him. Sickert was a regular visitor to the Great College Street flat, and Rayner's *'Mr Sickert and a lady'* etching was done during one of those visits, as Hewitt and Theresa were preparing for their 1934 trip to the Isle of Wight. The property is no longer there.

1937
49 Twisden Road, in Gospel Oak, north London. It looks as if for some reason Hewitt planned to move to 5 Lismore Circus while his wife was in hospital. He had clearly been trying to have his post redirected, because on 11th October he received a letter from the District Post Office pointing out that mail redirection was not normally allowed to premises that were shared, but that in 'the exceptional circumstances of the present case' this would be allowed. The redirection service was set up to run until 15th December.

1937
5 Lismore Circus, in Gospel Oak, north London. Hewitt lodged there while Theresa was in City Hospital giving birth to their second daughter Kay. All the houses in Lismore Circus were demolished around 1970 as part of a major redevelopment of the area.

    Marylebone Road. Hewitt gave this address for a sonnet published in *The Indicator* on Friday 26th November 1937, although no other references to any such address have been found.

1939
Herbert Street NW5, between Belsize Park and Gospel Oak, north London. No street number known. This is the address given by Hewitt when he wrote a letter to the editor of the *Cavalcade*, published in the 31st October 1939 issue, and also referenced in the *Hampstead Express* of 23rd February 1945. Hewitt's daughter Frances described the family's two-room flat at this address in her own autobiographical writing. At some stage, wrote Frances, the family moved back to Lismore Circus, and were there when air raid shelters were built.

1940
69 Mansfield Road, Gospel Oak. Several letters from Theresa covering the periods when she and the girls were living in Leicester in November are addressed to Hewitt at 69 Mansfield Road. This is the studio that was damaged by bomb blast in November 1940. Hewitt stayed there for a while, and then moved to Allcroft Road.

1941

18 **Allcroft Road, NW5**. Letters from Theresa in Cambridgeshire to Hewitt through July, August and October 1941 carry this address. He continued to live here through into early 1943, since it is given as the family's address in an article in the *London Evening Standard* in January that year.

1943

45 **Herbert Street, NW5**. Letters from the National Gallery of Victoria in Melbourne, Australia, dated May and September 1943, are addressed to Hewitt at this address.

1943–1955

Mansfield Road, NW5. Frances recalled the relocation from Herbert Street to Mansfield Road, with a van carrying most of their possessions, but her father carefully carrying his important papers and art.

The Rayners lived first at **number 64** (on the north side of the road), and then after the building was affected by bombing they moved to **number 121** (on the south side) around 1944. This remained the family home until they moved out of London to Ramsgate in August 1955. While living there, they were burgled three or four times, according to a letter from Hewitt to his mother.

It was a two-storey end-of-terrace building with habitable attic, plus sub-basement, and stone steps leading up to the front door. The Rayners rented the first floor plus the attic, giving them two bedrooms, a large living room and a kitchen. The small toilet was shared by all residents of the building. Rayner usually directed visitors to arrive via Camden Town underground station.

Number 121 no longer exists, having been demolished around 1970 as part of a major local authority housing project.

1955–1958

39 **Duncan Road, Ramsgate**. On 30th August 1955 the family moved out of London to this house, using part of the legacy from Hewitt's mother in Australia to pay the £600 purchase price. The house is one of a small block of four known as Ventnor Villas. This move was part of Hewitt's grand plan to set up his Sickert Art Group. Frances was working by this stage, and spent some of this period living and working in London. In 1957 Hewitt took his own life at the Duncan Road house.

1958 onwards

22 **Crane Road, Tottenham**. On 6th October 1958 Theresa, Frances and Kay moved back to London, to this terraced house. They continued to live there until their deaths in the 1990s.

A5: New information about two Sickert addresses in Islington

Sickert had various home and studio addresses in central London between 1920 and 1934. New information from the Rayner archive has revealed important new facts about the Barnsbury Park house, as well as useful information about the Noel Road studio (both in Islington).

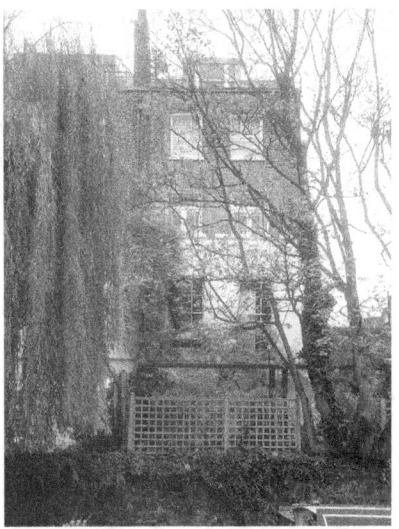

A5.1 The rear of 54 Noel Road in 2006. The castellations over the first-floor extension are still visible. PHOTO RS.

54 Noel Street (nowadays called Noel Road)

Biographical references to Sickert include a rented studio at number 26 Noel Street, Islington in the mid 1920s. Since then, not only has the street name been changed – to Noel Road – but the houses have also been renumbered. As a result, the address given for Sickert's Noel Street studio in published references has not been consistent.

Matthew Sturgis got it right in his masterful 2005 biography of Sickert, and information from Hewitt's archive confirms that the house in which Sickert had his studio is the house that today carries the number 54. The evidence from the Rayner archive also confirms that it was this house containing Sickert's studio that featured in his '*Hanging gardens*' and '*Fading memories of Sir Walter Scott*' works.

Noel Road runs East-West. The houses on the South side of the street have short gardens leading down to the Regent's Canal towpath. Hewitt visited Sickert in Noel Road on several occasions, and sat and worked with him on the far side of the canal, looking back at the houses. On their left, the canal disappeared into Islington Tunnel. On the right, it passed under Danbury Bridge, which carries Danbury Road across the canal. The scene today is very little changed from the 1920s, except that large trees obscure much of the view of the houses. Danbury Road cuts between what are today numbers 54 and 56 Noel Road.

Hewitt wrote: 'Sickert's house was right against Danbury Bridge, a quiet hidden spot. The old three-storied houses along this drab yet strangely lovely stretch of water in Islington were grey and possessed battlements which stood over the dark waters of the canal like little knightly castles. We settled ourselves against the canal railings by Danbury bridge. Sickert was finishing a painting that was to become '*the fading memories of Sir Walter Scott*.' And the house he drew was that in which he worked.'

Only number 54 Noel Road fits all these details, being next to Danbury Bridge, and having castellations along the first-floor roof line. The reference to the canal railings is also important – across the canal facing numbers 56, 58 and up is a well-aged brick wall, not railings.

Evidence that the house was today's number 54 also comes from Sickert's painting '*Laylock and Thunderplump*'. This was done in the ground floor front room of the house, and the view through the window shows the houses across the other side of Noel Road. They are the correct size and style for the properties facing number 54. The houses facing number 56 are smaller and different in style.

Number 12 Barnsbury Park, not number 14

The previous note about Noel Road is a matter of adding to the weight of existing evidence regarding the house where Sickert rented a studio in the mid 1920s.

In the case of the Barnsbury Park house where Sickert lived in the early 1930s, something altogether more exciting has emerged from the research for this biography.

It is well known from contemporary sources that the property the Sickerts acquired in 1931 was number 14 Barnsbury Park. What was not known until now is that the Sickert's home was not in the house that today carries the number 14. It was the next-door property that today is number 12.

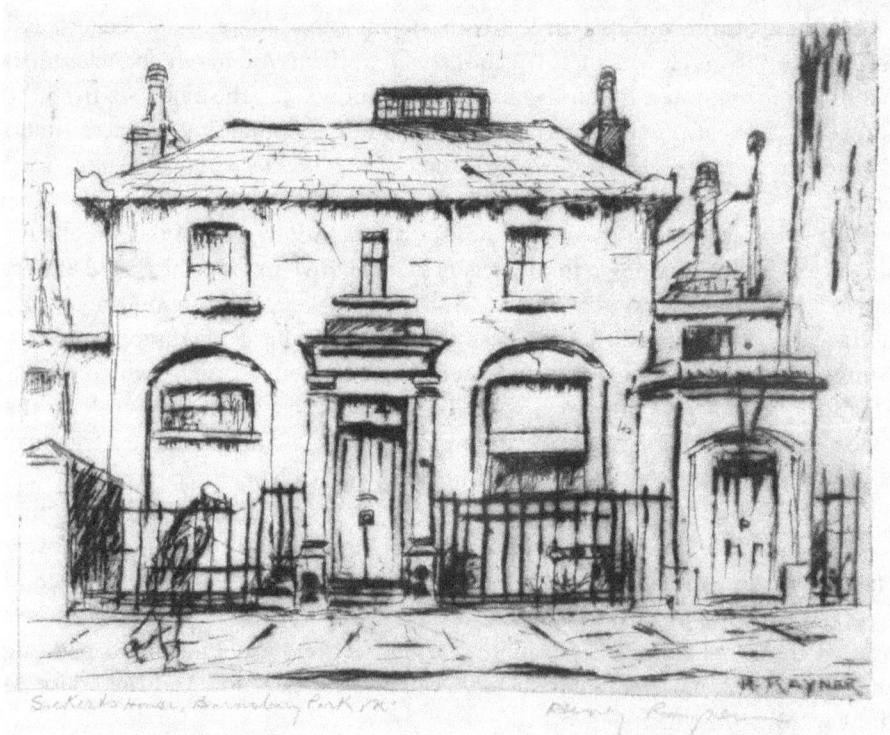

A5.2 Rayner's drypoint of Sickert's home in Barnsbury Park. In the 1930s it was number 14. Nowadays it is number 12. The structure on the roof is probably the toplight that Sickert had fitted to provide more daylight for his studio. Drypoint, 1932, 125x158mm. sw.

This fact only came to light when a 1931 drypoint etching by Hewitt was found in the Rayner archive. This shows Sickert's Barnsbury Park home – a large and imposing detached house with a central doorway, symmetrical window arrangement, steps down to the pavement, and number 14 above the front door.

A visit to the road showed immediately that this is the house that today carries the number 12. Everything matches.

Once this breakthrough had been made, some information in 'Walter Sickert: a life', by Matthew Sturgis, became even more meaningful. He wrote how Sickert had the ground floor front windows modified in the interests of privacy, to prevent passers-by from looking in. This chimes exactly with the detail visible in Rayner's drypoint, which shows partially bricked-up ground-floor windows. Even today, one of the ground floor windows is still bricked up.

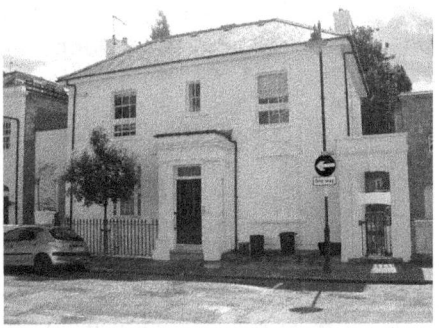

A5.3 The Sickert's home as it is nowadays, number 12 Barnsbury Park. Without doubt the same house depicted in Hewitt's 1931 drypoint. PHOTO RS.

The author approached Mark Aston at Islington Local History Centre with this new information. Islington holds the collection of paintings, drawings and etchings found in Sickert's studio at the time of his death, along with an archive of his photographs and personal papers. [You can read more on the website devoted to 'Walter Sickert and the Sickert family collection in Islington'].

Mark looked into the matter and found that the street numbering in Barnsbury Park had changed in relatively recent times, and that's why the number of Sickert's house changed from number 14 to number 12.

A6: The 1945 Brook Street Art Gallery exhibition

This is the complete text of the catalogue for Henry Rayner's 1945 one-man show.

Although scheduled to run only from the 14th to the 30th June, in the event it was so successful that its run was extended for an extra week.

Interesting First Exhibition of
DRY-POINTS BY HENRY RAYNER
The OFFICIAL OPENING of the Exhibition will take place on
Thursday, June 14th, at 3 p.m. by Mr. W. I. JORDAN,
High Commissioner for New Zealand.

BROOK STREET ART GALLERY LTD.
14, BROOK STREET, W1.

**From June 14th to June 30th
Open Daily from 10 to 6. Sat. 10 to 1.**

CATALOGUE

1. A Soldier of New Zealand .... 12 gns.
2. To New Zealand .... 14 gns.

GROUP 1. RELIGIOUS.

3. The Last Supper 1941 (Trial print, Royal Collection, Windsor) .... 20 gns.
4. Christ at Emmaus, 1944 (First trial print) .... 15 gns.
5. Jesus and Magdalene (To Dufy) .... 14 gns.
6. The Last Supper, 1939 .... 12 gns.
7. Christ Presented to the People .... 14 gns.
8. Jesus Rides into Jerusalem (2nd impression) .... 14 gns.

GROUP 2. BALLET AND CIRCUS.

9. Les Sylphides, Enamel Drypoint (British Museum Collection) .... 15 gns.
10. Les Sylphides, No. 8 .... 8 gns.
11. Les Sylphides, No. 3 (In Royal Collection) .... 10 gns.
12. Les Sylphides, Rehearsal .... 8 gns.
13. The Lambeth Walk, No. 1 (Trial print) .... 10 gns.
14. The Lambeth Walk, No. 2 (Early print) .... 9 gns.
15. Prima Ballerina .... 9 gns.
16. The Clowns, No. 1 .... 8 gns.
17. Clowns and Horse .... 8 gns.
18. Circus (Trial print) .... 6 gns.
19. Circus Night (First proof) .... 10 gns.
20. Circus Girl (First proof) .... 8 gns.
21. The Running Clown .... 8 gns.
22. Clowns and Dogs .... 10 gns.
23. Clowns' Rehearsal (First proof) .... 14 gns.
24. The Laugh .... 6 gns.
25. Me and My Gal .... 8 gns.
26. Songs of the Nineties (Trial print) .... 7 gns.
27. Allegro (Trial proof) .... 6 gns.
28. 7 a.m. (Colour Drypoint) (Only one made) .... 15 gns.
29. The Pattering Clowns (First proof) .... 15 gns.

GROUP 3. CHELSEA SCENES.

30. The Old Mangle Works, World's End, Chelsea, 1926 .... 8 gns.
31. Cheyne Walk, 1935. Destroyed by enemy action (British Museum) .... 8 gns.
32. Cheyne Walk, small plate, 1928 .(Trial proof) .... 6 gns.
33. Cheyne Walk, No. 4 .... 8 gns.
34. Chelsea Reach, Saturday (Rare early print) .... 8 gns.
35. Evening from Chelsea Reach .... 9 gns.

36. The Duke's House, Chelsea ....6 gns.
37. Chelsea, 1938 (showing Power House) ....6 gns.
38. Chelsea Old Church (Destroyed 1941) ....7 gns.
39. The Lombard Cafe, Chelsea (Destroyed by enemy action) ....8 gns.
40. Chelsea Reach (Rare early print) ....10 gns.
41. Chelsea Pier, 1937 ....6 gns.

GROUP 4. SICKERT MEMORIES.
42. R. W. Sickert, 1925 (Fitzroy Street) (Trial proof) ....10 gns.
43. Mr. Sickert at Barnsbury Park, 1931 (British Museum) ....10 gns.
44. Walter Sickert in Kensington Gardens, 1925 ....7 gns.
45. Walter Sickert, 1931 (Square plate (First proof) ....7 gns.
46. Sickert's Studio, Barnsbury Park, N. ....6 gns.
47. Sickert, 1940 ....15 gns.

GROUP 5. PORTRAITS.
48. Teresa, 1940 (Trial proof) ....8 gns.
49. Teresa ....10 gns.
50. My Daughter Frances, 1940 ....6 gns.
51. Study of a London Boy, 1940 ....6 gns.
52. My Daughter Kay (Trial proof) ....9 gns.
53. Henri Gaudia Brzeska, 1914 ....6 gns.
54. Mr. G. B. Shaw, 1939 (Rare early proof) ....12 gns.
55. The Etcher (South Kensington Museum) ....7 gns.
56. My Mother (Trial proof) ....14 gns.
57. Selfportrait, 1939 (Royal Collection) ....7 gns.
58. Selfportrait, 1943 ....8 gns.

GROUP 6. LANDSCAPE.
59. A Farm near Isle of Ely, 1941 ....8 gns.
60. The Fen Field ....10 gns.
61. The Lane, Hampshire ....7 gns.
62. The Fen Village ....8 gns.
63. Two Cows and a Bull (Early proof) ....8 gns.
64. Ely Cathedral ....8 gns.
65. The Little Wood, Norwich (Artist's proof) ....8 gns.
66. A French Farm, 1930 ....6 gns.
67. Old Regent's Park, 1939 (Artist's proof) ....12 gns.
68. Lismore Circus, London, N. ....8 gns.
69. The English Landscape ....6 gns.
70. The End of the Road (Leicester City Art Gallery) ....10 gns.
71. Old Paddington, 1941 ....8 gns.
72. The Marshy Wood (Artist's proof) ....9 gns.
73. Old Regent's Canal, Regent's Park, 1928 ....10 gns.
74. The Harvesters ....7 gns.

GROUP 7. AUSTRALIAN SCENES.

75. Bush Bullocks, 1924 (Rare early print) .... 10 gns.
76. The Bullock Plough (Artist's proof) ....8 gns.
77. Evening Muster, Australia, 1921 .... 10 gns.
78. The Bullock Team, Australia, 1930 (Cardiff Art Gallery) ....8 gns.
79. The Rising Horse ....8 gns.

GROUP 8. WAR SCENES.

80. The Incendiary Bomb from South Kensington Museum, 1940 (Acquired by the
New Zealand Government) .... 10 gns.
81. Heavy Explosive Bomb, Chelsea, 1941 ....8 gns.
82. The Heart of London, 1941 (First proof) ....8 gns.
83. Rescue during Blitz, Chelsea, 1940 (First proof) ....6 gns.
84. St. Paul's District, 1941 (Artist's proof) ....5 gns.

GROUP 9. MISCELLANEOUS.

85. Study in Drypoint (Nude) (Artist's proof) ....5 gns.
86. Study of Tramp ....6 gns.
87. The Flowers of Iron (Rare early print) ....7 gns.
88. Mother and Son, London, 1940 ....6 gns.
89. The Old Turk's Head, Wapping (Destroyed), 1927 .... 14 gns.
90. The Fish ....5 gns.
91. The Leopard ....6 gns.
92. Study No. 5: Jesus chases Moneylenders from the Temple .... 10 gns.
93. Study No. 6: When We Stood Alone, 1941 (Etched under Fire) (Acquired by the
Australian Government and Walter Nash, Australian Bush, Deputy Prime Minister
of New Zealand. Went before Queen Mary early in the War)
.... 12 gns.
94. Study No. 7: Anton Dolin in the Bluebird Ballet (Indebted to Gjon Mili)
.... 14 gns.

HENRY RAYNER

Henry Rayner, one of the interesting figures in Modem British Art, a man of outstanding personality and character, was born of Australian worker-pioneer parents in
Melbourne, 19th September, 1902.

He began drawing at two years of age; a delicate child who soon threw himself
into the common fight. After a varied life at the jeweller's bench, as a cowman on a
New Zealand farm, for a while a motormechanic in the wildest parts of the Southern
Australian Bush, painting and drawing at every available moment, learning about the
ancient inward and outward manifestation of Beauty, and their ancient difference,
an inner gentleness keeping his artist's vision pure, and he preferring to live close to
nature, he came to England with little in his pocket in 1924.

After passing the difficult entrance test, was entered into the Royal Academy
Schools, where, with his earnest impassioned nature and his modem, progressive
outlook, he led the student strike, and was for some years after regarded as an
untouchable rebel by the authorities.

He met McEvoy, Wilson Steer, and studied under 'that great colourist' Charles Sims; but Walter Sickert made him his protégé and friend. They painted and drew together at his studio and in Kensington Gardens.

Rayner was in deep poverty. He married Miss Theresa Zecchin in 1926 and continued to evolve his art theories. His extreme sensibility, his deep feeling for everything in nature, enabled him to avoid so much of the formlessness and hypocrisy in Modern Art; and he loved all that was best in living art; and, though he is in the line of best Tradition, he cannot be considered to belong to any 'School'.

Like all men of pioneering and progressive spirit he has cut new ground and has evolved a technique of his own. He took from the old what he wanted for the new and living. His method approaches that of the Impressionists. He does not believe in cluttering his surfaces, or indulging in grand eloquent phrases. He wants to say something and get it said poetically, succinctly. Simplicity and purity of line is his aim.

He is a superb draughtsman, and his work finished craftsmanship. This present exhibition is rich in examples of a master. It reveals a character full of courage, deep humour and humility a man of whom Sickert once said: 'He possesses mighty gifts'. But Rayner's work is known more widely in France and Russia than it is here.

In 1939 Queen Mary purchased from him an unconventional portrait of the present King; and works of his were acquired by the British Museum and the Victoria and Albert Museum.

Early in 1940 his Studio was blasted by parachute landmine. Rayner was injured, but he worked on despite his condition. Soon he became very ill ; then his painting arm was smashed. A famous surgeon saved it enough for the fingers to just hold the etching needle. In this condition he has worked since, his body mending but slowly.

He determined to stick it out in London 'with the others', and went through all the blitz. In 1942 the Queen had a command inspection of his work at the Palace, and purchased a picture. Later three of his works were acquired for the King's Collection, Windsor. The British Council had his work on exhibition. Augustus John, who greatly admired his drypoints, supported him in his application for a post as war artist.

Again in 1944 Rayner received shock in a flying bomb incident, but helped the victims for two hours. During the visit of the Dominions' Premiers, Mr. Curtin, Mr. Walter Nash, Mr. Fraser and General Smuts acquired his war pictures. The New Zealand Government took three, and the Canadian Government acquired another. The Belgium Government acquired several. Recently he has made a portrait of the Princesses for the Queen.

Henry Rayner is represented in the Ashmolean Museum, Oxford ; The Royal Library of Belgium ; The Rijksmuseum ; The Melbourne National Gallery ; The National Museum of Wales ; The Industrial Museum, Aberdeen ; The Manchester Art Gallery, and The Congressional Library, Washington, U.S.A.

But for the efforts of Mrs. Rayner, who has devotedly nursed the artist through his long illness, and the kindly support of Mr. H. Harben, this exhibition would not have taken place.

Note: All exhibited prints have been 'pulled' by the artist at his own press ; each proof having the qualities that the artist desired. The editions are limited from ten to fifteen prints, according to the life of the burr.

A7: The 1960 Richmond Hill Gallery exhibition

[This retrospective exhibition was at the Richmond Hill Gallery, 47 Hill Rise, Richmond, Surrey, in March 1960.]

[Print prices are quoted in Guineas (gns). One Guinea was £1.1.0.]

Henry Rayner was born in 1902, worked in Australia and New Zealand before coming to this country where he studied at the Royal Academy, and was befriended by Sickert. His work is in the Royal Collections and in many galleries and private collections throughout the world. His struggles against ill health and adversity culminated in his tragic and untimely death in 1957.

Etchings on show

Title	Price in Guineas
1. A soldier of New Zealand (Art Gallery, New Zealand)	16
2. To New Zealand, Christ over every city	17
3. Self portrait	21
4. The last supper (1941 trial print in Royal Collection, Windsor)	44
5. Christ at Emmaus (1944, first trial print)	50
6. Jesus and Magdalene (to Dufy)	45
7. Christ presented to the people	45
8. Jesus heals the earth proud	45
9. Christ enters into Jerusalem	44
10. Christ betrayed	46
11. The Crucifixion	60
12. Jesus in the field of corn	43
13. Jesus chases money lenders from the Temple	55
14. Richard Sickert at Fitzroy Street 1925	21
15. Walter Sickert at Kensington Gardens 1925	20
16. Mr Sickert at Barnsbury Park 1931 (British Museum)	21
17. Richard Sickert 1932	30
18. Walter Sickert 1940	17
19. Old Mangle Works Chelsea 1926 (British Museum)	15
20. Chelsea Old Church (destroyed 1941) Q. Mary Collection	18
21. Cheyne Walk Chelsea 1929	15
22. Thames at Chelsea I	14
23. Chelsea Study II black and white 18gns, gold	23
24. Chelsea Reach	14
25. Les Sylphides No. 3 (British Museum)	35
26. Ballet 48	60

27. Les Sylphides 15
28. The Lambeth Walk (Industrial Art Gallery Aberdeen) 23
29. Prima Ballerina 14
30. Anton Dolin (Bluebird Ballet) 40
31. Harlequin 15
32. Circus (Sir Arthur Bliss) 21
33. The laugh 15
34. Clowns and horse 15
35. Rehearsal, Les Sylphides 10
36. K George VI (in galleries home and abroad, USA) 100
37. Henry Gaudier Brzeska 1 40
38. My daughter Frances 15
39. Henry Gaudier Brzeska 1914 II 50
40. Boy's head 15
41. T E Lawrence 1929 (Lon., Ashmolean Museum, Oxford) 15
42. Mother (Melbourne Art Gallery) 20
43. Sir Winston Churchill (British Museum) 40
44. Augustus John (National Portrait Gallery) 30
45. Dame Sybil Thorndike 30
46. Mr Bernard Shaw (Oldham Art Gallery) 30
47. Theresa 21
48. A London Boy 15
49. Old Regent's Park 1939 15
50. The Turk's Head, Wapping 1929 30
51. Old Regent's Park Canal 1935 30
52. Lismore Circus London 1938 30
53. Old Market Street Shepherds Market 15
54. A French farm 20
55. Old Park Lane 1939 23
56. The Fen village 30
57. The dream .... NFS
58. The incendiary from V&A Museum, New Zealand Govt 35
59. Mother and son 25
60. The etcher 20
61. My studio after 1940 blitz 10
62. My path is a rose even as this plain 50
63. There is no shelter 55
64. The man with the asses head (Leeds Art Gallery) 50

All these Rayner etchings were on show alongside paintings by a New Zealand artist called Glyn Collins.

A8: Complete exhibition listing

There have been four significant one-man exhibitions devoted to the work of Henry Rayner – three of them during his lifetime, and one after his death.

Material surviving from Hewitt's archives also reveals a number of other events at which his work was shown. The following list includes all known exhibitions at which his work could be seen, in date order.

Old Lombard Cafe, Chelsea 1927 or 1928
There are no records of this exhibition, just a passing mention. It was the period in which Rayner started his series of drypoints of Chelsea scenes. The Old Lombard Café was itself the subject of a Rayner drypoint (repeated several times, suggesting it sold well). The Old Lombard Café was in one of the oldest surviving buildings of Cheyne Walk, near Old Chelsea Church. It had a first floor balcony that was Rayner's favourite place from which to watch the river, and in particularly the sunsets. The building was in a poor state, and was pulled down for redevelopment in the 1930s.

Regent's Park, 1929
In Theresa's reference list there is a mention of a 'private exhibition' in Regent's Park. That is all that is stated. This may indicate that it was at someone's house. Or maybe even in the Rayner's own home.

Melbourne 1932
There is a passing reference in Theresa's reference list of Rayner's portrait of Sickert titled '*Barnsbury Park*' being shown in Melbourne. Nothing further is known.

Kentish Town, 1937
The *Hampstead and St John's Wood News* of 16th September 1937 referred to an exhibition of work by Henry Rayner the previous month in Kentish Town. '*...where some arresting portraits of Chelsea notabilities caused considerable comment. They were executed in a fresh vigorous style, as were the etchings and drypoints.*' No other references to this exhibition have yet been found.

Guild Theatre exhibition, Jan/Feb 1939
Nothing is known about this exhibition, apart from a surviving invitation card worded:
> Art Exhibition
>> Guild Theatre Studio
>> 3 Roger Street, Gray's Inn Road
>> Friday 27th & Saturday 28th January 1939, from 2pm to 5pm
>> Etchings & watercolours by Henry Rayner
>> Watercolour paintings by Cecil Skelly
>> Architectural designs and cartoons for frescoes by Margaret Radford

A reply will be appreciated by Anne Trotman, 23 Parliament Hill, NW3
Hon secs R Ricardo, Margaret M Radford
Also Inaugural Meeting of Troubador Poets Club

International Circle of Arts and Letters, March 1939

Keen's Chop House, Great Turnstile, Holborn, Wednesday 8th March 1939.
At 7pm there was a talk entitled 'The Chop Shop as the future ICAL Home'. The
RSVP name and address is Miss Anne Trotman, 23 Parliament Hill, NW3.
A handwritten note by Hewitt on the reverse of the invitation card notes that he
exhibited eight works, unframed, at this ICAL event.

Royal Society of Amateur Artists, 1939

Hewitt exhibited his portrait of H M The King, at the request of Dame Alice
Godman. The portrait was acquired by Queen Mary, with three other proofs.
This was the start of Rayner's media recognition.

Royal Institute of Ray Therapy, 1939

Eight Rayner drypoints were exhibited and sold, and the proceeds donated by
Hewitt to the new clinic

Private exhibition at the home of Miss Buckley, c1939

Theresa's reference list notes that 14 proofs were sold at this show, at the home
of Miss Buckley ('the Australian'). Purchasers included Lady Grey Egerton, Miss
Bridges, and Mrs Valentine Williams.

The Wertheim Gallery exhibition, 1939

Although Hewitt would later describe his Brook Street exhibition as his first
one-man exhibition, in truth it was this 1939 event at the gallery owned by the
legendary Lucy Wertheim, 3–5 Burlington Gardens, London W1, that should
have been his first one-man show.

Lucy Wertheim ran a gallery to showcase work by the younger generation of
artists, who found it difficult to get gallery space elsewhere. The Rayner exhibition was rudely cut short by the outbreak of what he generally described as 'the
Hitler war'. It seems that Rayner's would be the last exhibition to be held at the
Wertheim Gallery; and it's possible that it never actually opened, since war was
declared the day before the exhibition's planned opening day.

Leicester Art Gallery, 1940

Twelve works by Rayner were shown in an exhibition arranged by director
Trevor Thomas, and three were purchased for the gallery.

New York, c1940

Rayner's 'The etcher' was shown at the New York British Contemporary Art
Exhibition.

A very private exhibition, 1942

In November or December this year, Queen Mary (mother of the then King) viewed a selection of proofs by Rayner, and bought a portrait of the King. According to hand-written notes on a proof in the author's collection, one of the other proofs presented was the 1938 Rayner self portrait.

Belgian Ministry 1942

There are no records of this event, apart from a mention that it was arranged at the Belgian Government in Exile in Eaton Square by a Miss Cloquet, and that the Chef de Cabinet of the Belgian Minister of Education, a Mr Nieuwenhuys, purchased the portrait of The King, for presentation to the Prime Minister of Belgium.

Belgian Institute, Belgrave Square, August 1943

Patrons listed in Theresa's notes are Madame Els, M Castelein (the artist), Madame de la Putta. Several sales are listed: to Lt. Beaurens, 'Military Minister' (one work), Mr Henroteaux (three works), British Columbia through the Ambassador (five works). Lady Wolseley of Eaton Square purchased a Lawrence of Arabia proof.

British Council exhibitions 1943 and 1944

Theresa's reference list mentions various exhibitions arranged by the British Council at which Rayner proofs were exhibited, including Palestine, Czechoslovakia, Poland and Mexico. A letter dated 6th October 1943 from the Director of Fine Arts at the British Council informed Hewitt that two of his etchings had been selected for inclusion in an exhibition in Palestine. They are *Chelsea 1941* and *Old Regent's Park Canal*. Hewitt must have sent others for consideration, since the letter invited him to collect the other prints 'as they are liable to get damaged if returned through the post'.

A letter a month later from Mr L D Harvey at the British Council informed him that one more of his etchings has also been selected. 'I showed your latest portrait of Sickert to Mr Campbell Dodgson, and he was very much taken with it,' wrote Harvey. 'He would like it to be included in our Palestine Exhibition, to make a group with the other two prints we have already selected.'

Sales resulted, and specific drypoints mentioned are *Regent's Park*, *Sickert* and *Cheyne Walk*. The inclusion of Rayner's work in this travelling exhibition may have been to soften the blow of his being turned down for a position as an Official War Artist.

City of Dudley Municipal Art Gallery, 1944

An exhibition of Rayner's work was held in January and February.

Alfred Wilson Booksellers, Hampstead, date unknown

A small advertisement in a Hampstead newspaper tells of an exhibition of drypoints by Henry Rayner to be held from 12th October to 10th November at Alfred Wilson Booksellers, 11 Hampstead High Street. 'This is the sixty-sixth of a series of exhibits by living artists which will be on view. We hope that Hampstead residents will find pleasure and interest in visiting them.'

The Brook Street Art Gallery exhibition: June 1945

The one-man exhibition at the Brook Street Art Gallery from 14th to 30th June 1945 was a milestone event for Rayner. Arranged with the help of his friend Henry Harben, it was opened by Mr W J Jordan, New Zealand's High Commissioner in London. The exhibition catalogue shows a list of 96 etchings, with prices ranging from 20gns (£21) for '*The last supper, 1941*' to 5gns for '*The fish*' and others. Most of the prints are priced in the range 6 to 10gns.

26th May 1948

Hewitt organised an exhibition at his own home at 121 Mansfield Road. Titled (for unknown reasons) 'The Henry Rayner Anniversary', it featured some of his wartime drypoints and some of the works from the 1945 Brook Street Art Gallery exhibition, together with war photographs by Thomas Hennell and an unknown photographer called Bly. Some of the photographs showed Hewitt out sketching in the remains of bomb-damaged buildings. He prepared a big poster for the event.

1948/49, Sept to January

A letter dated 3rd October 1948 from the Foreign Service of the USA acknowledges receipt of further etchings from Hewitt for an 'Exhibition of art by Henry Rayner at the American Library, Sept 1948 to Jan 1949. Etchings and coloured work'. There were nine etchings in total. Nothing else is known.

The Australia House exhibition, January 1953

The invitation describes this as 'An official winter exhibition of the paintings and drypoint etchings of Henry Rayner', and was held under the auspices of the Australian Government at its embassy in The Strand. Rayner was assigned one of the main windows of the embassy, and the prints and paintings were arranged according to his own plan.

The Richmond Exhibition, March 1960

This was a retrospective exhibition of Rayner's work held at the Richmond Hill Gallery, 47 Hill Rise, Richmond, three years after his death. It was organised by Theresa, then living at 22 Crane Road, Twickenham.

There were 65 drypoints on show. The last picture sold at the exhibition, noted Theresa, was a portrait of Sickert at Fitzroy Street, bought by Sickert's sister-in-law Andrina Schweder.

A9: Theresa's list, 1925–1960

This list of major events in her husband's career from 1925 onwards was compiled by Theresa Rayner. She probably prepared it in 1960 as background information for the Richmond retrospective exhibition. She titled it 'A reference list of the distribution (public) in part of the works of Henry Rayner'. Much of it is a listing of the institutions and well-known individuals who purchased or accepted prints by her late husband. It is reproduced here exactly as written by Theresa, apart from some minor tidying up of spelling and punctuation.

1925: Won Ivory (medallion) Royal Academy Schools, London. RW Sickert bought probation painting '*The Dying Clown*', and accepted him as a pupil.
- Wilson Steer bought '*Chelsea Reach*'.
- Watercolours, portraits and paintings went to Australia and New Zealand.
- Portraits of the artist's Mother sent out. The 1925 portrait of Sickert was finished in drypoint. Sickert bought the portrait.

1926: Portrait of MeEvoy finished. McEvoy purchased the drypoint. Fitzroy street portrait of Sickert was finished and sold to him.

1927: Portrait of René Quinn sold to B. in America.

1927–28 Set of Chelsea drypoints begun in March.
- Chelsea Exhibition at the Old Lombard Café.
- Portrait of Shaw commenced.
- Chelsea Library acquired a scene of '*Chelsea*', '*Cheyne Walk*' and '*the Old Lombard Café*'.

1929: Private exhibition, Regent's Park.
- Finished portrait of T.E. Lawrence of Arabia.
- Several works went to Australia, New Zealand and France, America and Russia.

1932: Sickert's portrait '*Barnsbury Park*' sold to Sickert. This was shown in Melbourne.
- Worked with Sickert at Barnsbury Park. Made etchings of his house. Chelsea set completed for 1934. The Sickert 1931 portrait completed in the large plate. (This was later bought by Lord Methuen, 1945).

1934: Portraits of Theresa since 1926 go to Australia.
- Portraits of Captain Fordham, and Hal Gillard, self portrait in paint and drypoint.
- Altogether 9,000 drypoints have been sold.

1939: Mrs. Anthony Eden purchased '*The Cold Joint*' an etching.
- Dame Alice Godman acquired a Chelsea scene and a head of Frances, the artist's daughter.

- Portrait of H.M. The King is exhibited at the Royal Society of Amateur Artists at the request of Dame Alice Godman. Queen Mary acquired the portrait of H.M. The King, with three other proofs.
- The King and Queen Elizabeth acquire two portraits for the collection at Windsor. One is an early proof of the Royal portrait. Portrait of His Grace the Duke of Windsor is completed, and acquired by him on 19th September, 1939. The Royal Institute of Ray Therapy exhibits eight drypoints sold, but proceeds given by the artist to the new clinic. British Museum acquire (1939–1952) *'Les Sylphides'*, *'self portrait'*, *'portrait of Winston Churchill'*, *'The King (drypoint)'*, *'The Old Mangle Works, Chelsea'*, *'Cheyne Walk, Chelsea'*. The Victoria and Albert Museum acquire self -portrait *'The Etcher'*, *'Richard Sickert'*, *'The King'*.
- Private Exhibition at the home of Miss Buckley, the Australian, at Hans Mansion. Lady Grey Egerton, Miss Bridges and Mrs Valentine Williams bought proofs from the show. 14 were sold in all.
- Dealers Brown and Philip bought a portrait of the King and hold other works. Sickert gave Henry Rayner a letter authorising him to teach in Australia.
- Mrs Anthony Eden bought 12 prints of Chelsea. Mr James Quinn bought the Chelsea scene.
- Sir Charles McCann purchased three works.
- Mr. Bernard Shaw acquired a portrait of himself by Rayner (The Bernard Shaw portrait was an early proof by the Oldham Art Gallery Committee). Princess Galitzine and Prince Vladimir Galitzine purchased six works in Berkeley square Crisis Exhibition, held at the gallery of Mrs. Lucy Wertheim (Sept 2/5th 1939), Burlington Gardens. Five works sold. This was the first one-man public exhibition by Henry Rayner.
- Colnaghi's had offered to take the work and acquired three, by the Manager Wright.
- Portrait of Theresa sent to Australia.

1940: Blitz pictures and etchings are made up to the time of injury November 1940. Portrait of Mr Parr, Manager, Rubber Co, Lots Road, Chelsea, is finished.
- The Leicester Art Gallery, under the director Trevor Thomas, show twelve works and buy three for the gallery. *'When we stood alone'* completed and further works made around the blitzed area of St. Paul's and the West and East ends of London, also in Chelsea where a new portrait of Wilson Steer is made. Steer takes portrait etching of a boy by Rayner. Major Athee's portrait in drypoint is finished.

1942: Miss Cloquet holds an exhibition of Rayner's works at the Belgian Ministry [Belgian Government in Exile] at Eaton Square.

- Mr. Nieuwenhuys, Chef de Cabinet, Belgian Ministry of Education, buys the portrait of the King. The Prime Minister of Belgium is presented with the portrait.

1943: Exhibition at the Belgian Institute in August, 1943 – Patrons Madame Els, M.Castelein (the artist), Madame de la Putta etc. Lt Beaurens, Military Minister, takes one work, Mr Henroteaux three works, British Columbia, through the Ambassador, takes five works. Lady Wolseley of Eaton Square purchased Lawrence of Arabia.

1943: The Editor of the *Belgian Message* publishes Rayner's portrait of General Montgomery.
- Sir Louis Busseau, Agent General for Victoria, Australia, buys one work. The Belgian Minister of Finance buys Ballet scenes.

1939–40: Works in museums and galleries:
- Royal Collection, Windsor holds: *'The Last Supper'*, *'Les Sylphides No. 3'*, *'Self Portrait'* and two portraits of the King.
- The Rijksmuseum, Amsterdam, one work 1939.
- The Royal Library of Belgium one work (The King) 1939.
- The Academic des Beaux Arts, one work 1939.

1943: National Portrait Gallery, London holds portraits of Augustus John, The King and Lawrence of Arabia. The National Gallery, Melbourne, holds a portrait of the King and the artist's Mother, 1943.
- The John portrait was made in the months of June 1943 at John's studio, Tite Street. Augustus John holds three of Rayner's works.
- The British Council, Palestine Exhibition, Czechoslovakia, Poland etc. These sell Rayner's works including *'Regent's Park'*, *'Sickert'* etc, 1943.
- Ashmolean Museum, Oxford take five works including *'T.E.Lawrence'* and *'Les Sylphides No. 5'* etc.
- Aberdeen Industrial Museum buy three works including blitz scene in Chelsea.
- National Museum of Wales buy three works.
- Glynn Vivian Art Gallery, Wales, take one work.
- Plymouth Art Gallery, one work
- Library of Congress, Washington, one work
- The Rochdale Art Gallery, March 1944, one work, a portrait
- Work shown at the Contemporary British Artist's Exhibition, 1940.
- New York British Contemporary Art Exhibition showed *'The Etcher'*.
- Exhibition of Rayner's works held at the Dudley Municipal Art Gallery January and February 1944.
- British Council Mexican Exhibition sold one work: *'Cheyne Walk'*.
- Norwich Art Gallery, two works.
- Fitzwilliam Museum, Cambridge, two works.

- Portsmouth Museum, Oct.1943, four works including the '*Presentation at the Temple*' and '*Christ presented to the people*'.
- Merthyr Tydfil Art Gallery, Wales, three works including '*The Last Supper*'.
- Nottingham Art Gallery, one work 1942.
- Cheltenham Art Gallery acquires Sickert and McEvoy portraits by Rayner.
- Lady May of Weybridge, one work.
- Christie's were given eight works for auctioning to help the Red Cross. 1942.
- Royal Collection Windsor take further works in April 1943.

1942: On 19th December the Queen views work at the Palace and buys a portrait of the King by Rayner.
- Swansea Art Gallery buy '*The Last Supper*'.
- The Queen, Jan 1943, acquires three etched portraits of herself.
- City of Derby Art Gallery buy '*Regent Canal*' 1943.
- Queen Mary buys two works: portraits of the King and '*Old Chelsea Church*', 27th November 1942.
- Stoke-on-Trent Museum buy two works, March 1943.
- Manchester Art Gallery one portrait.
- Birmingham Art Gallery, two works, April 1941.
- McDougall Gallery, Christchurch, New Zealand are presented with '*The Last Supper*' by N.Z. patron.
- The National Art Gallery, NZ, and Dominion Museum are given Rayner's '*A Soldier of New Zealand*' (by Mr. Walter Nash sold to as well).
- Professor Einstein acquires '*Les Sylphides*', 1947.
- Leeds Art Gallery buys '*the Man with the Ass's Head*'.
- Belfast Art Gallery buy portrait of John, May 1947.
- The Queen acquires Rayner's portrait of Queen Mary April 1948.
- Auckland Art Gallery are presented with a portrait of King George VI by Mr. Hewitt Edwards of Auckland, 1947.
- Portrait of Dame Sybil Thorndike is completed and Dame Sybil buys it and '*Crucifixion*' by Rayner.
- Royal Society of British Artists Council buy Rayner's '*portrait of Sickert*' for their Council Chamber.
- Lord Methuen buys two works.
- Sir Arthur Bliss buys one circus scene, 1945.
- The Queen takes ballet scene showing the Princesses, Feb '45.
- Field Marshal Smuts takes Rayner's '*When we stood Alone*' to Africa in 1944.
- Mr.John Curtin buys three works, May 1944.
- Canadian Government buy '*Hospital during Air Raid*' April 1944.
- Portrait of Irene Vanbrugh made June 1946, she takes '*Les Sylphides, No.10*'.
- The Queen buys another proof (The first artist's proof) of the King, 5th Dec 1951.

1945: Life work exhibition held at the Brook Street Gallery, 1945 was a gesture of regard for Australia and New Zealand. Jack Lindsay was present.

1953: Exhibition held at Australia House, London, for one month, January 1953, with a varied number of works (drypoints).

1957: In Febuary Queen Elizabeth purchased for her private collection a portrait of the late King George VI.

1957: Henry Rayner died at his home in Kent April 25th 1957.

1960: A retrospective exhibition of dry points, 65 works – the last picture sold being a portrait of Sickert at Fitzroy Street, to Andrina Schweder, sister-in-law to Sickert, at Richmond Hill Gallery.

A10: Finding Rayner's childhood home in Brighton, Victoria

Trying to find the house in Brighton, near Melbourne, where Hewitt spent most of his childhood, proved to be quite a challenge. He had left numerous false clues – the biggest of which was to give the house a completely false name. He wrote that the family home was called 'Wildways'. Then he wrote that it was built of bluestone. This was another false lead. Historic houses built from the local bluestone in the Melbourne area are rare, and tend to be well-documented and protected.

There were other clues from Hewitt's writing, however, that would turn out to be more reliable. For example, he wrote that his father's local pub was the Marine Hotel. He said the family would go down Park Street to the shore on a hot evening, to swim and paddle. He wrote about returning home from a visit to 'Granny Day's' along Church Street. All of these reminiscences, plus others such as the smell from the gasworks, and going to Sunday School nearby in a bluestone building, made complete sense when the location of the family home was eventually identified.

A further hurdle lay in the street numbering. The initial local research in 2004 into old Brighton street guides and council rate books showed a Henry Redstone Rayner living at number 165 New Street. But a walk past number 165

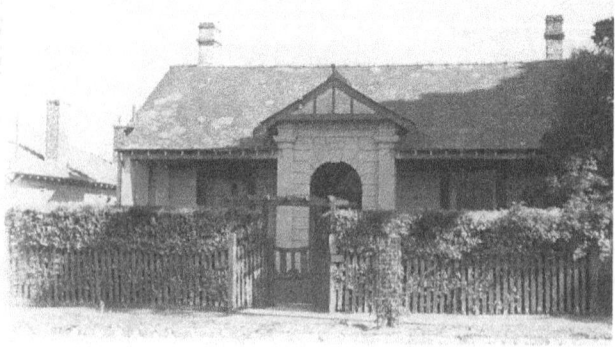

A10.1 Grey Lynn in 1949. The property just visible to the left is still there (2005) and may have been built by Hewitt's father. sw.

showed that it didn't fit Rayner's descriptions in any way. It was too far to the south along New Street.

Where was the house?

This is what Hewitt had written about the family home 'Wildways' in his manuscript.

His father had spotted an empty commercial building for sale in New Street, Brighton. In an inspired move, he purchased it. The building had served several different uses including an assembly room, library, school, courtroom and even business premises. But Hewitt's father had seen that the large grounds would give him room to store wood and other building materials for his planned house-building activities. And in due course the plot could probably be subdivided.

Hewitt wrote that the plot of land on New Street was part of what had originally been known as Brighton Park – the extensive property of Henry Dendy, an important figure in the early history of Brighton. However, an 1842 map of Brighton shows that the location of the Rayner home was on the opposite side of Park Street from the old Dendy estate, so this information may be incorrect.

'This corner was the site originally chosen for the township by Dendy himself,' Rayner wrote. 'Our house stood almost on the ground where he pitched his tent in the bush. New Street was made the centre of the township.'

According to Hewitt, writing many years later, there was a local rumour that beneath the building's foundation stone was a cache of money hidden by a previous mayor. The building was also believed by locals to be haunted. It was generally referred to as 'the old hall', and evidently this continued even when the Rayners had turned it into a family home.

Hewitt recalled that as part of the conversion, his father had removed from the front of the building a cement cast of a bearded Greek head, said to be of the god Zeus. For years, this lay in the grass next to the wall dividing the Rayners' property from the next-door property – a two-storey building that served as a vicarage.

Some aspects of the conversion project were not completed immediately, because the recession and the ending of the 'land boom' meant money was still tight. In 1914 a sleeping hut was added in the grounds behind the house, and this became Hewitt's bedroom.

Hewitt captured the style of the building in a pencil doodle never intended to be seen. It shows a single-storey dwelling with a porched door in the centre, and windows symmetrically either side. A photo from the period has also survived, showing that the house changed very little over the decades that followed.

But where was the property?

In the event, it took a visit to Brighton, and in particular to the offices of the Brighton Historical Society, that solved the mystery. The BHS is a tremendous resource for anyone researching Brighton's past. They have a file on the house, because in 1984 there had been a plan to demolish it. This provoked fierce public opposition, with a campaign to have the building added to listed buildings register. In the file were all the press clippings, with photographs of the building as it was in 1983 and 1984.

The debate was centred on the building's history as possibly the oldest surviving civic building in Brighton, and the fact that it may have been originally designed by a famous local architect.

Melbourne's *Herald* newspaper ran a big story about the fight in the 19th June 1984 edition. Under a main headline 'Knock down row over historic home', it reported that the property had been bought at auction by the owners of the adjacent Brighton Lodge nursing home in 1983. A demolition permit had been sought from Brighton Council, but the Historic Buildings Preservation Council (HBPC) had imposed an order that barred any demolition work.

A spokesman for Brighton Historical Society, which was on the side of the HBPC, stated: 'Grey Lynn was one of Brighton's oldest buildings. We believe it is of great historical significance to Brighton.' One of the new owners stated that Grey Lynn had been vandalised and was in poor condition. Doors and windows had been stolen, and the building had been used by squatters. He was of the view that Grey Lynn was so damaged that there was no scope for developing the building as part of Brighton Lodge.

The final words of this press report summarised what little was known of the building's past, from the Brighton Historical Society records – that Grey Lynn had been built in 1861 as a Mechanics Institute, was opened by John Pascoe Fawkner, and was later used as a meat factory, a school and a home.

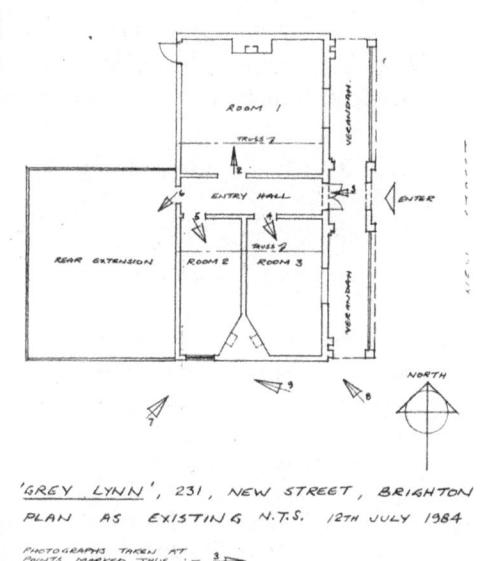

'GREY LYNN', 231, NEW STREET, BRIGHTON
PLAN AS EXISTING N.T.S. 12TH JULY 1984

PHOTOGRAPHS TAKEN AT
POINTS MARKED THUS :-

A10.2 This plan was drawn at the time of the impending demolition of Grey Lynn in 1984. It shows clearly the outline of the original Mechanics Institute building and the front porch and extra room at the rear added by Hewitt's father. IMAGE COURTESY BRIGHTON HISTORICAL SOCIETY ARCHIVES.

When the controversy about the building's future was raging in 1983/4, nobody knew that it had been the childhood home of Henry Rayner the artist. Although given that Rayner was almost unknown in those years, it is debateable whether this knowledge would have made any difference to the outcome.

The photographs in Brighton Historical Society's files show the house exactly as described by Hewitt, even to the extent of the blue roof tiles, red ridge tiles and rendered stone effect walls, with the name still visible above the doorway. Not 'Wildways' at all, but 'Grey Lynn'. It remains a mystery why Hewitt created a fictitious name for his autobiography.

In the Brighton Historical Society file on the house was a hand-written letter written to Brighton Council dated May 1912 from the house owner, expressing concern about water discharge from the local gasworks onto land where he was building a house. The householder's name was Henry Rayner. Definite confirmation that this was the house where Hewitt grew up. The reference to a nearby gasworks also ties in with his comment about smells.

Further confirmation came much later in the research for this book, when a bible given to Hewitt as a Sunday School prize in 1913 turned up. On the flyleaf was written 'Hewitt Rayner, 165 New Street, Mid Brighton'.

Once the true location of the Rayner family home had been established, then it was possible to refer to the authoritative and fascinating book *A history of Brighton* by Weston Bate for more historical data. This shows that the building had been designed as a Mechanics Institute and erected on land donated by architect Charles Webb. Before this, the Mechanics Institute meetings were conducted in Brighton's Devonshire Hotel.

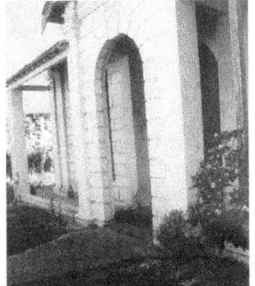

A report in the *Argus* of 18th October 1860 records that at a meeting there on Tuesday 16th October 1860, after a talk titled 'Shakespeare's Fools in *As You Like It* and *King Lear*, with readings', the audience was invited to take a look at Charles Webb's plans for the proposed new home for the Mechanics Institute. There was to be a public meeting a week later to discuss how the necessary building funds were to be raised.

A10.3 Even in 1983, the 'Grey Lynn' name was still clearly visible in the stone-effect render Hewitt's father had applied to the doorway in 1908. PHOTO COURTESY BRIGHTON HISTORICAL SOCIETY.

The new Mechanics Institute was officially opened by the hon. John Pascoe Fawkner (the founder of Melbourne) in 1861. It had cost £503. In the years that followed, the new premises were used as a venue for lectures and 'penny readings', and were available for other 'improving' activities. By 1871, however, having lost money, and with the library books in poor condition, and a dwindling membership, the Mechanics' Institute was closed. The premises were acquired by Charles Webb that year for £250. An item in the *Melbourne Argus* of Friday 20th December referred to the property as the 'Assembly Hall (late Mechanics Institute)'.

It seems that from then on the premises were rented out for a variety of commercial and educational purposes. In 1900 it was home to O'Hara's co-educational school – one of many small private schools that existed in the town.

The *Victorian Historical Journal* published an article with reference to the Brighton Mechanics' Institute in 1970 (volume 41 page 411, issue 161–2).

An old faded photograph of the house is in the Rayner archive. On the reverse of the print, he had written: 'My boyhood home, Brighton, Melbourne, 1914'. Comparing this photo to the picture of the house in the 1983 newspaper clippings shows that the building was virtually unchanged from 1914 to the 1980s. The only obvious difference was that in 1914 there were fabric curtains that could be drawn across the front of the veranda to cut down the sunlight and keep out

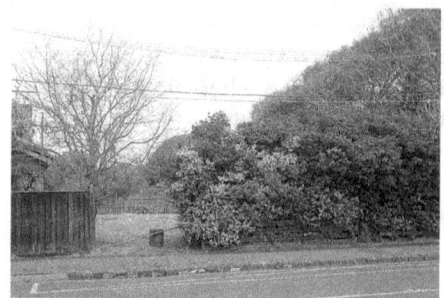

A10.4 The empty plot at 231 New Street, Brighton, where the Rayner family home stood until 1983. PHOTO RS

the dust from what was then an earth road in front of the house.

The name 'Grey Lynn' was still clearly visible above the front door – a tribute to the craftsmanship of Hewitt's father, who had created it some 70 years earlier.

Because residential plots of land in Australia were so large a century ago, and later sub-divided, the number of houses on a street tended to increase. As a result it was common for the properties along streets to be completely renumbered. This is what had happened to the Rayner home. Today, Grey Lynn is not number 165 New Street, but number 231.

Or, rather, it was. Sadly, the attempts to save the building in 1984 failed, and it was demolished. In 2004 the plot of land was still there, a small grassy, empty meadow. No sign of the house. Or the sleepout where Hewitt Rayner slept in his teenage years. Or the wooden shed at the bottom of the garden where his father kept his trade tools. Or the chicken run alongside it.

The adjacent property on the right, a vicarage in Rayner's childhood, has also gone, to be replaced by a nursing home.

But the house standing to the left of this plot, nowadays number 229, may well provide a direct link back to the Rayners. Hewitt described the location of the family property in his 'when my ship comes in' manuscript as 'near the corner of New Street and Park Street'. That suggests that the Rayner land may have originally reached right as far as the corner where the Marine Hotel is.

If this is so, then number 229 would have been built on land originally belonging to Hewitt's father. It's not unreasonable to conclude that the property was actually built by Hewitt's father. Certainly, in Hewitt's autobiography there is an account of watching his father at work building a house on a nearby plot of land.

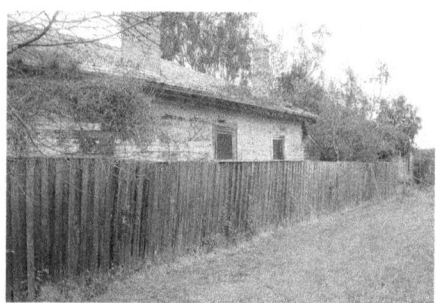

A10.5 The house next to the site of Grey Lynn, number 229 nowadays, was probably built by Hewitt's father on land that originally belonged to the old Mechanics Institute. PHOTO RS.

The Brighton rate book for 1911 records that the land area of number 165 New Street measured 100 x 250 feet; whereas the 1921 rate book gives the land area as 50 x 132 feet. This indicates that the plot had already been subdivided, perhaps into four plots, and reinforces the possibility that the building at what is today number 229 was erected by Hewitt's father.

If you stand in what would have been the gateway to Grey Lynn, looking back across the road, there in front of you is the small terrace with two shops described in the 'Child' manuscript. Hewitt recalled watching as a funeral procession set out from one of the houses, with a child's coffin.

Over to the right is the garage, and across the junction the old Marine Hotel. Over to the left is the spire of St Andrews church, and the turning into Church Street, still a main shopping street. The church building looks different from how it would have looked in Hewitt's childhood, as it was rebuilt after a fire in 1961. But the adjacent original bluestone building where Hewitt attended Sunday School is unchanged.

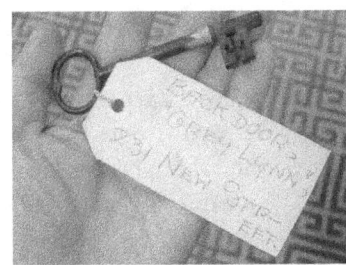

A10.6 The only surviving item from Grey Lynn is this backdoor key, kept in the files of the Brighton Historical Society. PHOTO RS.

Because of the legal arguments about the planned demolition of number 231 in 1984, a floor plan had been sketched, and this is also in the Brighton Historical Society file. It shows a building with a central corridor leading from the front door to the rear extension Rayner senior had built. Just as Hewitt described in the 'Child' manuscript. There are two bedrooms on the left, and one large room on the right of the corridor. This is the room where the Sunday family and friends gatherings took place. The plan shows that each room had a fireplace.

The only surviving piece of the Rayner family home is the door key, 'souvenired' from the back door by a local council executive during the debate about planned demolition. This is carefully kept in the Brighton Historical Society files. The size and weight of the key suggest that it is an original item from the building's early civic role, rather than a domestic house key.

An interesting reference to the property turned up in the Rayner archive, in the shape of a 1951 letter from an old school teacher with whom he had been put back in touch. 'Fairy' Thomas, 82 years old in 1951, remembered Hewitt from his Brighton schooldays 37 years earlier, and told him a story about the former Rayner home on New Street.

'About 59 years ago,' she wrote in the letter dated 21st November 1951, 'I was a junior teacher at dear old 1542 Wilson Street School, Brighton. Some of the rooms wanted painting, so our nice Headmaster, Mr J Elvins, sent me and my class over to the courthouse for some time. Some years after, the old courthouse was pulled down, and here your dear father bought the land and built your house, in which you spent your boyhood. Just fancy, where I taught. That must be the connecting link between us!'

It is interesting that 'Fairy' Thomas referred to the Rayner home as a former courthouse. The letter was about events around 1892. Brighton's original courthouse at the corner of Wilson and Carpenter streets had been demolished in 1883. So if her recollection was correct, it suggests that for a while in the late 1880s and early 1890s the Rayner home may have been used as a courthouse. She was, of course, wrong in recounting that Hewitt's father had demolished the building. In fact he simply converted the existing structure, and gave it a new look.

A11: The Rayner archive

Hewitt Rayner rarely threw anything away. At least, not anything written. He was a prolific note-taker and writer throughout his life, noting down observations and thoughts for later use. In addition, he kept a wide variety of other material – letters to and from family, friends and customers, receipts, medical certificates, sketchbooks and notebooks, his passport and even his day-passes for the British Museum. Copies of invitation cards, posters and other promotional material for his exhibitions were carefully kept, as well as press cuttings.

After his death, his widow Theresa continued to look after everything. As a result, most (but not all) has survived. It is this archive from the artist's estate that became the primary source for this book. For this reason, rather than provide detailed footnotes on a page-by-page basis (which would anyway tend to refer repeatedly to the same sources), it is perhaps more helpful to provide a general overview of the material on which this book has drawn.

Hewitt worked hard to capture the things he saw in drawings, paintings and etchings. But there was another side to his creative instincts. He wanted to capture events and ideas in the written word. This showed up at an early age, when he initiated a school magazine at the State School in Brighton, Melbourne.

During the early years in London, from 1924 onwards, he tried his hand at writing poetry, and sent a book of verse to John Middleton Murry, the former partner of New Zealand-born Katherine Mansfield, for comment. The response he received was rather lukewarm. 'I don't know … you may be a poet,' Murry replied.

Hewitt regarded this reply as positive. 'It left me very hopeful,' he noted. 'I kept to my brush and etching needle, but still continued to read Keats.'

Later in life he worked on two large autobiographical manuscripts that he tried (and failed) to get published. One, called *Child, when my ship comes in* was an account of his childhood and growing up in Australia up until his departure for England in 1924. The other, called *Red Violet* chronicled the years from his arrival in England up to the 1940s. Essentially this was the story of his friendship with Sickert.

As well as the complete manuscripts themselves, masses of scribbled notes have also survived, with ideas and recollections that were either included in the main works or abandoned. Many of the documents have been annotated by Hewitt, almost as if he was preparing the material for a later biographer.

In 1935, he had submitted a manuscript to Hodder & Stoughton, receiving a final rejection letter from Paul Hodder-Williams on 6th December. Unfortunately, there is no mention in the letter of a manuscript title, so it is not clear whether this was an early version of the *Red Violet* or *Child* works, or something else. Another possibility is that it was an account of his 1934 visit to the Isle of White, to research his family origins, which by 1954 had become one chapter of the *Red Violet* work.

During the years of the 1939–1945 war, he wrote (but did not send) regular letters to his children. He referred to these as his 'war letters'. He had decided to stay put in London, even though his wife and daughters had been evacuated to safer places. The letters, he later said, 'were a form of escape for me in those days of very grim trial', and were intended as something his daughters could read when they grew older.

In June 1946 Theresa was trying (unsuccessfully) to get Walter Nash to write an introduction to a proposed book of these letters. [Nash would later become Prime Minister of New Zealand, from 1957 to 1960]. This document has not survived, and was perhaps never more than an idea, but some of the letters were included in *Red Violet*.

Hewitt also had aspirations as a poet, and through the second half of 1937 regularly had sonnets published in the British media.

Hewitt and Theresa worked assiduously to raise his reputation, and regularly told the press whenever he sold a work to an art gallery, museum or individual of note. Some of these press background briefings, press releases and press cuttings are useful for dating purposes, and some also mention facts not recorded elsewhere.

One press cutting in particular provides valuable facts about his childhood (and covers a period that is omitted from the *Child* manuscript). This is from an edition of New Zealand's *Waikato Times* newspaper in 1952, and was based on information supplied by Hewitt himself.

He had the habit of writing lengthy letters to his mother, some of which were never posted. They are more like essays than letters. Many of these are very spiritual in tone, but most also contain factual information that helps fill in details about his life.

His mother wrote regularly from Australia, and many of these letters were kept. These provide insights into a somewhat tortured, but nevertheless loving, relationship.

He and Theresa wrote frequently to each other during the war years when they were separated, although with one or two exceptions only Theresa's letters have survived.

There are also examples of little creative works he did for his wife and children. These include illustrated children's story books using a character called Cheribinks, which he remembered from his mother's storytelling when he was a child.

The value of this material is that taken together it provides a mass of factual information about Hewitt Rayner's life and work over a period of 55 years, as well as insights into the experiences of a family trying to stay together and survive through financial adversity, ill health and a war.

The information contained in the two unpublished autobiographical manuscripts is so valuable that it is worth reviewing those in more detail.

Red Violet

This is a largely factual and autobiographical work about Hewitt's life and experiences after he arrived in England in 1923, as he struggled to make a reputation (and a living) through his art. It covers the period up to around 1940. A note made by Hewitt on a scrap of paper says: 'It has taken me 30 years to write this book.' He was still working on it in 1956.

Inevitably, given the long-lasting influence Walter Sickert had on the young Rayner, there is much space devoted to Sickert, his views, and his advice. Some of the information is especially interesting, as it provides fresh perspectives on a relatively undocumented period of Sickert's life.

In putting his recollections of Sickert on paper, Hewitt must have been very conscious of comments Sickert had made about the biography of him written by Dr Robert Emmons. 'Sentimental tosh,' he commented to Hewitt, and then added one of his little wordplays: 'One has to be of stature to write about a man of stature.'

Other friends and acquaintances are mentioned. Hewitt also includes frequent comments about his health, his beliefs, and his passions. There is a large section devoted to the extended visit he and Theresa made to the Isle of White in 1934 to research his family history. He usually referred to this trip as the 'Saga', and sometimes as the 'Pilgrimage.' Initially, he had intended to write a book solely about this visit, and what he found. He had been working on it on and off ever since the trip itself. His notes, when he finally picked up the project after the 1939 war, were singed by heat and damaged by the water from fire hoses.

Towards the end of the writing, in the spring of 1954, he contacted Sylvia Gosse and invited her to contribute some recollections of Sickert. She declined, explaining: 'Having given all the small help I could to Dr Emmons when he wrote his 'life', I do not feel I have anything to add. Nor inclination to do so if I had, for I do so strongly believe that an autobiography should consist purely and solely of the knowledge and experiences of its author, and not the second-hand contributions of other people. What will be interesting in your book is what *you* saw, did and thought.'

Andrina Schweder had already given Rayner a copy of the same notes she had given to Dr Emmons when he was researching his 1942 book on Sickert, and some of this information on Sickert's earlier years Rayner used in his manuscript.

In 1954 Hewitt submitted the finished manuscript to Angus & Robertson Ltd, Publishers, of 105 Great Russell Street, London WC1. This company was registered in New South Wales, so Rayner may have felt his chances of publication would be higher if he offered the manuscript to a firm with Australian connections.

Their reply (23rd September 1954) to Rayner at 121 Mansfield Road, says simply:

> ... we have now received reports from our readers. These have been moderate but not sufficiently good to warrant publication.

The title of the work is not explained by Hewitt in the text, although there are some clues. It seems that he thought of the mid-1920s as the Red Violet era in art. And he linked it specifically with Sickert. His exact words in the opening of one chapter of the *Red Violet* manuscript are:

'The era of Red-Violet was at its height … the era of the Sickert touch.'

In one of the many jottings found in his archive, there is a long note about how Sickert prepared his canvases. This includes the comments: 'He then squared up a large canvas, usually of the coarse absorptive sort, which he primed either with copious white lead or white lead and indian red, which gave the red-violet glow to many of his paintings.'

From a purely technical perspective of course, the term red-violet refers to the colour obtained when red and blue are mixed with more red than blue. In the colour wheel, the primary colours are red, yellow and blue. If you mix these three primary colours in pairs, you achieve the three secondary colours orange, green and violet. The so-called tertiary colours are the six colours that fit in between the primary and secondary colours: yellow-orange, red-orange, yellow-green, blue-green, red-violet and blue-violet.

So, if you mix blue and red in equal proportions, the result is violet. Add more red, and the result is red-violet.

Child when my ship comes in

The other major manuscript is a story of early 20th century Australia as seen through the eyes of a child, in the years before, during and after the Great War. Hewitt started working on this project in 1925, and continued up to 1936.

Subtitled '*An Australian workman's story*', it is essentially a tale of a boy growing up in the small town of Brighton, south of Melbourne, Australia, more or less woven around Hewitt's own life. It traces his childhood from the earliest memories, through his teenage years and the death of his father, and his work as a motor mechanic. It ends with his departure for England in 1923.

It isn't the whole truth – there are some events that he omitted, because they were just too painful. And it isn't only the truth, because there are some events that he exaggerated, or in a few cases entirely imagined. But overall it constitutes a reliable source of information on the first 21 years of his life.

The title of his manuscript, '*When my ship comes in*', was one of his father's endlessly amusing responses whenever the young Hewitt asked when something would happen.

The final version of the manuscript, dated 1938, has survived, together with an earlier draft, and an even earlier compilation of notes. Only hand-written copies of the manuscripts have survived, so it may be that Rayner never submitted it to a publisher. Or he may have submitted it in handwritten form.

An earlier draft completed on 11th April 1935 has also survived, together with a book of ideas, memories and notes, some of which were used in the final version. Hewitt had tried various subtitles for the work – '*A reconstruction of my life*', '*Story of a colonial boy*', '*the autobiography of a dreamer*', and '*the autobiography of a nobody*'

Some of the information in the notes was not used in the final version, and some of the stories differ in the amount of detail given. This makes it necessary to study all three documents, in order to extract the fullest and most accurate picture.

On one of the first pages of the final version, Hewitt wrote: 'Several of the names of people and places in this book have been changed.' It took a visit to Melbourne to check out Hewitt's accounts of his childhood years, using the '*Child*' manuscript as a guide. Despite the fact that he had changed the names of people and places, and dramatised some of the events portrayed, it is clear that it is a genuine recollection of what it was like to grow up in Brighton as a child in the years leading up to the First World War. Hewitt himself described the manuscript as 'a semi-autobiographical account of his childhood.'

It is more difficult to identify the characters that appear in the book. Particularly frustrating is the real identity of someone who Hewitt refers to as Frederick Chappy. He had a lasting influence on Hewitt's spiritual beliefs. Hewitt wrote that he was a carpenter and joiner in Brighton, a friend of the lady who ran the shop (now demolished) at the junction of Carpenter and Wilson Streets, and a regular visitor to the Rayner family open-house Sundays. To date his real identity has not been established. There is scope here for further research, if anyone wishes to expand the story of Hewitt's childhood years in and around Brighton.

At the end of the final (1938) version of the 'Ship manuscript, Hewitt wrote:

> I leave these records to my children, for I am no scribe and wish only to leave the simple story of my thoughts and experiences to those who may actually need them – at least those who should rightly inherit them.

This seems to indicate that by this stage he no longer had any expectations of getting the work published.

Bibliography

This is not intended to be an exhaustive bibliography, just a few suggestions about books that may be of interest if you want to dig deeper into the places, people and events that figure in Hewitt Rayner's life story.

A history of Brighton, by Weston Bate, Melbourne University Press, 1962. An invaluable reference resource about the history of Brighton, Victoria, Australia, where Hewitt Rayner grew up between 1908 and 1918.

Adventure in art, by Lucy Carrington Wertheim, Nicholson and Watson, 1947. This book is about the pioneering Wertheim Gallery in London's Burlington Gardens. The very last exhibition held at the gallery in September 1939, and abruptly cancelled, was of Henry Rayner works.

All my yesterdays by Clifford T. Rayner (b.1902). Insights into the Rayner family of Shanklin, Isle of Wight, by a cousin of Hewitt's.

Among the bohemians, experiments in living 1900–1939 by Virginia Nicholson, Penguin Group, 2002.

Artists and bohemians: 100 years with the Chelsea Arts Club, Tom Cross, Quiller Press, 1992

Augustus John, 3 volumes, by Michael Holroyd, Heinemann, 1975.

Australian Surrealism: The Agapitos/ Wilson Collection by Bruce James, The Beagle Press, Sydney, 2003. The book that accompanied the exhibition at Australia's National Gallery in Canberra. Four works by Rayner are included.

Burning to speak, the life and art of Henri Gaudier-Brzeska, Roger Cole, Phaidon, 1978.

By Chelsea Reach, by Reginald Blunt, Mills & Boon, 1921. This and the companion volume *Red anchor pieces* offer glimpses of the Chelsea that was fast disappearing by the time Rayner came to the UK.

Chelsea Old Church, bombing and rebuilding, 1941–1950, by Leslie Matthews and Miss Moberly Bell, 1958, New Forest Printing Co, 13 Spicer Street, London SW11.

Gaudier-Brzeska, life and art by Evelyn Silber and David Finn, Thames & Hudson, 1996.

Georgian and Victorian Shanklin, a pictorial history 1700–1900, Lindsay Boynton, date and publisher unknown.

Hip! Hip! Hip! RA, an unofficial book for the Royal Academy's bicentenary 10th December 1968, Robert Wraight, MW Books, 1968

History of the Royal Academy 1768–1986, Sidney Hutchison, Robert Royce Limited, 1968.

Modern painters, the Camden Town Group, edited by Robert Upstone, Tate Publishing, 2008.

Permanent Londoners: an illustrated guide to the cemeteries of London, by Judi Culbertson and Tom Randall, Robson Books, 1991. ISBN 0–86051–735–7. Rayner's grave in Highgate Cemetery gets a mention, and there is a pretty accurate synopsis of his life.

Savage Messiah, a biography of the sculptor Henri Gaudier-Brzeska, by H S Ede, Heinemann, 1931. Brzeska held a strong fascination for Rayner, probably because of what he learnt from Nina Hamnett.

Sickert, edited by Lillian Browse, Faber & Faber, 1943.

Sickert paintings and drawings by Wendy Baron, published by Yale University Press, 2006, ISBN 0–300–11129–0. The definitive reference work.

Sickert, the painter and his circle, by Marjorie Lilly, Elek, London, 1971.

The life and opinions of Walter Richard Sickert, by Robert Emmons, Lund Humphries, 1992. A reprint of the 1941 book.

The Royal College of Art, one hundred & fifty years of art & design, Christopher Frayling, Barrie & Jenkins, 1987.

Walter Sickert, a biography, by Denys Sutton, Michael Joseph, 1976.

Walter Sickert: a life, by Matthew Sturgis, published by Harper Collins in 2005, ISBN 0–00–257083–1. The most recent and most comprehensive biography of Sickert.

Walter Sickert and the Camden Town Group', Maureen Connett, David & Charles, 1992.

Walter Sickert as printmaker, Aimée Troyen, Yale Centre for British Art, 1979.

Walter Sickert: drawing is the thing, published by the Whitworth Art Gallery, University of Manchester for the 2004 exhibition of the same name.

Wartime Britain 1939–1945, by Juliet Gardiner, Headline, 2004.

Whistler, by James Laver, Faber & Faber, 1930, second edition in 1951.

Index